THE XANUE

THE XANUE

BEFRIENDING THE BIGFOOT FOREST PEOPLE

By Dr. Matthew A. Johnson, Psychologist
Foreword by Dr. Daniel Reilly, Psychiatrist

PO Box 221974 Anchorage, Alaska 99522-1974
books@publicationconsultants.com—www.publicationconsultants.com

ISBN Number: 978-1-59433-944-8
eBook ISBN Number: 978-1-59433-945-5

Copyright © 2020 Matthew A. Johnson
Cover artwork created by Terry Thomas
—First Edition—

All rights reserved, including the right of reproduction in any form, or by any mechanical or electronic means including photocopying or recording, or by any information storage or retrieval system, in whole or in part in any form, and in any case not without the written permission of the author and publisher.

Manufactured in the United States of America

"If you want to find the secrets of the universe, think in terms of energy, frequency and vibration"

Nikola Tesla

For in Christ, all things were created, things in Heaven and on Earth, **visible and invisible,** whether thrones or dominions or rulers or authorities. All things were created through Him and for Him. He is before all things, and in Him all things hold together.

The Apostle Paul (Colossians 1:16 – 17)

Let the heavens be glad and the Earth rejoice; let the sea resound, and all that fills it. Let the fields exult, and all that is in them. **Then all the trees of the forest will sing for joy before the LORD,** for He is coming—He is coming to judge the Earth. He will judge the world in righteousness and the peoples in His faithfulness....

King David (Psalm 96:11 – 13)

You will indeed go out with joy and be led forth in peace; the mountains and hills will burst into song before you, **and all the trees of the field will clap their hands**.

The Prophet Isaiah (Isaiah 55:12)

Endorsement

My name is Scott Taylor. I live in Washington State. I grew up in the Pacific Northwest, in Oregon. Hunting and fishing were my passions. I have a degree in Mechanical Engineering Technology from Oregon Institute of technology. Since graduating from college 36 years ago, I have done engineering work in national laboratories, defense manufacturing, and commercial aerospace. I had my first sasquatch encounter in October 2005 in western Washington State while walking out of a place I had been hunting. The realization that they were real was profound. That experience was life-changing.

As a result of my encounter, I became obsessed with learning about these creatures. At that time, I didn't know much about them other than seeing the Patterson-Gimlin film, and *In Search-Of* with Leonard Nimoy. I thought it strange that although my experience was frightening, I wanted to know more and see more of them. Why? I felt this odd "connection." I didn't know why. I read a lot on the internet. I found sites that had stories of other people's encounters. It was fascinating. I ran across the Bigfoot Field Researchers Organization (BFRO) website, and read a ton about sightings that were published there. I also noticed that they had public expeditions that people could sign-up for. I just had to do that!

I signed up for the August 2006 expedition to the Washington Cascades. When I arrived at the Main Base Camp, it felt like I had just met 35 new lifelong friends. There were people there who are still important to my life, and we still go squatching together. There were "newbies" there, on their first expedition, like me, and old timers who had been doing this for decades. I met Matt Moneymaker there, and Bob Gimlin, who has since become like a second father when we are in camp together. We had a great time on that expedition. There were sightings. I discovered the great fun of walking logging roads in the dark with no light. I saw eye-glow on my first night walk. We heard wood knocking. I got to spend an afternoon with Mel Skahan, a Yakima Indian Nation Forrester. What an education! I learned about what people already knew about sasquatches, and I also learned about the Native American understanding of them. Mel taught me that they are people, so I kept that in mind always. That perspective set me on a path that would lead me to the truth. You see, the Native American, and First Nations people have been living alongside them for thousands of years. You think that they don't know exactly what they are all about? They know.

After that expedition, I began networking with other expedition "newbies" as well as the experienced "Old timers" (they aren't old, just far more experienced than most). Seeing my sincere and serious commitment to the subject, I was asked to join the BFRO as an investigator. I jumped at the chance. Kristine Walls took me under her wing to show me how to do investigations, and write good reports. I was doing two to three investigations per month. Some were great, with profound discoveries and learnings about their behaviors, and some others were duds where the witness won't answer the phone or call you back. Most of them were legit though. My work situation changed, and I had to slow down with reports, but I still love it, and when I retire, I will be investigating a lot of them again. I have to-date investigated 176 reports. I have learned a lot. A lot more than I ever expected to learn.

When I started doing investigations, going on expeditions, and studying what we call "habituation sites," I was under the impression that I was looking for a primitive cave-man like creatures who were closer to what bears are than people. Not real smart, wild, elusive, masters of stealth, not needing fire or technology to live, tough as nails, and extremely large. Very vocal and loud. Stinky. Probably dangerous. However, as I wrote up investigation after investigation, attended many expeditions, studied habituation sites (some of which are still on-going over the last 10 years), there was a certain "weirdness" that crept into the subject.

First there was that nagging "connected" feeling that I had towards them. I discovered that others felt the same. There was eye-glow; a self-illumination in the absence of other light. This was hotly debated by people with Ph.D. behind their names and was said to be impossible (go watch a squid or octopus for an example of self-illumination). We were all seeing it. Infrasound, a low-frequency vocalization that gives people the "heebie-jeebies," making them want to leave the area. I heard about cloaking, just like in the movie Predator. I actually saw it for myself more than once. I and several others experienced a huge creature run-by in an open clearing on a moon-lit night, but couldn't see it, although we should have been able to see it because I could clearly see part of our group 100 yards away. From Ron Moorhead's Sierra Sounds, I learned that they have language. I also heard about orbs, and little blue lights that can pass through the fabric of a tent. I knew people who had a giant hand reach through the fabric of a tent without making a hole and touch them. One friend experienced some sort of being inside his tent who was lying next to him. He could feel its arms, and the hair. It just appeared…and was not a threat, nor a dream. That is very weird.

People were reporting mind-speak, and mental images that were played like a slide show in their minds. On one occasion, a sasquatch was sitting on the opposite side of the log that this person was laying alongside. When the mental slide show started, it was playing his memories. I heard of this experience from several people, including the author of this book, Matthew Johnson. I did experience this myself once. There was clearly something very strange, and much more profound going on than me chasing some wild, primitive cave-man/wood ape. As with most weird, unexplained things, I filed them away in my mind for later. Always, there was something that happened to confirm and validate this "strangeness." This paranormal experience became what some people termed "The woo." They were quite threatened and hostile towards the idea and the people who dared speak of it. That is another story.

Back in 2010, at the second Oregon Sasquatch Symposium, Dr. Matthew A. Johnson was speaking about post-traumatic stress disorder (PTSD) in connection with bigfoot sightings. That struck a chord in me. I was an experiencer of PTSD resulting from my Marine Corps experience, and had learned that very many terrified witnesses suffer from the same. I saw that as part of my investigations, I was helping people to cope with PTSD just by listening and validating their stories. At that event, Thom Powell (author of *The Locals, Shady Neighbors* and *Edges of Science*) cornered Matt privately and asked, "What really happened at the Oregon Caves?." You see, for a long time, Matt was a "Flesh and blood only" believer. However, he kept a secret inside that was constantly bothering him. The one he saw, materialized in front of him. It uncloaked. That made it doubly terrifying and incomprehensible. He had never told anybody about it before that day.

Matt decided that he needed a new approach, so he started the Southern Oregon Habituation Area (SOHA). He invested many years, thousands of dollars, fuel, and miles of traveling to the same place once or twice per month for three or four days at a time. It took a long time to gain their trust, and it paid off. He would take people there with him, who would be sworn to secrecy about the location. They experienced what he experienced. They could vouch for what he reported. There were the stainless-steel dog bowls used for gifting that had giant non-human fingerprints on them, finger prints on the vehicles, a lantern being swished off the hood of his truck by something that was not visible (cloaked) and much more. He accumulated audio recordings of speaking and singing. He was getting somewhere that others were not. This spawned jealousy on some people's part because he was getting results, and they weren't. Rather than learn along with Matt, they attacked him. He didn't give up nor back away.

Matt moved up to Puyallup, Washington from Grants Pass, Oregon. He hadn't been here long when he invited myself and some others over to his house to talk bigfoot. While there, he said, "Scott, I am new to the area. Where would you recommend, I go to do research?." I just pointed out his back window and said, "Right down there." You see, in my investigations, I learned that they live very near to populated areas. Matt took my advice, and the area became the Washington Habituation Area, WAHA. Matt had great interaction there, which I took some part in. On one occasion, he was physically bumped and spun around by a cloaked sasquatch. Many people went with him on night sits and had some great experiences.

Matt also started a monthly gathering at the restaurant at the Pierce County Airport. It was always great fun to attend that meeting. There were speakers, including me, from time to time. Barb Shupe showed her "Cloaker" video publicly the first time at one of these gatherings. It was also an opportunity to hear of the latest experiences and discoveries from his continuing work at SOHA. A portal was discovered there! This was witnessed by Adam Davies, John Carlson, Matt, and his son Grady.

Through some trial and error, and observations, Matt discovered the key to how to make the portal open. Seeing this, the forest people asked him for help in trying to find a way to hold the portal open. They told Matt that there were people on their home planet who were stranded there, with their sun dying, who could not use the portals to get here. Finding a way to save their people was their whole agenda. Then SOHA got compromised by some unethical trolls. They stayed 15 minutes, made a short video, and pronounced the whole SOHA site to be a hoax.

By this time, Matts relationship with the forest people had reached the point of knowing their names and having conversations. They warned him that "Camp 7 is coming." Matt called me and asked me, "Do you know what Camp-7 means?" I knew from other experiences here in Washington State what that meant and who they were referring to. I won't name that person. The forest people told Matt that they would relocate him to a different place, and they would put the image in his mind so he would know it when he saw it….and they did. There were actually two places. The first place ended up being on a small sliver of private property which was unknown to Matt until the owners caused some trouble. So, the forest people directed Matt to another place, which became the Southern Oregon Interaction Area (SOIA). The activity and interaction there were spectacular.

When Matt started looking for some help with some way to hold the portals open, he went on the Coast to Coast radio show to talk about it. A retired physicist from MIT who heard the show contacted Matt and said that they had been working on the same thing and maybe he could help. However, it became clear that this person really just wanted to catch one coming through the portal and kill it. That ended that deal. However, there was a man named Steve Bachmann, who lived in Bonney Lake, Washington who liked to build the devices that Nikola Tesla invented, just to see if he could make them work. He e-mailed Matt offering to help with a device he had built. Matt jumped at the chance. Until then, Steve had had no interest in bigfoot research. All this is told in his previous book *Bigfoot-A Fifty Year Journey Come Full Circle*. I was not there at SOIA when the EXODUS happened. However, I heard about it from Matt immediately after he returned home. My wife and I were invited to his house to be told something important. Arriving there, I found Lt. Col. Kevin Jones (ret.) had also been invited, and Anita Hlebichuk. Steve Bachmann was there too. I had never met Steve before. The device was there too. I looked it over, and knew right away how it worked and what it did.

Matt and Steve told us the whole story of how he, Steve and Mike Kincaid went to SOIA with the device and helped the forest people, the Xanue, to rescue 23,542 of their people. It all made perfect sense to me. I also knew all the people involved well enough that I knew what they were telling me was true. Remember that "connectedness" I mentioned before? Something from that connectedness was telling me it was all true too. The Xanue are a connected race of beings. When you have a close interaction with them, it is possible for them to connect with you, and through that they can teach you, communicate, and are a part of your life.

In 2018, I was asked by another researcher to take over a BFRO investigation, as he was moving out of Washington State. I agreed to take it on, and contacted that witness. I went to the witness's home several times, finding evidence, doing a night sit, and questioning the witness about the strangeness going on there on his property. He was hearing their mind-speak, and not knowing what it was thought that he might be going crazy. Some people are very good at receiving their thoughts. I helped him to understand what was going on. For some reason, they took an interest in him. As with many similar witnesses, through questioning I find that they have been having sasquatch interaction their whole lives and don't know it. I was wanting to believe what this witness was telling me, but needed a way to validate it.

I called Matt and explained what was going on. He told me to ask this person "Who is the leader of the council of twelve?" I did that, giving the witness no clue as to what I meant. I just asked him to trust me and keep asking them. We corresponded through texts for months. I downloaded and saved all the texts. He kept saying that they are repeating "North," "North." Finally, he got it. They told him the name was Zorth. Right answer and a validation of Matts first book, *Bigfoot-A Fifty Year Journey Come Full Circle*.

So now Matt has written a second book. This new book is about the origins of the Xanue people, ambassador #13, Zorth's response to questions, and testimonials from people who are experiencing interaction with the Xanue. I highly recommend and endorse this book. There will be insights and teachings that will amaze you. Now, if you are not ready for what is contained in *Bigfoot-A Fifty Year Journey Come Full Circle* or in this new book, all I can advise is to keep an open mind and keep on squatching. In time, you will run into these things yourself, and then you can go back and read the books again.

Scott Taylor, BFRO Field Investigator, and Bigfoot Witness (Spanaway, Washington)

Table of Contents

Endorsement	7
Foreword	19
Acknowledgments	27
Introduction	35
Memoirs from Zorth's Daughter-In-Law	39

PART 1—THE XANUE

Chapter 1: In The Beginning	53
Chapter 2: The Garden of Eden	59
Chapter 3: The Mustard Seed	67
Chapter 4: The "COCO DE MER" Seed	73
Chapter 5: Do These Two Things	89

PART 2—THE XANUE AMBASSADOR ("THE 13")

Chapter 6: Faithful Failures	95
Chapter 7: The Younger Years (K-12)	103
Chapter 8: The University of Alaska - Anchorage	131
Chapter 9: The Graduate School Years	147
Chapter 10: The Oregon Trail	155
Chapter 11: How Not To Find Bigfoot	161
Chapter 12: How To Find Bigfoot	173
Chapter 13: The Xanue Ambassador	199

PART 3—QUESTIONS & ANSWERS WITH ZORTH THE LEADER OF THE XANUE COUNCIL OF TWELVE

Chapter 14: The Universal Language   219
Chapter 15: Q&A with Zorth   225

PART 4—MULTIPLE EYEWITNESS TESTIMONIALS

Chapter 16: Multiple Eyewitness Testimonials	317
Steve Bachmann	325
Cindy Barger	331
Andrea Billups	337
Brittany Bosen	341
Ruth Cameron	345
Mike Collier	351
Timothy Collins	353
Andrew Cunningham	357
Bill Cunningham-Corso	361
Karen Davies-Johnson	365
Jacqui Davis, MS, LPC	371
Gordon Dodds	375
Paul Glover	379
Howie Gordon	387
Stuart Hill	393
Regina Horne, D.V.M.	405
Cindy Johnson	411
Joel Kaminskas	423
Kevin Kehne	431
Alex Kerson	437
Gary Luke	443
Christine MacDonald	447
Donna Mansfield	459
Cheryl Lee McAuley	465

Charlene Peters	473
Chris Pettross	475
Thomas Potter	483
Amy Rajek	489
Pamela Roberts-Aue	493
Faydra Romero	497

PART 5—A SECOND OPEN LETTER TO MY PROGENY

Dear Biological Descendants	503

PART 6—HOW TO GET IN TOUCH WITH DR. JOHNSON

Contact Information	512

Foreword

By Dr. Daniel Reilly, Psychiatrist

Reading Dr. Matthew A. Johnson's book, "The Xanue: Befriending The Bigfoot Forest People," will get you well on your way to interacting with, developing a relationship with, and understanding the Xanue People.

My name is Daniel Reilly and I am a physician with a specialty in Psychiatry. I trained at Menninger and practiced for nearly thirty years. The past twenty of those years at the Monroe Clinic in Monroe, Wisconsin.

I have been interested in Sasquatch or Bigfoot for many years, dating from junior high school years when "Patty" from the Patterson-Gimlin film first took the front page of a well-known magazine in my school library in the late 1960's. By the time I came upon YouTube videos of Dr. Johnson in the summer of 2016, I had already read many books about this phenomenon.

Watching the first video, in which Dr. Johnson spoke about his Toy Fox Terrier interacting with the Sasquatch, I had a strong impression that Dr. J. was a front-runner, on the cutting edge of Bigfoot research, and a person "in the know." I felt compelled to contact him and I did so via email. Three months later, after several times trading emails and phone calls, we finally connected via cellphones and proceeded to converse for over an hour. By the end of that call, Dr. J. trusted me sufficiently to invite me as one of his guests to visit his very remote Southern Oregon Interaction Area. Of course, I jumped at this opportunity. It was then scheduled to occur immediately following his Bigfoot University Conference of April 2017. So I and a group totaling up to twelve, part of the time, camping for five days.

THE XANUE

At that remote camp, I and others began experiencing amazing events from the very first night. As I describe this story, I highlight my personal experiences, but keep in mind that fellow campers had many others!

The first night, I awoke to the sound of heavy bipedal footsteps which I perceived coming from the middle of our camp. During the second night, I and others heard Forest People speaking. It sounded like high-pitched, quickly vocalized gibberish.

Throughout our stay, we tried to maintain Dr. J.'s protocol. After dark, we did not have camp fires, and avoided the use of flashlights as best able. We sat as a group, sharing, laughing, enjoying the company, singing, and putting out lots of positive energy and love towards these people. Matt played a selection of music from his blue tooth speaker many times around the perimeter of our camp.

My most remarkable experience happened on the third night. Prior to bedtime that night, I offered the Forest People a song, "Thankful," recorded by Josh Groban, which I sang a capella to them and straight from the heart. Before sleep, I prayed to Jesus Christ for safety from all harm for all of us. I also asked the Forest People to be especially gentle with me, as I was a somewhat anxious newbie at this, and not yet ready to view a nine-foot tall hairy being beside my cot!

The weather was not great – it was spitting rain upon us most of the night. Everyone had a tarp or similar covering them as they lay snug inside sleeping bags.

Suddenly, it happened! Someone began putting pressure upon my right ankle. They worked their way up my leg to my abdomen! I began a panic attack! Now Dr. Johnson had cautioned us to put on our bravest Navy Seal self if Forest People approached us. He also made it clear that freaking out was not acceptable and that he would personally "haul your ass" off the mountain if you did so! I quickly cut off the panic attack my switching to thoughts of gratitude for their interacting with me, and putting out loving thoughts.

Then I remembered having with me inside the sleeping bag a beautiful polished lapis stone that I intended to gift to them with. I grabbed the stone with my left hand and thrust it out from the sleeping bag and wet tarp. One of them snatched the stone from my palm. My sense is that it was a younger female. She then proceeded to gently place one of her hands over mine and one underneath, drew my hand to her lips and tenderly kissed my fingers! At that moment, I felt very joyous and loving towards her and them. I left my hand outside the tarp for a few moments longer in hope that one of them would touch or shake my hand. This was not to be. I withdrew that hand back inside the sleeping bag and immediately checked the time on my night-glow watch. It was 3:40 am.

Further events continued over the next couple of days, some involving me, although space does not permit sharing these in detail here.

Dr. Johnson informed us that often times, when the Forest People get to know you, they may follow you home or those local to your home area may befriend you. This appears to explain events that began happening upon my return home from this trip. Back in Iowa, I did a little research for where might be the best chance of having contact with the Bigfoot. In June of 2017, I packed the dog and camping gear. I headed two hours northeast of home, to the rugged Yellow River State Forest near the Mississippi River. As I prepared my campsite, I realized that I needed a cutting utensil which I had failed to pack, so I flagged down the park ranger and borrowed his.

The park ranger noticed my beautiful rough-coat purebred Collie. When I commented how far I had to travel to find her, he questioned if it were Hickory Creek's Collies. I was stunned and acknowledged "yes," then learned that the breeder was his sister! What's more is that the only reason he was on duty this particular weekend was because he had given his coworker the weekend off! I knew at that moment that I had selected just the right camp spot!

That night, the Collie spent the night in the car. I drug the cot into the woods, a short distance from the campsite. During the night, more strangeness ensued. I seemed to be in an altered state, perhaps lucid dream, and had the perception of a toddler Squatch climbing upon me inside my sleeping bag, and playing. Suddenly, the mother appeared to the left of my face. She was calm and kind. Her face was very human looking, pretty, with oriental features, and straight bangs. Her face, while directly lacking hair, was framed by the long dark hair. She leaned closer and communicated that the Forest Person out in Oregon that took the stone out of my palm was the one that some of Dr. J.'s campground guests referred to as "Chatty Cathy." Nothing else was communicated.

The next morning, in excitement, I contacted Dr. J. to get his perspective on the night's events. He believed the experience to be more than just a dream, and ultimately, I concluded the same. Consider the following: Up to this event, I had never had dreams in which the content centered upon me sleeping in the actual setting and bed that I was physically in. That just does not occur for me in my dreams, and was primary in convincing me that this was more than just a dream.

The following night at camp, one other peculiar event occurred. Around 10:30 pm, I heard what sounded like a pack of Coyotes in the distance. However, it was not the usual, disjointed yip, yip, yipping that I have come to know as Coyotes. This was rather melodious, as if a lead Coyote would howl a pretty note and others would respond in a pleasing chorus. Very strange!

Other events played out at my acreage. For example, the sounds of large Owls hooting from trees in the backyard or near the driveway, when usually, Owls are not around my property. In addition, the hooting begins only after I just stepped out the door to go do chores. Likewise, a chorus of the sounds like a pack of Coyotes starting up immediately as I leave the backdoor to do chores. I began finding wild Turkey feathers strewn along the path to the burn barrel, but nowhere else in the yard or pasture. A large rock was discovered in my horse's rubber feeding tub in the yard. An acorn squash mysteriously relocated from beside the driveway where I had left it, all the way over to the Oliver tractor with no bite or claw marks or other visible changes! Loud noises like wood cracking happened repeatedly in the master bedroom, always in the same two locations near the ceiling.

One time, I purposely let the horse out of the yard gate, with the gate left open, so he could avail himself of a section of good grass.

Later, I discovered that he was back inside the yard and the gate was latched! To my knowledge, a neighbor has never wondered over and dealt with my horses.

When Dr. J. heard about these strange events occurring at my residence, he suspected that Forest People were around. He strongly encouraged me to start sleeping on a cot in the backyard. This seemed to invite more peculiar events.

The very first night was in September of 2017. I was awoken to the sound of a deep male voice, presumably of a Forest Person. Next, a toddler Forest Person appeared playing with the toes of my left foot and proceeded to move up next to my left elbow beside the cot. He or she was a very attractive child, and I exclaimed, "You're so cute!" Just then, the mother appeared at the right side of my cot near the knee. One could tell by the similarity of looks that these two were mother and child. The mother had straight dark bangs and appeared familiar to me, so I inquired if she were the same one that appeared to me at Yellow River State Forest, to which she acknowledged, "Yes."

I inquired as to her name and thought she answered, "Bob," which I found humorous. Shen then told me about her children, a teenager, one nearly a teen, and the toddler. Note that this whole sequence flowed smoothly and was very clear in details, unlike usual dreams for me. Next, a young male Forest Person appeared at the foot of my cot, followed by many more Forest People filing into the backyard through the dog-kennel gate. The mother seemed reluctant to reveal how many were in her clan, however, I stopped counting at thirty but estimate around forty total in my backyard around my cot.

In all, I have experienced these nighttime events about six times since May of 2017. It is from these events that I have been given three very specific names of Forest People that have appeared: "Bob," whom I learned from Dr. Johnson through Zorth, is actually "Bah-Eeb," "WhaYa," and "Sheltie."

In October of 2018, I was involved in a life-threatening motorcycle collision with a large corn-fed doe. She jumped into me from the right side of the highway. The right side of my helmet was splattered with deer blood and skin. The deer was found dead on the highway in the lane that I was traveling in. I and the motorcycle were thrown into the oncoming traffic lane landing about fifty-feet apart on the pavement.

I was hospitalized for nearly a month and underwent two major surgeries. The first was an emergency laparotomy to repair a late discovered stomach rupture, thoroughly cleanse peritonitis, and explore for any other internal injuries. I already had a hemo-pneumothorax and chest tube in place on the left lung, along with a fractured left clavicle and scapula, and then fractured ribs on the left, most of those in two places. I had true "flout-chest," my blood pressure bottomed out, and they could not get my pain under control. I went into respiratory failure after the first surgery and had to be placed on a ventilator . I had hovered near death for days. My family was distraught and mourning the possible loss of me.

I had amnesia for the first ten days of hospitalization. I later learned that there were many, many people praying for me: My large family, friends from throughout my life, relatives near and far, Bigfoot community friends from east and west coasts and in between.

When I became lucid, I learned from Dr. Johnson that I had been assigned two Xanue Forest People to be with me daily in the hospital. I have screen memories that two or three times in the hospital beds, something sunk onto the mattress at my side. Looking to see who was there, I saw no one.

I began to make astounding physical improvement, to the point that it was now time to address the rib fractures. The second surgery involved fileting the left side of my back open from the spine to the left side to expose the ribs. I now have permanent individual hinged titanium plates providing structural support for my ribcage. During subsequent weeks in the hospital, I made remarkable improvement that surprised my caregivers greatly.

After an extended period of recovery and physical therapy, I am nearly pain free. I can tolerate food normally again, although I do have some restrictions of the ribcage and left shoulder. I believe that the love and healing energy of family, friends, medical personnel, guardians,

Forest People, and Divine Intervention all worked together to bring a miraculous healing to me.

So what to make of all these experiences involving the Xanue Forest People (AKA Sasquatch, Bigfoot, Beings of Light) over the past three years? I don't just believe that they exist, I have a knowing that they exist. I am honored that they have chosen to interact with me. I know that if you're a good person with a kind loving heart and an open mind and you reach out to them, they will reach back and interact with you. In my experience, where I asked them to be extra gentle with me, I cannot conceive of a kinder, more gentle and tender interaction than what was offered me – gently taking my hand and kissing it. They totally respected my human emotions.

From a psychological standpoint, experiencing these beings has forced me, in a good way, to completely re-evaluate my concept of the world in which we live. I have become much more open to the possibilities of what all our world contains, and stand in awe of it. As a psychiatrist, I fully recognize how "crazy" or "psychotic" these experiences can sound to the inexperienced. The problem with considering these experiences to be hallucinations (i.e., perceiving things through our senses that are not present in reality) or delusions (i.e., belief in things not based in reality) is that these experiences are reality and experienced by so many witnesses. Statistically, imagine the minute possibility that each and every one of us experiencers are actually psychotic. So minute as to render the possibility zero!

Dr. Johnson has been identified by Zorth as Ambassador to us humans for the Council of Twelve. Given the accuracy of the numerous things and information that he has relayed on behalf of Zorth, head of said council, I have no doubt that Johnson is indeed that Ambassador. I highly recommend Dr. Johnson and his book as a solid source of information from which to learn more about the Xanue People, who are true Beings of Light.

Dr. Daniel Reilly, Psychiatrist
(Mt. Vernon, Iowa)

Acknowledgments

When my family encountered a Bigfoot on the mountainside above the Oregon Caves National Monument Park on July 1, 2000, I had no idea how my world would be turned upside down. Although my older three children participated in some of the subsequent media shoots and expeditions, their mother chose to shelter them from allowing our family encounter to turn their world upside down too. However, eventually, my third born child, Micah, chose to involve himself with my research for a little while. It was amazing to watch his desire and excitement to participate grow so quickly. I thank him for his limited involvement and for the father and son time we shared together up in the mountains. We had fun together. I'm grateful.

On the other hand, my fourth child from my second marriage, Grady, has been out in the research field with me since the age of two. His mother has been very supportive and encouraging of his involvement in my life and in my research of the Bigfoot phenomena. To be quite honest, he's become a better tracker than most adults I bring into the research field with me. This young man knows no fear and he loves the Bigfoot Forest People. He's hooked too. I'm grateful for him as well.

Also, the participation of my third and final wife, Cynthia, has been a godsend (i.e., Third time is a charm). If it wasn't for her, I would have thrown in the towel regarding my Bigfoot research on several occasions. She has been there for me in so many ways. I would have to write another book just to share with you all of the ways she has supported me. Perhaps, she will write her own book someday regarding her experience with both the Xanue and with me. Her children have participated as well and have been very supportive. I love all my family members. I respect their choices to participate or to not participate in my Bigfoot research. I'm grateful for their support, encouragement, and interaction with me in life and for hanging out with me up in the beautiful Siskiyou mountains and at our mountain top home west of Chehalis, Washington.

In addition, I would never have guessed how many wonderful people I would meet, get to know, and interact with online and in the Bigfoot research field as the result of my family's encounter on that fateful day (July 1, 2000). I have met Bigfoot researchers and armchair enthusiasts from all walks of life. Interest in the Bigfoot phenomena cuts across all lines, including geographical location, age, gender, socio-economic status, education, political affiliation, religion, ethnicity, professional status, and sexual orientation. In short, almost everyone is interested in the Bigfoot phenomena. Most of them are wonderful human beings. Some of them are trolls, haters, and mean spirited people. Ultimately, all of these individuals have impacted my Bigfoot research and my personal life in a positive manner. I am thankful to all of them. Yes, even the trolls, haters, and mean spirited people too.

I'm grateful to the Bigfoot Forest People, who refer to themselves as the Xanue, who stepped into my life unexpectedly, grabbed me by the scruff of the neck, dragged me into the Siskiyou forest, showed me who they are, and invited me to join their families and clan. My mind has been blown, my body has been healed, and my heart is filled with respect and love for them, my family, friends, and our world.

Finally, it's also pretty cool to have the Xanue living with us on our property on a mountain top fifteen miles west of Chehalis WA. I appreciate all of the friendships that we have made with the people who have traveled so far to visit with us at our home. They're all kind people with good hearts and open minds.

We host "Night Sit/Sleep Over" weekend events at our mountain top home every June, July, and August. We have ten acres of forest and our property is adjacent to five-hundred thousand acres of Weyerhaeuser Timber Property. Sign up via www.Xanue.com to attend our summer weekend events. We would love to have you come join us and add you to our list of newfound friends. The Xanue would like to add you to their list of newfound friends too. Our motto: "Camp Xanue, where connections are made."

In loving memory of Robert Quinn, my good friend and fellow admirer of the Xanue. He spent his entire life pursuing the truth via many paths. When he finally found and befriended the Xanue, he was like a kid in a candy store. He loved, loved, loved the Xanue. He couldn't get enough of them. He was intelligent, funny, kind, supportive, encouraging, and most important of all, loving. He genuinely cared about others. The greatest of these is love. I look forward to seeing you again, my friend.

"The universe is a pretty big place. If it's just us, seems like an awful waste of space. Somewhere, something incredible is waiting to be known."

— **Carl Sagan**

"You don't have a soul. You are a soul. You have a body."

— **C. S. Lewis**

"Only a life lived for others is a life worthwhile."

— **Albert Einstein**

Introduction

Note: From this point on, for the purpose of clear communication, throughout the rest of my book, I will be using the name, Xanue, while I'm referring to the Bigfoot Forest People. I'm doing so because Zorth and the Council of Twelve have informed me that they refer to themselves as the Xanue – not Bigfoot, Sasquatch, Yeti, Yowie, Yeren, etc.

Please allow me to begin by stating the obvious regarding my book on the Xanue phenomena: I'm either a lunatic, a liar, or I'm telling the truth.

For those of you who think I'm a lunatic, the trolls and haters filed complaints in the past with the psychologist licensing board in the State of Washington alleging psychosis and drug abuse. However, the licensing boards swiftly rejected their complaints as bogus, citing that I've shown no signs of psychosis, drug abuse, nor have I injured any of my patients as a practicing psychologist. They also responded to the complainants by saying that they're not in the habit of regulating the hobbies of psychologists. Finally, I'm still gainfully employed as a Licensed Clinical Psychologist in private practice. Just saying.

For those of you who think I'm a liar, although I'm far from perfect, I'm a "born-again" Christian and I value my honesty and integrity. I don't lie and I don't hoax. If I say it happened, guess what? It happened. The cool thing is that I have at least 500+ witnesses who've joined me in my research areas in southern Oregon and who've attended our "Night Sit/Sleep Over" weekend events on our property west of Chehalis, Washington. Over the past twenty years, they have all vetted and validated my work. If it was just me, all by myself, reporting what I'm finding, experiencing, and learning, then it would be easy to blow me off as being dishonest. It would be easy to call me a liar.

THE XANUE

However, when you include 500+ people confirming my research findings via their YouTube video testimonials and written testimonials in the back of my two Bigfoot/Xanue books, you don't get to call me a liar. You simply have to admit that the issue really lies within you. You're the problem – NOT me.

You're not willing to believe the truth, even if 500+ people are telling you that I speak the truth. The real issue is that you're unwilling to climb out of your little rigid box where you feel safe. You don't want me messing with your current worldview. But, if you proceed with reading my book with an open mind and allow me to blow your little rigid box to smithereens, I'll show you a world full of wonder, love, respect, and connection to God, others, and our planet.

For those of you who believe I'm telling you the truth in my book, I thank you for your confidence and trust in my honesty and integrity. However, I caution you before you proceed to read my book. Some of you will also have your minds blown too by what I'm about to share. Some of you will also learn that there's much more to the Xanue than you were aware. Our world is about to get a whole lot bigger and different than you could ever imagine. In the end, I hope to encourage and assist you in developing a trusting relationship with the Xanue as well as with our mutual Creator – God.

Finally, for those of you who don't know me, I've always been a passionate educator about the issues and topics that grab my attention. For example, during my junior year in high school, a fellow student died in an alcohol and drug related car accident after attending a party in west Salem, Oregon after we won the Valley League Basketball Championship in 1979. His death hit me so hard that I spent the remainder of my junior year and my entire senior year speaking at all of the local elementary schools and middle schools on the topic of Alcohol and Drug Abuse Prevention. I used my local celebrity status as an All-State and Honorable Mention All-American basketball player to passionately educate the younger members of our community from the ill effects of alcohol and drug abuse. I didn't want them to end up like my friend.

Introduction

Also, after we intervened on my mother and her alcoholism, I became passionate about becoming a State and Nationally Certified Alcohol and Drug Abuse Counselor. I also went on to obtain my first Master's degree (MSW) at Rutgers University in New Brunswick, New Jersey. I obtained my second Master's degree and Doctorate degree in Clinical Psychology from George Fox University in Newberg, Oregon (i.e., A Christian liberal arts institution located halfway between Portland OR and the Oregon coast).

I also wrote a book, "Positive Parenting with a Plan (Grades K-12): FAMILY Rules" and spoke in eighty cities per year for twelve years as I passionately educated thousands of professionals and parents regarding how to implement order and structure into their lives as they utilized a successful game plan for parenting in their homes.

Are you seeing a pattern yet? In other words, when something grabs a hold of my attention, it's been my natural response throughout my lifetime to engage in passionate education about the topic. My goal has always been to help others understand and to help improve their lives one way or another.

Regarding the Xanue phenomena, how will learning about them help to improve your life? Well, if you have a better understanding of who they are, where they're from, and why they're here, that information will hopefully cause you to engage in self-reflection and cause you to improve your connection with God, your neighbors, yourself and our planet.

As a Licensed Clinical Psychologist, with a professional reputation and licenses to maintain, I have everything to lose and nothing to gain by taking the risk to tell you the truth. I hope you appreciate this fact. On the other hand, you have nothing to lose and everything to gain by taking the time to read my book. In the end, I hope you feel blessed with newly acquired knowledge, understanding, wisdom, respect, and love for God, your neighbor, yourself, and the Xanue.

Memoirs from Zorth's Daughter-In-Law

I met Zorth on my first trip to the Southern Oregon Interaction Area (SOIA) in early June of 2016. Matt and I had spent the afternoon exploring the area. Matt showed me around and oriented me to everything before night fall. Not long after we settled in for our night sit, I walked forward to the tree line, facing into a cove of open ground surrounded by trees. Between the tree canopy and the lack of moon, it was extremely dark, and very still. I began playing my flute, and almost immediately became aware of a huge shimmering figure to my left, standing at the edge of the trees. Matt verified that he also saw the figure, and identified him as Zorth.

I turned to face Zorth, and walked a few steps closer, stopping about 8 feet from the figure. I could not only see the shimmering shape, I could also feel a palpable sense of presence and energy. I greeted Zorth as calmly as I could in spite of my pounding heart. I was not afraid, but I was in awe, and ecstatic to be standing so close to Zorth. Matt told me Zorth was enjoying my music, and would I please resume my playing. I did so, and as I played, Zorth slowly faded back into the trees.

We were still working toward the EXODUS at that time, totally unaware that later in this same month Matt, Mike, and Steve would help the Xanue achieve their goal and rescue the remnants of their people stranded on their dying home world. I also didn't know that Zorth would eventually adopt Matt, making him my father-in-law when Matt and I married.

At the time, Matt was living in southern Oregon and he came to visit me after the EXODUS. He was still jazzed with all of the energy that filled the SOIA area the night of the EXODUS, and still processing all that had happened. We went into the green belt one of those nights, and though I was unable to see the figures that surrounded us, Matt described how they were coming by and thanking us for our efforts and sharing their joy in having their friends and family safe and reunited at last.

During one of our trips to the woods, we went through my favorite grove of cedar trees. There was one tree in particular that always pulled me to it, feeling a warmth through the bark against my palms. On that day as I pressed my hands against the tree I felt a brush of consciousness, and a sense of love like I have never experienced before. It was a fleeting experience. Although I returned to that tree many times after that, I never again felt that presence or that loving warmth again.

Matt had often spoken of writing a book to share his experiences, and teach what he had learned. After the EXODUS was completed, Zorth spoke to Matt and told him the time had come to write his book. We talked about the book when Matt was visiting one weekend. When Matt left to return to Oregon, he headed out via Yakima, Washington. Bob Gimlin had agreed to write the forward for Matt's book. Therefore, Matt was meeting Bob and Lt. Col. Kevin Jones, Retired U.S. Army, to tell them the story of the EXODUS so Bob would know exactly what he was putting his name on. Matt called me after he left the restaurant, excited about Bob's response and acceptance of his story, and ecstatic that Bob had agreed to write a foreword for the book.

The following couple of months were chaotic. Matt was writing quickly, the story flowing through and out of him. At times, he reported that it felt like he had help in the writing the book as ideas and words took shape so quickly in his mind. We were in a rush to get the book published in time for the 3rd Annual Bigfoot University conference in Bremerton, Washington in April of 2017. Matt would send out sections of the book as he finished them to me and several other people to edit as he finished. Matt was also busy talking to people about contributing testimonials and relating their experiences to add to the corroboration of the events in the book. Additionally, Matt was talking to the individuals being invited to speak at the conference. He told the story of the EXODUS over and over, explaining to the people writing for the book and planning on speaking so they would understand the magnitude of the message that Matt would be sharing.

Matt finally finished his book and sent it off to the publishers. Pre-orders were already flowing steadily in. I had labels printed, and stocks of shipping envelopes on hand. I thought I was organized until the books arrived at the house. Matt was still living in Southern Oregon at that time, so all of the packaging and shipping of the books fell on me. I had boxes of addressed and packaged books on every available inch of floor space in the house, with only a narrow walkway left.

After initially trying to take small loads of books into the post office each night on my way home from work, my sanity was saved when I stopped into a small local independent shipping and copy center. I gave them all my information and delivered my boxes of books to them. When they had quiet times during the day they processed and shipped out all the books. As more orders came in, I would deliver more books to them. They continued shipping them for me through all of the entire processing of the pre-orders, and the initial flood of orders once the book was published.

The Spring 2017 Bigfoot University Conference was scheduled for the last weekend of April, as usual. After work each night, I would update the attendance list, load names for name tags, and make lists of people who had ordered the book to be delivered at the conference. Then, I received a phone call from one of my older brothers. My father, dependent on a walker after breaking both hips in falls, had been struck in the back of the head by a very heavy, old-fashioned garage door and had been badly concussed. Dad was in the hospital, and they were still assessing the extent of his injuries.

I headed to Salem, Oregon that weekend. I was able to spend a couple of days with my father in the rehabilitation center. He was unstuck in time, drifting through events in his life. He wanted his briefcase and drawings for a meeting with customers, after being retired for over twenty-years. He explained to my brother and I the importance of the positioning of the antennas on the tower. He needed his briefcase to make certain that the drawings of the towers correctly showed the locations of the antennas. He kept saying over and over again that he didn't know what to do, but could not explain what he meant. Yet, when staff came into his room, he would sit up and coherently and correctly introduce us to them. My sister-in-law brought my mother to visit every day, and we all spent the hours we could together.

Two weeks later, my brother made arrangements to move my father back home on hospice care. The rehabilitation center staff were confused by his request, they were confident my father could and would recover. I don't know exactly what my brother saw or sensed, but his instincts were right. My father returned home on Wednesday morning. He never spoke again after he was loaded into the van that returned him to my mother. The home they had lived in together for fifty years. Two days later, he slipped quietly away as my mother held his hand.

Friends pitched in over the next two weeks to help me finalize all of the arrangements for the conference in Bremerton. I handed over all of the registration sheets, book orders and books, meal tickets, and lanyards to a group of friends and started my drive south for the funeral of my father.

I was still north of Portland when Matt called me in tears to ask if I remembered when I had seen Zeus last, and to inform me he was missing. At that point I became totally numb, overwhelmed, and unable to help in any way. Matt called back around half an hour later to let me know that Zeus had been found, cold, unresponsive, but alive. They were taking him with them to Bremerton and many people were taking turns holding Zeus and keeping him warm.

My family spent all day Friday together at the house with my mother. She was quiet, fragile, and achingly bereft. She and my father were high school sweethearts and had been married in 1945. After seventy-one-years together, a part of her had been torn abruptly from her.

The only comfort we could provide was by being there, a testament to their life and the family they built and nurtured together. Six children, in-laws, and grandchildren all grieving together in their own ways.

Memoirs from Zorth's Daughter-In-Law

My parents had been active and involved members of the community through-out their years living in Salem. The church I had grown up in, connected to the elementary school I attended, was packed even though it is a huge facility. I saw many familiar faces as we walked down the center aisle to the pews reserved for family in the front of the church. My eldest daughter had accompanied me to Salem, and was a rock and a comfort as we all said our final good-byes to our father and grandfather. The service was a blur, as was the following reception. My only vivid memory was the presence of a friend from elementary school I had not seen in years. She was there for me, to try to provide solace and comfort in any way she could. I was incredibly touched by her taking that time to be there for me after all of those years apart.

After the reception, I changed clothes, climbed in my car and began the long drive north from Salem, Oregon to Bremerton, Washington. My goal was to get there before Matt began his presentation. I knew what he was to present would not be palatable to everyone, something he was keenly aware of. He was putting everything on the line to speak the truth of a journey that had taken us in unimaginable directions. We had had time to process the implications and impacts of what Matt had learned from Zorth, but now he was going to deliver all of the information at once to a group of people who had no idea of the magnitude of the events they were about to experience through his story.

I arrived during the dinner break, just in time to get oriented before Matt began to speak. There was a tremendous out-pouring of condolences and support from everyone I met who knew I had spent the morning at my father's funeral. However, there was also a palpable tension in the room, and Matt's level of stress was evident to everyone around us.

One woman told me that she and some friends had taken to hanging out in the bathroom because the level of energy was so intense. Another woman, one of the speakers from earlier in the day, looked seriously shaken up. I tried to thank her for helping to care for Zeus,

THE XANUE

but she was miles away when she responded, and her eyes showed confusion and hesitation before Matt even began to speak. Then the hour arrived, and Matt took the microphone. The only thing I could do was be there for him, stand with him, and stand with the truth. I sat on the stage behind him as he began to present, a silent testimony of support and love that I hoped he was aware of.

The fallout after the conference was about what we expected. There were those who were unable, and some perhaps unwilling, to accept what Matt experienced as real. The truth regarding the nature of the entities previously known as Bigfoot was more than some could or would absorb. However, there were also those who embraced the knowledge, supported the message, and by doing so - encouraged us.

We were unsure of what would come next. Matt moved back to Puyallup, Washington from Grants Pass, Oregon. We decided it was time to move south of the Olympia area, into the country and to a quieter environment. Beyond that, we didn't know what our lives would hold.

We put the Puyallup house on the market, and I expected it to sell quickly. I loved the house and the setting, and we had put a lot of work in the yard since we moved in. We went out house hunting south of the Olympia area. Late in the afternoon, at the southernmost house we had found to view, we found the Chehalis house where we now live. It was a perfect setting, snuggled in the woods, in the countryside west of the small town – Chehalis, Washington. The house was beautifully finished. It was the dream house of the couple who had built it slowly around them. We made an offer that day, contingent on the sale of our house.

Time passed and our house didn't sell.

I was frustrated and stressed. People told me if I buried a statue of St. Joseph upside down in the backyard, the house would sell. It turned out that was a very real superstition. There were many St. Joseph statues available on-line with instructions on how to bury them in the yard. As our offer got close to expiring, I bought one and buried it in the flowerbed outside the sliding-glass-door. The house still didn't sell. Our offer expired.

I gave up, deciding that there must be a purpose in our remaining in Puyallup, Washington. Matt and I discussed the situation, and decided to let the listing lapse and try again in the spring. I had been blocking open a window for the cats to use as a pet door. However, we worried about the dog trying to jump from the window and hurting himself. So, after I gave up and turned the eventual sale of our home over to God, I went to the pet store and brought home a pet door we could install in the sliding glass door. It took me most of an afternoon, but I finished the installation, and the cats took to it immediately. Shortly thereafter, we got an offer on the house. We renewed our offer on the Chehalis home and it was accepted. Suddenly, we were packing and boxing and preparing to move. Apparently, letting go and trusting God really does work.

In October of 2017, Friday the 13th to be exact, we spent our first night in the new house sleeping on foam pads, in sleeping bags on the floor. We could hear the frogs in the wetlands and an occasional call of a barred owl. I lay awake for a while, cataloging the sounds of the new house and the surroundings. The stars were brilliant, visible through the skylights in the ceiling above. The next day, the movers arrived with our belongings, and suddenly the house was filling with familiar furniture. The house was really ours!

Unfortunately, I did not think to log the events that occurred after we moved in. I can't promise that these events occurred in the order in which I describe them, but I will try to keep a somewhat chronological sequence.

Two weekends after we moved in, Matt left to spend a weekend with Grady in Grants Pass, Oregon. I was still unpacking boxes and slowly organizing the house. I still shudder when I see packing boxes and wrapping paper. I was in the living room, during the afternoon, when I heard voices. Clearly, two individuals were talking to each other. It sounded like they were in the guest bedroom, right off the entry way to the house. I walked into the entry way and glanced into the bedroom. It was empty. I walked out to the front porch, there was no one in the driveway or on the road above the house. I smiled as I turned back to go into the house and called out 'hello'. That wasn't the first time the Xanue had let me know they were around, while Matt was out of town.

We had an open house in January of 2019 for our Bigfooting friends. We actually got a break in the weather, and we were able to invite people to see our new home and sleep out on the property. Given the time of year, we had an excellent turn-out. We had several groups spread out over the property doing night sits. Matt, Steve Bachmann, and I worked our way from group to group, visiting with them and hearing about their experiences. Almost every group was hearing movement, seeing Orbs and lights, and flickers of energy.

One group, deep under the canopy of the trees at the bottom of the hill, was not so fortunate. It was so dark where they were sitting that they were unable to see anything. About a hundred yards away, the group along the wetlands were having an amazing experience. When I caught up with them, they told me the trees on the far side of the wetlands were filled with lights in the tops of the trees, and larger orbs had been seen closer. I turned around to talk to one of the people there and saw two pale blue Orbs, about the size of a dodge ball floating behind us. All I could say was 'wow' which made everyone laugh.

In the spring of 2018, Grady came up north and spent some time with us during his spring break. We brought a friend of his down from Puyallup for company. We had put up trail cameras on the property to identify what wildlife we had hanging around. When we later watched the still shots from the camera at the top of the hill, we captured Grady and his friend running up the hill on the trail from the woods. Stepping through the pictures, we could also see a distortion in a vaguely humanoid form moving directly behind the boys.

Matt left to take Grady back home, and I started work planting flowers in the planter boxes along the hill. Matt had cleaned them all out for me, so all I had to do was add dirt, and work in the flowers. When I got to the first of the large round planter boxes, I discovered a circle of rocks carefully laid out in the planter. In the center of the circle of rocks was a bone. Most of the rocks were similar to the ones on the ground around the house, but one of the stones was a pale blueish white, with round darker blue spots. I took a picture of the arrangement and sent it to Matt. I asked him if he or Grady had left the rocks in the planter. I knew the answer, but I had to be certain. Sure enough, Matt and Grady replied 'no' - the rocks were not from them. The Xanue apparently liked the flowers that I was planting.

The success of the night sit with our open house had gotten Matt thinking. When he first brought up the idea of hosting events at our house, having people stay a few nights, sleep out, and learn how to interact with the Xanue, every introverted cell of my body shuddered. I have never been comfortable in large groups of people. However, I have come long way out of my shy shell during the time I have been with Matt, and I was able to push aside my initial reaction. I was still absolutely terrified, but agreed that the conference setting didn't give us the opportunity to help people fully experience and understand the impact of interacting with the Xanue.

I learned a lot about what could be improved with the mechanics of hosting the Camp XANUE weekend events that first summer. But those were not the important lessons. The important lessons were the ones I learned from the people who came to visit, and became our friends. Watching the connections that people made during their time at our home, listening to their experiences, and the impacts on their lives was awe-inspiring. In two to three days, groups of strangers were coming together and forging bonds that remained long after they left. Some people experienced physical healing. Other people experienced a profound personal interaction that touched their hearts. A few people experienced nothing, but when they returned home, interactions in their areas began. Matt and I both felt confident that we had found our path forward, and our way of sharing the connection with the Xanue.

Zorth had told Matt that when we found our new house he would have a family waiting there for us. Kontue, the local clan leader, his wife Sayreah and their children Gouthda, Merta and Boetree made their presence known immediately, and over time we became familiar with the personalities of the children. Boetree is fascinated by electronics and mechanical devices. He has turned on the wipers in my car, plays music on Matt's MP3 player, and is intrigued by the riding lawn mower. Merta loves the animals, the cats in particular.

The second summer we were at the house we received a wonderful surprise, Ceska and his little sister Nipkia (aka 'Chatty Cathy') were visiting from SOHA. Ceska requested that Matt play 'Baker Street' his first night there, always his favorite song. As we started sensing more Xanue in the house during the evenings, and the level of interactions increased during our events, Zorth confirmed to Matt that seven additional families had moved into the area in order to be part of the events and reaching back to the people who were reaching out to them. Even Zorth has become a regular, easily identifiable by his height and the impact of his energy. The Xanue were definitely reinforcing our choice to host the events on the property, and the impact on the people attending was growing.

My previous commute home ended in the south hill area of Puyallup. Congestion and traffic kept my nerves on edge until the final turn into the subdivision. The Chehalis house lies fifteen miles west of town, on a hill top, in the middle of farming country. The long winding road leading to the foot of the hill winds through a pastoral valley, peaceful and beautiful in every season. When I drive home on a clear night, I can see the stars from the inside of my car. There is so little light pollution, that the stars stand out vividly even with the headlights on. I arrive to our new home in a very different mental state than I used to in Puyallup.

I have had two very unusual events occur along that country road driving home. The first event occurred not long after we had moved in. It was still daylight as I was driving home. From the right-hand side of the road, I saw a large reddish orange ball rolling out of a yard into the road. As I got closer, I realized that there was no one in the yard. Also, I notice that there was something peculiar about the color and texture of the ball, and it appeared to be floating above the ground rather than rolling on the ground. I slowed down and the ball appeared to pass under my car. I felt a jolt as if it had hit the inside of the driver side front wheel. I looked in the rearview mirror expecting to see a collapsed ball or some kind of debris in the road. There was nothing. When I got home, I checked to see if there was anything lodged under the car but there was no evidence of a rubber ball, or any trace of what hit the wheel.

The second strange event occurred in January of 2020. We had a few days of freezing weather, and some periodic snow squalls. The temperature was up and down, and fronts were passing through on a daily basis. My sinuses were complaining about the constant changes in pressure. One night, a wind squall hit as I was driving home. The trees were lashing, and debris were blowing across the road. Heading into the first curve on the country road, I slowed down as my car was buffeted by the wind. As I came around a bend in the road at milepost five, I had to hit my brakes. Ahead of me, about twenty-feet in the air, was a blindingly bright white-blue light. I expected to hear the explosion of a transformer but it was quiet.

Blueish green sparks began to shoot upwards from the light. I crept forward slowly, keeping my foot on the brake, just in case the anticipated explosion finally occurred. When nothing happened, I began to wonder if someone was setting off fireworks. The light faded away. I moved into the lane of on-coming traffic to maintain space between myself and the location of the light. I could see nothing but a white fence marking the driveway of a house. All their lights were on, as were the lights of the houses around them. If a transformer had been damaged in the wind, the power to the houses would be cut, and there would be no lights. I maintained a slow speed moving forward, worried there would be more fireworks or possibly a broken power line.

Around the next corner, I spotted a tree across the road. It appeared that I was not going any further. As I got closer, I realized the tree was in small pieces scattered across the road. It was a frozen cottonwood that had sheared off in the wind, shattering when it hit the pavement. I picked my way through the debris driving forward cautiously. A few corners later, I encountered the final surprise of the night. I drove from wet pavement into packed snow and ice, swirling snowflakes replacing the earlier rain.

THE XANUE

Two days later, I drove by the house where I saw the brilliant explosion of light. There was no sign of heat damage, and there were no transformers or power poles on the right side of the road, they were all on the left side of the road. That blinding light caused me to slow down and drive even more cautiously that night, just before encountering the tree debris and snow and ice coming around a corner. The Xanue have warned Matt about potential dangers facing him while driving; I believe that the Xanue were trying to get my attention that night in order to get me to slow down because of the debris on the road as well as the snow and ice.

On January 1, 2020, during our wedding vows, Matt and I both acknowledged the 'rabbit hole' that has become so much a part of our lives together. 'Curiouser and curiouser' is a common response for us as we move along a path that neither of us ever anticipated in our lives. I wouldn't ever want for our lives to shrink back to its previous dimensions, this path has led me to so many extraordinary people, and life-changing experiences. We would love for all of you who can, to join us for one of our summer weekend events, and interact with the families on our property. If you are unable to make the trip, please remember that if kind people with good hearts and open minds reach out to the Xanue, the Xanue will reach back to them. Then you can join us in the rabbit hole from where ever you may live.

So, the journey continues, and whatever comes next, we will keep you posted.

PART 1
THE XANUE

CHAPTER 1
IN THE BEGINNING

What I'm about to share with you has come from Zorth via mind speak (i.e., telepathic communication). Mind speak? Telepathy? Zorth? If you're asking yourself these questions, then that means you haven't read my first book in this four-volume series: "BIGFOOT: A Fifty-Year Journey Come Full Circle."

May I strongly suggest that you put this book down, go online, and order my first Bigfoot book from Xanue.com. Once you read my first Bigfoot book and catch yourself up to speed, then please come back to this book so you can learn a whole lot more about the Xanue and how to befriend the Bigfoot Forest People.

Wait a second! What are you doing? If you haven't read my first Bigfoot book, I just asked you to put this book down, go online, order my first Bigfoot book, and read it from the front cover to the back cover. I understand that you may be sequentially impaired. I understand that you may have a contrary personality and feel compelled to do the exact opposite of what others suggest that you do. Hopefully, you'll eventually work through your possible anti-authority issues.

In the meantime, please do exactly what I have suggested. Read my first Bigfoot book so this book will make much more sense to you. If you read my Bigfoot books out of order, you're simply not going to get it. You won't understand half of what I'm sharing with you. Therefore, be a good reader, step away from this book, and go read my first Bigfoot book. I'll see you back here after you have completed your very necessary assignment in the proper order. Resistance is futile. You will be assimilated.

THE XANUE

What I'm about to share with you is not a religion. This is not a cult and I am not a cult leader. I have asked no one for their money and earthly possessions. I am simply the messenger. I'm committed to sharing the truth. The Xanue do not claim to be demigods. Rather, they view themselves as being fellow children of God. They claim to be our brothers and sisters because all sentient beings have been created by God. Therefore, we are all children of God.

The Xanue have no desire to be worshipped. Instead, just like us, they worship the Creator. They live and walk by faith, hope, and love. The greatest of these is love. They take great offense to anyone who implies otherwise about them (i.e., Demons, Nephilim, etc.).

The Xanue are not monsters or demons. They are a people of faith. Unlike the human race, they never fell from grace. They are connected with God, with one another, and with the Earth. What one Xanue knows, they all know. What one Xanue feels, they all feel. They are all individuals, yet they're also one corporate body (See I Corinthians 12:12 - 31).

On the other hand, because of humanity's fall from grace, we are disconnected from God, from one another, and from the Earth. That's why humans hate, slander, envy, steal, lie, rape, murder, troll, and go to war with one another. For this reason, the Xanue keep their distance from the human race. For the record, humans are not the apex species on the planet.

Although the Xanue occasionally reach out to us in an attempt to help us, in many cases, they withdraw their attempts because many humans are not very kind to one another. But wait! Don't give up hope. There's so much more to the story.

In the beginning, God created the heavens and the Earth. The opening sentence of the Old Testament clearly states that God is the Creator of all things. He's not only the Creator of the Earth but he is also the Creator of the heavens too. The heavens are comprised of everything else out there, including a countless number of stars, planets, and other sentient life forms.

In the book of Colossians which is found in the New Testament, the Apostle Paul wrote: "**Jesus is the image of the invisible God**, the firstborn over all creation. For in him all things were created: things in heaven and on Earth, **visible and invisible**, whether thrones or powers or rulers or authorities; all things have been created through him and for him. He is before all things, and in him all things hold together."

In a nutshell, no matter how you choose to view it – Evolution or Creationism, God spoke all life into existence. Life can only spring forth from life. Life does not spring forth from non-life. God created all things in heaven and on Earth, **visible and invisible**. It doesn't matter if it took six days or six billion years to create it all. The fact of the matter is that God created it all and Jesus holds all things together (i.e., The God particle). Most important of all, the Xanue know this to be true and they want me to share this information with you.

Before you get all upset and accuse me of interjecting my Christian faith into the subject of the Xanue, I would like to point out to you two very important things for your thoughtful consideration:

(1) Right now, you're doing the same exact thing that you're accusing me of doing. You don't believe in God or Jesus Christ and, therefore, are interjecting your lack of Christian faith into the subject matter. For you, the explanation has to be free of God and Jesus Christ. It has to be any other possible explanation that does not include God and Jesus Christ into the discussion. Believe it or not, you have your own biases.

You'll keep an open mind regarding any other possible explanation except for the inclusion of God and Jesus Christ. You'll entertain the possibility of alien manipulation of DNA, or a military experiment gone awry, or that the Xanue might be the Nephilim or Demons. The last two theoretical possibilities, I might add, most definitely require the existence of God and His creation. However, you open mindedly accept the created sentient beings without being willing to accept the existence of the Creator. Go figure.

The fun and all of the possibilities don't end there. Nope. You might possibly be contrary in nature. If you were raised Democrat,

THE XANUE

you chose to be a Republican. Perhaps you were raised Republican and chose to become a Democrat, just to spite your parents. You may have been raised Christian but chose to become Hindu, Buddhist, Muslim, Jewish, or an Atheist just to spite your parents or your community.

Finally, for example, you may have been raised in a North American Native community and refuse to open mindedly accept the existence of God and Jesus Christ. Rather, you are sticking to the beliefs that you were raised with regarding the Xanue that have absolutely nothing to do with the Trinity. Regardless of your personal reasons and unresolved struggles, you're doing the very same thing that you're accusing me of doing. You're interjecting your life experiences and beliefs into the subject of the Xanue. You're guilty of the very same bias that you just accused me of engaging in.

In reality, you don't have an open mind at all. Matter of fact, your heart and mind are closed to the possibility of God and Jesus Christ being involved because of your unresolved issues from your childhood (i.e., "My parents made me go to church and I didn't like it" or "My parents were hypocrites" or "Christianity is the white man's faith" even though Jesus wasn't white. Rather, Jesus was a Middle Eastern Jew). You may have had a negative experience with the church as an adult like I did. I saw three different churches, within a two-year period of time, lynch their pastors for political reasons - not scriptural reasons. It was horrible to witness how ugly some alleged Christians could become (i.e., Lying, gossip, slander, malice, etc.).

Finally, the nail in the coffin for me was when I divorced my first wife after twenty-two years of marriage. Not one member of our church bothered to talk with me or my parents about our side of the story. We all lived with her and witnessed her repeated actions. The church members simply swallowed my ex-wife's side of the story as the gospel truth without any verification. They kicked me to the curb over a dump truck load of lies and false allegations. My parents and I knew the truth. This was the final straw and left a very bad taste in my mouth regarding the church. I could no longer trust those in positions of leadership in the local church. They were not seekers

Chapter 1: In The Beginning

of the truth. Rather, they were enablers of gossip, slander, lies, and dysfunctional behaviors.

This leads me to my second point that I want to make regarding your allegations that I'm interjecting my Christian faith into the subject of the Xanue:

(2) You're one hundred percent wrong and here's why: In light of what I just disclosed above, I was not a big fan of God, Jesus Christ, and the church. I was angry with God for what He allowed to happen in my life. It seemed like I gave Him my best and He gave me His worst. Please don't get me wrong, I never chucked my Christian faith. However, I also wasn't a big fan of breaking bread and fellowshipping with other Christians. As a result of my negative experience with Christians, the mountains became my church and the logs and stumps became the pew that I sat on to engage in worship of the Creator.

Because of the betrayal I experienced, I no longer trusted Christians. In my mind, most Christians were back stabbing hypocrites. They weren't interested in the truth or living the truth. They were all simply politicians vying for ecclesiastical power. They weren't any different than any other group of people at work, at school, or in the Baseball Little League. Therefore, you're wrong. I had absolutely no motivation or desire to interject my Christian faith into the subject matter of the Xanue. Instead, the Xanue did it in spite of my issues and lack of enthusiasm and trust in the Christian community.

If you have a problem with God and Jesus Christ being interjected into the Xanue phenomena, then you have your argument with the Xanue – not me. I'm merely the messenger.

The Xanue brought me back to my spiritual roots. Over a twenty-year period of time, they slowly but surely reeled me back into a strong faith in God and Jesus Christ. They helped me to experience unconditional love. They taught me the importance of letting go of my hurt and subsequent anger. They encouraged me to forgive my enemies, and sometimes, buy them lunch. Finally, they patiently steered me back on course regarding walking the talk of my Christian faith by focusing on things above rather than on the world below. They helped me to set my mind on the Spirit rather than on the sinful nature of the flesh.

None of the above had anything to do with my upbringing whatsoever. Instead, it had everything to do with what the Xanue actually know to be true. They know that God is the Creator and that all things were created, **visible and invisible**, by Him and for Him and through Him. They know that Jesus Christ holds all things together (i.e., The God Particle).

The Xanue simply speak the truth and they expect me to do likewise. I'm not interjecting my Christian faith into the subject of the Xanue. Rather, they are interjecting God and Jesus Christ into the Bigfoot phenomena because the truth matters to them. They believe that it is important for humanity to know and live the truth. They want to help us reconnect with God, our neighbor, and to be good stewards of the Earth. We have much to learn from them.

Therefore, please stop attempting to interject your life experiences and your beliefs, or lack thereof, into the Xanue phenomena. Instead, simply let go of your preconceptions, kick on back and relax, open up your mind to the truth, because the Xanue are going to take you for a revelatory ride, on an informational highway, and straight down the Rabbit Hole to a world that most of you never knew existed. Buckle up! Here we go!

CHAPTER 2
THE GARDEN OF EDEN

In the beginning, God created the heavens and the Earth. As previously mentioned, the heavens consist of the countless number of created stars, planets, and all sentient beings. The heavens also consist of the creation of the planet where all sentient life forms begin, otherwise known as the Garden of Eden.

According to Zorth, C.S. Lewis is correct: "We don't have a soul. We are a soul. We have a body." In other words, when God creates a new sentient being, He creates them as Beings of Light or souls (i.e., Orbs). The Orb is who we are. The Orb is our soul.

From this point forward, I will be including scriptural references that support what I am sharing with you. I want to encourage you to actually take the time to look up the scriptural references and read them for yourself. If you don't own a Bible, don't worry about it. You can simply take a scriptural reference such as "John 4:24" and type it into the Google Search Engine. Then in a blink of an eye, the passage of scripture will show up on the screen of your smartphone or laptop computer. There are many translations available online. I would avoid the King James Version (KJV) because the "Thees" and "Thous" are hard to sort through. I suggest you select the New International Version (NIV) or the New American Standard Bible (NASB). They are much easier to read and understand for most people.

God is a Spirit of Light (John 4:24 and I John 1:4-6) God creates all sentient beings in His image (Genesis 1:27 and Genesis 5:1). Jesus Christ, in physical form, is the image of the invisible God and the first born of all creation (Colossians 1:15).

THE XANUE

The newly created sentient Beings of Light (Orbs), who have been created in the image of the invisible God who is a Spirit of Light, are given a predominant body that they can shape shift into if and when they want to do so. For example, humans look like, well, humans. The Xanue look like tall, upright, hairy, bipedal beings that look somewhat human. Naturally, they look very different from one another just like humans look different from one another too.

God has created countless body types with varying physical features for all sentient Beings of Light to shape shift into. Just read through the book of Revelations at the end of the New Testament to learn about a few of the unique looking sentient beings (Revelations 4:6-8). Also, watch Howard Storm's five-minute YouTube video on "Life in The Universe." Both sources of information are incredibly revelatory. While you're at it, please take the time to watch Howard Storm's complete testimonial video. It will blow your mind.

According to Zorth, after each sentient Being of Light has been created, they're tested on the life giving planet – the Garden of Eden. All new species are told that they can eat from any tree in the garden. However, they are forbidden to eat from the Tree of the Knowledge of Good and Evil (Genesis 2:9 and Genesis 2:15-17) as well from the Tree of Life (Genesis 3:22-24).

If you have read my first Bigfoot book, then you know that Zorth revealed that they are Beings of Light (Orbs) and they live in the trees during the day. The morning after the EXODUS, Zorth requested that I share the following message: "Please tell everyone that we are in the trees and the trees are everywhere." Although, they're not in every tree.

Their primary source of food or sustenance is energy from the sun. They obtain energy from the sun during the day while resting inside the trees. They also obtain nutrients from the roots of the tree. Finally, when they choose to shape shift into their physical form, they can eat the fruit from the trees.

Like all newly created sentient beings, including humans, the Xanue had their own Adam and Eve. However, their names were Gromene and Istra. Eventually, their time of testing came to an end.

Chapter 2: The Garden of Eden

They both chose to obey God's directive. They did not fall from grace by defiantly breaking God's rules.

As a result of successfully passing the test in the Garden of Eden, God sent Gromene and Istra through a portal to their new home world. Because they did not fall from grace, they continued to remain connected with their Creator, one another, and the planet God gave them to be good stewards of. They lived in peace, harmony, fellowship, and love for a very, very long time. In short, they were living the lifestyle that God had planned for all the sentient beings that He has created. By the way, God continues to create new worlds and sentient beings to live on those planets. God's universe is endless and exists in multiple dimensions. We can't begin to fathom it all.

One day, long ago before the creation of man, the Xanue all sensed a slight difference in the energy that their sun was producing. As previously mentioned, they feed off of the sun via resting in the trees during the day. It would be similar to a human noticing the change in the taste of the well water when you realize it's time to change the filter in the pump house. If you don't change the filter, the taste of Sulphur in the well water becomes stronger and stronger. In a similar way, their sun was slowly losing its intensity of energy and light. After much contemplation, the Council of Twelve concluded that their sun was slowly dying. It was beginning to slowly burn itself out. Although they had time, because a sun does not burn itself out quickly, they decided that the Xanue needed to take action. It was time to send scouts out through the portals in search of a new compatible planet to colonize.

Before I continue, please allow me to refresh your memory with some information that I revealed in my first Bigfoot book. Zorth shared that a long, long time ago, an ancient alien species created portals on many of the planets to help expedite their travels from one planet to another planet. One of those portals was placed on the Xanue's home world.

Eventually, some of the Xanue figured out that they had the ability to manipulate the portal and go through it on their own. They weren't able to take anyone else through the portal with them. They could only go by themselves. It turned out that only about twenty-five percent of the Xanue population were born with the ability to manipulate and travel through the portals.

After much exploration, the Xanue scouts returned to their home world and reported on what they had learned during their travels to millions of other planets. Please remember when it comes to the Xanue, what one knows, they all know. What one feels, they all feel. Therefore, when the scouts returned from their explorations, they were like thumb drives that downloaded their thoughts and feelings to the collective Xanue corporate body and the Council of Twelve.

After much deliberation, the leaders decided to colonize Earth in order to save their species. They sent all of the Xanue, who were able to manipulate the portal, on to colonize the Earth. The remaining seventy-five percent of the Xanue remained behind on their home world.

The Xanue first migrated from their home world to the Earth near the very end of the Cretaceous period, approximately sixty-five million years ago. They adapted to the Earth fairly quickly. They enjoyed the vibrant sun and the energy it provided for the Earth. They witnessed many changes on the Earth over millions and millions of years. Yes, they witnessed the end of the dinosaurs. They also witnessed the coming and going of other alien species, including one alien species that mined the Earth and left the Treykon behind. Finally, they witnessed the arrival of the human race on the Earth several thousand years ago. We are mere babies in the greater scheme of God's grand creation.

Just like all other created sentient beings, the human race had its turn in the Garden of Eden. We were also created in God's image (i.e., A spirit of light; an Orb). Next, humans were assigned a predominant physical body to shape shift into if we so desired. Finally, Adam and Eve were tested just like all other newly created sentient beings were tested.

Adam and Eve were told that they could eat from any tree in the Garden of Eden except from the Tree of Knowledge of Good and Evil or from the Tree of Life. That meant that they could go inside the trees and enjoy soaking up the energy the sun and the nutrients from

Chapter 2: The Garden of Eden

the roots or they could shift into their physical form and eat the fruit from the trees. They could eat from any and every tree except the two forbidden trees.

However, unlike the Xanue, the human race flunked the test. By their actions, Adam and Eve rebelled against God's directive. They decided that they wanted to become like God knowing good and evil. Therefore, they went into the forbidden tree and ate from it. First, Eve, and then, Adam. When they were done feasting and returned to their physical form, they realized that they were naked, created cover via sewing fig leaves together, and then try to hide from God (Genesis 3:6-8).

Uh oh! Someone was in trouble. God was not a happy camper. He scolded Adam and Eve regarding their sinful and rebellious behaviors and booted them out of the Garden of Eden (Genesis 3:9-24). However, not without promising them eventual redemption first (Genesis 3:15). He prophesied that Jesus Christ would eventually be coming to bruise Satan on his head while he would only manage to bruise Christ on his heel.

As the result of Adam and Eve rebelling against God in the Garden of Eden, several things occurred:

1. They realized that they were naked because they had acquired the knowledge of good and evil. They no longer were innocent like a child (Matthew 18:2-4).
2. They became disconnected from God and from one another. They were both attempting to hide from God. Also, Adam threw Eve under the bus by blaming her (Genesis 3:6-12).
3. They sinned against God and, therefore, the human race was locked into their physical bodies. Humans could no longer shapeshift into their Orb form and enjoy the easy life of going into the trees and feed off the energy from the sun and the nutrients from the ground. Instead, because Adam and Eve became locked into their bodies, humans were cursed to toil the ground, eat the plants of the field, and eat bread (Genesis

3:17 – 19). No more living the easy life like the Xanue still do today.
4. Finally, throughout the history of the human race, we have historical documentation, over and over again, as to just how our rebellious sinful nature has disconnected us from God, one another, and the Earth (i.e., Racism, discrimination, hatred, stealing, lying, murder, rape, wars, genocide, pollution, human trafficking, addictions, infanticide, trolling, etc.).

What a sorry mess Adam and Eve got us all into. The fall of man in the Garden of Eden was devastating. However, to be fair to Adam and Eve, we all start off as childlike too. Nevertheless, we all eventually, one way or another via our attitudes and behaviors, rebel against God. We sin one way or another and miss the mark. We all fall short of the glory God that He intended for all of us to experience as his children. Also, we try to become as God and attempt to take control of our lives and our destiny. "The Big Lie" is if we believe that we can become as God, then we will have no need for God because we are God. This lie couldn't be further from the truth. As a result of buying into this lie, we become disconnected from God, one another, and from the Earth. All humans have sinned and have fallen short of the glory of God (Romans 3:23). Thank goodness God gave all of us a way out of the pit: "For the wages of sin is death, but the gift of God is eternal life in Christ Jesus our Lord" (Romans 6:23).

The Xanue know this to be true and are wanting to help the human race to understand this very important truth. Unfortunately, the human race is disconnected, working overtime to be like God and be in control of their lives and destiny, and many of our hearts and minds are closed and locked up tight. Instead of being open to the TRUTH, we attempt to become as God and decide to create our own truths which really turn out to be falsehoods in the end.

The apostle Paul stated it the best: "I know that nothing good lives in me, that is, in my flesh; for I have the desire to do what is good, but I cannot carry it out. For I do not do the good I want to do. Instead, I keep on doing the evil I do not want to do. And if I do what I do not want, it is no longer I who do it, but it is sin living in me that does it. So this is the principle I have discovered: When I want to do good, evil is right there with me. For in my inner being I delight in God's Law. But I see another law at work in my body, warring against the law of my mind and holding me captive to the law of sin that dwells within me. What a wretched man I am! Who will rescue me from this body of death? Thanks be to God, through Jesus Christ our Lord! (Romans 7:18 – 25). Thanks to God and Jesus Christ, we have a way out of this mess. Happy dance.

CHAPTER 3
The Mustard Seed

The mustard seed is one of the smallest seeds on the Earth. Mustard seeds are the small round seeds of various mustard plants. The seeds are usually about 1 to 2 millimeters in diameter (0.039 to 0.079 inches) and may be colored from yellowish white to black. Most seeds on the Earth don't get much smaller than this.

Just a public service reminder, I'm not interjecting my Christian faith into the Xanue phenomena. As you previously read, I had been soured by the hypocrisy of many Christians in the church. I simply spent almost two decades in search of the truth regarding the Bigfoot phenomena. It was the Xanue who led me to this conclusion. I'm merely the messenger conveying to you what Zorth and the Council of Twelve would like you to know. Please don't shoot the messenger.

When Jesus ministered on the Earth for three years before his crucifixion and resurrection, he said the following to the twelve disciples, "If you have faith the size of a mustard seed, you can say to this mulberry tree, 'Be uprooted and planted in the sea,' and it will obey you" (Luke 17:6). Then Jesus told them, "I tell you the truth, if you have faith and don't doubt, you can do things like this and much more." (Matthew 21:21).

Did you catch that? Do you understand what Jesus said to his disciples? Once again, Jesus more or less said if you have faith the size of a mustard seed, and don't doubt God, you can do things like this and much more. That's right! We can do things like this and much more. Wow! All it takes is a little itty bitty faith about the size of a mustard seed and we can perform apparent miracles too.

It's very important to understand the above, and to truly let it sink into to your mind, if you're going to be able to make sense out of the rest of this chapter. All of the above seems like hogwash to most humans because we aren't all running around turning water into wine, healing the sick, walking on water, raising the dead, helping the blind to see and the lame to walk, or calming storms. Therefore, Jesus must have simply been messing with his disciples' minds by telling them that they could pull off the apparent miracles that he was doing, knowing full well that they couldn't. What a prankster or jerk, right?

Well, now wait just a minute, Buckwheat. In my short fifty-eight years on this planet, I've seen a few humans who were able to replicate some of the miracles that Jesus said we all could do if we had the faith the size of a mustard seed. In short, I've seen humans being used by God to heal others. I have a friend who's a traveling pastor and God uses her faith to heal many people. I've seen the power of prayer change the course of an individual's physical, psychological, and/or spiritual life. I've seen the love of Christ transform the souls of many people, including my own. That's a freaking miracle of faith.

Did you know that Jesus was falsely accused by the Pharisees and Sadducees of being possessed by a demon? The Jewish religious leaders of the day alleged that Jesus was casting out demons because he was possessed himself by Satan. How crazy is that accusation?

"Then Jesus entered a house, and again a crowd gathered, so that he and his disciples were not even able to eat. When his family heard about this, they went to take charge of him, for they said, "He is out of his mind." And the teachers of the law who came down from Jerusalem said, "He is possessed by Beelzebub! By the prince of demons, he is driving out demons." So Jesus called them over to him and began to speak to them in parables: "How can Satan drive out Satan? If a kingdom is divided against itself, that kingdom cannot stand. If a house is divided against itself, that house cannot stand. And if Satan opposes himself and is divided, he cannot stand; his end has come. In fact, no one can enter a strong man's house without first tying him up.

Then he can plunder the strong man's house. Truly I tell you, people can be forgiven all their sins and every slander they utter, but whoever blasphemes against the Holy Spirit will never be forgiven; they are guilty of an eternal sin." He said this because they were saying, "He has an impure spirit" (Mark 3:20-30).

Okay, let's do a quick review. The Xanue want everyone to know that God is very real and that He is the Creator of the heavens and the Earth. This includes being the Creator of all sentient beings. The human race rebelled against God in the Garden of Eden but the Xanue obeyed. The human race is disconnected from God, one another, and the Earth. On the other hand, the Xanue are connected with God, one another, and the Earth. The Xanue also want everyone to know that Jesus Christ is God's only begotten Son. Everything was created by Him, for Him, through Him, and He holds all things together (i.e., The God Particle).

During his three years of ministry on the Earth, Jesus performed many miracles. His own family thought he was out of his mind. They probably would have had Jesus committed to a psychiatric hospital if there was one in Israel two-thousand-years ago. He told his disciples that if they had the faith the size of a mustard seed, one of the smallest seeds on the planet, they could do what he did and more. The Jewish religious leaders accused Jesus of casting out demons because he was possessed by Beelzebub (Satan). Jesus more or less told the Pharisees and the Sadducees that they were going to Hell because they committed the unforgivable sin (i.e., Blasphemy of the Holy Spirit - accusing Jesus of having an impure spirit).

With all of the above stated, I have to ask this question for you to wrestle with. Lord knows that I've wrestled with it, off and on, for many years. Based on the fact that there have been numerous reports about the Xanue alleging that they possess paranormal abilities (i.e., Cloaking, mind speak, reading through memories, healing, seeing into the future, Orbs, etc.), how do they manage to pull it off? Are the Xanue possessed by demons or do they have the faith the size of the largest seed in the world? The "Coco De Mer," which is the seed of a palm tree. It can reach about 12 inches (30 cm) long, and weigh up to 40 pounds (18 kg).

If the Xanue are possessed by demons or, in fact, happen to be demons, then why are they so interested in helping humanity reconnect with God and Jesus Christ? Why do they want to help humanity reconnect with one another and the Earth? Why do they heal people? For Pete's sake, they saved my life by getting rid of a humongous Deep Vein Thrombosis (DVT), in my left leg, that went from my groin to my knee. The vascular surgeon was flabbergasted. He just sat there with Cynthia and me with an amazed look on his face. He said, "You should be dead" a bazillion times. It was a miracle.

According to the Bible, demon-possessed people can be extremely violent (Matthew 8:28) and self-destructive (Mark 5:2–5). They lose all sense of decency (Luke 8:27). The Bible also shows that demons can possess or influence people to make them spiritually, psychologically, and physically sick.

Why do so many people who I've come to know over the past twenty-years claim, including myself, that their faith in God and Christ has grown exponentially because of their relationship and interactions with the Xanue? Finally, why are the Xuxiko (i.e., Fallen Angels/Demons) trying to stop the Xanue from sharing their message with the human race. It makes no sense at all. Jesus said that Satan doesn't work against himself because a divided kingdom will not survive.

What we do know is that Jesus said if we had the faith the size of a mustard seed, we could perform the miracles that he did and do more than what he's done. Please keep in mind that the Xanue never fell from grace in the Garden of Eden. Unlike the rebellious human race, the Xanue chose to obey God. Therefore, to this very day, they continue to commune with God and Jesus Christ via faith the size of a "Coco De Mer" seed. The largest seed in the world. They have absolutely no problem at all with living and walking by faith. On the other hand, the human race has to struggle with conjuring up enough faith to equal the size of a mustard seed. No wonder why the Xanue keep their distance from the human race. They're pure in heart and the human race is, well, not so pure in heart. Lord, please forgive us and help us for we know not what we do. Thank goodness, He did.

CHAPTER 4
THE "COCO DE MER" SEED

Jesus said, "If you had the faith the size of a mustard seed, you can do what I do and more." Well, based on my observations and interactions with the Xanue over the past twenty-years, I would say that they have faith the size of the "Coco De Mer" seed – the largest seed in the world that can weigh up to forty pounds. Since they never fell from grace in the Garden of Eden, it's only natural for them to live and walk by faith. Therefore, it also makes sense that they can do what Jesus could do and more.

Reading Through Memories

Jesus demonstrated his ability to read through the memories of individuals. Let's take a peek at some verses found in the gospel of John, chapter four:

1. Now Jesus learned that the Pharisees had heard that he was gaining and baptizing more disciples than John— 2. although in fact it was not Jesus who baptized, but his disciples. 3. So he left Judea and went back once more to Galilee. 4. Now he had to go through Samaria. 5. So he came to a town in Samaria called Sychar, near the plot of ground Jacob had given to his son Joseph. 6. Jacob's well was there, and Jesus, tired as he was from the journey, sat down by the well. It was about noon. 7. When a Samaritan woman came to draw water, Jesus said to her, "Will you give me a drink?" 8. (His disciples had gone into the town to buy food.) 9. The Samaritan woman said to him, "You are a Jew and I am a Samaritan woman. How can you ask me for a drink?"

(For Jews do not associate with Samaritans.) 10. Jesus answered her, "If you knew the gift of God and who it is that asks you for a drink, you would have asked him and he would have given you living water." 11. "Sir," the woman said, "you have nothing to draw with and the well is deep. Where can you get this living water? 12. Are you greater than our father Jacob, who gave us the well and drank from it himself, as did also his sons and his livestock?" 13. Jesus answered, "Everyone who drinks this water will be thirsty again, 14. but whoever drinks the water I give them will never thirst. Indeed, the water I give them will become in them a spring of water welling up to eternal life." 15. The woman said to him, "Sir, give me this water so that I won't get thirsty and have to keep coming here to draw water." 16. He told her, "Go, call your husband and come back." 17. "I have no husband," she replied. Jesus said to her, "You are right when you say you have no husband. 18. The fact is, you have had five husbands, and the man you now have is not your husband. What you have just said is quite true." 19. "Sir," the woman said, "I can see that you are a prophet.... 23. Yet a time is coming and has now come when the true worshipers will worship the Father in the Spirit and in truth, for they are the kind of worshipers the Father seeks. 24. God is spirit, and his worshipers must worship in the Spirit and in truth." 25. The woman said, "I know that Messiah" (called Christ) "is coming. When he comes, he will explain everything to us." 26. Then Jesus declared, "I, the one speaking to you—I am he." ... 28. Then, leaving her water jar, the woman went back to the town and said to the people, 29. "Come, see a man who told me everything I ever did. Could this be the Messiah?" 30. They came out of the town and made their way toward him.... 39. Many of the Samaritans from that town believed in him because of the woman's testimony, "He told me everything I ever did." 40. So when the Samaritans came to him, they urged him to stay with them, and he stayed two days. 41. And because of his words many more became believers. 42. They said to the woman, "We no longer believe just because of what you said; now we have heard for ourselves, and we know that this man really is the Savior of the world."

Chapter 4: The "COCO DE MER" Seed

Once again, the Xanue are a people who live by faith in God and Jesus Christ. Because of their great faith, they're able to do what Jesus did and more. They have read through my memories (please read my first Bigfoot book). I know a few people who've also had their memories read through by the Xanue. Trust me, it's a mind blowing experience. I saw my whole life flash before my mind's eye like I was watching a movie screen. It was a majorly cool experience. However, as far as I can tell, it doesn't happen to very many people.

Healing Others

There are many documented stories in the Bible of Jesus healing others. Here is an example found in Matthew 8:14-16:

14. When Jesus came into Peter's house, he saw Peter's mother-in-law lying in bed with a fever. 15. He touched her hand and the fever left her, and she got up and began to wait on him. 16. When evening came, many who were demon-possessed were brought to him, and he drove out the spirits with a word and healed all the sick.

Here is another example found in Luke 6:17-19:

17. And Jesus came down with them and stood on a level place with a crowd of His disciples and a great multitude of people from all Judea and Jerusalem, and from the seacoast of Tyre and Sidon, who came to hear Him and be healed of their diseases, 18. as well as those who were tormented with unclean spirits. And they were healed. 19. And the whole multitude sought to touch Him, for power went out from Him and healed them all.

Finally, although there are numerous occasions of Jesus healing others, I simply don't have enough room in my book to share them all with you. Please crack open your Bible and read the stories for yourself. However, here is one last example that I would like to share with you which I found in Luke 7:1-10:

1. After he had finished all his sayings in the hearing of the people, he entered Capernaum. 2. Now a Roman centurion had a servant who was sick and at the point of death, who was highly valued by him. 3.

THE XANUE

When the centurion heard about Jesus, he sent to him elders of the Jews, asking him to come and heal his servant. 4. And when they came to Jesus, they pleaded with him earnestly, saying, "He is worthy to have you do this for him, 5. for he loves our nation, and he is the one who built us our synagogue." 6. And Jesus went with them. When he was not far from the house, the centurion sent friends, saying to him, "Lord, do not trouble yourself, for I am not worthy to have you come under my roof. 7. Therefore I did not presume to come to you. But say the word, and let my servant be healed. 8. For I too am a man set under authority, with soldiers under me: and I say to one, 'Go,' and he goes; and to another, 'Come,' and he comes; and to my servant, 'Do this,' and he does it." 9. When Jesus heard these things, he marveled at him, and turning to the crowd that followed him, said, "I tell you, not even in Israel have I found such faith." 10. And when those who had been sent returned to the house, they found the servant well.

The Xanue are also able to heal others. I can personally testify to the fact that they saved my life from a humongous DVT that was in my left leg between my groin and knee. The DVT should have killed me because no one lives through what I had, according to the vascular surgeon. The Xanue also healed my prostate. They removed a tumor from my colon. Finally, they worked on my lymphatic system and removed cancer from my body.

I know many others who have also been healed by the Xanue and their faith in God and Jesus Christ. Among my friends and acquaintances, the Xanue have healed them from an over-sized heart, colon cancer, macular degeneration, kidney stones, heart arrhythmia, leukemia, bone spurs, and they even grew out my friend's leg which was one-inch shorter than the other leg.

Finally, during the August 2019 weekend event at Camp Xanue located on our property in Chehalis WA, approximately forty-five people witnessed a woman, Ruth Cameron, who was crippled from three previous strokes, experience a total and complete healing. She came to our event dramatically physically impaired and had to hold on to her husband, David Cameron, in order to walk around inside our home and outside on our property. Yet, near the end of her weekend stay at Camp Xanue, she was walking unassisted. She was also running up and down the hill all by herself. As a matter of fact, Ruth was also jumping up and down with excitement and she was praising God and Jesus for her healing mixed with much appreciation for the Xanue too. It was a jaw dropping experience for everyone in attendance to actually witness this firsthand account. Amazing miracles of faith. Thank you God and thank you Jesus!!!

By the way, the Xanue will not heal anyone if it's not within the will of God. They are very mindful to seek God's permission and guidance before they begin the healing process. Sometimes the Xanue, by faith in Jesus Christ, are able to pull off an immediate miracle. On other occasions, they have to spend several days or weeks working on someone to help them heal their bodies. Steve Bachmann's local Xanue worked on him for over a week to help rid him of his colon cancer. It's an amazing story and you should ask him about it sometime. He's a humble gentleman who enjoys sharing about his faith in Jesus Christ as well as his experiences and friendship with the Xanue.

The Transfiguration

The transfiguration of Jesus Christ is one of my favorite passages in the Bible because it clearly demonstrates that we are all beings of light. God is light (1 John 1:15), Jesus is the image of the invisible God (Colossians 1:15), Jesus is the firstborn among many brethren (Romans 8:29), and, therefore, we are the light of the world (Matthew 5:14-16) and we are required to walk in the light with God and Jesus (1 John 1:5-7). What a privilege and blessing we have and the Xanue want us to understand this truth. The Xanue want all of us to live this truth. They are believers too.

Here is the passage in the Bible that refers to the Transfiguration event (Matthew 17:1-9):

1 Six days later Jesus took with Him Peter and James and his brother, John, and led them up on a high mountain by themselves. 2

And He was transfigured before them; and His face shone like the sun, and His garments became as white as light. 3 And behold, Moses and Elijah appeared to them, talking with Him. 4 Peter said to Jesus, "Lord, it is good for us to be here; if You wish, I will make three tabernacles here, one for You, and one for Moses, and one for Elijah." 5 While he was still speaking, a bright cloud overshadowed them, and behold, a voice out of the cloud said, "This is My beloved Son, with whom I am well-pleased; listen to Him!" 6 When the disciples heard this, they fell face down to the ground and were terrified. 7 And Jesus came to them and touched them and said, "Get up, and do not be afraid." 8 And lifting up their eyes, they saw no one except Jesus Himself alone. 9 As they were coming down from the mountain, Jesus commanded them, saying, "Tell the vision to no one until the Son of Man has risen from the dead."

Can you imagine being Peter, James, or John and actually witnessing the Transfiguration of Jesus and also seeing a cloud of light and hearing God speak from within it? What a freaking mind blowing experience that would be, right? Yet, it all makes absolute and complete sense. God clearly wanted Peter, James, and John to see the light (pun intended). God wanted them to see Jesus in his true form, acknowledge who Jesus really is, and listen to His beloved Son. Man was no longer obligated to listen to Moses (The Law) or Elijah (The Prophets). God now wants us to pay attention to Jesus who came to fulfill The Law and The Prophets.

Now since God is light, and Jesus is the image of the invisible God, then it only makes sense that the firstborn among many brethren (i.e., Jesus) would be light too, right? Since Jesus is the firstborn among many brethren (i.e., All created sentient beings throughout the universe), then it only makes sense that we are all Beings of Light too. As C.S. Lewis wrote, "We don't have a soul. We are a soul. We have a body." In other words, just like God and Jesus, we are all Beings of Light. The Xanue are Beings of Light too. All created sentient lifeforms are Beings of Light.

Chapter 4: The "COCO DE MER" Seed

The only difference between the Xanue and the human race is that they never fell in the Garden of Eden but we did. Therefore, we are locked into our physical form as a consequence of the fall of man. On the other hand, because the Xanue did not fall in the Garden of Eden, they are free to shapeshift back and forth between their Orb form and physical form. That is why there are so many reported experiences of Bigfoot researchers seeing Orbs in the woods while they're looking for Bigfoot (i.e., The Xanue).

During my first ten years of Bigfoot researching, I silenced anyone who brought up seeing Orbs while on our expeditions. I was afraid that they were going to damage our credibility as a Bigfoot research team. Matter of fact, I politely kicked two of them out of our group. I wished I knew how to contact those two individuals today so I could humbly apologize to the both of them. They were both right and I was terribly wrong. My closed mind and inflated ego wasn't willing to deal with the truth of the matter at that time. Some of you are in the same boat right now and reading all of this is most likely causing you to contort yourself. Relax, you'll eventually work through your denial.

In November of 2013, I brought two friends, Gunnar and Mike, to the Southern Oregon Habituation Area (SOHA) with me. At night, they were sitting with their backs up against the side of my suburban while I was using my smartphone to play music videos on the perimeter of the SOHA basecamp. I moved from the 9 o'clock position on the perimeter to the 12 o'clock position and on to the 3 o'clock position. I went back and forth around the perimeter of the basecamp for several minutes.

I walked back over to where Gunnar and Mike were sitting and reported to them that I counted a total of fourteen Bigfoot toddlers, juveniles, and adolescents on the perimeter who were all enjoying watching and listening to the music videos that I was playing on my phone. Gunnar and Mike asked me to go count them again for confirmation so I did. I was right, there was a total of fourteen Bigfoot toddlers, juveniles, and adolescents on the perimeter.

However, during my last headcount around the perimeter, while I was standing at the 9 o'clock position, I saw two tall Beings of Light. They were standing a ways back in the woods. The Beings of Light were translucent. Although I could see through them, I could make out the shape of body with head, shoulders, arms, hands, trunk, legs, and feet.

Suddenly, there was a fog of light emanating from their feet and it was covering the ground like dry-ice fog on a Broadway stage. The whole area was lit up with this fog of light. The three-belly crawling juvenile Bigfoot on the other side of the berm at the 9 o'clock position were still totally captivated by the music video on my smartphone. They were totally ignoring the Beings of Light, like it was no big deal to them.

During this experience, which lasted for a couple of minutes, I felt the complete and total unconditional love of God permeating my entire body and soul. I never felt anything like it before. All of my worries, troubles, and pain were gone. It was heavenly. The unconditional love was such a strong feeling that I wanted to walk closer to the beings of light. However, I decided not to do so because I didn't want to startle the three belly crawling Bigfoot juveniles by walking into their space. As suddenly as the Beings of Light appeared, they vanished as if a light switch was turned off. Everything was dark again.

I walked back over to Gunnar and Mike with tears streaming down my cheeks. They asked what had happened and I told them everything. They shared that they didn't see the Beings of Light because of where they were sitting. However, they most definitely saw that the area at the 9 o'clock position on the perimeter was lit up and then went dark again a couple minutes later.

By the way, when we retrieved the gifting bowls the next morning, there were only two peanut butter and raspberry jelly sandwich halves left in the two bowls. The other fourteen peanut butter and raspberry sandwich halves had been taken and consumed (i.e., A confirmation that there were actually fourteen young Bigfoot hanging around the perimeter of the SOHA basecamp, just as I had counted and reported). Oh yes, fingerprints were left behind on the gifting bowls too. Majorly cool beans.

Chapter 4: The "COCO DE MER" Seed

CLOAKING

Over the decades, there have been numerous reports of Bigfoot researchers seeing a Bigfoot (Xanue) cloaking or uncloaking. I have seen and experienced these phenomena on a few occasions. Please remember that Jesus told his Disciples that if they had the faith the size of a mustard seed, they could do what he did and more. The Xanue never fell in the Garden of Eden. Trust me, they have a truckload of faith.

Believe it or not, there's actually a story in the Bible that shares that Jesus has cloaking abilities. I'll share the passage of scripture (John 20:19-29) with you that talks about Jesus uncloaking on two separate occasions. Then I will explain it to you afterwards:

19 It was the first day of the week, and that very evening, while the disciples were together **with the doors locked** for fear of the Jews, **Jesus came and stood among them**. "Peace be with you!" He said to them. 20 After He had said this, He showed them His hands and His side. The disciples rejoiced when they saw the Lord. 21 Again Jesus said to them, "Peace be with you. As the Father has sent Me, so also I am sending you." 22 When He had said this, He breathed on them and said, "Receive the Holy Spirit. 23 If you forgive anyone his sins, they are forgiven; if you withhold forgiveness from anyone, it is withheld." 24 Now Thomas called Didymus, one of the Twelve, was not with the disciples when Jesus came. 25 So the other disciples told him, "We have seen the Lord!" But he replied, "Unless I see the nail marks in His hands, and put my finger where the nails have been, and put my hand into His side, I will never believe." 26 Eight days later, His disciples were once again inside **with the doors locked**, and Thomas was with them. **Jesus came and stood among them** and said, "Peace be with you." 27 Then Jesus said to Thomas, "Put your finger here and look at My hands. Reach out your hand and put it into My side. Stop doubting and believe." 28 Thomas replied, "My Lord and my God!" 29 Jesus said to him, "Because you have seen Me, you have believed; blessed are those who have not seen and yet have believed."

THE XANUE

First things first, I need to provide you with some context for the scripture that you just read (John 20:19-29). The disciples had just spent three years following Jesus. They walked with him, talked with him, ate with him, laughed with him, slept alongside him, ministered with him, and prayed with him for three long years.

After those three long years with Jesus, the disciples still didn't realize who He was. Even after the Transfiguration, Peter, James, and John still didn't get it completely. Suddenly, as Jesus foretold his Twelve Disciples, he was swiftly taken from them and crucified. They were totally caught off guard. Their faith and hope were shattered by Jesus' horrific death on the cross.

What did the disciples do after the crucifixion? They hid themselves from the Jewish religious leaders and from the Roman soldiers who were looking for them. They did not want to suffer from the same inhumane death that Jesus experienced. They were hiding in the upper room while other individuals were keeping them informed, fed, and watered.

It is important to note that the author of the scripture, the apostle John, wrote twice about the fact that the doors were locked (i.e., **"with the doors locked"**). Why is this important to note? Well, it's important to note because, in spite of the locked doors, **Jesus came and stood among them**. In other words, He appeared out of nowhere (i.e., Jesus uncloaked himself on two separate occasions). He didn't come walking through the doors because the doors were locked. He wasn't in the room the entire time because John wouldn't have stated that he "came" and stood among them. Besides, everyone would have already seen that Jesus was in the room with them. In other words, Jesus wasn't there and then suddenly He was there. Shazam! Jesus uncloaked.

The fun doesn't stop there, Jesus uncloaked on other occasions too (Luke 24:36-49):

36 While they were telling these things, He Himself stood in their midst and said to them, "Peace be to you." 37 But they were startled and frightened and thought that they were seeing a spirit. 38 And

Chapter 4: The "COCO DE MER" Seed

He said to them, "Why are you troubled, and why do doubts arise in your hearts? 39 "See My hands and My feet, that it is I Myself; touch Me and see, for a spirit does not have flesh and bones as you see that I have." 40 And when He had said this, He showed them His hands and His feet. 41 While they still could not believe it because of their joy and amazement, He said to them, "Have you anything here to eat?" 42 They gave Him a piece of a broiled fish; 43and He took it and ate it before them. 44 Now He said to them, "These are My words which I spoke to you while I was still with you, that all things which are written about Me in the Law of Moses and the Prophets and the Psalms must be fulfilled." 45 Then He opened their minds to understand the Scriptures, 46 and He said to them, "Thus it is written, that the Christ would suffer and rise again from the dead the third day, 47 and that repentance for forgiveness of sins would be proclaimed in His name to all the nations, beginning from Jerusalem. 48 "You are witnesses of these things. 49 "And behold, I am sending forth the promise of My Father upon you; but you are to stay in the city until you are clothed with power from on high."

Once again, please allow me to provide you with some necessary context. In short, Jesus was blowing the disciple's minds with his constant cloaking and uncloaking before them. He would come and go and come again. They thought they were seeing a ghost. Therefore, he had to convince them that he wasn't a ghost. He had His disciples look at his crucifixion wounds and touch him. If that wasn't enough, he asked for some food so He could eat it in front of them. Finally, He opened up their minds so they could understand the scriptures and who He actually is – The Son of God.

Do you know any knuckleheads like doubting Thomas and the other disciples? You know the type. I'm talking about the individual who says unless I see a God, Jesus, Bigfoot, a Being of Light, or an Orb with my own eyes, I won't ever believe what you're saying. It's like they're taking the slogan from the State of Missouri way too seriously (i.e., "The Show Me State").

They close their eyes and stick their fingers in their ears while saying, "Nah! Nah! Nah! Nah! I can't see or hear you!" They don't want their minds blown like Jesus blew the minds of the disciples. They feel much more comfortable keeping their minds inside their small, rigid, black and white, theoretical boxes and with their head stuck deep down in the sand. They live in a blue pill world (i.e., watch the Matrix movie). Yet, blessed are those who have not seen and yet have believed. I'll take the red pill any day of the week because I want to see the truth, speak the truth, and live the truth. I'll take reality over theoretical fiction every time.

SEEING INTO THE FUTURE

Around the world, human history is full of prophesies regarding future events (i.e., Seeing into the future). More specifically to this discussion, in the Bible, the Old Testament is full of prophecies regarding the coming of the Messiah - the Son of God - Jesus Christ. Matter of fact, Jesus made some of his own predictions too. He predicted his own death and resurrection (Mark 8:31):

31 Then Jesus began to tell them that the Son of Man must suffer many terrible things and be rejected by the elders, the leading priests, and the teachers of religious law. He would be killed, but three days later he would rise from the dead.

Jesus predicted the destruction of Jerusalem (Luke 19:41-44) which happened 70 years after his death and resurrection (i.e., 70 AD):

41 When He approached Jerusalem, He saw the city and wept over it, 42 saying, "If you had known in this day, even you, the things which make for peace! But now they have been hidden from your eyes. 43 "For the days will come upon you when your enemies will throw up a barricade against you, and surround you and hem you in on every side, 44 and they will level you to the ground and your children within you, and they will not leave in you one stone upon another, because you did not recognize the time of your visitation."

Chapter 4: The "COCO DE MER" Seed

Jesus predicted the destruction of the Temple in Jerusalem which also happened 70 years after his death and resurrection (Luke 21:5-6):

5 And while some were talking about the temple, that it was adorned with beautiful stones and votive gifts, He said, 6 "As for these things which you are looking at, the days will come in which there will not be left one stone upon another which will not be torn down."

Finally, Jesus predicted his second coming (Mark 13:24-27). Although his second coming has yet to happen, it will most definitely happen just as certainly as all of the other Old and New Testament prophesies which have already been fulfilled:

24"But in those days, after that tribulation, the sun will be darkened and the moon will not give it's light, 25 and the stars will be falling from heaven, and the powers that are in the heavens will be shaken. 26 "Then they will see the Son of Man coming in the clouds with great power and glory. 27 "And then He will send forth the angels, and will gather together His elect from the four winds, from the farthest end of the Earth to the farthest end of heaven."

Based on this last passage of scripture, it looks like Jesus might be returning around the time that the Earth is engulfed in an all-out nuclear war or after an asteroid hits the Earth followed by meteor showers. However, to be clear, neither man nor the angels know the day or hour of the second coming of Christ. Not even Jesus knows himself. Only the Father knows (Mark 13:32). Therefore, any other individual who claims that they know exactly when Jesus Christ is returning or when the world is going to end is a false prophet.

With all of the above said, please remember that Jesus did say that if we had faith the size of an itty bitty mustard seed, we could do what he has done and more. Once again, the Xanue have a truckload of faith. Like many others of God's faithful servants throughout history, they're also able to see into the future with great accuracy.

Case in point, in January of 2018, Cynthia and I invited several friends to come to our property and join us in a night sit and sleep over.

Fortunately, the weather cooperated and the weekend was absolutely amazing. However, prior to everyone's arrival, I had to get up early and weed whack the trails in the forest behind our home so no one would get injured or lost.

While I was weed whacking the trails, I kept hearing the same mind speak over and over again: "Stay off the trails." I would respond in my mind by stating, "I have to weed whack the trails to make sure that my guests are safe from injury and that no one gets lost." It took me a couple of hours but I managed to weed whack all of the trails successfully, in spite of their repetitive nagging. When I was done, I told the Xanue in my mind, "Neener! Neener! See! I'm fine and nothing happened." Then everyone arrived and the fun began.

When it got dark, we split up everyone into different groups in order to spread out all over our property for the various night sits. Steve Bachmann, Cynthia, and I planned to rotate around the property together and spend time with each night sit group. First, we spent about thirty minutes with the group sitting near the fire pit and woodshed. Next, we spent about thirty minutes with the group halfway down the hillside.

On our way down the hillside in the dark, the three of us hit the steepest part of the wet slick trail. In a split second, my legs slipped out from underneath me and I ended up twisting my right ankle and right knee. Steve and Cynthia fell too. Steve landed on his back. Cynthia landed on her stomach. Fortunately, neither one of them were injured.

Suddenly, I heard a mind speak, "Stay off the trails." I had to chuckle because they had the last laugh. I believe that was the Xanue's very kind, gracious, and loving way of saying, "Neener! Neener! See! We told you so!" Well, I decided to stop arguing with them after that.

Since that time, whenever I receive a mind speak from the Xanue warning me about something in the future, you better believe that I'm giving them my undivided attention and doing exactly what they advise me to do. I appreciate the fact that the Xanue are believers in God and Jesus Christ and that they walk by faith. Finally, I'm grateful that they are able to see into the future and are loving, kind, and caring enough to want to help keep me safe and sound.

CHAPTER 5
DO THESE TWO THINGS

Jesus was constantly scrutinized by the Jewish religious leaders. They were jealous of the fact that the multitudes were spending their time listening to his teachings rather than the Pharisees and the Sadducees. The religious leaders were not pleased that Jesus was healing people, especially on the Sabbath. How could they compete with this guy for the attention of the Jewish people? Also, they feared that the Roman empire would interpret Jesus' impact on the nation of Israel as a rebellion that they would have to put down. In other words, some of Jesus' followers thought that he was there to help lead the Jews into war against the Roman empire in order to win Israel's freedom. That would mean the destruction of their synagogues and temple. Therefore, the Jewish religious leaders agreed that they needed to work together to find a reason to accuse Jesus of blasphemy so they could have him put to death.

Jesus wasn't dumb. He happened to be fully God in human flesh. He knew what they were up to. He had to constantly watch his back when he was around the Pharisees and Sadducees. He once called them white wash tombs (Matthew 23:27): "Woe to you, scribes and Pharisees, you hypocrites! You are like whitewashed tombs, which look beautiful on the outside, but on the inside are full of dead men's bones and every impurity." Jesus didn't hesitate to call them out on their crap and they were not very happy about it.

In Matthew 22:34-40, we read the following:

34. And when the Pharisees heard that Jesus had silenced the Sadducees, they themselves gathered together. 35. One of them, an

expert in the law, tested Him with a question: 36. "Teacher, which commandment is the greatest in the Law?" 37. Jesus declared, "'Love the Lord your God with all your heart and with all your soul and with all your mind.' 38. This is the first and greatest commandment. 39. And the second is like it: 'Love your neighbor as yourself.' 40. If you do these two things, you fulfill all of the Laws."

Well, once again, Jesus managed to dodge the bullet and the Jewish religious leaders were not happy. You see, at that time, there were a little over six-hundred commandments that the people had to live by in order to be good Jews. Nevertheless, Jesus simplified the commandments by boiling them down to two things: (1) Love God, and (2) Love your neighbor as yourself.

Needless to say, the Jewish religious leaders were very frustrated. They certainly couldn't tear their robes and cry out, "Blasphemy!" over Jesus' message of love. Also, they had just mistakenly pitched the ball right over the plate to Jesus, in front of the multitudes, and He smacked the ball right out of the park. A grand slam homerun!

Jesus just taught the crowd that they don't need to live by the onerous six-hundred plus rules anymore. All they needed to do was simply (1) Love God, and (2) Love their neighbor as themselves. If they would do these two things, they would fulfill all of the Laws.

To be fair to the Jewish religious leaders, both the Catholic and Protestant churches aren't any different today. Neither are many of the other world's religions. Although they don't have over six-hundred plus rules in a Torah to live by, they most certainly have just about as many written and unspoken rules that their members are supposed to live by in order to be good believers. Apparently, Jesus' message to do these two things fell through the cracks during the historical development of the church.

Believe it or not, as previously stated earlier in this section of my book, the Xanue consider themselves to be children of God. They are our fellow brothers and sisters in Creation. They worship the Creator and do not want to be misunderstood and worshipped by others. They are not the Nephilim, Demigods, or Demons. They are sentient beings who never fell in the Garden of Eden. They want to connect with the human race, like big brothers and big sisters, and help us to reconnect with God/Jesus Christ, our neighbors and ourselves, and the Earth that God gave us to be good stewards of.

There is absolutely nothing in the message of the Xanue that contradicts the scriptures or that can justify the ignorance of accusing them to be something that they are not – Nephilim, Demigods, or Demons. They are faithful and loving children of God. Just like you and me. They're simply much farther down the spiritual path of faith, hope, and love than we are and they are very interested in helping us to get there too.

The Xanue continually work on me every day, hand in hand with God's Holy Spirit, to change my attitudes and behaviors to become a better Christian. They have helped me to love my enemy and pray for them. They have encouraged me to be a better husband and father. They have inspired me to stop some negative behaviors while starting to engage in new positive behaviors. As the result of my friendship with the Xanue, I'm becoming a better human being in spite of my many imperfections.

Finally, Zorth and the Council of Twelve want me to convey the following message: "You can't have one without the other." In other words, Zorth is trying to say that if you believe in the existence of the Bigfoot Forest People (i.e., The Xanue), then you must also believe in God and Jesus Christ. It's a package deal. You can't have one without the other. Zorth says, "We do not exist apart from the existence of God, our Creator, nor his blessed Son, Jesus Christ. If you want to commune with us, you must learn to commune with them. Without God, there is no Xanue."

The morning after the EXODUS in June of 2016, Zorth told me, "We are in the trees and the trees are everywhere." He also stated, "If a kind person with a good heart and an open mind reaches out to us, we will reach back to them." I know hundreds of people who can testify to the fact that Zorth and the Xanue have and still are delivering on their promise.

PART 2
THE XANUE AMBASSADOR ("THE 13")

CHAPTER 6
Faithful Failures

I've been working in the mental health field for thirty-eight years. I've been a licensed clinical psychologist for twenty-five of those thirty-eight years. Over almost the past four decades, I've worked with thousands and thousands of children, adolescents, adults, couples, and families. Although they all have a variety of differing primary problems that bring them into my office such as depression, anxiety, bipolar disorder, physical or sexual abuse issues, alcohol and drug addiction, eating disorders, seasonal affective disorder, anger issues, cutting and suicide attempts, ADD or ADHD, schizophrenia, and personality disorders, most of them have low self-esteem in common (i.e., they don't think very highly of themselves). All of the above listed primary problems usually chip away at an individual's self-esteem.

Many of the above people would be considered by others as being successful in life. They are professionally successful. They are financially successful. They are successful with their marriage and family. They are active in their school, church, and community. They have many friends. They're physically attractive. They're smart, funny, and have a pleasant personality. Yet, they're just not quite good enough. They believe that everyone else has it better than them. Everyone else actually is better than them. They feel like failures bogged down by low self-esteem. Some of them seriously believe that their family and the world would be better off without them.

There could be many reasons why they consider themselves to be failures. As a child, they endured parental neglect. Perhaps they were victims of verbal, physical, and/or sexual abuse. Maybe they were born with a physical deformity or childhood disease that has plagued them throughout their entire life. However, most common of all, they consider themselves to be failures because they have simply made what they consider to be as one or more serious mistakes in their life. They have dropped the ball one or more times in a major way. They have let others down. They have let themselves down. They're not perfect. They're failures.

Can you imagine walking around from day to day, forging through life, with this invisible heavy monkey on your back? What a burden it must be everyday to strive to appear to be outwardly successful while always feeling internally disappointed in one's own self. There are many people who live like this and believe that they have absolutely nothing to contribute to the wellbeing of others and to the world. They are convinced that they are unforgivable failures and that God could never use them to accomplish great things. They believe that they have missed the train. That's all she wrote. The fat lady has sung.

I recently read a Facebook meme that is apropos. It said, "If you think that you've blown God's plan for your life, please rest in this fact: You, my beautiful friend, are not that powerful." All too often, people who've made mistakes are way too hard on themselves. They judge themselves rather harshly. They are their own judge, jury, and executioner. They are their own worst enemy. Although the people who verbally, physically, and/or sexually abused them in their childhood are long gone or dead, they have now become the perpetrators of their own ongoing emotional abuse.

I work hard to help these individuals to see the fact that although the truck is muddy, it can be washed. Although the windshield is cracked, it can be replaced. Although the tire is flat, it can be repaired or changed. Finally, although the engine is sputtering, it can be tuned up. There isn't anything that we have said or done that can't be dealt with, one way or another. God can and will take our life's mistakes and messes that we make and cause them all to work together for His good if we allow Him to do so and believe that He will do so (Romans 8:28). In short, God uses faithful failures.

THE HALL OF FAITH: In the book of Hebrews, Chapter 11, verse 6, we are reminded that "without faith it is impossible to please God, because anyone who approaches Him must believe that He exists and that He rewards those who earnestly seek Him." Throughout the rest of Hebrews, Chapter 11, we are given numerous examples of how God used imperfect people to accomplish His perfect plans. God used Noah, a drunkard, to build the Ark and save his family. God used Abraham, who almost murdered his own son, to bring about the nation of Israel. God used Moses, a murderer, to lead his chosen people out of Egypt. God used Rahab, a prostitute, to help His people at the wall of Jericho. God used Sampson, who gave into his own ego and sexual temptation, to accomplish His purposes. God also used David, an adulterer and murderer, to be the King of Israel and to govern His people. The stories of God using faithful failures to accomplish His plans just go on and on.

To be fair to the previously mentioned Biblical characters, to all of my clients, and to those of you who are reading this book, I can totally relate to feeling like a failure sometimes because of making mistakes and bad choices in my lifetime. I have whooped on myself plenty of times for the choices I made in my life. Guilt! Guilt! Guilt! I have been hurt by people and I have hurt people. I felt the pain of my parents' poor choices and my children have felt the pain of my poor choices. Absolutely no human being is perfect. No one. Well, okay, you just might be the exception to the rule. Oh wait…. NOT!!!

Even Paul, the greatest Apostle of all time, struggled with the same inner conflict that we all do from time to time. Paul wrote the following in Romans 7:18-25:

18 I have the desire to do what is good, but I cannot carry it out. 19 For I do not do the good I want to do. Instead, I keep on doing the evil I do not want to do. 20 And if I do what I do not want, it is no longer I who do it, but it is sin living in me that does it. 21 So this is the principle I have discovered: When I want to do good, evil is right

there with me. 22 For in my inner being I delight in God's law. 23 But I see another law at work in my body, warring against the law of my mind and holding me captive to the law of sin that dwells within me. 24 What a wretched man I am! Who will rescue me from this body of death? 25 Thanks be to God, through Jesus Christ our Lord!

Fortunately, God grants all of us a clean slate through faith in His Son, Jesus Christ (I John 1:9):

9 "If we confess our sins, he is faithful and just to forgive us our sins and to cleanse us from all unrighteousness."

We don't have to live out the rest of our lives weighted down by our struggles and imperfections. We don't have to surrender to the false belief that there's no way to get off of the insane merry-go-round of self-doubt and low self-esteem. We can finally move forward, knowing full well, that God uses faithful failures to accomplish His purposes. We simply aren't powerful enough to take ourselves off of His radar. No matter what, He can and will still use us as long as we remain faithful and simply believe.

WHY ME? Since my family's encounter with a Bigfoot up on the mountain above the Oregon Caves National Monument Park on July 1, 2000, the past twenty years have been absolutely incredible and mind blowing. Although the journey down the Rabbit Hole has been eye opening, it hasn't come without a whole lot of questions. However, the most obvious question being, "Why me?" I've had plenty of people tell me over the past two decades that "You were chosen" or "God wanted you to help the Xanue."

Many thoughts have gone through my mind such as, "This is not the path I saw myself walking on when I was a kid." Instead, I saw myself growing up to become an NBA player and eventually a Pastor. Also, I've even thought, "Am I being deceived and used by Satan to mislead everyone down the wrong path?" Finally, I've thought "Out of all the seven billion people on the planet, why was I called or compelled to walk this path in order to help the Xanue?" In short, the "Why me?" question has caused me to dig deep down inside and wrestle with my own imperfections and unworthiness. I've prayed a whole lot, talked

Chapter 6: Faithful Failures

with a lot of people, prayed a whole lot, read through the scriptures, talked with a lot of people, and prayed a whole lot. Then I talked and prayed some more.

The conclusion I arrived at was, although I'm not worthy, I am a faithful failure and God can still use me to accomplish his purpose. I concluded that absolutely no individual has failed so much that God can't use them. All we have to do is confess our sins and ask for forgiveness and then raise our hand and say, "Here I am, send me" (Romans 10:14-15).

God can and will use our faithfulness to do His bidding in all areas of our lives. Besides, we are never alone. We are always accompanied by family, friends, coworkers, and strangers at just the right time to help us accomplish God's plan in our lives and in the lives of others. Living by faith is a team sport and there's no "I" in team.

GO TEAM: Truth be told, it was never just me alone. I couldn't have accomplished anything pertaining to helping the Xanue if it wasn't for a cast of supporting characters such as my first ex-wife and our three children (i.e., I would have never gone on the hike on the Big Tree Loop Trail above the Oregon Caves if we hadn't gone to the park together that day on July 1, 2000). My second wife encouraged me to continue with my research even though the death of my colleague and friend, Dr. William York, took the wind out of my sails. She encouraged me to take our son, Grady, out with me into the forest and continue my research regarding the Bigfoot phenomenon. Grady and I had lots of fun adventures together.

I most certainly couldn't have discovered who the Bigfoot Forest People (Xanue) are, where they're from, and why they're here without the love, encouragement, and ongoing support from my third and final wife, Cynthia. She has supported me in so many ways that it would take writing another book just to tell you. Suffice it to say for now, no Cynthia equals no EXODUS.

Also, without the friendship and assistance of Mike Kincaid and Steve Bachmann, there most definitely wouldn't have been an EXODUS for the Xanue. Mike's friendship and companionship kept me going back out into the forest repeatedly over the years. We shared many Rabbit Hole experiences together. Steve Bachmann, a very humble salt of the Earth type of guy, built the electromagnetic pulsating device from Tesla's design. We used Steve's device at the Southern Oregon Interaction Area (SOIA) to help the Xanue keep the portal open so their loved ones could make it from their dying home world to the Earth. Hence, the EXODUS.

Finally, there were so many other people who were supportively involved and who came out with me into the forest over the past twenty-years, including teachers, principals, businessmen, hairstylists, pharmacists, military personnel, law enforcement officers, media personalities, psychiatrists, mental health counselors, ITD personnel, construction workers, avid hunters, and so many more. This doesn't even include the great number of people who've joined Cynthia and I over the past two years at Camp Xanue, on our property, during the months of June, July, and August.

So to answer the question, "Why me?" Well, it turns out that there was no me. Rather, there is we.

A team of faithful failures working together to help the world to understand that God has created many sentient beings. To help the world to understand that the Xanue are our fellow brothers and sisters in Christ. They are here to help us reconnect with God, with one another, and with the Earth that God gave us to be good stewards of.

Without the entire Chicago Bulls basketball team working together, there would be no multiple championships for Michael Jordan. Without the entire Patriots football team, there would be no multiple championships for Tom Brady. Without the Jackson Five band of brothers, there would be no singing career for Michael Jackson. Without the U2 band, there would be no Bono. Without the Maroon Five band, there would be no Adam Levine. Finally, without the twelve disciples (i.e., Jesus' faithful failures), the gospel of Jesus Christ and the early church would have never gotten off the ground. Team! Team! Team!

Nevertheless, all of the above "teams" had a point man, a team captain, an inspirational leader who kept everyone focused and moving ahead together to get the job done. Without an inspired and gifted team leader, many teams would have failed. Yet, everyone working together under the guidance and inspiration of the team leader, helps to accomplish the successful obtainment of the desired goal. A leader doesn't just take charge. He takes care of those whom he's in charge of. I've tried my best to do so.

During the remainder of this section of my book, I'm being asked to share with you why I was appointed to the team leader position. You're probably thinking, "Wait! What? Who's asking you?" Well the answer would be both God's Holy Spirit as well as Zorth, the leader of the Xanue Council of Twelve. For whatever reason, they want this story documented. It seems rather self-serving but there's no one else who knows as much as I do who can accurately document my story. Therefore, I'm stuck with writing my own autobiography section. Ugh! But somebody has to do it. I'll try my best. May you find it to be inspirational. Go Team!!!

CHAPTER 7
THE YOUNGER YEARS (K-12)

ASTORIA, OREGON

I have been told by many people that I have not lived an ordinary life. Matter of fact, I totally agree with them. I believe that I've lived an extraordinary life with a pinch of fun adventures and a dash of crazy. Okay, maybe a dump truck load of crazy. However, with all of the misadventures, unexpected detours, epic failures, and painful disappointments, I wouldn't change a thing because all of my yesterdays, the good, the bad, and the ugly, add up to making me who I am today.

I can't start my story without first mentioning both my father and mother. My father, Arthur H. Johnson, shared a memory with me that he had from prior to his birth. His memory consisted of being in the clouds while sitting on the stairs of a Parthenon. He was looking down from the heavens and viewing the Earth. He was then shown his parents who were awaiting to give birth. He was told that that their names were Clarence and Goldie Johnson. Finally, my father was told that it was time to go be with his parents. However, my father objected. He didn't want to leave his comfortable and serene environment. The next thing he remembered was that he was being born.

My mother, Joann, never shared any early memories with me. However, when I was very young, she did share with me that she had special abilities too. I was confused by what she was saying because I was simply talking with her about the people that I was seeing inside the house, in the backyard, and in the woods behind our home. I wasn't quite sure why it took special abilities to see and talk with people. She said that God made me just the way I am and that I had nothing to worry about. She said that God was everywhere and would keep me safe from the bad people. As a four-year-old, I just accepted what my mother said and went on from there. Therefore, I kept talking with God in the woods behind our house in Astoria, Oregon.

Over the years, my mother encouraged me to learn more about my special abilities. She would give me various articles to read and would watch some psychic and paranormal TV shows with me. However, she never talked openly about her abilities ever again. Matter of fact, based on twenty-twenty hindsight, my mom apparently couldn't handle living with her abilities. Because she stuffed her thoughts and feelings inside of herself for so long, she ended up drinking and smoking herself into a premature death.

This truth was recently confirmed by one of my three sons who had a chat with my parents, his grandparents, while he was meditating. I understand that this all sounds crazy to some of you. However, I guarantee all of you that it's one-hundred percent true. Two out of my four children are gifted just like my parents and me.

My earliest personal memory was at the age of two-months-old when my parents had me go through infant baptism at the Lutheran Church in Astoria, Oregon. I remember being scared that they handed me to a strange man dressed in funny looking clothes. Then he had the audacity to sprinkle water all over my head and face. It really pissed me off. Seriously, it did. I cried and cried because I was so angry. After that, I remember fearing who else my parents were going to hand me to in the future and what were they going to do to me. There was definitely a feeling of my trust being violated at that moment in time.

At the age of one, I remember my mom laying me on the floor to change my diaper. While she was leaning over me, I remember seeing a cigarette dangling out of her mouth. The ashes on the end of the cigarette were long and about to fall off. I remember being afraid that they were going to drop on me and burn me. Another trust issue.

Chapter 7: The Younger Years (K-12)

Just past the age of two, I remember my parents watching news reports regarding the assassination of President John F. Kennedy. I remember seeing my parents crying over his death. I also remember my parents bringing my little brother home from the hospital three weeks later. I remember feeling demoted from the baby of the family to just another kid in the middle, along with my older brother and sister. Needless to say, I was just a tad bit jealous of my little brother and tried to encourage him to swallow pennies and other objects too. Now I was creating the trust issues. What comes around goes around.

At age four, I learned to be very friendly and social as I met and talked with various individuals who came to visit with me in our home and outside our home. Although some of the visitors were kids my age, most were older people with grey hair. Sometimes, they were shadow people too. All I knew is that it was okay to visit with them and that my mom told me that God would protect me from the bad people.

If you read my first Bigfoot book, then you will remember that at the age of five, I was playing in a large lumber pile in the front yard of my friend's home. He lived just up the street from our home in Astoria, Oregon. He had another friend over to play too. Eventually, we got bored and walked on a trail into the woods behind his home. Once we got fairly deep into the woods, the other two boys pointed up into the trees and screamed, "Bear!" They turn and ran back down the trail to my friend's home.

For some reason, I couldn't move. I just stood there and watched the Black Bear climb down the tree. When the Black Bear made it all the way down the tree to the ground, it walked over to me on two feet (i.e., bipedal steps). At that point, I was looking face to face with a hairy human looking kid. He wasn't a Black Bear. Then he said, "Hello" to me with his mind. I turned around and ran back down the trail to my friend's home. I passed my friends in his yard, and ran straight back to my home. I never went back to my friend's home again.

That same year (1966), I entered Kindergarten at John Jacob Astor Elementary School. The same school they used, long after my childhood, to film the movie, "Kindergarten Cop" with Arnold

Schwarzenegger. My claim to fame is that I actually flunked Kindergarten at that very school. Arnold would have been disappointed in me. I was very tall for my age, extremely awkward, and I had hearing problems which created speech impediment issues on top of it all.

Matter of fact, I underwent speech therapy sessions at that same school on late Saturday mornings. We met on the top floor in the hallway. My speech pathologist was a cranky old woman straight from Nazi Germany. At least it seemed like she was from Nazi Germany. Anyway, she wasn't very kid friendly. Matter of fact, she would yell and scream at me quite often. Therefore, I chose not to cooperate with her.

As a result of my lack of cooperation, she would leave me sitting alone at the table, in the middle of the hallway on the top floor for an hour as punishment. I didn't remember the above scenario until I watched the movie, "Kindergarten Cop."

The movie caused me to have nightmares about my childhood speech therapy experiences with Brume Elda. Fortunately, the Goonies movie, the Short Circuit movie, and the Teenage Mutant Ninja Turtles III movie, all filmed in Astoria, Oregon, never triggered any unpleasant memories for me.

After my eardrums were lanced, I was able to hear normally. As a result of improved hearing, I was able to eventually start talking normally too. I passed Kindergarten the following year and my parents' friends no longer thought that I was mildly mentally retarded. If you're a politically correct type of individual, sorry. That's what they called in back in the 1960's (i.e., Mildly mentally retarded).

While we were living in Astoria, I remember sitting on my father's lap while we were watching Lew Alcinder (AKA Kareem Abdul Jabbar) play on the TV for UCLA (1966-69). My father told me that I was tall for my age and that I was going to be a tall young man. He said that if I practiced hard enough, I could go to college for free someday just like Lew Alcinder. The only problem was that we didn't have a basketball hoop for me to practice on the 35th Street hill in Astoria, Oregon.

Chapter 7: The Younger Years (K-12)

SALEM, OREGON

My father was an Oregon State Trooper for twenty-five years. After patrolling the highway for the first ten years of his career, between the cities of Astoria and Seaside, he was promoted to a desk job in Salem, Oregon. He spent the rest of his career working in the fingerprint bureau. When he retired in 1985, the fingerprints were just starting to be digitally stored. Prior to that, all of his work involved painstakingly looking over thousands of paper cards stored in rooms full of filing cabinets. He was very good at what he did and helped to catch many bad guys.

When we moved to Salem in 1969, the State Capitol of Oregon, I was in the middle of the second grade. I really enjoyed the move for several reasons. First, we moved into a bigger and nicer home with a half-acre of fenced property. Second, there was a creek in the very back of the yard that we could fish in for crawdads. Third, we also had lots and lots of trees in our backyard that we could climb and make a tree fort. Fourth, we had two types of cherry trees, one apple tree, two plum trees, and a walnut tree. We also had a ton of very tall Cottonwood trees down by the creek. Finally, and most important of all, we had a basketball hoop on the garage in front of the home.

I could finally start practicing hard to earn my college scholarship like my father suggested a year earlier. He told me that while I was practicing shooting hoops in the driveway, I would earn one dollar per every basket that I made towards my college education. Please keep in mind, I had absolutely no idea in the second grade what college or a scholarship were. I just knew that it was important enough for my father to suggest the idea and it sounded like a lot of money to me. So I practiced shooting baskets in the driveway for the next ten years until I graduated from high school.

In the middle of the second grade, I started attending Morningside Elementary School in Salem, Oregon. I was not excited about going to my new school. I had been bullied at John Jacob Astor Elementary School because of my height, awkwardness, hearing problem, and speech impediment. However, my mom was very positive about the new school and enthusiastically encouraged me to attend with a positive attitude because it was going to be a completely different experience than the previous school that I attended. I quickly learned at my new elementary school that I was the new cool kid on the block. All of a sudden, everyone wanted to be my friend. What a positive change that was in my life. My mom was right. I liked my new school.

As the elementary school years progressed, I took on two new roles among my peers: (1) I was everyone's Ann Landers or Dear Abby. In other words, all of my peers came to me to talk about their problems; and (2) I became the protector of the students who were being bullied at school. Although I never got into a fight, I most definitely used my size to act as a nuclear deterrent in order to get the bullies to stand down and walk away. As a result, I became everyone's friend, including the bullies eventually. I guess they figured that if they couldn't beat me, they should join me.

Also, I enjoyed being the teacher's pet, year after year, during elementary school. I accelerated academically. I also did well in art, drama, choir, and in sports. I enjoyed playing Boy's Club basketball and football. I loved playing Little League baseball too. My size and strength definitely gave me the competitive edge on the fields and the court. I competed with everything I had and I always played for the winning teams that brought home the championship trophy at the end of the season. Fortunately, participation trophies did not exist when I was a child. Therefore, I always had to work hard to win, win, and win some more if I wanted to obtain a trophy.

In 1973, I was in the sixth grade. I was at the top of the elementary school food chain. I was 5'11" tall and I was kicking butt in all of the sports I played: basketball, football, and baseball. I also remember that I could barely fit into the bathtub by that age. I loved taking baths. I didn't start taking showers until the seventh grade.

Chapter 7: The Younger Years (K-12)

THE BATHTUB VISION

Anyway, during the summer between my sixth grade and seventh grade years, one night I was taking a bath as usual. While I was reclining in the very warm water, I somehow slipped into a spiritual trance. I visualized myself as standing in the middle of a very bright white light. However, it was not a blinding white light. My eyes were wide open and all I could see is the bright white light. There weren't any floor, walls, ceiling, windows, or doors. Just a warm, bright light, and a whole lot of unconditional love. I remember feeling confused by where I was and why I was standing there.

Suddenly, a voice started talking to me. It was a serene, kind, caring, and loving masculine voice. He started telling me about how my life was going to turn out. He told me that I would become a successful athlete, especially in the sport of basketball. He told me that I was going to go to college. He told me that I was going to get married and have several children. He said that I was going to be a well-known Bigfoot researcher. He said that God would use me to help thousands of families. Finally, he told me a few other things that are simply too personal for me to share with you in this book or in person so please don't ask me. However, I can tell you that some of these more personal things have been coming true, thus far.

I was then asked if I would accept God's plan for my life and try my best to live it out to the fullest. Naturally, I said, "Yes," even though I really didn't understand completely what the heck was going on. Then, as suddenly as the vision began, it was over with. I found myself laying in the water in the bathtub completely perplexed. What just happened to me? Was I dreaming? No! I didn't fall asleep. I was simply transported in my mind to another place for this future telling meeting. I kept it to myself. I waited for about forty years before I first told Cynthia about it. Eventually, I recently started telling others too.

I have to tell you that I thought about the vision quite often. However, the only part that I found totally confusing was the well-known Bigfoot researcher prediction. What the heck did that mean? Searching for Bigfoot was most definitely not on my childhood radar or agenda. But that successful basketball player prediction was most certainly inspiring. I continued to shoot baskets in the driveway, adding up dollars for my college scholarship. I wanted to become an NBA player.

SLEEPING UNDER THE STARS

During the warm summers in Salem, Oregon, I was in the habit of sleeping outside in the backyard on the chase lounges with my friends, brother, and sometimes my father. After the bathtub vision, while sleeping outside under the stars, I began to occasionally have repetitive dreams where a kind and gentle voice was calling me to come down the hill to the backside of the property where the creek was. In the dreams, I would walk down the hill in the dark and follow the voice to the very tall and plentiful Cottonwood trees alongside the creek. Then out of the corner of my right eye, I would see a Bigfoot pop out of a Cottonwood tree. He would start walking toward me with a friendly look on his face. However, in my repetitive dreams over the years, I would always turn around and run away right back up the hill to my house. Then I would wake up out of the dream, sweating, and with my heart pounding rapidly. I was scared. Then I would eventually realize that it was only a dream and I would fall back to sleep while staring up at the bright stars above.

CAMPING AT SILVER FALLS PARK

Silver Falls State Park is located in the state of Oregon, near the community of Silverton. The state park is about twenty-miles east-southeast of Salem, Oregon. During the summer between my sixth grade and my seventh grade years, and after the bathtub vision experience, a friend and I rode our ten speed bicycles approximately twenty-five miles from our neighborhood to Silver Falls State Park. We set up our pup tent in the camping area and locked our bikes up to an adjacent tree. Then we spent the rest of the day hiking the trails and swimming in the creek. It was an awesome day for two young kids to spend together.

That night, we were exhausted and crawled into our pup tent and into our sleeping bags. Keep in mind that it was a small pup tent and we had to leave the door unzipped. I needed to stretch my legs outside the front opening of the tent. During the middle of the pitch dark of night, I was slightly awoken by the sound of heavy footsteps outside our pup tent. Suddenly, I became wide awake when I felt two hands grab the bottom of my sleeping bag where my feet were. I was slowly being pulled across the tent floor and outside of our small pup tent.

My heart was pounding. I didn't know what to do. I jerked my legs, while bending my knees, up to my chest. I managed to jerk the sleeping bag out of the hands of whoever was slowly pulling me outside of the tent. I laid there quietly, with my heart pounding rapidly, as I listened to the heavy footsteps walk back into the forest. I told my friend what happened the next morning. He laughed at me and made fun of me. I laughed too. Then we ate our breakfast, packed up our gear, and rode our ten speed bicycles twenty-five miles back to our neighborhood in Salem, Oregon.

By the way, if you ever get the chance to visit Silver Falls State Park just outside of Salem, Oregon, it will be well worth your time. Plan on spending an entire day hiking the trails and viewing the ten waterfalls. Also, there are more than twenty-two miles of multiple use trails. They have room for a couple hundred campers. They also have space for RVs. Silver Falls is Oregon's largest state park. Enjoy!

FRESHMAN YEAR AT LESLIE JUNIOR HIGH SCHOOL

Although I was still everyone's Dear Abby and Ann Landers, the go to guy for everyone's problems, I was somewhat socially shy. I succeeded in athletics but I didn't fit into any one particular clique or social group. I had friends in all of the groups. I was a free floater. Also, although my parents found themselves in the low middle class socioeconomic group, I was attending the ritzy rich Leslie Junior High

School. Sometimes, because I was from the other side of the financial tracks, I didn't feel like I fit in.

One day, near the end of my eighth grade year, two close friends persuaded me to run for the ninth grade student body president. At that time, Leslie Junior High School was attended by seventh, eighth, and ninth grade students. My friends said that they would support me and even help me write my campaign speech. We made some campaign posters with "The Fonz" from the TV sitcom series, "Happy Days." We added the following slogan to the poster of "The Fonz" which said, "Don't be a nerd. Vote for the Bird" (i.e., My nickname at that time was Big Bird). To change my image, I gave up my bowl haircut and got one of those 1970's parted down the middle, feathered haircuts. Then I delivered a totally awesome humorous campaign speech to a bunch of seventh and eighth grade peers and I won by a landslide. This was a perfect way to end my eighth grade year. I couldn't wait for the ninth grade year to begin.

My ninth grade year was full of the good, the bad, and the ugly. The good involved my success on the basketball court. I was finally beginning to grow into my paws. I was fifteen years old, six foot and seven inches tall, and I was averaging thirty points a game. In one game, I only played the first three quarters and managed to score forty-seven points. The other team beat me by two points because they scored a total of forty-nine points. Fortunately, my teammates scored an additional twenty-eight points so we won seventy-five to forty-nine. Whew! Team! Team! Team!

I was the talk of the town and constantly in the local newspaper. Even Paul Harvey wrote about me in his nationally syndicated weekly newspaper column: "Did you hear about the ninth grader in Salem Oregon who called up his local newspaper to ask if it was legal to dunk the ball during a junior high school basketball game?" Younger kids recognized me in the grocery store and at the mall and would ask me for my autograph. All four high school basketball coaches secretly recruited me to play at their high school but denied having done so when a sports writer interviewed them about the topic. I didn't throw any of the coaches under the bus. I enjoyed riding the wave of success and popularity.

However, during my freshman year, my mother's alcoholism kicked in. I didn't know anything about alcoholism other than my mother was a completely different person when she drank her one glass of wine. By the way, her one glass of wine every night was big enough to fit the entire bottle of wine inside of it. She started yelling at me, treating me meanly, and she would occasionally physically abuse me. I was confused by the fact that she treated me nicely when she wasn't drinking her wine. I knew that she loved me. I just didn't understand the change.

Also, during the ninth grade, my first bout of Seasonal Affective Disorder (SAD) kicked in. I had absolutely no idea why I was so depressed during the winter months. Overall, life was going pretty good for me. Other than my mom's alcoholism being a problem, I was the freshman student body president, I was the star basketball player, and I had the new girlfriend who just moved in from out of State. All the guys were after her but I was the lucky one who reeled her in.

I DON'T NEED JESUS

During the summer between my freshman year at Leslie Junior High School and the starting of my sophomore year at South Salem High School, I had a friend named, Scott. From the seventh grade until this point in my life, Scott was always a part of my life. We enjoyed both our classes and sports together. We had fun on the weekends too. There was just one problem with Scott. He was continually inviting me to church and kept telling me that I needed to have Jesus be the Lord of my life.

I repeatedly told Scott that I was a good guy and that didn't need anyone to save me. I told him that I loved him like a brother but that he needed to stop talking about this Jesus guy. Well, Scott never stopped talking about Jesus. Finally, while picking strawberries during the summer to earn some spending money, Scott asked me if I wanted to go to a Church Youth Group Retreat with him at the Oregon Coast.

THE XANUE

He said that his parents would pay for me to go. There would be lots of fun, food, and females. I finally saw my opportunity to shut Scott up.

I said to Scott, "I'll make a deal with you. If I go to the Church Youth Group Retreat on the Oregon Coast with you, and I don't accept Jesus as my Lord and Savior, then you will keep your mouth shut and never talk with me about Jesus again. Deal?"

Scott gulped and said, "Let me talk with my parents first. They're the ones who are paying so they should have the final say about the deal. How does that sound?" I agreed with his proposal.

The next day, while picking strawberries in the field, Scott told me that his parents accepted the deal. I attended the Church Youth Group Retreat that following weekend. The guest speaker was an ex-convict who had served time for armed robbery and murder. He was six-feet and four-inches tall. He was also very broad and had tattoos on his arms. At that time in the 1970's, only antisocial people who skirted the law and conventional norms and values had tattoos on their body. Although he had a tough guy exterior, he was a gentle teddy bear on the inside who wouldn't harm a soul. He said that Jesus changed his life while he was in prison. Although his message resonated with me, I did not accept Jesus as my Lord and Savior during the weekend retreat.

During our last week of picking strawberries, Scott talked with me about anything and everything but he kept his word and didn't talk with me about Jesus. Then that following Saturday night, I called him up and asked him when he and his parents were going to pick me up on Sunday morning to take me to church. Scott literally dropped the phone. I heard it hit the floor. He picked it back up and asked for a confirmation regarding my question. I laughed. Scott and his parents picked me up the next morning for church.

At the end of the summer, I attended a Christian Rock n' Roll Concert at the First Conservative Baptist Church in downtown Salem, Oregon. I was really ministered to by the music and the message. At the end of the concert, I left my pew seat and met with some gentlemen who helped me to pray, confess my sins, and ask Jesus Christ into my life and to be my Lord and Savior. I was officially 'born again'.

Chapter 7: The Younger Years (K-12)

I GUESS I DO NEED JESUS

That night, when I got home from church as a brand new 'born again' Christian, I actually got to sleep in my own bedroom for the very first time. My older brother had just moved out of the home so I was promoted to my own bedroom. He hadn't even moved everything out yet and I hadn't moved anything in to the room. All that mattered at that moment in time was that I finally got to sleep in my own bedroom. No more sharing a bedroom with my younger brother.

I turned off the lights and climbed into my bed. While I was laying on my back and rejoicing in my new found Christian faith and my new bedroom, I suddenly sensed an evil presence coming from the closet in the corner of the bedroom. The next thing I knew, my chest was straddled by someone sitting on me. I was being pushed down into my mattress.

Although I couldn't see anything, I could hear an evil, deep, raspy voice in front of my face. The voice said, "You think just because you became a Christian that life is going to be easy for you now. Well, we are going to be all over your case for the rest of your life." Then I heard some evil chuckling and laughter from others in the room. I tried calling out for my dad but nothing came out of my mouth. Then I managed to call out the name of Jesus and they were immediately gone. I laid there for hours, scared to death, but I finally fell asleep.

That Sunday night, I went to the Youth Group meeting with Scott. The Youth Pastor was asking if anyone had any prayer requests before he started sharing his lesson for that night. I raised my hand and told him and everyone else about my bedroom encounter on the previous night. Well, he jettisoned his planned message and spent the rest of the time teaching all of us about how to rebuke demons in the name of Jesus Christ.

I went to bed in my new bedroom again. On the second night, once again, I sensed an evil presence coming from the closet in the corner of the bedroom. Once again, I had someone straddling my chest and pushing me down into my mattress. He was laughing and the others were chuckling. He said, "I told you that we were going to be on your case for the rest of your life." I immediately rebuked all of them in the name of Jesus Christ and they were gone, just as quickly as they appeared.

The next morning, I opened up the window blinds to let the light inside my new bedroom. I turned on the lights. I grabbed a flashlight and approached the closet door. I opened up the closed door and turned on the closet light. In spite of all of the light, I was still using my flashlight too. I looked through the items on the floor that my older brother had left behind in the closet. Nothing. I looked through some of the clothes that were hanging in the closet. Nothing. I looked at the items up on the closet shelf from my right to my left. Nothing. However, there was a blanket hanging over the shelf on the left side. I slowly lifted up the blanket and I found an Ouija Board.

THE XUXIKO BOARD GAME

One year earlier, at the age of fourteen, before I became a 'born again' Christian, I was bored on a rainy Saturday morning. My mom could tell that I was bored and told me to ride my bike to the Fred Meyer retail store in south Salem and find a board game to play with my younger brother. As my mother directed, I road my bicycle in the rain for one mile to get to the store. I took my time looking through all of the board games until I came across the Ouija Board game. Twenty-twenty hindsight, I can't believe that a store would put a Ouija Board in a game section and allow children to purchase it.

Anyway, I took the Ouija Board home with me. Later that night, while my parents were downstairs in the basement watching the TV, my friend, my younger brother, and I closed all of the drapes in the living room, lit several candles, and turned off the lights. We began to play the Ouija Board game. We got lots of answers. We all swore that we were not moving the triangle piece with intention. Finally, we asked our final question: "Are you a good spirit?" The answer came back, "No."

We turned on the lights, blew out the candles, and opened up all of the drapes. My friend ran all the way back home. My brother and I ran downstairs to the basement and told my parents everything. They both laughed and thanked us for telling them a good story. Then they told us that it was time to go to bed. We both simultaneously said, "No! We aren't going upstairs to go to bed!" It took my parents approximately three hours to get us to go to bed. We never saw the Ouija Board game again until I found it under the blanket on the left side of the shelf inside the closet of my new bedroom.

When I found it, I grabbed the Ouija Board and immediately took it downstairs to the basement. I started a fire in the fireplace. I knew that I was going to be late for my first period class but it didn't matter. I needed to take the time to burn up that Ouija Board. Once the fire was going really good, I placed the Ouija Board into the flames. It burned for about two minutes. Then suddenly, the Ouija Board was engulfed in major flames and was hissing while the room grew bright. Then, just like that, the Ouija Board was gone. It just suddenly vanished. Needless to say, I was praying the entire time and thanking God and Jesus when it was over. I was never attacked by the demons (Xuxiko) in my bed ever again.

THE GOOD, THE BAD, AND THE UGLY

Although I was excited about my new found Christian faith, I was also saddened because it meant that I was going to have to break up with my ninth grade girlfriend. She wasn't a Christian. Also, she thought that Christianity was a crutch for weak people. Finally, we had just started having sex and I didn't want to do that anymore. I was way too young and I wasn't ready for that kind of relationship. Although it was very difficult, I broke up with her. I needed to focus my life in a more positive direction, which included keeping my pants zipped up. My faith was a good thing, breaking up with her was a bad and sad thing, but I still think often about the subsequent ugly thing every day of my life.

During the first week of my sophomore year at South Salem High School, the best friend of my ex-girlfriend approached me in the parking lot every day after school. She kept telling me that I needed to talk with my ex-girlfriend. She wouldn't tell me why but she insisted that I really needed to talk with her. I asked her if my ex-girlfriend was suicidal and she said, "No."

Then I said, "Well then, since she's okay, I'll leave her alone. I have no desire to get back into a relationship with her."

She responded, "Even though she's not going to kill herself, she's not okay. You really, really need to talk with her."

I said to her, "We are done dating. Nothing she can say will convince me to return to her. We are incompatible because we strongly believe differently about important matters. I'm sorry. Please stop bothering me. Please leave me alone."

After desperately pleading with me on behalf of her friend, my ex-girlfriend, for five straight days during the first week of school, she left me alone. I was a fifteen-year-old kid. I missed all of the clues. It wasn't until decades later that I had it indirectly conveyed to me by a mutual friend that I had gotten her pregnant. She ended up aborting our baby.

I reached out to her over ten years ago by sending her a very sincere letter of apology. She wrote back to me, told me to go to Hell, and told me to never ever write her again. I have respected her boundaries.

A day doesn't go by that I don't think about what our child would be doing today? Where would they be living? What would their hobbies be? Would they be tall like me or short like their mother? Every year I think about how old our kid would be and that we would have grandchildren by now.

That is an ugly burden that I must carry with me every day. I know that I'm forgiven by God and His Son, Jesus. I know that I will see our child someday in Heaven. Nevertheless, I wouldn't wish this experience on anyone. As I've previously stated, I'm a faithful failure.

Chapter 7: The Younger Years (K-12)

DELIVERING THE STATESMEN JOURNAL

I delivered the morning newspaper, The Statesman Journal, between my sixth and sophomore grades in school. A total of five years of getting up at 5:00 am every morning to make sure that the newspapers were all delivered by 6:30 am every day. As previously mentioned, my parents were in the lower middleclass socio-economic group. Although they had good jobs, they didn't make great money. Therefore, I had to mow lawns, pick strawberries during the summer, and deliver newspapers year-round to pay for my school clothes, school supplies, summer basketball camps, and for desired odds and ends such as a ten speed bicycle, a Pioneer Home Stereo System, a used car, and to pay for my own car insurance.

One dark winter morning during my sophomore year of high school, I was walking down this dark street, Pheasant Avenue, toward some homes that were located on McGilchrist Street.

These homes were located at the top of the heavily treed hill overlooking the Gilmore Baseball Field below. The baseball field was located on Hoyt Street in Salem, Oregon.

Anyway, there were no street lights and the people didn't keep their porch lights on at night. In other words, it was pitch dark. I was not a big fan of the dark.

I'll be honest, I was always scared to walk on this part of my paper route. There were lots of tall pine trees that blocked out the moonlight and the stars. While I was walking in the fog and the pitch dark back down Pheasant Avenue toward Cedar Way where there were a few street lights, I heard heavy footsteps following me on the gravel road. The steps weren't that far behind me.

When I stopped, I would always hear the individual make one or two more footsteps before they stopped. When I resumed walking, so did the individual following me. Once again, when I stopped, I would hear one or two additional steps before they stopped. When I started walking, they started walking. Yet, when I would stop and turn around, there was never anyone there. Even on the lighted Cedar Way.

After experiencing this for three mornings in a row, I finally told my father about it. My dad's Oregon State Trooper instincts kicked in immediately and we drove the route that night so he could devise a game plan to catch the stalker. He was worried that my local fame as a high school basketball star was motivating some psycho to stalk me and possibly kidnap me. I wasn't going to argue with my father.

For the next week, my dad would dress every morning completely in black, walk up a half-hour before me to Pheasant Avenue, and hide in the tall hedges on the side of the gravel road. Eventually, I would walk by him down the dark gravel road, deliver the newspapers to the houses in the dark, and then walk right past him again and hang a right on Cedar Way.

Only on the first morning did my father hear the heavy footsteps following me on the dark and foggy gravel road. I had passed my dad and about thirty-seconds later, the heavy footsteps were passing my dad. He jumped out with his flashlight on and said, "Caught you, sucker!" However, there was no one there. My dad was perplexed because the sound of the footsteps were approximately six feet in front of where he was hiding in the tall hedges. He shined his flashlight everywhere and there was no one to be found. The person who was following me simply disappeared. Vanished into thin air.

Afterwards, for the next six mornings, we both heard absolutely nothing. However, my dad wasn't convinced that the stalker had left the scene. So he drove me around for the rest of the month and then made me quit my paper route. He said that I could get a job somewhere else. No more morning paper routes. He wanted me to be safe. He may have had his own imperfections such as anger management issues, but he most definitely loved his family and kept us safe to the best of his ability.

Chapter 7: The Younger Years (K-12)

LOOK BOTH WAYS TWICE

On October 30, 1977, my sixteenth birthday, I obtained my driver's license. It was my sophomore year at South Salem High School and I was beginning to enjoy my independence. Although I was going to high school and playing basketball, I also had an awesome job in the evenings at the Southgate Movie Theater in south Salem. I worked the concession stand for a few months until I was promoted to the projectionist when the manager's boyfriend walked out on her.

I had the projectionist booth all to myself. All I had to do was keep the movies running in all of the theaters. I could even do my homework upstairs in the booth while the movies were running. In the meantime, I could also go downstairs to the concession stand and consume as much popcorn and soda as I wanted to. Most important of all, I was making better money as a movie theater projectionist than I was delivering newspapers in the early morning hours.

With my increased earnings came the opportunity to purchase a 1962 Chevy Bel Air from the neighbor across the street. Dale was an auto mechanic and his hobby was to buy cars, fix them up, and resell them. I was fortunate because he really liked my father and decided to give me a deep discount sale price since it was my very first car. We painted it cherry red and nick named my car, "The Bomb." I was very popular with all of my high school friends who didn't have their driver's license yet. Although my car was nicknamed "The Bomb," it actually ran perfectly. I drove it to and from school as well as to and from work during my sophomore year without any problems whatsoever.

In May of 1978, I was driving my car home from school. I drove south on Summer Street until the road T-boned at Fairview Avenue. At this point, you could only turn right or left. Fairview Avenue, just like all other residential streets in Salem had a speed limit of twenty-five miles per hour. I looked right up the Fairview Avenue hill. I looked left down the Fairview Avenue hill. My parents' home was to the left. I looked right up the hill one more time and it was all clear. I pushed down on the gas pedal with my right foot and began to turn left when my car suddenly stalled. My car came to a sudden and complete stop. I looked up and a car coming down the Fairview Avenue hill zipped by me while going approximately ninety miles per hour. It wasn't there a second ago but now it was passing in front of me at dangerous speeds. It was a fellow classmate of mine. I chewed his butt out the next day in school.

I'm sharing this story because "The Bomb" never stalled on me before that moment in time. Also, my car never stalled on me again after that moment in time. If my car hadn't stalled when Lance was driving by at ninety miles per hour, I believe that we both would have died in a tragic car accident. It most definitely was not a coincidence that my car stalled at that exact moment in time. I thank God for saving my life that day. Since that time, I always look twice before I drive through an intersection.

BASKETBALL BLUES

Although I started receiving recruitment letters from college basketball coaches during my sophomore year at South Salem High School, the recruitment letters really started arriving during my junior year. I received five to ten or more letters per day at home and at the high school. I was the only student at South Salem High School who had his mail personally delivered on a daily basis during the fifth period class.

After every daily lunch period, the students and teacher would gather around my desk during the fifth period class. They wanted to see who was recruiting me today to play for their college or university. I received recruiting letters from at least one school in all fifty States, including Duke, Kentucky, North Carolina, Indiana, UCLA, Notre Dame, Gonzaga, Hawaii, Stanford, Harvard, Princeton, Yale, Cornell, the Naval Academy, the Air Force Academy, and West Point.

One day, while looking at my mail, one of my classroom peers standing behind me asked "Why don't you go play basketball for the University of Alaska?"

I responded to her in my youthful arrogance, "Are you kidding me! Even if Alaska had a basketball team, that would be the last place on Earth that I would ever play."

In my mind, I was hoping to play for North Carolina, Duke, Kentucky, UCLA, or some other basketball powerhouse school. I wanted to play for a good school so that I would have a real shot at making it into the National Basketball Association (NBA). I wasn't going to throw it all away and play for some Podunk school like the University of Alaska. Well, apparently, God heard me. Keep on reading.

Because of my basketball success, I was constantly in the media with newspaper, radio, and TV interviews. Although the reporters were obviously primarily interested in talking with me about basketball, I always used the interview opportunities to share my Christian faith with the consumers of the various media outlets. As a result, I was not only known in my community as a basketball player but I was also known for my outspoken Christian faith. Therefore, I was invited to a few churches and banquets to speak and share my Christian faith and testimony.

During my junior year, our season record was twenty-five wins and only one loss. One might say that's not a bad season. However, we lost the wrong game during the State Championship playoffs and took third in the State of Oregon. I felt like I had let my parents down, the school down, and the city of Salem down. At the age of seventeen, I put a lot of my value and self-worth eggs in the basketball success basket. When I returned home to Salem with anything short of the State Championship, I considered myself a major failure. I took off the following week from school and drove to a family friend's ranch on the Oregon coast to clear my mind. To be honest, I was very depressed and suicidal.

Although my parents insisted that I go to school, they knew that if they didn't support my going to our family friend's ranch on the Oregon coast, that there was a good chance that they might lose me. I used their fear to manipulate them into letting me go. However, along the way, I almost killed myself.

I was driving the car about ninety miles per hour on the freeway. I was about to drive straight into a concrete pillar under one of the overpass bridges when I literally heard the voice of God scream inside my head, "No!!!" I pulled out of the planned point of death at the last second and drove sanely the rest of the way to the ranch. During my week of clearing my mind, God assured me that everything was going to be okay. All I had to do was trust Him and His plans for my life.

THE CLASSROOM DEBATE

Near the end of my junior year at South Salem High School, my friend, Scott, and I were taking a science fiction class together for elective credits. The teacher, Mr. Johnson (no relation to me), assigned the class to read "The Martian Chronicles" by Ray Bradbury. We had one week to read the book and then we would all discuss the book in class on Friday.

Well, Friday arrived and Mr. Johnson started facilitating the classroom discussion. Several students shared their interpretations of the book. After they were done, Mr. Johnson gave them his feedback. Then both Scott and I started sharing our interpretations of the book. We both thought that there was some obvious Christian symbolism woven in and out of his story. When we were done, we concluded that we both liked the book very much.

Apparently, we pushed some buttons that we didn't know that Mr. Johnson had and he exploded on the both of us. He yelled at both Scott and me and told us how stupid we were for believing the mythological Christian fairy tale. He then proceeded to use the rest of the class period to totally shred the Christian faith. In conclusion, he assured the class that there was absolutely no Christian symbolism woven in and out of "The Martian Chronicles" story. He also assured everyone that there was absolutely no God and that Jesus never existed. It was all made up.

Chapter 7: The Younger Years (K-12)

As fate would have it, there were three more minutes until the bell rang to end the class period. Therefore, Scott and I were not going to allow Mr. Johnson's tirade regarding God, Jesus, and Christians to go unanswered. Scott took the first minute and politely countered Mr. Johnson's arguments and conclusion. Then I grabbed the battle axe and finished the job. I told Mr. Johnson, point blank, "You are an arrogant and ignorant man. How dare you mock God, Jesus, and Christians in the disrespectful manner that you just displayed. If you have any brains at all, you will find it within yourself to humbly ask God for His forgiveness. Otherwise, you are not going to enjoy where you will be spending eternity apart from His presence. You better repent, Mr. Johnson."

In retort, Mr. Johnson stated in front of the entire class, "Hell will freeze over before I ever repent to your fairytale God and Savior." Then the classroom bell rang and we all left the room to get to our next class. Scott and I were looking at one another in disbelief and we were shaking our heads. Some of our peers said, "Wow! You really let him have it." I said, "I wouldn't want to be Mr. Johnson right now."

The weekend passed and Monday had arrived. Scott and I were back in Mr. Johnson's Science Fiction class. However, Mr. Johnson wasn't there. Instead, we had a substitute teacher filling in. One of the other students asked if Mr. Johnson was home sick today. The substitute teacher responded, "No, he's not home sick today. Unfortunately, he died over the weekend due to a brain aneurysm."

Immediately, the whole classroom looked at Scott and me. One of the students spoke up and said, "Whoa! Apparently God was listening to your debate on Friday. I wouldn't want to be Mr. Johnson right now."

The substitute teacher had a quizzical look on his face. Another student explained the Friday debate to him and suggested that the teacher not argue with Scott and Matt about Christianity. The teacher gave both of us a blank stare and his face was as white as a ghost. He replied, "Don't worry. I share their Christian faith. It might not be as strong as their faith but I most definitely won't be arguing with them about it."

After class was over, several students talked with Scott and me about our Christian faith. They all wanted to know more because they didn't grow up in the church. As a result, we added several new students to our Youth Group at church and several friends gave their lives to Jesus Christ. I wonder what Mr. Johnson would think about the fact that his arrogance, ignorance, and unrepentant heart helped to add more young individuals to the Christian faith?

MORE BASKETBALL BLUES

During the summer between my junior and senior year of high school, I made an Oregon All-Star Team and played in a National High School All-Star Tournament in Provo, Utah. We took third in the nation. Not too shabby for the State of Oregon. Also, I attended a summer basketball camp in San Diego, California for the best one-hundred high school players in the country. By the time my senior year started, I had obtained both All-State and Honorable Mention All-American status. I was feeling pretty good about the fact that all of those years of dribbling and shooting hoops in the driveway was finally paying off. The college and university basketball coaches were really turning up the heat on the recruitment process now.

By the end of my senior season of basketball, we were first place in the Valley League and we were ranked second in the State. We were kicking everyone's butts off the basketball court. Without a doubt, my team felt confident that the Oregon State Championship was going to be ours this year. In addition, I had college and university basketball coaches calling me every night at dinner time and on the weekends. They all knew that was when they could catch me at home. It was nice to be wanted by at least one school in all fifty States. Life was good.

Then with three games left to go in our regular season play, we were in a real tight game against South Albany. I dove on the floor to grab the loose ball. The guard from the other team dove too and landed on my lower back with both of his knees. The game stopped and I was laying

Chapter 7: The Younger Years (K-12)

on the floor in pain. Filled with adrenaline, I managed to get up and finish the game. We won. Then I collapsed in the shower after the game.

I had injured my back so bad that my season was over. I had cracked and crunched some of my lower vertebrae. I spent the next month laying on the floor at home. I listened to the State Championship game on the radio. Corvallis High School, the number two team in our league behind us, managed to cakewalk through the playoffs and win it all. We had manhandled them twice during the regular season. That was our State Championship to win. Instead, I lay injured on the floor and listened to our rival team win our championship title.

As previously stated, I lay on the floor at my parents' home for a month. My bed was not firm enough. I was in so much pain that it took everything I had to crawl to the toilet and back. My mom left me with food and beverage by my side because I couldn't fend for myself. I watched a lot of TV, cried a lot, and yelled at God too. I was pissed.

Within a two-week period of time, the college and university recruiting letters and phone calls stopped. Apparently, news of my injury made its way through the recruiting grapevine rather quickly. No one wanted me anymore. I was no longer worth their time or money. I continued to lay on the floor while watching TV, crying, and yelling at God. Then after a month, I finally picked up my Bible. I apologized to God for my anger and I asked Him to please give me some hope. I really needed some hope. Please.

I randomly opened my Bible and was directed to read Romans 8:28:

"And we know that God works all things together for the good of those who love Him, who are called according to His purpose."

I closed my Bible and prayed. I thanked God for loving me and I said, "I know that you're going to help me get my college education, even if I'm in a wheelchair."

Well, God heard me. My back slowly began to heal and feel good enough to eventually return to school. I missed so much school that I was lucky if I would graduate. Fortunately, my teachers were very understanding and bent over backwards to help me catch up in all of my classes. I felt silly walking around school with my pillow which was needed to make sitting in the classroom chairs more comfortable. I eventually healed up enough to start working out. I wanted to see if I could play basketball again.

One night, during dinner time, the phone rang. We all looked at each other. My dad answered the phone. He smiled and said, "Coach Bliss from the University of Alaska at Anchorage wants to talk with you." By this point in time, I didn't care who was calling me. If I could get a free college education, I was going to play for them. We talked. He informed me that he was in the Pacific Northwest on a recruiting trip. He asked if he could drop by our home this weekend to visit with me and my parents. The visit went very well.

Coach Bliss flew me up to Anchorage, Alaska the following weekend. I received a tour of the University of Alaska at Anchorage (UAA) campus, the city, and the Alyeska Ski Resort. I prayed that night, while staying in the Captain Cook Hotel with an incredible view of Anchorage. I woke up the next morning with the peace of God in my heart that this is where He intended me to be all along. I signed the letter of intent to play for UAA and then returned to Salem, Oregon. You should have seen the look on my classmate's face when I told her that I was going to play for the University of Alaska at Anchorage. She smiled and said, "Never say never." I shrugged my shoulders and laughed. She was right. Never tell God never.

THE MIDDLE OF THE NIGHT AWAKENING

Approximately two months before I graduated from South Salem High School, I was sound asleep in my bed. In the middle of the night, my alcoholic mother came into my bedroom drunker than a skunk. She proceeded to slap me out of my sleep while yelling at me about how I was such a disappointment to her. She ended her five-minute tirade with, "I wish you were never born."

My mom left my bedroom feeling better. However, I laid in bed, crying, and staring up at the dark ceiling, asking God, "Why did you stick me in a family like this?"

Five minutes later, my mom came back into my bedroom. She was crying, feeling horrible, and was apologizing to me. She wanted me to forgive her. She wanted a hug and a kiss before she left my bedroom. I didn't want anything to do with her. She smelled like a brewery. If a match was lit at that moment in time, I'm sure that my bedroom would have blown up.

I quickly realized that she wasn't going to leave my bedroom until I gave her a hug and a kiss. I complied with her wish. Once again, she left my room feeling better. I lay in my bed, crying, and staring up at the dark ceiling, asking God why, why, why?

The next morning, while I was getting ready for school, my mother sat in her living room chair reading the newspaper. She was acting like nothing ever happened the night before. It wasn't until several years later that I learned that she had experienced an alcoholic blackout. She had no way of remembering what she did or said to me.

HASTA LA VISTA, BABY!!!

Because of my dysfunctional family, I couldn't wait to leave home as quickly as possible. I graduated on a Friday evening from South Salem High School with five-hundred-twenty-four other students. We were the class of 1980. The very next morning, on Saturday, I gave the invocation at the Governor's Prayer Breakfast at the State Capitol in Salem, Oregon. Before I prayed, I referenced Psalm 104:32:

"God looks at the Earth, and it trembles; He touches the mountains, and they smoke."

You see, only one month earlier, on May 18, 1980, Mt. St. Helens erupted and covered Portland, Oregon with a whole lot of ashes. Fortunately, we only received a light dusting of ash in Salem, Oregon. Anyway, the above scriptural reference was apropos for the reverent occasion. It was also a very cool way to end my time in the State of Oregon.

After the Governor's Prayer Breakfast was over, my parents drove me to the Portland International Airport. I gave them hugs and kisses. I boarded the Alaska Airlines jet and flew to Anchorage, Alaska to begin my life as a young adult. I was now free from my parents' dysfunctional home. Although we loved one another very much, I could no longer tolerate being around my mother's alcoholism or my dad's anger management problems. Let the Alaskan adventures begin.

CHAPTER 8

THE UNIVERSITY OF ALASKA - ANCHORAGE

LIGHT IN THE MIDST OF DARKNESS

Anchorage, Alaska looked beautiful from the air as we flew over the Chugach Mountains. I was excited to live in the land of the midnight sun. The last frontier. The 49th State. I could see the city below and couldn't wait to start my independent life as an eighteen-year-old young man. I had worked hard for this moment of independence in my life and now it was finally here. No more putting up with an angry dad. No more putting up with an intoxicated mom who would yell at me for no justifiable reason at all. It was now just me, myself, and I. I couldn't wait to see what God had in store for me as I lived in Anchorage, while playing basketball for the University of Alaska at Anchorage (UAA). I was finally going to get my free college education.

During my freshman year at UAA, I started a weekly Bible Study meeting in our apartment located on Tudor Road. Believe it or not, we managed to cram about fifty college kids into our large apartment living room every Tuesday night. We had some great lessons and enjoyed singing together while praising the Lord.

One Tuesday night, just before the Bible Study meeting was going to start, I had to walk out to my car to get my Bible. I had forgotten to bring it back inside earlier that day. It was a beautiful winter night. There was snow on the ground and the skies were clear. The stars were bright and beautiful. I felt the Spirit of God within me and I was full of joy. I grabbed my Bible out of the car and walked back through the snow to get back inside the apartment complex. We had a great time of fellowship that night.

The next day, after basketball practice had ended and most everyone was showered and gone, one of my teammates and I were still getting dressed in the locker room. By the way, all of us basketball players all lived in the same large apartment complex. In 1980, UAA did not have dorms for students to live in. Anyway, David asked me if he could tell me something very strange. I said, "Sure. Go right ahead." I'll never forget what he said to me.

David said, "Last night I was studying for one of my classes and I went into my bedroom to grab a text book. I looked out my third floor window and saw you walking across the parking lot to your car. This is going to sound strange but you were glowing like a light bulb."

I chuckled and said, "David, don't you think it was a combination of the snow and the light poles in the parking lot making me look that way? Besides, I was wearing a dark coat and stocking cap."

David immediately retorted, "Matt, I'm not stupid. I know what I saw. You were glowing like you were a translucent Being of Light. You were looking all happy and at peace. It was incredible."

I thanked David for sharing that with me. He was right. It was strange. However, what you don't know is that David was a very serious individual, a perfectionist, and OCD. He didn't drink or do drugs. He always worked his butt off in practice and maintained good grades in school. He eventually became an Alaska State Trooper. In a nutshell, I believe that David saw what he said that he saw. I just couldn't figure out how it happened because I didn't notice anything different at all. All I saw was my Bible and the snow. However, David evidently saw the light.

ATHLETES IN ACTION (AIA)

I had a fun and successful first year of college. I enjoyed my university classes and also playing for Coach Bliss. I started several games

Chapter 8: The University of Alaska - Anchorage

and was developing my confidence as a collegiate player. That season, I scored my first two collegiate points on ESPN TV against North Carolina in the Great Alaska Shootout. I also got half my picture in Sports Illustrated magazine. My silly teammate was in the way of the other half. At the end of the season, I was asked to play with Athletes In Action (AIA) on a summer travel team to Brazil. AIA is a Christian ministry that uses sports as a platform to share the gospel of Jesus Christ with people around the world.

I worked very hard to raise the three thousand five hundred dollars necessary to travel to Brazil during the summer of 1981. I received a lot of help from my church, Muldoon Community Assembly of God. Once it was all raised, I flew from Anchorage, Alaska to Portland, Oregon. I spent a week at my parents' home in Salem, Oregon. I thought it was important to spend some time with my parents before I flew to Florida for a week's worth of training camp and then on to Brazil. In spite of my dad's anger issues and my mother's alcoholism, they were still my parents and I loved them very much.

One day, while sitting in the living room at my parents' home, the phone rang. I answered it and it was an accountant at the main office for Athletes In Action (AIA) in Colorado Springs, Colorado. She told me that I was still eighty dollars shy from reaching my goal and that I needed to send the remaining money in before I would be allowed to go on the trip to Brazil. My heart sunk. I didn't have a summer job and I most certainly didn't have any money. As I shared previously, my parents had good jobs but they didn't make great money. We were in the lower middle class socioeconomic group. They weren't going to be able to come up with the money either.

A couple of hours later, my mother came home from work. She was an attendance clerk at North Salem High School. If you remember, I attended South Salem High School. Therefore, there was a little bit of rivalry between my mother and me. However, I knew that she was always rooting for me when our two schools competed.

Mom walked into the living room and said, "I talked with my coworkers today and they asked about your upcoming trip to Brazil.

Although I didn't solicit anyone, three coworkers gave me donation checks to help you with your trip with Athletes In Action." She handed me the three checks. Guess what? Yup! They totaled exactly eighty dollars. I was blown away to the point of tears. At that point, I told my mom about the phone call from the AIA office in Colorado. Mom was blown away too. We both agreed that God was in charge and met my financial need.

We played twenty-seven games in thirty-five days while competing in Brazil. About half way through our five-week trip, we competed against the Brazilian Junior Olympic Team. The 10,000 seat arena that we were playing in was known to contain violent fans who would throw eggs and beer bottles full of sand at the visiting opposing teams. Therefore, they had staged six military guards with rifles strapped to their backs around the entire basketball court. All six soldiers had German Shepard police dogs sitting at their sides. In my entire life, I had never played in a basketball game with armed soldiers needing to keep my team safe. Apparently, Brazil didn't want to start an incident with the U.S.A.

During the first half of the game, I grabbed a defensive rebound and pivoted around with my elbows out to the side, just like I was taught to do in high school and college. Well, one of my elbows caught the opposing team's big man and knocked him to the floor while he was trying to prevent me from throwing an outlet pass to one of our guards.

Their big man was on the floor and he was kicking up at my crotch. The referees blew their whistles and stopped the game. They deliberated at the scorer's table for about five minutes. During the five-minute delay in the game, the crowd was growing more and more agitated. They were standing on their feet, yelling, screaming, booing, and hitting or kicking their seats. Their focus was on the guy who unintendedly threw their big man on the floor – me. Suddenly, the six military soldiers took their rifles off of their backs and cocked their weapons. The German Shepard police dogs were barking. I hadn't been that scared in a long time. There were 10,000 Brazilian fans who were not happy with me.

Chapter 8: The University of Alaska - Anchorage

After five minutes of deliberation, the referees decided to throw the other big man out of the game for attempting to kick me in the crotch. Immediately, the crowd became even more angry, loud, and crazy. I was seriously concerned that I might not make it out of the arena alive. I was also concerned that the soldiers actually might start shooting people. These fans were worse than fans that you would find attending a soccer game or hockey game.

The Brazilian Junior Olympic Team substituted another big man into the game. I thought, "Crap! This guy is much bigger than the other big man." I nick named him, Bruno. I'm only six feet and nine inches tall. Bruno was a solid seven-footer, maybe seven foot and one inch tall. He clearly outweighed me by at least sixty pounds. I looked tiny next to him and I'm not a tiny guy.

The game started back up. Within the first minute of resumed play, Bruno grabbed a defensive rebound, looked me right in the eyes, smiled, and then planted his elbow right into my big Irish nose. I went crashing backwards to the floor. I was experiencing a tremendous amount of pain and thought, "Bruno just broke my nose!" My eyes were watering and I couldn't see a thing. The crowd began cheering with much joy. They were obviously pleased at Bruno's retribution to me. However, I was thinking, "Give me a break! I didn't even hurt the other guy."

Our team trainer ran out on to the floor and had me lay there for a couple of minutes until he could thoroughly examine me. He used a towel to clean up the blood and then had two of my teammates escort me back to the end of the team bench. I still couldn't see anything because my eyes were watering so bad. Then the team trainer put some ice on my nose and face and told me to keep my head tilted back. The game resumed and the crowd quieted down. They were satisfied with Bruno's Brazilian basketball justice.

As the game continued, I remained sitting at the end of the team bench, with my head tilted back, and holding the ice on my nose. A young Brazilian boy, approximately ten years old, tapped me on my shoulder and said, "For you, mister. For you." I said, "Thank you but I'm okay." I was in so much pain, I had ice on my nose, and the towel was covering my eyes. Honestly, I was trying to be polite but I didn't want to be bothered at that moment in time.

The young boy responded, "No mister, for you! For you! Please take." I felt him tapping my shoulder with a small book. I reached out my hand and took his little book. I smiled at him and thanked him. He walked away with a smile on his face. He had just handed me a pocket book of the New Testament with both English and Portuguese translations side by side. I thought it was a very cool gift.

The game finished and we won. We better have won. We had beaten their Olympic team a few days earlier. The opposing coach and his son took me, our team trainer, and our team translator to the local hospital. It took about four hours to get in and out of the emergency room. The doctors had concluded that I had broken my nose and that there wasn't any other damage done to my skull. They told the team trainer that I probably shouldn't play for the next week. I was not happy. I didn't travel to Brazil to sit on the bench. I was a starter – not a bench warmer.

During the four hours at the hospital, I had the opportunity to share my Christian faith with the opposing coach's son. I would speak to him through our team translator. Then I would look up scripture in English in the pocket New Testament that the young boy had given to me during the game. Then I would point to the Portuguese translation on the adjacent page and have him read it. This continued throughout the four hours. By the time we made it back to my hotel room around 2 am in the morning, the opposing coach's son had prayed to give his life to Jesus Christ. I was grateful that the young boy was persistent with me and that he gave me the pocket New Testament in both English and Portuguese. What are the odds of all that randomly coming together? God was definitely behind it all. That was well worth a broken nose.

THE ALASKAN COACH FROM HELL

During my sophomore year at the UAA, Coach Bliss was fired for political reasons. The Athletic Director liked the assistant coach better and wanted to clear a path for him so he could become the head

Chapter 8: The University of Alaska - Anchorage

coach. The assistant coach didn't like me because of my Christian faith. Matter of fact, he ridiculed me in front of my teammates every now and then. He especially didn't like me when I led a group of students who stopped the basketball boosters club from securing a liquor license for the campus pub. Anchorage had enough bars already and we didn't need any alcohol on the UAA campus.

I had a teammate with a drinking problem and he would show up to practice intoxicated and smelling like a brewery. I was concerned for him and other students on the campus. We won and the basketball booster club lost. I was young, altruistic, naïve, and politically inept. I didn't realize it at the time but I just secured a spot on top of the blackball list in the athletic department. I unknowingly angered a lot of people.

All of a sudden, I went from starter to permanent bench warmer. It was crazy because I was clearly one of the best players on the team. I would dominate my teammates in practice but that just didn't matter. The assistant coaches, as well as several of my teammates, would encourage me to keep playing hard in practice. They didn't want me to quit. They all knew that I should be starting.

Meanwhile, the head coach was acting out the script of the movie, "One on One" with Robby Benson. He was doing everything under the sun to emotionally and occasionally physically abuse me. He was trying to break my will and get me to quit. I refused to give up. I kept giving one-hundred and ten percent during every practice. I made it obvious to everyone that I deserved to be a starter. I'm not a quitter.

THE ALASKAN WIFE FROM HELL

During this year, I met my first wife. I fell head over heels in love with her. I married her after only eight months of courtship. I lost a twenty-five dollar bet to my dad because I got married before I turned twenty-one years old. She was twenty-two years old and obviously robbed the cradle. Matter of fact, her younger brother and I were born on the same day and year.

He was the same brother who told me two nights before our wedding day, "I can't believe that you're going to marry the bitch."

I said, "She's not a bitch. She's never been mean to me or anyone else around me. Besides, if she was a bitch, she's obviously changed."

Her brother responded, "Matt, I grew up with her. She's a bitch."

Well, unfortunately, I chose to keep my head in the sand. Other kids that went to high school with her in Anchorage tried to warn me about her too. I chose to ignore everyone because she wasn't showing me any negative side to herself. Then seven days into our honeymoon, she let her hair down. She lambasted me in front of everyone in the Wildlife Safari parking lot just south of Roseburg, Oregon because I accidentally locked the keys in the car. She yelled, screamed, and cussed like a sailor. Everyone in the parking lot heard my angry and out of control wife.

An older man in his seventies approached us and said, "It sounds like you two are having a problem."

I responded sheepishly, "Yes, sir. We are on our honeymoon and I just accidentally locked my keys in the car."

He said, "No problem, son. I used to break into cars all of the time in my youth. I'll just go back to my RV and grabbed a coat hanger. In the meantime, you calm yourself down, ma'am. I'll be right back."

Sure enough, the elderly man returned with a coat hanger in hand. My wife and I were on the passenger side of the car, looking through the window, and watched him as he bent the hanger, shoved it down inside the driver's door, and popped the lock open. He grabbed the keys out of the ignition, waved them over the roofline and said, "Are these the keys that you're missing ma'am?"

She yelled at him with a loud and angry tone of voice, "Yes!"

He looked shocked by her ungrateful response, tossed the keys on the driver's seat, locked the door, and closed it.

My wife literally started to jump on top of the roof of the car to go after the elderly man. I had to grab her by the legs and pull her off of the roof and back down to the passenger side of the car. The elderly man yelled, "Ma'am, now you just calm right down. I'll have those keys out in a jiffy."

Sure enough, within a couple of seconds, he popped the lock again, grabbed the keys off of the driver's seat, and tossed the keys over the roof at me. I caught the keys. He looked directly into my eyes and said, "You have yourself a wonderful marriage, son." Then he rolled his eyes, turned, and walked away. I knew right there and then that I was screwed. I was never going to become a pastor being married to a woman like that. However, I didn't get married to get a divorce. Therefore, I was committed to loving her into becoming a better person. Stay tuned.

THE RED HOT POKER

It was my junior year at UAA and I had just returned from playing for Northwest Basketball Camps overseas in Australia. We only played fifteen games in three weeks, including beating their Olympic basketball team. No broken noses this time. In spite of my repeated success overseas, I was still on top of the boosters' blackball list. I went from an overseas starter who helped to beat both the Brazilian and Australian Olympic Teams back to an Alaskan politically incorrect bench warmer. Apparently, I hadn't paid enough penance yet for the liquor license issue.

I continued to bust my butt during practices and dominated my teammates. The assistant coaches and my teammates were shocked that the head coach was continuing to punish me for successfully preventing the basketball booster club from obtaining a liquor license for the campus pub. They kept encouraging me to practice hard and said that the coach will eventually pull his head out of his butt and start me.

Well, after the first ten games of eternally sitting on the bench, the coach tried to put me in the game during the last two minutes. I didn't like him treating me like I was some inept player and that he was graciously giving me some playing time at the end of the game. I responded, "No! I'm not going into the game." He had to find someone else to put into the game. He was fuming mad at me. I didn't care. He called me into his office the next day and chewed my butt out for not following his directive by refusing to go into the game. He sat there quietly waiting for my response.

I responded, "You're an idiot. You're benching the best player on your team because of booster politics. I've paid my dues for winning the battle over the liquor license. You need to knock it off and move on. You either start me for now on or you won't have me back for my senior season. I have enough credits to graduate and I don't have to put up with your crap anymore."

Well, my head coach heard me loud and clear. He started me every game after that meeting. He would start me and play me for one or two minutes and then bench me the rest of the game. This was worse than his waiting to put me in during the last two minutes of the game. He was a real jerk.

Finally, during the last game of the year, he started me as usual. However, there were no dead balls. No whistles were blown. The game kept going on and on uninterrupted for five straight minutes. He didn't want to waste a timeout just to take me out of the game. At the end of those five minutes, we were winning 17 to 12. I had scored 14 of our 17 points in only five minutes' time. There were still thirty-five minutes left to play in the game. The coach took me out and benched me for the rest of the game.

During the rest of the first half of the game, the crowd was shouting and stomping on the bleachers in unison, "We want Matt! We want Matt! We want Matt!" I stood up and faced the crowd. I smiled at everyone and then motioned with my hands to please quiet down. Then I sat quietly on the end of the bench satisfied that I finally got a chance to show everyone what was going on.

After the game, the local sports writer wanted to interview me in the locker room. He sat there quietly staring at me for about thirty seconds. Then he asked, "What's going on? You scored 14 of your team's 17 points in the first five-minutes of the game. You were single handedly beating the other team all by yourself and then the coach

Chapter 8: The University of Alaska - Anchorage

benched you for the rest of the game. I saw it and the crowd saw it. Please tell me what's going on?"

Finally, I was provided with an opportunity to let my coach and the boosters club have it for the way they treated me for the past two years. However, my Christian faith kicked in and I chose to take the high road.

I responded, "Everyone has their role to fill on the team. I simply stepped on the court and did my job to the best of my ability. I'm glad my team won the game."

The sports writer smiled at me, nodded his head, got up, and walked over to another teammate to interview him. He knew that I wasn't going to give him the juicy gossip story that he was looking for. I wasn't going to allow him to use me to publicly disparage the basketball program at UAA just so he could help sell a few more newspapers. Truly, he didn't care one iota about me. He just wanted a good story for his readers.

The season had come to an end. Two weeks later, the head coach ran into me near the balcony overseeing the hockey rink in the athletic center. He sheepishly approached me and apologized for how he treated me during the past two years. He said, "I didn't realize it until I watched the video after the game but you played really well during those first five-minutes. You were beating the other team all by yourself. I can't believe that you had fourteen of our seventeen points."

What an idiot! He knew that I was All-State and Honorable Mention All-American in high school. He had the coaches' reports from my Brazilian and Australian summer tours. He knew that I started in all of the games and helped to beat their Olympic Teams. He saw me dominating my teammates every day in practice for three straight years. Now he thought he was going to convince me that he never knew that I was that good. Like it was a real surprise to him. Give me a break.

I just stood there looking at him. I didn't say a word to him. The coach looked awkward and gulped. Then he said, "Anyway, I would love to have you come back and play for your senior season. I promise that I will start you and that you will stay in every game. I won't pull you out anymore. You've earned the position."

THE XANUE

I smiled and said to the coach, "I earned the starting position during my freshman year when I played for Coach Bliss. You took it away from me the following year when I helped to win the battle over the liquor license for the campus pub. You catered to the boosters' club demands that I sit on the bench. You even tried to get me to quit the team. You verbally and physically abused me. Then when I finally had the chance to play for five straight minutes and outscored the other team, you were so blinded by your agenda that you couldn't even see what the entire crowd and sports writer saw. Now you want me to trust you and come back for one last season? I already have all of the credits that I need to graduate."

My coach said, "You could start taking graduate classes. Your athletic scholarship will cover graduate classes just like it covers the undergraduate classes."

I said, "You saw 'One on One' with Robby Benson, right?"

My coach responded, "Yes."

I replied, "Then you know what you can do with that red hot poker." I turned, walked away, and never spoke to him again. He had some of my teammates beg me to come back for one more year but I had hit the wall. I had enough of collegiate basketball politics. Besides, I had obtained the goal that my father had set out before me. I had practiced enough basketball to go to college for free. I had traveled all over the USA, including Hawaii twice. I had played basketball in Brazil and Australia. It was time for me to move forward with my life.

THE ALASKA SOCIAL WORKERS FROM HELL

While attending UAA for four years, I had managed to help start the Inter-Varsity Christian Fellowship (IVCF) chapter on the campus. I had also managed to be one of only two males who made it through the Social Work program. The angry, liberal, man-hating-feminists had managed to drive three other men out of the program. However, I stood firm and refused to let them win.

Chapter 8: The University of Alaska - Anchorage

During every class, the Social Work instructors would make fun of my Christian faith and conservative morals and values. I would dish it right back to them. If they wanted a classroom debate, I wasn't going to back down. Besides, they couldn't affect my playing time on the basketball team because I was already being forced to warm the bench.

One day, I went into talk with one of my Social Work instructors. I showed her my report cards and said, "I get A's and B's in all of my other classes, semester after semester. However, all you ever give me is C's. I've even showed my papers to fellow classmates and they tell me that my papers are good enough to receive A's and B's but you keep giving me C's."

She responded, "Matt, you're just a dumb, white jock and you don't deserve anything other than C's."

I laughed with a surprised look on my face and said, "Well, thank you for pitching that ball right over the plate. You just won me a multimillion dollar lawsuit against you and UAA. However, I will give you just this one chance to put all of that behind you if you go back and retroactively change all of my grades to the A's and B's that I deserve."

She changed my grades and never harassed me again after that day. Matter of fact, during the five-year reunion for our graduating Social Work class, she pulled me aside and said, "I want to personally apologize to you for the way I treated you several years ago while you were going through the Social Work program. I was battling alcoholism and I took out my anger and frustrations on you. I sincerely apologize and I'm so sorry for the way I treated you."

I smiled at her and said, "Don't worry. We're good. I appreciate you apologizing to me. I hope life is going much better for you now."

She smiled and nodded her head in the affirmative. I gave her a nice long warm hug. She had a tear coming down her cheek. I smiled at her again. Then we returned to the reunion party and mingled with everyone else. That was the last time that I ever saw Myrna.

GOD'S REWARD FOR MY PERSEVERANCE

Before I move on, I must say that the best reward that I ever received for putting up with all the Hellish crap that I suffered from my head basketball coach and the angry, liberal, man-hating feminists Social Work instructors at UAA, came immediately right after my last class ended. I was out in the hallway, celebrating with the other Social Work students. We were done. No more college classes. We were all going to graduate.

I was approached by a young lady of African American descent. She asked me if she could speak privately with me. I followed her down the hallway, through the doorway, and into the stairwell. I thought this was strange. We had never talked during any of our social work classes.

She sat down on the stairs in front of me and said, "I've been watching you for the past few years in all of the Social Work classes that we shared together. I saw how they attacked you, your Christian faith, and your conservative morals and values. You always took the high road. You stood out to me like a bright light in a dark room. Because of you, I want to know what I need to do to become a Christian. Can you help me?"

Needless to say, my jaw hit the floor. She saw tears coming down my cheeks and apologized for upsetting me. I said, "You're not upsetting me at all. These are tears of joy. I now understand that you're the reason I endured all of the crap that I suffered while attending UAA. You are worth every bit of disappointment and frustration that I suffered. Sure, I would love to help you."

I first shared with her about the fact that God loved us (the world) so much that he sent His only begotten Son to die for us on the cross for our sins. Jesus did not come to condemn the world, rather he came to save the world because he loves us so very much (John 3:16). Then I talked with her about what it took to become a Christian. I shared that she needed to understand that we are all sinners and have fallen short of the glory of God (Romans 3:23) and that the wages of sin is death (Romans 6:23). Then I shared that without faith, it's impossible to please God because anyone who approaches Him must believe that He exists and that He rewards those who earnestly seek Him (Hebrews 11:6). Then I shared that if we confess our sins, He is faithful and just to forgive us our sins and He will cleanse us from all unrighteousness (I John 1:9). Finally, I shared that everyone who calls on the name of the Lord shall be saved (Romans 10:13).

She had tears flowing down her cheeks and said, "Now it is my turn to cry. I'm sorry."

I told her to not worry and asked her if she wanted to pray at that very moment to ask Jesus Christ to be her Lord and Savior. She said, "Yes." We prayed together in the stairwell and she gave her life to Jesus. When we were done praying, she gave me a big hug and thanked me for my time. I encouraged her to start attending a strong Bible believing church as soon as possible. She agreed to do so. We parted ways and I never saw her again after that day.

As I shared earlier in this book, my plan was to become an NBA player and eventually a pastor of a church. However, God had other plans for my life. My college years soured me regarding the politics of the game of basketball. Also, I had married a woman for life who most definitely wasn't going to be suitable as a pastor's wife. Now that I was done with undergraduate school, it was time to seek God's guidance regarding the career that He had planned for me all along. I was now in a space and frame of mind where I could listen to Him and follow His lead.

CHAPTER 9
THE GRADUATE SCHOOL YEARS

During the next fifteen years, I would end up doing what I most definitely had never planned on doing with my life. Thanks to the influence of my mom's alcoholism on my life, I would go on to become a State and Nationally Certified Alcohol and Drug Abuse Counselor. I first worked in a residential facility for emotionally disturbed youth at Alaska Children's Services. I was also the volunteer Campus Life Club Director at Service High School in Anchorage, Alaska. We had the largest club in town averaging about one-hundred plus kids in attendance per week. It was an awesome ministry. Finally, I worked for a private psychiatric hospital – Charter North Hospital on Debarr Road in Anchorage, Alaska.

While working at Charter North Hospital, I created a job position for myself – Pastoral Services Coordinator. I had convinced the hospital administration that creating a bridge of trust between the psychiatric hospital and the religious community of Anchorage would help keep our beds filled. However, my real motivation was to provide the necessary education for free that the religious community of Anchorage was missing and their parishioners where suffering as a result. While attending seminary, the clergy were never educated about mental health issues or alcohol and drug abuse issues. I created a win/win scenario for everyone.

Over a ten-week period of time, I helped to train over one-hundred-fifty clergy and laymen from every possible denomination and faith (i.e., Catholics, Protestants, Jews, Mormons, Universalists, Greek Orthodox, Russian Orthodox, Unity, Baha'i, etc.). The program went so well, the Charter Corporate Office flew me down to Atlanta, Georgia to train dozens of the hospital chaplains from their hospitals in the southeast USA.

In 1988, we drove approximately five-thousand miles from Anchorage, Alaska to New Brunswick, New Jersey. In short, we drove ten hours per day for ten straight days, averaging about five-hundred miles per day. Halfway through the trip, our little dog was begging me not to get back into the truck to continue our journey. Nevertheless, we persevered and I began attending Rutgers University to obtain my Masters of Social Work (MSW) degree.

At this time, the MSW program at Rutgers University had a partnership program established with the Master of Divinity (M.Div.) program at Princeton University. Once I completed my MSW education at Rutgers, they offered me one-hundred percent free tuition to complete the M.Div. degree at Princeton Theological Seminary. What a dream come true. However, as I've previously mentioned, I was not married to a woman who would make a good pastor's wife. She had way too many unresolved personal issues to make this career/ministry path possible.

While attending Rutgers University, I was still in shape and I was playing basketball with a group of local elite players who had recently graduated from various colleges and universities. By this time, I could pretty much shoot the 3-point shot with seventy percent accuracy from anywhere inside the half-court line. I could shoot farther away from the basket than most guards could.

One day, after we were done playing, I was approached by a representative of the New Jersey Nets (now the Brooklyn Nets) who asked me if I would be interested in trying out for their team. It took me only a few seconds to say, "Thank you, sir, but no thank you."

He asked, "Why not?"

I responded, "Because I've been accepted into a Doctor of Psychology program out west and that's where my calling and my future happens to be."

What I didn't tell him is that I got soured on formalized basketball because of the internal politics. As a result of my collegiate experience,

Chapter 9: The Graduate School Years

I didn't see the NBA being any better than the crap I experienced at UAA. The New Jersey Nets were the worst team in the NBA and I would have most likely been the bench warmer for the worst team in the NBA. Finally, I was married to an angry, controlling woman who made it clear to me that it was time to grow up and be a man and stop playing sports or else our marriage would be over. I didn't get married to get a divorce. She knew this and had control over me because of it. She was always threatening to divorce me and to trash my reputation if I didn't do what she wanted me to do.

I obtained my second Master's degree in Clinical Psychology from George Fox University (1992); and my Doctorate degree in Clinical Psychology from George Fox University (1994). Then I went on to become a Licensed Clinical Social Worker, and a Licensed Clinical Psychologist when we returned to the State of Alaska.

If you remember reading in the previous chapters, my claim to fame was that I flunked Kindergarten. My parents' friends thought that I was mildly mentally retarded because of my lack of coordination, hearing issues, and speech impediment. Matter of fact, after I graduated from Rutgers University with my first Master's degree, my mother was sitting in the back of the car and was shaking her head. I saw her in my rearview mirror while I was driving away from the Rutgers University campus.

I asked my mother, "Why are you shaking your head?"

My mother responded, "I never thought I would see this day. You just graduated with a Master's degree and now you're going after a second Master's degree and a Doctorate degree."

I asked her, "Why does that surprise you?"

My mother responded, "You were always my slow boy."

Well, that ended the discussion rather quickly. I laughed and changed the conversation. However, she was kind of correct but not completely. My grades in high school weren't the best, not because I was her slow boy, but because I hated school. I hated reading the books. I hated the anxiety involved in studying for the tests as well as taking the tests. I didn't realize it until decades later but I had an Attention Deficit Disorder (ADD).

The only reason I went to high school and college was for my friends, the girls, and playing basketball. I wasn't going to make it into the NBA if I didn't play high school and college basketball. That's why I went to school even though I hated school.

Now here I was, married to a woman who would never make a good pastor's wife because of her anger and control issues. I wasn't going to make it into the NBA because of the liquor license snafu while attending UAA which ended up souring my love for the game. Also, my wife told me it was time to grow up, stop playing sports, and become a man. Finally, I had attended a total of ten years of college when I had originally planned on attending for only four years. Now I was a Licensed Clinical Psychologist instead of an NBA player and eventually a pastor. The best laid schemes 'Of Mice and Men' go oft awry.

Upon our return to Anchorage, Alaska in 1993, I did both my pre-Doc and post-Doc internships at Charter North Hospital. I had worked there years earlier before my graduate school trek across North America. They liked me and wanted me back again. I was good for their business. During these two years, I volunteered at our church as the Children's Ministry Director (K-6th grades). The Youth Pastor was in charge of the middle school and high school kids. By this time, we had three young kids and we both wanted them involved with the church.

When I completed my post-Doc internship, I immediately became a Licensed Clinical Psychologist. Charter North Hospital promoted me to the Clinical Director position of their outpatient counseling center in Fairbanks, Alaska. We moved north to Fairbanks which was located only one-hundred miles south of the Arctic Circle. When we arrived there, several people said, "Welcome to the real Alaska" because the temperatures routinely dropped from twenty to forty below zero during the winter months. It got so cold in Fairbanks that you had to keep your car running when you were inside the store shopping for groceries. Also, you had to plug your car in to the electrical outlet to keep your engine oil warm. Otherwise, the engine oil would freeze.

Chapter 9: The Graduate School Years

Our move to Fairbanks, Alaska was timely because I had just seen a third pastor lynched for political reasons rather than any kind of spiritual and ethical violations. The first two pastoral lynching's occurred while I was attending graduate school in Oregon. Now our Anchorage church hung their pastor because of a controlling Elder Board.

I enjoyed the five years of living in Fairbanks, Alaska. I managed to bring the Charter North Counseling Center out of the red and back into the black. The previous Clinical Director had run the clinic into the ground financially. Also, I enjoyed my private practice as a Licensed Clinical Psychologist. Finally, I enjoyed teaching the College/Career Singles Sunday School class at the new church we were attending. It was nice to be attending a healthy church where no one had overblown egos. There were no pastoral lynching's in Fairbanks.

While living in Fairbanks, my angry and controlling wife forced me to get a vasectomy against my will. Can you imagine the outrage if a husband forced his wife to get her tubes tied? Well, if I didn't comply with her wishes, she was going to cut me off sexually. It was already bad enough, we weren't having sex but one to two times per every two to three months whether we needed it or not. I complied with her demands.

However, before the surgery, I had a vision of a small blonde hair boy looking at me with concern. He said, "What about me daddy?" Obviously, this was my fourth child waiting to be born. I told my wife about the vision but she didn't care.

While on the operating table, the doctor could see that I was crying silent tears. He said, "Matt, you don't have to get this surgery if you don't want to do it."

I told him, "You don't understand my situation with my wife. If I don't do it, she will make my life worse than it already is."

He complied and I got the vasectomy. The fourth child would have to wait until later for his turn to be born. God works miracles.

Finally, the straw that broke the camel's back that caused me to leave Fairbanks was when I took on the school district publicly. I had

151

noticed while practicing in Fairbanks over a five-year period of time that kids of all ages were going undiagnosed and untreated regarding their Attention Deficit Disorder (ADD) and Attention Deficit Hyperactivity Disorder (ADHD). As a result, they were falling through the cracks and running into academic problems, family problems, peer problems, and substance abuse issues.

I organized parents and teachers to publicly take on the school district since the superintendent wasn't willing to work with us. They weren't willing to admit that they had a "Don't Ask/Don't Tell" policy regarding ADD/ADHD. In other words, they would not allow their teachers to bring up the possibility of ADD/ADHD to the parents if they saw that their child was struggling with their academics. They were afraid that the school district would have to pay for the professional evaluations so they forbid teachers to discuss the issue at all.

The public debate continued via newspaper articles and radio interviews. One day, a friend and School Board Member took me out to lunch. He warned me not to push the issue any further. He told me that if I didn't drop this hot potato issue with the Fairbanks School District regarding the "Don't Ask/Don't Tell" policy concerning ADD/ADHD, then they were going to shut down my private practice. Well, needless to say, he was no longer my friend. We continued our push and eventually won the dispute after a local physician provided me with a copy of the school district memo that was circulated eight years earlier. I was impressed that he held on to the copy of the memo for so long.

The memo hit the front page of the local Fairbanks newspaper and we had won the war. Two days later, the Fairbanks school district offered a formal public apology and freed their teachers to talk with parents about the possibility of their kids having ADD/ADHD. Now the children and adolescents in Fairbanks were going to start getting the help that they needed and deserved.

One month later, as threatened and promised, my private practice was shut down. I couldn't believe that they pulled it off. Somehow, someway, someone on the school board managed to cut off all of my

Chapter 9: The Graduate School Years

business phone calls and my private practice dried up instantly. I suspect that they worked in the local phone company or had a friend who worked there. Anyway, no phone calls equal no business. It was now time to pack up and move back down to the Lower 48 States. Specifically, to Salem, Oregon and eventually, to Grants Pass, Oregon.

CHAPTER 10
THE OREGON TRAIL

I have no intention of rewriting my first book all over again within this book. As I strongly suggested at the beginning of this book, please read my Bigfoot books in their proper sequential order. If you want to understand this book, you must begin by reading my first Bigfoot book (i.e., Bigfoot: A Fifty-Year Journey Come Full Circle). Otherwise, you're simply not going to get it.

With all of the above said, I'm only going to highlight events in this book that I think matter regarding your understanding as to "Why me?" Who am I? Was I actually chosen to be the ambassador for the Bigfoot Forest People (i.e., The Xanue) or did I earn it? Why is it important for the Xanue to have an ambassador (i.e., "The 13") speaking for them? So once again, please read my first Bigfoot book before you read this book if you really want to truly understand everything.

We moved from Fairbanks, Alaska down to Salem, Oregon and stayed with my parents for a few months while I established my new private practice in Grants Pass, Oregon. The kids finished out the school year in Salem and then everyone joined me in Grants Pass near the end of June. We had just moved into our rental home and the kids were itching to get outdoors and play. They had done a lot of hiking with their mother and me while living in Alaska.

On July 1, 2000, we took a tour at the Oregon Caves National Monument Park. The caves make for an awesome tour. If you decide to take a tour, please wear a coat or hoodie because it's very cold inside the caves. After the tour of the caves, we decided to hike the "Big Tree

THE XANUE

Loop Trail." That's when we ran into a Bigfoot about one mile up the mountainside. More specifically, that's when we ran into Zorth, the leader of the Xanue Council of Twelve. If you don't know what I'm talking about right now, that's exactly why you need to read my first Bigfoot book. Now please go do so.

Anyone who's very familiar with the story of my family's encounter with a Bigfoot (i.e., Zorth) will remember that I was very traumatized (i.e., PTSD). I had horrific nightmares for the following month and occasional bouts of uncontrollable tears. Every night in my dreams, I saw a Bigfoot ripping my family apart and there was nothing I could do about it. It helped to talk with family and friends. The endless number of radio and TV interviews also helped me to process my thoughts and feelings.

Please keep in mind that my family was absolutely in no danger whatsoever. I can say this based on twenty-twenty hindsight. All of the fear and danger was created in my own mind because of my "Fight or Flight" response created by the encounter. It had nothing to do with the behavior of the Bigfoot (i.e., Zorth). All he was doing was watching my family. He made no threatening gestures whatsoever. Just like many other people who have had a Bigfoot encounter, I created all of the fear and danger inside my own head. Retrospectively, there was absolutely nothing to fear but fear itself.

But just so you understand what was going through my mind at the time was the fact that I not only saw a very tall and buff Bigfoot, I also saw him uncloak and cloak again. How was I going to defend my family against something so much taller and larger than myself that could appear and disappear again? In my mind, we were all going to die and there was absolutely nothing that I could do about it. I was so relieved when we actually got off the mountain an hour later.

My wife and I sent the three young children into the Gift Store to pick out an item for being such good little hikers. They had no clue what was going on. In the meantime, she and I talked about the pros and cons of filing a report at the administration office at the Oregon

Chapter 10: The Oregon Trail

Caves National Monument Park. We agreed that the public safety issue trumped our fear of the media pestering us for our story.

She went into the Gift Store to help our three young children make their choices while I walked over to the administration office and filed a report. Ranger Beverly Churner took the report. I was in tears and thought that she was going to think that I was crazy. Instead, she reassured me by telling me that new species are discovered every year on our planet. She also told me that anyone who thinks that we have discovered all of the existing species on our planet is practicing ignorance. At this time, my wife and oldest son came into the administrative office and confirmed the story.

Two days later, Ranger John Roth took my family back out on the trail along with two Bigfoot Field Research Organization (BFRO) investigators. We walked them through the entire event (i.e., Where we smelled it, heard it, and where I saw it). I even made them come up the hill off the trail and confirm the fecal matter and toilet paper on the ground (i.e., Where I was standing when I claimed to have seen the Bigfoot watching my family). Although they were understandably reluctant, they confirmed the viewing area for me.

Ranger John Roth had all of us remain on the trail while he explored the area below the trail. After a while, he called us all down to an animal trail that he had found. He told us, "Something very large has moved through this area during the past twenty-four to forty-eight hours. I also found this very large track on the ground."

The track dwarfed my size sixteen tennis shoe which is fourteen and one-half inches long. Also, the ground was baked hard because of the prolonged heat during the day. Therefore, whatever made the footprint in the ground had to be very heavy. I jumped up in the air and slammed my foot on the ground and I couldn't even dent the turf next to the very large track.

Ranger John Roth was squatting on the ground while the rest of us were standing around him. He looked up at all of us and said, "This is not a Black Bear track. This is a Bigfoot track."

Then he looked up at us and said, "You need to know that the park has a policy where we will not make a public acknowledgement with the media regarding the existence of the Bigfoot species within our park boundaries."

We all looked at each other and I'm sure we were all pretty much thinking the same thing: "What the heck did he just say? The park has a policy not to acknowledge the existence of the Bigfoot species within their park boundaries? Wait a second! You can't have a policy unless a bunch of people sit around a table in a private room and discuss the need to make such a policy. Also, you wouldn't discuss the need to make such a policy unless encounters with the Bigfoot species had already occurred within the park boundaries. Wow!"

Whether or not he realized it, Ranger John Roth revealed a lot of information to us in that simple little Oregon Caves National Monument Park policy statement. Within a month, I had thirty plus confirmations come to me via phone calls, emails, and face to face discussions regarding various individuals who encountered the Bigfoot species within or near the park boundaries (i.e., Park employees, hikers, campers, miners, hunters, etc.). My mind was blown. I had no idea that the Bigfoot species really existed outside of folklore, myth, and legend.

At this point in my life, I found myself facing a major personal dilemma. I had grown up in and around the woods my entire life. I loved to hike, camp, and fish. Now that I knew that the Bigfoot species existed, was I willing to go back out into the woods or was I going to let the fear of the unknown keep me out of the woods for the rest of my life?

Well, I opted to go back into the woods with a vengeance. I was going to go back into the woods, grab Bigfoot by the scruff of the neck, drag him out of the woods, and show the world that the species existed and that I wasn't crazy for saying publicly to the world that I saw one.

Over the years, I had some family and a whole lot of new found friends join me in my quest to prove that Bigfoot existed. The media also tagged along with us. In the past twenty-years, I've been on fifteen TV shows and I've participated in over three-hundred radio interviews. To this date, I've had over five-hundred people participate in my

Chapter 10: The Oregon Trail

quest to prove the existence of Bigfoot via my research areas and via attendance to our weekend events during the Summer months at Camp Xanue (i.e., Our ten acres of forested property on a mountain top, approximately fifteen miles west of Chehalis WA, which is surrounded by half a million acres of Weyerhaeuser timber property).

As previously mentioned, if you haven't read my first book yet, please stop reading this book and go read my other Bigfoot book first. Otherwise, you're truly missing out on a whole lot of detail that I'm simply not going to repeat for you in this book. Suffice it to say for now, the next two chapters of this book will highlight what I believe to be the important events to demonstrate who the Bigfoot really are and why I was selected to become their ambassador/spokesperson (i.e., "The 13").

CHAPTER 11
How Not to Find Bigfoot
("THE SCIENTIFIC METHOD")

I began my quest to find Bigfoot via utilizing "The Scientific Method" which can be summarized as follows: (1) Make an observation; (2) Ask a question; (3) Gather background information; (4) Create a hypothesis; (5) Create an experiment to test the hypothesis; (6) Analyze the results of the experiment; (7) Draw a conclusion; and (8) Share the conclusion.

In other words, (1) On October 20, 1967, Patterson and Gimlin allegedly observed and filmed an upright, hairy, bipedal, female, humanoid being walking away from them at Bluff Creek, California; (2) Did Patterson and Gimlin actually see and film a Bigfoot? (3) The Patterson/Gimlin research team heard that a Bigfoot might be in the area, filmed it, and collected multiple foot casts; (4) I expect that if researchers spend an inordinate amount of time in the forest, there will be more sightings, film/video captured, foot casts collected, and possibly DNA collected via hair samples and/or blood samples; (5) I will go out into the woods with other researchers in order to collect more film/video, foot casts, and hopefully obtain some DNA via hair samples and/or blood samples; (6) If we obtain DNA samples, we will have a credible DNA expert analyze the samples; (7) Hopefully, the collected, analyzed, and newly identified Bigfoot DNA samples will set the species apart from all other species on the Earth; and (8) We will share this data with the rest of the world.

I began my Bigfoot research under the tutelage of Dr. William York (AKA Bill), a British wildlife biologist with over forty-years of experience in Africa. He was a former big game hunter, former game warden officer, and eventually became a wildlife biologist. He actually took the Queen of England on a guided Safari in Africa. He was also a wildlife consultant for the Walt Disney World Animal Kingdom in Orlando, Florida as well as for the Wildlife Safari Park in Winston, Oregon (i.e., Just south of Roseburg, Oregon). Toward the end of his forty-year stint in Africa, he became a primate specialist. He fully understood animal behavior and tracking. He was the perfect research team member who also became my mentor, best friend, and father figure.

Also, at the very beginning of my quest to find Bigfoot, I was under the tutelage of Matt Moneymaker, the founder of the Bigfoot Field Research Organization (BFRO). We talked a lot on the phone and sent emails back and forth. He taught me about the predominant school of thought regarding what the Bigfoot species was: A descendant of Gigantopithecus (i.e., A dumb giant mountain ape or wood ape).

I was taught that scientists had found a fossil record for Gigantopithecus in some caves located in China. I didn't find out until years later that this whole theory came from a very large tooth that was found in a cave in China. There actually isn't a fossil record after all. Just a tooth theory (i.e., Like a Tooth Fairy). Gigantopithecus was believed to be approximately ten-feet tall. The predominant theory was that their decedents, the Bigfoot species, migrated across the Bering Sea Land Bridge into North America. According to my many communications with Matt Moneymaker, the best way to look for Bigfoot was with the use of any and all technology available at the time.

Therefore, we proceeded with our quest to find Bigfoot while employing the commonly used and approved trail cams, video cams, seismic sensors, night vision equipment, and speakers to blast out screams at night. In addition to utilizing the commonly used technology, our research team also adopted the BFRO method of screaming into the darkness (i.e., Bobo screams) and hitting trees with big heavy

Chapter 11: How Not to Find Bigfoot

sticks. Then we would patiently await a response, which more often than not, never came.

After my first year or so in the field, Matt Moneymaker and I eventually parted ways. My family and I had shared two meals with him while we vacationed twice in California. He seemed like a nice guy. However, we had a falling out when I refused to refer the various inquisitive TV film crews to him. Instead, we chose to represent ourselves while giving our own interviews regarding our family's encounter at the Oregon Caves National Monument Park. After he realized that we weren't going to automatically send the TV film crews to him and the BFRO, he no longer had any use for me and my family.

My research team continued with our quest to find Bigfoot in southern Oregon. We continued to employ the use of technological equipment. Although we were finding numerous foot tracks and dried up scat piles, we seldom had a visual or heard any vocals or tree knocks. However, we were able to conclude the following from our research: (1) Some Bigfoot families appeared to have a Cougar or a pack of Coyotes as pets (i.e., Based on foot tracks and scat piles, they were clearly hanging out together in a symbiotic relationship); (2) They slept in the same patterns when we found their bedding areas (i.e., Dad on the left, mom on the right, and kid(s) in the middle); (3) Sometimes, they would travel parallel to a logging road with dad always walking closest to the road and mom and the kid(s) would walk twenty-five to fifty-feet away from the road (i.e., If we found dad's tracks, we usually found mom's and the kids' tracks within spitting distance from dad); (4) They would mark the boundaries of their territory with snapped off trees, large rocks, and X's (I will comment more about this in the next chapter); and (5) They would consistently avoid our Trail Cams/Video Cams when the infrared light was on and they would hit our bait piles when the infrared light was off (i.e., It was very clear that they could see infrared light).

During the Summer of 2003, we had just concluded a weekend expedition in an older research area. We had several people in attendance. After the last car departed, Don and I started to set up video surveillance to see if we could capture any Bigfoot images after we left the base camp. There was plenty of consistent evidence in the past that suggested that they visited our base camp after everyone left. We thought that we were going to be sneaky, hide the video camera inside a fake rock, and get them on film.

While Don was setting up the equipment, we both heard a very loud, prolonged, deep bass, guttural growl coming from behind him. Don's eyes were like saucers and he was scared to move. I told him that I couldn't see anything there behind him. He turned around and saw nothing. I told him that I was going to back up a little way and see if I could obtain a better view.

I backed up and I was looking and looking. Suddenly, I heard a loud, prolonged, deep bass, guttural growl coming from behind me. Matter of fact, the hot breath of whoever it was that was growling at me was breathing down my neck. That's right. I could feel the hot breath on the back of my neck. I seriously thought that I was a dead man.

I took one step forward and then slowly turned around because I wanted to see the Bigfoot that was going to kill me. When I turned around, I saw absolutely nothing. Yet when I reached my hand out in front of me, I felt a big hairy chest right around the level of my face. I'm almost seven feet tall (i.e., I'm 6'9" tall/6'10" tall with my shoes on). I immediately took a couple of steps back, turned around and walked back toward Don. I told him that I had one behind me too and that I thought that they wanted us to leave right away. He agreed and we left. No, once again, we never got anything on video. It was very frustrating.

On November 12, 2003, we lost Dr. William York to congestive heart failure. This was a very sad day for me. Matter of fact, it was a very sad following year or two for me. His death took the wind out of my sails. I had just lost my research mentor, friend, and father figure. On top of that, Bill and I were about ready to reorganize our research team because we had a couple of members misusing our nonprofit status for their own personal gain. We didn't want any problems with

Chapter 11: How Not to Find Bigfoot

the IRS. When Bill passed, I simply removed myself from the group and turned the reigns over to the unscrupulous individuals.

I went into hiding and into mourning. Well, I went into hiding from humans. However, that didn't stop the Bigfoot from coming to me. If you remember, earlier I said that I saw the Bigfoot (i.e., Zorth) on the "Big Tree Loop Trail," up on the mountain above the Oregon Caves National Monument Park, appear out of nowhere (i.e., Uncloak) and then disappear again (i.e., Cloak). The fact that I saw a Bigfoot was scary enough. But the fact that I saw a Bigfoot uncloak and cloak again was totally mind blowing.

By the way, I never told another human being about this. I didn't tell my wife, family, friends, research team, or Dr. William York. I told absolutely no one. I was taking enough of a risk with my professional reputation and private practice to simply publicly state that I saw a Bigfoot. If I added the fact that I saw the Bigfoot (i.e., Zorth) uncloak and cloak again, I would never hear the end of it from the general public, other Bigfoot researchers, the trolls, and the haters. I would have lost my private practice for sure. Therefore, I kept my mouth shut.

Nevertheless, while mourning Dr. William York's death and hiding from humans, the Bigfoot would occasionally come to me during my sabbatical. They would wait for me to come out of my office building at night, while standing next to tall bushes alongside the building. I would notice them as I walked to my vehicle. If I walked on the other side of the building at night to get to my vehicle, they would be waiting there for me too. They just stood there, next to the tall bushes alongside the building, and watched me walk to my car.

After Dr. William York's death, I met my second wife, Amanda. She was everything that I didn't have in my first marriage. Happy, kind, funny, playful, easygoing, caring, sports-minded, not controlling, and adventuresome. She had never been married before and did not have any kids. She wanted to have children very badly. I loved her very much. She moved to Grants Pass, Oregon and we began our life together.

One weekend, while Amanda was out of State visiting family and friends back home in Texas, I was sitting in the living room at night while watching a TV show. Suddenly, the two dogs sleeping on the living room floor next to my chair, jumped up on their four feet, wide awake, and began to bark ferociously at something standing in the doorway leading from the foyer to the living room. I about flew out of my chair.

Spencer was an Irish Wolf Hound and Sophie was a Chocolate Lab. I had absolutely no clue what they were persistently barking so loud at. I didn't see anything or anyone standing in the doorway. I told the dogs to quiet down. I yelled at them to stop their barking. I even whacked their butts. They wouldn't stop. Finally, after what seemed to be like a couple of minutes, they suddenly stopped barking just as quickly as they began. They looked nervous. They were wagging their tails. They wanted reassurance from me that they did the right thing. I loved on them and praised them for their bravery as they defended me from the invisible intruder. They laid back down and went to sleep by my chair.

After I was done watching the TV, I got up out of my chair, walked from the living room, through the foyer, to the computer nook on the other side of the kitchen. While I was on the computer, I heard three loud knocks at the front door. I got up, walked through the kitchen, and into the foyer and opened the front door. No one was there. I looked around and didn't see anyone. I went back to the computer and sat down.

Well, awhile later, the three loud knocks came again at the front door. Once again, I got up and walked through the kitchen, and into the foyer and answered the front door. There was no one there again. I had absolutely no clue what was happening. I walked back to the computer and sat down again.

A little while later, the third set of three loud knocks arrived at the front door. This time I was prepared. I grabbed a flashlight, called the two dogs, Spencer and Sophie, and we went running out the front door. We lived on two and a half acres that were fenced with a gate. Somehow, someway, some neighbor kids must have gotten into our yard and were playing a game with me. After covering all of the terrain, the dogs and I didn't find anyone. We went back inside the house.

Shortly thereafter, I heard this very loud crash that sounded almost like an explosion. The dogs were barking in response. We ran out the front door again to see what was going on. We found nothing in the front yard. We went in the backyard and walked down the hill going to the river. We found a very large tree that had fallen up hill, in a forty-five-degree angle toward the house. I went back inside the house, called Amanda, and explained everything to her. I thought I was going crazy.

First, I had two dogs barking at an invisible guest. Then I had three sets of loud knocks on the front door without anyone being there. Finally, I had a very large tree that fell over in the backyard with a very loud, explosive crash. Was this it for the night? Was anything else going to happen? Needless to say, I didn't sleep very well that night.

The next morning, I went out to investigate the backyard and discovered that the tree had fallen perfectly. It had managed to barely avoid hitting our inground benches and portable lawn furniture on both sides of the tree. When I say barely avoid hitting everything, I mean by one or two inches on both sides of the large tree. It couldn't have fallen more perfectly. It was like it was planned to perfection. Very strange.

As I previously shared, Amanda really wanted to have a child. Therefore, we decided to have me get a vasectomy reversal which was a very expensive and painful process (i.e., Equivalent to being kicked in between the legs a thousand times by someone who's wearing steel toed Army boots). As a result, my fourth child and her only child, Grady, was born in early 2007.

Do you remember, "What about me daddy," when my first wife forced me to get a vasectomy. Well, here he was. A ten-pound bundle of love. Two years later, while attending a Psychic Fair at the Josephine County Fairgrounds in Grants Pass, Oregon, a female Psychic told me that Grady was happy to be with me again. He had missed me. When Amanda returned from using the restroom, the Psychic looked at me and Grady, then looked at her, and then she looked very confused. I could tell that she thought that the three of us didn't belong together.

THE XANUE

While still taking a break from humans, I would occasionally hike on a trail along the Rogue River Highway. I loved walking in the forest away from people. Well, occasionally, I would smell "the smell" and/or sense that one or more Bigfoot were in the area. I would stop, look up the mountainside, and see one or two hiding behind the trees while they were watching me. It's like they wanted me to know that they were there. I would routinely ignore them and continued with my walks.

Regarding the activity on our property, you need to keep in mind that I was still very much in denial of the paranormal abilities of the Bigfoot species. Yes, I had seen a Bigfoot (i.e., Zorth) uncloak and cloak again. However, it was way too freaky for me to consider and I, more or less, repressed the experience because I didn't want to deal with it at the time. Therefore, I was more inclined to think that one or more ghosts were involved with the phenomena inside and outside our home.

For example, one weekend morning, Amanda and I were sitting in the living room and we were listening to the baby monitor, while Grady was playing with toys on the floor in his bedroom. To our surprise, we heard him talking with a young girl while he was playing. I got up right away and walked into his bedroom. There was no one else there. Grady looked all happy and continued to play while he was talking to someone sitting on the floor with him. This time, there was no response back to his communication.

A few months later, Grady was sick and had a fever. We had a queen bed in his bedroom for any guests to use if they stayed with us. I decided to take Grady out of his crib and sleep with him in the guest bed so I could monitor his health. During the middle of the night, I was woken up by the feeling of the top bedspread being slowly pulled off of us toward the foot of the bed. I just laid there pretending like I was still asleep.

After about two feet had been pulled off of us toward the foot of the bed, two-year-old Grady sat up, pointed his finger at the end of the bed and said, "Nana, no! Stop!" Immediately, the bedspread stopped being

Chapter 11: How Not to Find Bigfoot

pulled off the end of the bed. I reached down, grabbed the bedspread, and then pulled it back up to cover our upper bodies. Then Grady and I laid our heads back down on our pillows and fell asleep.

On another occasion, I had moved my private practice office to the large bedroom area on the northeast corner of the home with windows facing the Rogue River. It was a hot summer day and I had just walked an older female client to my office. As she sat down on the couch, I asked her if she would like a glass of ice water. She said 'yes' so I walked to the kitchen to get both of us some ice water.

Upon my return to the office, the older female client asked if my daughter had stayed home from school today. I said, "Why do you ask?" She told me that she saw her walk from the other bedroom, past the office door, and follow me into the living room when I went to get us both some ice water. I smiled, quickly changed the subject, and proceeded with her counseling session. I didn't tell her that it wasn't my daughter. No one else was in the house but my client and me.

Finally, on another day, one of the house cleaners witnessed the blonde teenage girl quietly walking from the back bedroom, next to my corner office, through the living room, and on into the kitchen area. Then she disappeared. We obviously had a guest in our home that was hanging out in Grady's bedroom.

That's why I thought all of the other activity in the house and on our property was simply ghost activity. It wasn't until later on that Zorth had confirmed with me that Lokue, the guardian of the house, was the one who stepped inside our home and caused the dogs to bark. Lokue was the one who knocked on the door three times. Finally, Lokue and some other Xanue were the ones responsible for bringing down the tree in a precise manner as to not harm any of the furniture in the backyard.

They brought the tree down because it was aging, rotting out, and they didn't want it falling on me or Grady. We constantly played together in the backyard right around the spot where the tree came down. It was nice to learn that we had unseen guardians looking out after our safety.

THE XANUE

On a side note, I was informed much later that Lokue lives in the tree right outside the front door of the home. Apparently, he was our designated guardian. Well, he still is Grady's guardian because he and his mother still live in the home. A few years ago, Grady actually saw Lokue walk down the backside of the property toward the river. He's never forgotten that moment.

Thanks to a friend, Jason, who worked at a local convenience store on the Rogue River Highway, I got hooked into Bigfoot research again. He managed to talk me into checking out some very large tracks beside a pond halfway up on the mountainside behind his home. I took my kids, Hannah and Micah, up the mountainside with me to find the tracks beside the pond. They were twenty-two inches long. I was casting a foot track when I heard a prolonged, deep bass, guttural growl on the other side of the knoll. The kids' eyes and my eyes widened like saucers, simultaneously. I got up and started walking toward the knoll. My kids yelled at me, "Dad! What are you doing?"

I responded, "There's a Bigfoot on the other side of the knoll. I want to go meet him."

They responded, "We know! What if he kills you? Then what happens to us? Get back here!"

By this time, I knew that we weren't going to be killed by a Bigfoot. Nevertheless, I didn't want to freak out my two young kids. I walked back over to them, finished casting the track, and then we left. I said, "Goodbye" in the direction of the knoll, to the Bigfoot, before leaving.

A few days later, I followed the tracks, through the brush, trees, and stickers, up to the top of the mountain. The tracks exited the trees on to a logging road along the top of the ridgeline. The following weekend, I drove around in my Suburban until I eventually found the logging road. I located the dead-end cul-de-sac that I would eventually establish as the base camp for the Southern Oregon Research Area (SORA). I continued with my research solo for a while until I was contacted by Howie Gordon.

Howie was a reality TV star who appeared on Big Brother, Seasons Six and All-Stars Season Seven. He didn't know it but he was my

Chapter 11: How Not to Find Bigfoot

favorite Big Brother contestant ever. He was hilarious and a big kid in a man's body. Just like Tom Hanks in the movie, "Big." I didn't know it but Howie was a major Bigfoot enthusiast. He was coming to Oregon and wanted to go out Bigfooting with me. He became my Bigfoot research buddy and came to Oregon on several occasions to look for the big hairy guy. Bigfooting with Howie Gordon is always fun. Now, Howie is a member of the morning edition team, as the weatherman, for KTUU, Channel Two, in Anchorage, Alaska. My old stomping grounds. It's a small world after all.

During this time, I was still incorporating the standard "Old School" techniques as I continued with my Bigfoot research. I put out food and had cameras on trees. I whacked on trees with large heavy sticks and Bobo screamed into the night. Nothing. Nothing. Still nothing. However, when I slept in my tent at night in the middle of the SORA base camp, I could occasionally hear them walking around. I have to admit; I was still scared.

I slept with the fly cover on the top of my tent because I didn't want Bigfoot looking down on me while I was sleeping. Besides, I felt safer inside my sealed-up tent. Everyone knows that the nylon walls of a pup tent possess special powers that can protect all campers from Black Bear, Cougar, and Bigfoot, right? Nothing can penetrate the nylon walls of a tent. There's nothing like a false sense of security.

One night, while Howie was camping with me at SORA, I was being poked in the right shoulder, as I lay on my back, through the tent wall by a very large finger that was the size of a cigar. It slowly poked me and then slowly withdrew. The finger slowly poked me again and then slowly withdrew. On the third slow poke, I gently grabbed it and held on to it. Eventually, the finger started to slowly pull away and rather than fight to hold on to it, I let it go. Good decision. That was an awesome experience. Naturally, Howie theorized that Bigfoot was poking me with something else. I told you that Howie was funny.

By this time, my two-year old son, Grady, began to join me on my campouts. He loved to go camping. He loved the campfires and smores. He also liked the idea that we were looking for something in

171

the woods even though he didn't completely understand the entire Bigfoot concept yet. He simply enjoyed time with daddy in the woods.

Finally, by this time, I had put ten years into the "Old School" approach to Bigfoot research. I hadn't gotten very far. Yes, I collected a truckload of foot casts but I gave most of them away. Unlike some other well-known Bigfoot researchers, I wasn't out there in the forest to see how many foot casts I could collect. Yes, I got some occasional vocals returned to me after Bobo screaming in the dark. Yes, I got a few tree-knocks back after whacking on trees with big, heavy sticks. Yes, we had some occasional visuals. However, after investing ten-years of my life trying to find Bigfoot, I had to conclude that this wasn't the way to go about doing it. Yet so many Bigfoot researchers just don't seem to get it or accept this fact. They keep doing the same approach.

I couldn't help but think about other "Old School" Bigfoot researchers who had been out in the forest much longer than me. Some for twenty or thirty years. Yet, they weren't any further along than I was (i.e., BFRO Researchers, The Olympic Project, Dr. Meldrum, etc.). Also, Peter Byrne, a well-known Bigfoot researcher, had been utilizing "Old School" scientific research techniques for over fifty-years and he still hadn't seen a Bigfoot, let alone obtained any DNA from a Bigfoot. Something wasn't right. All Peter Byrne and the others had managed to do was show the rest of us how not to find Bigfoot. I was done with the scientific method approach. There had to be a better way to prove the existence of the Bigfoot Forest People (i.e., Xanue). I'm a licensed clinical psychologist and a problem solver by nature. I wasn't going to quit. I was going to find a better way because I wanted to meet, cultivate a relationship, interact with, and learn from the Bigfoot Forest People species. Not just collect foot casts, hear screams or tree-knocks, see occasional silhouettes at night, and/or hopefully collect some Bigfoot DNA.

CHAPTER 12
HOW TO FIND BIGFOOT
(THE "TRILS" METHOD)

After ten-years in the Bigfoot research field, and much thinking and problem solving, I decided to dramatically change my approach and attitude to Bigfoot research. It became very clear to me that the "Old School" research approach, which utilizes the Scientific Method, was getting all of us absolutely nowhere at all. There had to be another way of solving the Bigfoot mystery. There had to be a better approach. Rather than continue to utilize the Scientific Method, postulating that the Bigfoot species were a bunch of "dumb giant mountain apes" that could be easily tricked and eventually caught in order to obtain their DNA, I decided to prove their existence via another method. After much thinking and problem solving, I decided to use an approach that I later coined as the "Targeted, Relational, Interactive, Learning, and Sharing method" (TRILS).

The Targeted, Relational, Interactive, Learning, and Sharing Method (TRILS) seeks to prove the existence of the Bigfoot (i.e., Xanue) species by (1) simply targeting the location of a family group of the Bigfoot species; (2) Developing a relationship with them; (3) Interact with them; (4) Learn from them; and (5) With their permission, share this knowledge with others around the world so they can also enjoy a relationship with the Xanue. In summary, "We interact with and learn from our large hairy bipedal friends, therefore, they are" (i.e., You can't target, befriend, interact with, and learn from someone unless they exist).

THE XANUE

Let me explain it another way, after my marriage had ended with Amanda due to various reasons of incompatibility, Cynthia and I met at our South Salem High School 30th Class Reunion. By chance or fate, we ran into one another in the lobby of the Grand Hotel in Salem, Oregon. We ate breakfast together and talked. Afterwards, we walked through downtown Salem together, ate lunch together at the food court in the Salem Center Mall, and then walked some more around downtown Salem. Then we attended the 30th reunion event together in the evening.

Afterwards, I drove away from the hotel, back to southern Oregon so I could catch my airplane at the Medford airport, fly back east, and speak about my "Positive Parenting with a Plan" program. Eventually, I moved to Puyallup/South Hill, Washington to live with Cynthia. After much time spent together as well as nonstop communication with one another, we got to know each other very well. After nine years of dating, we were pretty certain that we both existed, without having to utilize the scientific method to prove it. We decided to get married on January 1, 2020 in Las Vegas, Nevada. No! There was no DNA collection. Blood tests are not required to get married in the State of Nevada.

For the record, during our nine years of courtship, I never once searched Cynthia's bedding area for hair samples to capture her DNA in order to scientifically prove her existence. I never put Trail Cams up on the walls inside her home to capture pictures or video footage to prove her existence. I never took foot casts from her impressions out in the front yard or the backyard to prove her existence. I never yelled at her with Bobo screams in order to receive a response back from her. Finally, I never hit the outside walls of her home with a large stick or baseball bat to see if she would make knocking sounds back at me.

Matter of fact, I'm pretty certain that if I had tried any of the above methods to prove her existence, she would have booted me right out of her neck of the woods. Neither of us thought it was necessary to utilize the Scientific Method to prove one another's existence.

Chapter 12: How to Find Bigfoot

Through our ongoing relationship and interactions, confirmed by our experiences and five senses, we were pretty convinced that we both existed. The Targeted, Relational, Interactive, Learning, and Sharing Method (TRILS) was enough to satisfy our curiosity. No unnecessary Scientific Method was needed to cement our belief in and love for one another.

Anyway, after nine years of being in the same location, developing a relationship, interacting with one another, learning about one another, I now have Cynthia's permission to share with the rest of the world that she actually exists. I see her, hear her, smell her, feel her, and taste her. My satisfied senses have confirmed her existence. All of the above was accomplished without any DNA collection.

Now, if you come back at me saying that I have done nothing to prove that Cynthia actually exists and that she can't be proven to exist without utilizing the scientific method to collect her DNA evidence, I'm going to have "Let go and let God." All you have managed to do regarding your stubborn argument is prove just how closed-minded you are. You live in a safe and little rigid box with a very small worldview. I won't disturb your Blue Pill World with my Red Pill Truth.

For the record, you do realize that most humans believe in the existence of many things on the Earth, including the existence of God, without utilizing the Scientific Method to prove it, right?

Without any scientific proof at all, as far back as thousands of years ago all the way up to our present time, most humans believed in the existence of water, fire, Earth, air, the Moon, the Sun, mammals, birds, fish, reptiles, insects, trees, pumpkin pies, hot dogs, tacos, margaritas, beer, wine, fruit salad, houses, schools, airplanes, trains, cars, music, imagination, dreams, synchronicity, faith, hope, love, etc. To say that something doesn't exist simply because we can't measure it and replicate it is absolute nonsense and defies the common sense of everyday living as well as human history. There is more than one way to skin a cat.

Finally, if we're truly honest, we will admit that our science is in it's infancy. We humans are a bunch of science-minded infants crawling around inside the nursery of life thinking that we know it all. However, in reality, at this stage in the game of the development of the human race, our infantile science has only revealed the truths equivalent to one grain of sand on the beach in the entire universe. In contrast, look at all of the rest of the grains of sand on the beach that we know absolutely nothing about at all. There are a bazillion things that exists in the multidimensional universe even though our infantile science has yet to prove it. Don't be so closed minded. The human race and its scientific community has much to learn, Grasshopper.

Suffice it to say for now, the Scientific Method is not the only way to prove the existence of the Bigfoot species (i.e., Xanue). Not to mention the fact that after fifty plus years, the Scientific Method has come up empty handed time and time again. On the other hand, the Targeted, Relational, Interactive, Learning, and Sharing method (TRILS) can and has proven the existence of the Bigfoot Forest People (i.e., Xanue). We have located them, developed a relationship with them, continue to interact with them, learn from them, and have shared our experiences and the TRILS method with others. These individuals, in turn, have developed relationships with the Xanue and interact with them all over the USA, Canada, Europe, and Australia.

When I switched over to the Targeted, Relational, Interactive, Learning, and Sharing method (TRILS), I had to switch my way of thinking about the Bigfoot Forest People (i.e., Xanue) from being dumb giant mountain apes to intelligent sentient beings. My thinking was guided by several of the North American Indian stories that can be found online that describe the Bigfoot Forest People as very intelligent, spiritual beings with paranormal abilities. I simply could no longer think of them as descendants of Gigantopithecus (i.e., Dumb giant mountain apes). To continue to think this way, after fifty plus years of "Old School" research, utilizing the Scientific Method, has repeatedly turned up empty handed would be insane (i.e., Insanity is doing the same thing over and over again and again and expecting different results).

Also, rather than throw the food on the ground in a "bait-pile," for the dumb giant mountain apes, with a Trail Cam pointed at the food, I decided to "gift" the food in large stainless-steel dog food

Chapter 12: How to Find Bigfoot

bowls to the Bigfoot Forest People. I was going to utilize some of Dr. Jane Goodall's habituation techniques. I wanted to slowly but surely habituate the Bigfoot Forest People to me over time, as I built up their trust in me. After the trust developed, then we would officially have a relationship.

After one year of changing my attitude and approach, the local Bigfoot family finally started taking my food. They also started leaving fingerprints and handprints on the gifting bowls. We always cleaned the gifting bowls and delivered them at sundown while wearing surgical gloves. Then we would pick them up at sunrise while wearing surgical gloves. Therefore, any fingerprints or hand prints on the gifting bowls did not belong to us. Besides, the fingerprints and hand prints were much bigger than my very large hand that can palm a basketball.

For the record, over the subsequent years, the Xanue continued to routinely leave fingerprints and hand prints on the gifting bowls at SOHA. They even left some hand prints on the Suburban window and the Subaru window. It was amazing. Go watch our older videos on Xanue.Com or the YouTube videos on the TeamSquatchinUSA channel and see the fingerprints for yourself. Very cool stuff.

I guess I'm a little slow but after a few years, it finally occurred to me that the Xanue at SOHA were not taking the meat, vegetables, or fruit from the gifting bowls. They were only taking the bread products such as peanut butter and raspberry jelly sandwiches, donuts, Cinnabon rolls, cookies, Hawaiian sweet rolls, cheese bread, bagels, and cheese pizza (i.e., The Xanue picked off the olives and mushrooms from on top of the slices of pizza and placed them in the corner of the pizza box). They could get all of the fruit, vegetables, and meat that they needed out in the wild. However, they could not get bread products. They really enjoyed and appreciated the bread products.

Once again, I'm going to assume that you have read my first book: "BIGFOOT: A Fifty-Year Journey Come Full Circle." Therefore, I'm not going to rewrite that book within this book. I will assume that you already know the important factual details. In this book, I'm merely going to highlight the unusual events that appear to point in the direction of my inevitably becoming the Xanue Council of Twelve's choice as their Ambassador (i.e., "The 13").

While at SOHA for several years, I didn't begin to experience the Xanue psychic and paranormal phenomena until I stopped using the "Old School" approach of using the scientific method. I put the invasive electronic equipment away. No more Trail Cams, Night Vision or Thermal Imaging equipment, or Seismic Sensors. I was no longer trying to catch the dumb giant mountain apes on film. Also, no more attempting to gather hair samples or use Bobo screams or whack on trees with a big stick or baseball bat.

Instead, I started treating the Xanue as if they were intelligent sentient beings worthy of respect. I started approaching them with a humble attitude. I would talk out loud to them, let them know what I was up to, and what my intentions were. I also decided to switch from using invasive technology to passive technology. In other words, after I gave up the cameras and assisted vision equipment, night vision and thermal, I switched over to using a passive Bionic Ear Parabolic Microphone Dish hooked up to a tiny Sony Digital Recorder. I would place the passive equipment on top of my vehicle and record all night long. The equipment was positioned in base camp and not out in the woods away from our base camp. Therefore, it was passive and not invasive.

The Xanue didn't seem to mind the use of the passive equipment because they started to leave some interesting sounds for us to listen to later. We recorded wood knocks, screams, nine-hundred-pound owl impersonations, spoken language, singing, humming, drumming, and a crying infant who appeared to have just been born. The mother was comforting the newborn infant all night long with "Ah-Ooo, ah-ooo, ah-ooo."

One night, when Grady was four-years old, we were sleeping in the pup tent at SOHA. The older adolescent, Ceska, began to read through my life's memories. He began from my infancy and was working forward. It took me about ten or fifteen minutes of struggling in my mind but I managed to disconnect the memory reading process. Then I said in my mind, "This isn't fair. This isn't right."

Chapter 12: How to Find Bigfoot

Ceska responded with Mind Speak, "What isn't fair or right?"

I said, "If you want to read through my memories, then I get to ask you some questions. It's only fair."

Ceska responded, "I have to talk with the Elders first."

I replied, "Okay."

I laid there, inside the pup tent with Grady sleeping by my side. About an hour later, I heard two sets of heavy footed bipedal steps coming back towards our tent. Then the father began to Mind Speak with me by saying, "My son said that you had some questions that you wanted to ask."

I said, "Yes. Why is he reading through my memories?"

The Elder responded, "That's our way of knowing what's going on with the human race."

That made sense to me because it's not like they're watching the news on TV or listening to the radio. Then Ceska's father asked, "Do you have any more questions?"

I responded, "Yes. Who are you?"

Ceska's father responded, "We are the Guardians of the forest and we protect all who dwell within. Do you have any other questions?"

Well, by this point, my mind was totally blown away. My brain was on overload. I responded, "No. I'm good."

Ceska's father then asked, "May my son continue to read through your memories?"

I responded, "Yes. He can continue to read through my memories."

The Elder responded, "Thank you."

It took Ceska about an hour to finish the job. It was a very interesting experience because I just laid there and enjoyed the fast paced movie playing out inside my mind. It was quite the stroll down memory lane. When he was done reading through my memories, Ceska said, "Thank you," and then walked away back into the forest.

I laid there inside the pup tent, in the dark, wondering if I had merely been dreaming or had a psychotic break. It couldn't have been a drug induced psychosis because I don't do drugs. Suddenly, I thought to myself, "Oh no. What about Grady?"

As I rolled over to my left to take a look at Grady, he lifted his head up off of his pillow, looked at me and said, "They spoke to me too, Daddy." Then he laid his head back down on the pillow and went back to sleep. I immediately thought, "Crap. This really did happen. I just had a Bigfoot read through my memories." At that very moment, I blew up Cynthia's phone with text message after text message.

Shortly after this event, I was back home in Puyallup, Washington. Cynthia and I were asleep in bed. Something bumped the side of my bed and woke me up. Then I heard in my mind, "Come with me. Your friend, Kevin, is in trouble."

Suddenly, I was out of my body and we were flying over Puyallup, Washington. We were flying fairly fast to the north in the air until we were over the top of the 512 freeway. We headed west and hung a left on Interstate Five (I-5). We flew south over I-5 all the way past JBLM, Olympia, Centralia/Chehalis, Vancouver, Portland, Salem, Eugene, Roseburg, and to Grants Pass, Oregon. Based on the route he took me on, I think that the Xanue wanted me to recognize where I was going. We took Exit 58 at Grants Pass. We headed down 6th Street, through the city of Grants Pass, over the Rogue River, and out south on the Williams Highway. On the left hand side of the road was Kevin's rental home.

We managed to make the four-hundred-mile road trip in a total of fifteen minutes. That means that we were moving along at the speed of approximately 1,600 miles per hour. At that speed, in their Orb form, the Xanue could fly around the world in approximately 15.6 hours. However, please keep in mind that they can also use portals to get from one location to another location on the Earth in a matter of a couple of seconds. Recently, Zorth told me that in Orb form, they can fly up to 3,000 miles per hour and that they can get around the Earth in eight-hours.

The Xanue took me inside Kevin's home and into his bedroom. There was a dark mass of energy that appeared to be attacking Kevin. The Xanue told me, "Well, help your friend. Get that off of him and out of the house."

Chapter 12: How to Find Bigfoot

I remember thinking, "How am I supposed to do that? I don't even have a body. I don't have any arms or legs."

The Xanue responded, "Go grab him with your mind and push him out of the house."

So I went over to Kevin's bed, grabbed the dark force and pulled him off of the bed. I battled with the dark force on the floor. I felt like I was wrestling with pure evil. After a short bit of time, I felt like he was beginning to win as I was beginning to feel exhausted. I remember thinking in my mind, "Uhm, I could use a little help here, God. Please help me."

Suddenly, I felt super energized with pure love. I grabbed a hold of the dark entity and literally picked him up and threw him out of Kevin's home. I could see him flying away rather quickly. He looked like he feared that I was going to pursue him. Instead, I turned and went to the side of Kevin's bed. He looked peaceful and fell fast asleep.

The next thing I knew, we were flying back through Grants Pass, Oregon. We hung a left on I-5 and flew north at about 1,600 miles per hour to the 512 Freeway. Then, just as quickly as I had left my body, I was right back in it again. I laid there in the dark, staring up at the ceiling, wondering if it was just all a dream.

Cynthia and I woke up later in the morning and I told her all about my experience. As strange as it sounded to her, she believed every word. She knew that I wouldn't lie to her. Also, she remembered the memory reading that I had just experienced at SOHA.

After we were done talking, we laid in bed and checked our phone for messages. We also were in the habit of catching ourselves up on our individual Facebook accounts. Then my jaw dropped. I came across a posting from my friend, Kevin. He shared about how he was attacked by a dark entity last night while he was lying in bed. He then shared that he was rescued by an entity of light and love who kicked the dark force out of his home. I handed my phone to Cynthia for her to read what I just read. She dropped her jaw too.

I sent Kevin a personal message (PM) on Facebook and told him that the entity of light and love was me. I told him that I would give him a call and that we would talk about it. When he answered the phone, he laughed at me and called me a jokester. However, I told him where his new rental home was located and what it looked like. I reminded him that he had not told me that he had moved nor did he tell me where his new rental home was located.

Kevin became quiet and started listening. I shared with him about the wrestling event and how it all played out. I told him that I approached his bed and pulled the dark entity off of him. Then I told him that we wrestled around on the floor for a few minutes. Then I told him that I was on the bottom and the dark entity was winning because my energy was fading. I had then asked God for help and I immediately regained my energy. I became a brilliant force of light and love. I grabbed the dark entity and threw him out of the house. Then I came back to his bed and stayed there until he fell back to sleep.

Kevin said, "I can't believe it. That was you. That's exactly how the whole scenario played out. Thank you! Wait! How were you able to do that?"

I was silent for a moment. Then I said, "To be honest, Kevin, I really don't know. I'm still trying to figure it out myself. We talked for a few more minutes and then we hung up.

Please keep in mind that what I'm about to write is based on twenty-twenty hindsight. I didn't know any of this back then. In short, I have come to learn that the Xanue take all of us on individual journeys down the Rabbit Hole as we get to know them. They know who we are and what we are ready to experience. They also know that we are all gifted differently. Finally, they know that God has different plans for all of us in order to help accomplish His purposes on the Earth. Ultimately, The Xanue interact with all of us according to God's will and plans. The Xanue will never step outside the will of God.

On another occasion at SOHA, I was inside the pup tent all by myself. No other humans were with me. However, Atlas, my seven-pound Toy Fox Terrier was in attendance. At night, I was laying in my sleeping bag inside the pup tent. Atlas was inside my sleeping

Chapter 12: How to Find Bigfoot

bag. I positioned my Ruger Super Redhawk 44 Rem Magnum Stainless Double-Action Revolver (i.e., "Maggie") on the floor next to me. All I had to do was place my right hand towards the pup tent floor next to me and my hand would rest on the handle and trigger. The floor placement was perfect.

As I was trying to fall asleep, I heard some heavy footed bipedal steps coming towards the right side of my pup tent. I slowly and quietly reached out and placed my right hand on "Maggie." Immediately, I received a Mind Speak (i.e., Telepathic message), "Take your hand off of the gun." I took my hand off of the gun.

Then the steps continued to come closer to the pup tent. Once again, I slowly and quietly placed my right hand back on "Maggie." Then I heard the Mind Speak again, "Take your hand off of the gun." I took my hand off of the gun.

Suddenly, I became immobilized. Then he began to go through my memories from earlier that day. He showed me standing in the grocery store, buying wheat bread, creamy peanut butter, and raspberry jelly. Then he showed me making the sandwiches. Finally, he showed me put the gifting bowls out away from the base camp. Then he asked me, "What are your intentions?"

As I laid there immobilized, I felt a little frustrated. I thought, "Why is he asking me such a silly question? I've been out here all of these years doing what I'm doing. He knows what my intentions are." Therefore, I chose not to answer him.

For a second time, he took me through my memories from earlier that day. He showed me standing in the grocery store, buying wheat bread, creamy peanut butter, and raspberry jelly. Then he showed me making the sandwiches. Finally, he showed me putting the gifting bowls out away from the base camp. Then he asked me for a second time, "What are your intentions?"

Then I thought to myself, "Wow! Really? You're running me through all of my memories again and asking me the same obvious question?" My frustration began to grow. I became more stubborn. I refused to answer such a silly question. He knew what my intentions were.

My nonresponse generated a third trip down memory lane. For a third time, he showed me standing in the grocery store, buying wheat bread, creamy peanut butter, and raspberry jelly. Then he showed me making the sandwiches. Finally, he showed me putting the gifting bowls out away from the base camp. Then he asked me for the third time, "What are your intentions?"

Well, by this time, I realized that I had met my match. I thought to myself, "This Bigfoot is just as stubborn as me if not more stubborn. If I don't answer his question, this will probably go on all night long." So I responded to his question regarding what my intentions were. I said, "To earn your trust and friendship."

The Bigfoot responded, "Thank you!"

I not only heard his voice inside my head say, "Thank you!" I also felt his joyful emotions while he said, "Thank you!" I felt his emotions. He was truly happy. He was overwhelmed with joy. He truly wanted to be my friend.

I didn't learn until later that it was Ceska.

As I heard Ceska walk away from the SOHA base camp, I lay in my sleeping bag with a big smile on my face. I remember thinking, "I officially have a Bigfoot friend. He wants to be my friend. He's happy that he's my friend. Wow! It's working! I've earned his trust and friendship."

After this very significant moment in my journey with the Xanue, everything started taking off exponentially in a major way down the Rabbit Hole. Things started getting wild and crazy good. Better and better. Now, I'm going to fast forward through the next several years in SOHA and SOIA in order to highlight the significant experiences demonstrating how TRILS has continued to work along the way. In other words, I'll be skipping past several historical events that were highlighted in my first book because the focus of this second book is somewhat different.

After Ceska managed to get me out of my tent via the garbage bag dragging event and out of my Suburban via the window knocking incident, he had me right where he wanted me – on my cot, sleeping

Chapter 12: How to Find Bigfoot

under the stars at night. No more nylon tent walls or Suburban windows to get in the way of our future interactions and trust building at SOHA and SOIA.

In November of 2013, I saw two Beings of Light (i.e., Xanue) back some ways from the nine o'clock position on the perimeter of the SOHA base camp. They were very tall, translucent, and had a head, arms and hands, legs and feet. The most important thing that I learned from this interaction is their ability to transform from a flesh and blood, hairy, upright, bipedal humanoid to a translucent Being of Light. The other thing that I learned was the unconditional love that they had for me. Their unconditional love permeated my soul. It was like a love drug that replaced my worries, frustrations, and pain with love, acceptance, serenity and peace. While all of this was going on, a fog of bright white light emanated from their feet and covered the ground. It lit up the whole area which was witnessed by two other attendees.

During my first time to SOHA without any humans, my dog, or my gun, I experienced interacting with another Being of Light. But first, you need to understand that I was intentionally trying my best to demonstrate my trust to the Xanue by not bringing my dog or gun with me. My dog was my alarm system. He could smell, hear, and see anything approaching the SOHA base camp before my senses would kick in. I was completely vulnerable now.

Anyway, at night under the stars, I was in my sleeping bag on my cot near my vehicle. I heard and saw a translucent Being of Light walk into the SOHA base camp at the twelve o'clock position on the perimeter. However, this time, he was not bright white. This time, he was rainbow colored. His translucent body was radiating with a rotating radiant rainbow colored light. He walked over to the two o'clock position on the perimeter of the SOHA base camp. Then it appeared that he melted down to the ground and created a big sparkling rainbow colored blanket. The sparkling rainbow colored blanket moved across the ground toward my cot. Then it came up the side and completely enveloped me. I could feel the energy as the sparkling rainbow colored light was moving around me and through me.

THE XANUE

After about two minutes, the sparkling rainbow colored lights went back down on the ground and moved back to the two o'clock position. Then the translucent sparkling rainbow colored translucent Being of Light rose up from the ground back into humanoid form. He turned and walked out of the SOHA base camp at the twelve o'clock position. I lay there with my mind blown. I felt loved and rejuvenated. It took a while to fall asleep that night. The stars were extra beautiful that night.

As time progressed at SOHA, there were more visuals, vocals, and interactions experienced by myself and others. We had lots of physical sightings, silhouettes with varied colored eye glow, vocals, and healings.

In June of 2014, Adam and John were with me at SOHA. They accidentally discovered a portal. The first two nights of incredible Bigfoot activity on the perimeter, from the nine o'clock position to the twelve o'clock position and over to the three o'clock position was very overwhelming for them. So on the third night, they ended up hanging out with one another on the backside of my Suburban. They were filled with nervous laughter while smoking their Backwoods Cigars.

They eventually worked their way down toward the six o'clock position on the perimeter, which was the logging road that we drive up on to get to the base camp. Somehow, someway, they managed to trigger a portal and open it up. They were yelling for me to come over to them. I was a little irked that they were wasting their time on the other side of the Suburban when all of the Bigfoot activity was occurring on my side of the Suburban. I wanted them back with me because that's why they came to SOHA. Nevertheless, they kept yelling at me to come to them.

I walked around the Suburban to see what all of the fuss was about. When I rounded the corner of the backside of my vehicle, I couldn't believe my eyes. There was an open portal at the six o'clock position. You could see another world through the portal. It had red sky and dark scraggly vegetation. They asked me what it was. I said, "I don't know what that is. I've never seen it before. How did you two guys open it up?" They told me that they just walked in the direction of the six o'clock position and it opened up on them. Needless to say, the focus

Chapter 12: How to Find Bigfoot

during the next two nights at SOHA were divided between Bigfoot activity and portal activity.

It took me a year to figure out how to reopen the portal. I thought about those two nights over and over again. Finally, I realized that we had to have brought back some residual magnetic energy on our bodies from the Oregon Vortex. Otherwise known as the Oregon House of Mystery. After several experiments over a few months, I was able to reopen the portal on several occasions with a total of ten eyewitnesses. Except this time, the portal opened up and a fog of light came out of it. The fog of light was not blown around by the wind. It was stationary. Wind cannot blow light around. It was amazing energy.

In March of 2015, I finally made it into a cardiovascular surgeon's office to have my left leg evaluated. I had severed my Achilles tendon in a city league basketball game on Valentine's Day in 2012. A surgeon reattached my Achilles tendon two days later. No one told me that I wasn't supposed to go on an airplane two days after surgery. I flew to New Orleans, then to Las Vegas, and then on to Los Angeles to speak about my 'Positive Parenting with a Plan' program. At that time in my life, I was speaking in eighty cities per year, all over the USA, training thousands of professionals and parents about how to use my parenting program.

Since the surgery to reattach my Achilles tendon, my left leg was a ballooned elephant leg for three nonstop years. In a nutshell, the vascular surgeon said that I was lucky to be alive. He told me several times during the appointment that I should be dead. He then told me that I had what he would diagnose as a "big ass DVT" and that nobody lives through it. The DVT went from my left groin to my left knee.

The cardiovascular surgeon went on to say, "If you walked into my office with your DVT intact, I would tell you to get your affairs in order because you're going to die. If I try to operate to remove it, you're dead. If I give you blood thinners to remove it, you're dead. If it breaks up on its own, you're dead. There's absolutely no way out of it other than you're dead."

I asked, "Well, is the DVT still there?"

The doctor responded, "No. It's gone."

I was surprised and said, "Well then how do you know it was there at all?"

The cardio vascular surgeon responded, "Because of the aftermath which is clearly still there. The DVT completely blew out your vein. I'm not sure how you're still alive right now. It's a miracle. You should be dead but you're obviously not dead. It's a miracle." Then he told me to wear a compression sock every day for the rest of my life to help with the circulation and to bring my leg back to its normal size. He also told me to take aspirin every day to keep my blood thinned. After hearing a few more times that I should be dead and that it's a miracle that I'm alive, Cynthia and I left his office to go be by ourselves, thank God up above, and to celebrate the fact that I was still miraculously alive.

In July of 2015, while Cynthia and I were camping at SOHA, that's when I learned about the healing abilities of the Xanue. Apparently, with God's permission, the Xanue removed the "big ass DVT" from my leg shortly after my surgery in 2012. They were the reason that I was still alive. Truth be told, they have been monitoring my health for a very long time. The question is, "Why?" Did they know something that I didn't know? Was there a plan or purpose for my life to continue beyond an obvious DVT dead end?

In October of 2015, I took Miss Andrea to SOHA and we had a very eventful time interacting with the Xanue. We had incredible full body form visuals standing only five to six feet away from us. We also had a major multi-vocal display that went on for a very long time while we lay in our sleeping bags on our cots. Finally, while we were sleeping, a Xanue pulled a tarp over the top of us when it began to rain. You can watch Miss Andrea's testimonial video. You can also listen to the audio recording on line.

After I dropped Miss Andrea off at the Medford airport so she could return to her journalism teaching job at the University of Florida, I drove back up to SOHA to spend one last night with the Xanue. For years, I had been asking them to provide me with a teacher. I wanted

Chapter 12: How to Find Bigfoot

them to teach me their ways. The next morning, I was packing up my truck to return home to the State of Washington.

Before I climbed into my truck to drive away, I asked one last time if they would please provide me with a teacher. At that moment, I received a strong Mind Speak response, "You're our teacher. That's why we bring our children to you on the perimeter of your camp so they can watch, listen, and learn from you and your guests." My jaw dropped. That response blew my mind. I never considered that possibility at all. But when I started thinking about it, I began to understand why there was such a noticeable increase of young ones on the perimeter of the SOHA base camp at night.

The strong Mind Speak continued, "Because we have designated you as a teacher for our young ones, we have also given you a guardian to watch over you. It is our way of thanking you and honoring you."

Once again, not what I expected at all. However, I most certainly wasn't going to argue with them. This was a major step in the direction of developing a relationship with the Xanue and to eventually learn from them. By this point in time, my fifteen years of blood, sweat, and tears in the wilderness was finally beginning to pay off. I was officially interacting with the Xanue. I felt very blessed.

In November of 2015, I brought Mike Kinkaid to SOHA. By this time, Mike had become like a brother to me. I loved hanging out with Mike and the Xanue. We always had fun together. While at SOHA, it became clear that Mike was hobbling along the trail due to a recent basketball injury. He played basketball with a bunch of other older gentlemen just to stay in shape. Also, his arm was sore too. We walked the trail from the twelve o'clock position on the perimeter to the other end of the trail. It was a couple hundred yards long and increased by an approximate two-hundred-foot elevation.

Near the top of the trail, Mike had found a thick stick that was about three feet long. It had about a three or four-inch circumference. It had been snapped in two and was laying on the trail. Mike picked it up and was playing around with it. He was trying to put it back together like two puzzle pieces. He decided to lay it back down on the ground just in case it belonged to one of the Xanue children. We eventually made it back to the SOHA base camp and enjoyed an evening of interacting with the Xanue on the perimeter of the base camp.

The next morning when we woke up, Mike's tarp had been neatly folded and placed on the ground near the foot of his sleeping cot. A blanket had been folded over too. When he got up out of his sleeping bag and started to walk around, he realized that the pain was gone from his leg and arm. The Xanue had worked on him that night while he was sleeping.

We started to leave the SOHA base camp to go retrieve the gifting bowls. Mike was leading the way. I saw him stop for a second and look at the ground but then he kept on walking toward the gifting bowls. Once I got to the spot on the ground that Mike had quickly glanced at, I asked him to stop and come back to me. I picked up the thick stick that Mike had left the night before on the other end of the trail a couple hundred yards from base camp. Now it was on our end of the trail. Not only that, one of the two pieces had been snapped in half so now Mike's puzzle had three pieces to it. Mike thanked the Xanue for the gift and put the three pieces of the puzzle back together. He took it home with him.

On the last night that Mike and I ever spent together at SOHA, I had been recording all night long just like all of the other nights. During the night, I would wake up, roll over, and fall back to sleep again. While I was awake, I would hear Ceska standing at the head of my sleeping cot. I could hear the weight of his shifting feet. I could also hear him breathing. It was comforting to know that I had a guardian to protect me while I was staying at SOHA.

Normally, when I slept at night, I would wear a hoodie over the top of my stocking cap to keep my head warm at night. Also, I slept with a t-shirt over my eyes to keep the light out and to keep the bugs off of my face. Around four in the morning, I woke up again. This time, I heard nothing. No shifting feet and no breathing. As I lay there in my sleeping bag on my cot, I asked with my mind, "Are you still there?"

Suddenly, I heard heavy footsteps coming from the head of my cot to a position between myself and my truck which was only about

Chapter 12: How to Find Bigfoot

five feet away. The Bionic Ear Parabolic Microphone Dish and Sony Digital Recorder were on top of the truck recording all night long. Ceska leaned over me and said directly in my ear, knowing full well that he was being recorded, and responded verbally, "Yes. Right here beside you." Then he walked back to the head of my sleeping cot and stood guard.

I immediately pulled the t-shirt off of my eyes. I turned my head to see if I could sneak a peek of Ceska but he was cloaked. I could not see him at all. Not even a shimmering image. However, I could hear him shifting the weight on his feet again. I could also hear him breathing. I looked at my watch to pinpoint the time that Ceska verbalized, "Yes. Right here beside you." After I returned home, I fast forwarded the audio recording and, sure enough, found Ceska's audible response to the question that I asked with my mind. Amazing!

Unbeknownst to me at the time, but the Christmas night that Cynthia and I spent at SOHA in 2015, would be our last night there. We enjoyed singing Christmas carols to our Xanue friends. We could hear and see them moving about the perimeter of the base camp. We also saw some eye glow and Orbs. It was truly a magical evening.

A couple days later, the TROLLS found SOHA and posted the coordinates on the internet for the world to see. Cynthia and I cried. We felt like we had been kicked in the stomach. It turned out that an individual that I trustingly brought to SOHA with me decided to throw me under the bus by giving up the location. I know who he is. He knows who he is. Nevertheless, in spite of his bad intentions, God and the Xanue used it for good. I received a very strong Mind Speak and was told not to worry. They were going to move us to a new interaction area.

In January, I was guided to a new spot southwest of Grants Pass, Oregon. Jill, a mutual friend of Cynthia's and mine, accompanied me as we were led to the new location. It took a couple of hours of driving around the logging roads before we received major confirmation that we had reached the Xanue's desired location. We were provided with confirmation via Orbs, whistles, tree knocks, foot stomps, a very tall tree that was pushed over in front of us, and pictures of descending Orbs on our way home from the new location.

It was in this temporary location, while Cynthia and I were spending the night in our sleeping bags on our cots under the stars, that Onx woke me up in the middle of the night for a two-hour Mind Speak. During our chat, he informed me about how they used "Patty" and Patterson and Gimlin to get the world's attention. They wanted people to come into the forest to look for them. The goal was that they would eventually want to develop a friendship with them. Along the way, they were hoping that some of the curious individuals would stumble across a portal, not freak out, and eventually learn how to reopen it. Once that happened, they would seek help from the individual to assist the Xanue with the EXODUS.

Onx, a cousin of Ceska as well as Zorth's nephew, informed me that I was the first individual to figure out how to reopen a portal. He said that they had their eggs spread out into several baskets hoping that someone would come through for them. They couldn't invest all of their hope in just one human being because that person might get frustrated and quit their journey or they could get injured, sick, or die. Therefore, the Xanue were working on developing relationships with several people around the world in order to help them with the goal of the EXODUS.

Onx informed me that I was the first one to cross the finish line. He said, "We need a shunt. Can you help us with a shunt to keep the portal open?"

I was confused by what he was asking because, at that time, the word "shunt" was not in my vocabulary. I was wondering if he meant a stint but he stuck with the fact that a "shunt" was needed to help them bring their families and friends over from their dying world, through a portal, to the Earth. It turns out that a "shunt" helps the electrical flow to remain stable between points A and B. Onx knew exactly what he needed. The Xanue needed a "shunt" and not a stint.

It turned out that I had just been a guest on "Coast to Coast AM" and I was sharing about my experiences with the Xanue. During the

Chapter 12: How to Find Bigfoot

interview, I had mentioned the portal at SOHA and the associated experiences we were encountering when we reopened it on numerous occasions. This information got the attention of a retired physicist from MIT, Robert K. Gulka, who had been studying the Bermuda Triangle. He postulated that there was a humongous portal in the middle of the Bermuda Triangle that was demonstrating similar characteristics to the SOHA portal. Initially, he expressed an interest in helping us to work on developing a shunt to help the Xanue with the EXODUS. Then, for unclear reasons, he revealed that he wanted to kill one of the Bigfoot and turn their body over to science. That was the last time that I ever talked with him. We were back at square one.

Within a week, I received an email from Steve Bachmann. He shared how he had been following me on YouTube and that I was one of two people he believed were telling the truth. To make a long story short, Steve had worked in construction most of his life. He also enjoyed restoring antique tractors. At the end of his email, he informed me that he had made an Electromagnetic Pulsating Device from Tesla's design and attached a picture to his email. My jaw hit the floor. What were the odds of that happening so quickly? I began to understand about how the Xanue were working behind the scenes to influence people and accomplish their objectives. They are an amazing species.

It was right around this period of time that I had found a message on a piece of paper at this location. I thought we were camping on the State of Oregon BLM land. However, it turned out that we were on a small piece of private property surrounded by BLM land. The owner of the property had threatened to shoot me if I continued to trespass on his small tract of land. I showed the note to the Oregon State Troopers and to the BLM office. Both State employees strongly encouraged me to comply with the wishes of the property owner. Once again, I received a very strong Mind Speak and I was informed that they would lead me to another spot that would most definitely be located on BLM land.

Once again, Jill, a mutual friend of Cynthia's and mine, accompanied me as we were led to the new location. It took several hours of driving on the logging roads but we had reached our destination. We got a confirmation via a freshly torn, very large branch left in the middle of the Southern Oregon Interaction Area (SOIA). Also, we walked up the logging road and found a very fresh, warm to the touch, three foot Xanue turd left between two twenty-seven-inch foot tracks. The Xanue knew that I like collecting evidence so the three-foot turd was actually a gift. For the record, I later dried it out, shellacked it, and preserved it inside a display case. It amazes the crap out of people. Get it? Never mind.

While camping at SOIA, I had a vision while sleeping on my cot during the night. Onx had introduced me to his cousin, Mogdue. He was thanking me for my willingness to help them with the EXODUS. He was very excited about introducing me to his father, Zorth. During the vision, while I was sleeping, I felt a very large hand gently and lovingly massaging my head. The palm of the hand was at the base of my skull on the back of my neck. The very large fingers were reaching over my skull and massaging my forehead. It would take two of my very large human hands to reach that far.

The vision came to an end and I began to wake up. As usual, I was sleeping with my hoodie over my stocking cap. I also had a t-shirt over my eyes. While I was slowly but surely coming to my senses, I continued to feel my head being gently and lovingly massaged by the very large hand. Then I felt someone very large lean over me and speak into my ear in a very deep, bass like, guttural voice, "Zorth."

I asked with my mind, "Is that your name? Zorth?"

He responded, "Yes."

A few weeks later, on Sunday night, June 26, 2016, while Mike Kinkaid, Steve Bachmann, and I were sitting up on the mountain top to meet with Zorth and the Council of Twelve, I was informed via Mind Speak that the Xanue were Beings of Light (i.e., Orbs). During the day, they would go into the trees to absorb energy from the sun and nutrients through the roots in the ground. At night, they would come out of the trees and tend to their business of managing the forest and protecting those who dwelled within.

Chapter 12: How to Find Bigfoot

Zorth informed me that they were able to shapeshift into upright, flesh and blood, hairy, bipedal, humanoid beings when they chose not to remain in Orb form. He thanked Mike, Steve, and me for our willingness to help the Xanue with the EXODUS. He asked us to descend from the Council of Twelve hill, return to the SOIA base camp, start up Steven's Electromagnetic Pulsating Device, so that they could begin with the EXODUS. We gladly complied.

It took two nights to complete the EXODUS and those two nights were magical. The local Xanue would stand by Steve's device, charge themselves up, and then run back to the portal to help keep it open so that their families and friends from their dying world could make it from their dying home world to the Earth. Although they were cloaked, we could hear their heavy footed running back and forth between the device and the portal. Occasionally, we could see their shimmering images too.

After the first night was over, Steve had to return home to the State of Washington because he had work obligations and deadlines to meet. We thanked him for having been with us and for assisting us with the EXODUS. He kindly agreed to leave his Electromagnetic Pulsating Device with us so that we could complete the EXODUS. He explained to Mike how to operate the device and then returned home. Mike and I bought extra deep cycle marine batteries and charged them up just in case they would be needed. We also picked up my youngest son, Grady Johnson, from his mother's home and brought him with us back to SOIA so he could witness this monumental event.

On the second night, there were Orbs everywhere. While I was tucking Grady into his sleeping bag, we both saw an Orb inside his sleeping bag. It was down by his foot, made its way up his leg, and then popped up into the air above us and hovered for a few seconds before shooting back into the trees. Grady still remembers that moment to this very day. What a privilege it was for him, at the age of nine, to be there and witness the EXODUS. No other kid on the planet can say that they were there that night. Only Grady Johnson can claim that blessing.

Fast forward to Tuesday morning, June 28, 2016. Mike Kinkaid, Grady Johnson, and I had just helped the Xanue reach their goal of completing the EXODUS. With the aid of Steve's Electromagnetic Pulsating Device that he had left behind after needing to return home to the State of Washington, we had all worked together to help bring 23,542 souls over from their dying home world to the Earth.

Unfortunately, three older Xanue died within an hour or less of reaching the Earth. They had neglected using the dying vegetation on their home world to reenergize themselves and insisted that the younger Xanue use the vegetation instead. Although news of their deaths was very sad, at least they were able to reach the Earth and die in the presence of family and friends.

Once again, if you're reading this book, shaking your head, and wondering what the heck I'm talking about regarding the EXODUS, then that means you're a stubborn individual that is sequentially impaired. For the last time, stop reading this book and read my other book first: "BIGFOOT: A Fifty-Year Journey Come Full Circle." Once you're done reading my first book, then this second book will make much more sense. Thank you for your cooperation.

Anyway, the morning after the EXODUS had been completed. Zorth communicated with me via Mind Speak. He thanked all of us for helping the Xanue with the EXODUS. I accepted his gratitude on behalf of all of us. He informed me that, in appreciation for all that we had done, Mike, Steve, Grady, Cynthia, and I would receive Xanue guardians for life. Then I tearfully asked, "I'm free now, right? I'm free from this compulsion to come out into the woods in order to solve this mystery, right? I can freely go on with my life now, right?"

Zorth responded with a "Yes" but then informed me that the Council of Twelve would like me to consider staying onboard as their Ambassador. He told me that they wanted me to be the Xanue Council's "13." They wanted someone whom they could trust to convey what they had to share with the rest of the world. Zorth informed me that I had most definitely earned their trust and friendship (i.e., My stated intentions to Ceska a few years earlier in SOHA). He told me that they could think of no one better to serve as their Ambassador – "The 13."

Chapter 12: How to Find Bigfoot

Although Zorth told me several things (i.e., Read the first book), I wish to highlight the following: (1) Zorth informed me that it was him who I saw sixteen years earlier on the mountainside above the Oregon Caves National Monument Park; (2) Zorth asked me to tell everyone that the Xanue are in the trees and that the trees are everywhere. However, at a later date, he informed me that they're not in every tree; and (3) He told me that if a kind person with a good heart and an open mind reached out to the Xanue, then they would reach back to the human.

Based on twenty-twenty hindsight, although I intentionally broke away from the "Old School" approach of utilizing the scientific method to prove the existence of the Bigfoot species, I now truly believe that instead of me, it was the Xanue who successfully used TRILS to habituate me to them: (1) On July 1, 2000, the Xanue targeted me on the mountainside above the Oregon Caves National Monument Park; (2) In SOHA, the Xanue used Ceska to develop trust and a friendship with me; (3) Ceska and other Xanue continued to interact with me and my guests at SOHA and eventually SOIA; (4) Along the journey down the Rabbit Hole, I learned from Ceska, Onx, Mogdue, and Zorth about the Xanue; and (5) I was asked by Zorth and the Council of Twelve to become their Ambassador ("The 13") and share about them with the rest of the world. That's exactly what I've been doing online via social media, with my online video and audio files, with our annual conferences, our annual Camp Xanue experiences at our property during the Summer months, and via my books and media interviews.

The Xanue took charge of the situation while allowing me to believe that I was in control of habituating them to me. When I look back on the past twenty-years and see how it all played out, I have to chuckle because they were very wise, kind, gentle, loving, and tricky while they were teaching me to trust them, befriend them, interact with them, learn from them, and share with others about them. In the end, the TRILS method was successful. Since then, Cynthia and I have been helping many people to find Bigfoot. Sadly, the "Old

Schoolers" continue with their insanity via their ongoing use of the scientific method without any overall success. They are lost in the dark in the woods. They need to come join us on the Light Side of the Forest.

CHAPTER 13
THE XANUE AMBASSADOR
("THE 13")

During the summer of 2006, I took my second wife, Amanda, and my three older kids to San Francisco, California for Spring Break. Grady wasn't born yet. Over several days, we toured the entire city and surrounding areas. We even managed to catch a boat to Alcatraz Island and see the old prison facility. We really had a fun trip.

Just before leaving the city to return back home to southern Oregon, in the late morning hours, I stopped at a very large Shell gas station that had four rows of pumps. I parked the Suburban at the last pump on the outside row near the street. The timing couldn't have been better because we were running on fumes. It seemed like it was taking forever to fill up the thirty-two-gallon tank.

Three rows away at the opposite end of the pumps from us was a middle aged woman who was filling up the gas tank in her car. As I was leaning against the side of the Suburban, I notice that the lady was walking on a direct path straight towards me. She was walking through the aisles of pumps, with a smile on her face, trying to establish eye contact with me. I looked around and there was no one else there but her car and our Suburban. Quite frankly, the situation was feeling very awkward to me.

When she reached me, she smiled at me and said, "God wanted me to come over here and tell you that someday, you're going to help thousands and thousands of families. God wants me to tell you that He loves you and appreciates you. That's it. Can I have a hug?"

THE XANUE

I was standing there totally dumbfounded by what she just said. Before I could respond, she wrapped her arms around me and gave me a tight squeeze. She smiled at me again and said, "Go with God. Have a nice day." Then she walked back to her car and drove away. She smiled and waved as she drove by us. She didn't even know me or what I did for a living. This came smack dab out of the blue from nowhere.

Let me please remind you that at this point in my life, I had already spent a few years on the road speaking about my "Positive Parenting with a Plan" program in eighty cities per year all over the USA and Canada. I had already trained several thousand professionals and parents. Naturally, my mind went straight to this fact regarding my professional life and the process that I was already engaged in.

However, the confusing part to me was the lady's use of the words, "Someday, you're going to help thousands and thousands of families." In other words, she did not use past or present tense in the message that she relayed from God. Nope. She used future tense. She spoke as if I hadn't done anything yet regarding the helping of these alleged thousands and thousands of families. This was very perplexing to me. I couldn't do anything with it but tuck it away in the back of my mind.

Fast forward ten years and a couple of months. Tada! The EXODUS occurred and we helped thousands and thousands of families to move from their dying world to the Earth. Although it was unclear to me back then when the friendly lady delivered a message to me from God, it is most definitely very clear to me today. God used this faithful failure, along with a few other faithful failures, to help accomplish His purpose. Go Team!!! When I look back on my life and reflect on all of my experiences, it seems like I was born for this moment. God knows that I tried to throw the towel in on all of it on many occasions. Yet, He managed to guide the Xanue, me, Cynthia, Mike, Steve, and Grady to work together to make it happen.

On a side note, about a year ago, I took Grady and one of his friends to a Portland Trail Blazer NBA game. The boys were having a blast attending their very first NBA game at the MODA Center in Portland, Oregon. Popcorn, soda pop, hotdogs, and lots of three-point

Chapter 13: The Xanue Ambassador

shots and dunking. When the game was over, they announced that there was just over 23,000 people in attendance. My jaw dropped as I looked around the arena at all of the people. I tapped Grady on the shoulder and told him, "This is about how many souls we helped during the EXODUS to come from their dying planet to the Earth." Grady looked around the arena and he was blown away too. It was emotionally overwhelming to actually see over 23,000 people together in the same place.

In late September of 2016, I was contacted by an acquaintance named, Kevin. He's an Irishman who's living in the USA. He called me up and told me that while he was recently in Ireland for the purpose of marrying his wife, they were hiking through the forest and a tree started talking to him (i.e., Mind Speak). Kevin told me that the tree asked him to call and talk with Matt Johnson upon his return home to the USA. Kevin did exactly what was requested of him and called me. I was stunned by his phone call but I immediately knew that I needed to invite him and his wife to come to SOIA for our end of the year excursion in October.

Once we got to SOIA, I sat in the base camp while everyone else walked around in the woods. I had learned years ago that my guests liked to walk around the woods on their own to see if they could find any lighting or audio equipment that I might be using to hoax my guests. Obviously, no one ever turned up any kind of equipment because I wasn't using any lighting or audio equipment nor was I hoaxing anyone.

Kevin was the first individual back to the SOIA base camp. While the other guests were out and about still enjoying their hike, Kevin began to talk with me. He told me that while he was hiking up on the hill at the nine o'clock position on the perimeter of the SOIA base camp, a tree started talking with him. The tree was trying to tell Kevin about the Council of Twelve as well as "The 13." Kevin looked very confused and asked me if I knew anything about what the tree was trying to tell him. I sat there quietly and smiled at him.

I told Kevin to prepare to have his mind blown and then I explained everything to him, including the EXODUS. I shared about how although I was free to go on with my life, Zorth and the Xanue Council of Twelve asked me to stay on as their Ambassador – "The 13." His mind was most definitely blown. During Kevin's trips to SOIA, he reported having a bone spur removed from his heel. He also shared that his leg had grown an inch to the same length as his other leg. Matter of fact, Kevin ended up in the hospital in Grants Pass, Oregon because of all the energy that flowed through his body while the Xanue were working on healing him.

Finally, to top it all off, on Kevin's and his wife's last trip to SOIA, a Pterodactyl flew over the base camp from the east and hung a right and flew away to the north. I asked Zorth if that was one of the Xanue that shapeshifted into a Pterodactyl. He replied, "No. That was just a Pterodactyl."

I asked, "Where did the Pterodactyl come from? They're extinct."

Zorth said, "It came through the time travel portal on top of the nine o'clock hill."

I shrugged my shoulders. I thought that the Xanue not only have access to a portal that goes to other planets, and another portal that goes to anywhere on the Earth, but they also have access to a time travel portal? Go figure! Nothing surprises me anymore. The Rabbit Hole keeps getting deeper and deeper.

I have a friend, Ernie, who lives in the State of Massachusetts. One day, he contacted me to let me know about an experience that he had while hiking out in the forest in the adjacent State of New Hampshire. While he was hiking in the woods trying to locate a Bigfoot family to interact with, his smartphone in his coat pocket started playing a YouTube video about me talking about the Xanue. No matter what he tried, he couldn't shut off the video.

Then Ernie looked at the trees and asked if they wanted him to listen to me? Did they want him to learn from me about them? Ernie reported at that exact moment in time, he heard several tree knocks in response to his questions. After that experience, Ernie has been very active in our social media groups and has traveled out west to attend a conference and accompany us into the mountains in southern Oregon.

Chapter 13: The Xanue Ambassador

Ernie is an example of Zorth's promise: "If a kind person with a good heart and open mind reaches out to us, we will reach back to him."

Although I've had several people from all of the USA and Canada reach out to me because the Xanue told them to do so, the last story I wish to share with you along these lines is about Ryan from the State of New York. Ryan had called me because we had talked a few weeks earlier about how sometimes the Xanue will send a bunch of Crows or Blue Jays as a sign that they're in the area. Anyway, he was beside himself because of the number of Blue Jays that were in his backyard. He told me that he has rarely seen a Blue Jay over the years. Suddenly, after talking with me, his backyard was filled up with Blue Jays.

After we hung up, Ryan sent me a text message that he was receiving a Mind Speak. He was being told that he needed to listen to the man in a red shirt wearing a red hat. Well, he didn't know it at the time but I was wearing a red shirt and a red hat. I stopped my vehicle, took a selfie, and sent it too his phone. Once again, Ryan was blown away. Afterwards, I sent him a copy of my first Bigfoot book.

Unfortunately, just like many other Bigfoot researchers who've been bombarded with the truth by the Xanue, Ryan chose to go another way. Many Bigfoot researchers don't want to be spoon fed the truth. They want to discover it for themselves. Some are simply independent minded. Others, unfortunately, have egos much bigger than the one they accuse me of possessing. Now to be fair to them, I most certainly did possess a majorly big ego in the recent past until the Xanue started to break me down, slowly but surely, in a very gentle manner.

That became very apparent to me when they allowed the TROLLS to crash SOHA. Everything that I had worked for over a fifteen-year period of time was lost. Then the Xanue stepped up to the plate and let me know who was really in charge. It's next to impossible to have a major ego when they're telling me to forgive the TROLLS, take them out to lunch and apologize to them for goading them, and to submit and let the Xanue take the lead going forward.

Nevertheless, some Bigfoot researchers do have major egos that get in the way of their accepting the truth of the Xanue. These individuals don't want to accept the fact that the mystery has been solved and revealed. They don't want it to be true because then that means (1) they weren't the ones who solved the mystery, and (2) their researching days are over. What do they do now? It was never their goal to befriend and interact with the Bigfoot species. Their goal was to prove Bigfoot's existence so that they could become rich and famous.

Therefore, they blow me off as an egotistical psycho who is hypnotizing the masses to create a cult following to appease my ego. They cite how many years that they've been researching (i.e., 20, 30, 40, or 50+ years) and if they haven't discovered the truth yet, then nobody else can either. Well, what if they have been doing it wrong for 20, 30, 40, or 50+ years? Please think about this for a moment. The length of time involved with their research process means absolutely nothing if they've been doing it wrong all those years.

I've had plenty of Bigfoot researchers and enthusiasts disrespectfully blow me off over the years simply because of Bigfoot politics. It's kind of like the groups of social cliques in high school. The popular kids hang out with the other popular kids. Then there are those individuals who want to crack into the popular kids' club so they'll say or do anything to curry their favor. I've literally had people, based on Bigfoot politics, blow me off simply because of what their friends think or say about me. They don't look at and sift through the plethora of foot casts, fingerprints, hand prints, audio recordings of spoken language, pictures, video, and the five-hundred plus people who've been with me to SORA, SOHA, WAHA, SOIA, or who've attended Camp Xanue, on our property, during the summer months. They simply blow me off because the group of people they hang out with do not like me. If they're truly looking for the answers, why would anyone do that? People are funny.

Finally, some of the Bigfoot researchers will say that there's no such thing as a Bigfoot expert. They say this for two reasons: (1) They're trying to appear to be humble by saying that they're not declaring themselves to be a Bigfoot expert; and (2) They're most definitely discrediting anyone else who claims to be a Bigfoot expert. So my response to those stubborn and prideful Bigfoot researchers

Chapter 13: The Xanue Ambassador

is as follows: "I'm not claiming to be a Bigfoot expert. Rather, I'm claiming to be The 13." I don't know everything there is to know about the Xanue. I'm still learning about them on a daily basis. However, I am an Ambassador for the Xanue and they share their truths through me. Although it doesn't make me a Bigfoot expert, it most definitely makes me a Xanue spokesman. That's a title that no one else can claim until the Xanue decide that it's time for me to retire. When that time comes, they might pick someone to take my place. I don't know. We will see. Until that time arrives, Zorth has made it clear that he only speaks to me and that only I speak for the Xanue Council of Twelve.

Now, in order for me to be the Ambassador for the Xanue Council of Twelve, that means that I needed to learn how to listen to and hear Zorth's voice. Well, the first time I heard Zorth's voice was when he leaned over my cot at SOIA and verbally told me his name in a deep bass, guttural tone – "Zorth." He did so while he was gently massaging my head with his very large hand. Although he could have popped my head like an egg, he was kind, gentle, and loving.

Zorth began to teach me how to listen to his voice with a Mind Speak experience in early April of 2017. I was down in southern Oregon visiting with Grady. While I was in the area, I decided to drive up to SOIA to see if the snow had melted off the logging roads yet. SOIA is located at a 5,500-foot elevation. I wanted to see if the roads were clear because I wanted to bring a group of friends to SOIA after our third annual conference at the end of April. Jacqui and Brian accompanied me in their vehicle.

Well, we ran into snow at about the 4,500-foot elevation. I was disappointed because that meant that I couldn't bring my group of friends to SOIA after the conference. However, Zorth stepped in and sent me a Mind Speak message. He told me to turn my truck around and follow his lead as we went back down the logging road. He told me that Deer would be my sign that we were headed in the right direction. I got out of my truck, walked to Jacqui's and Brian's vehicle, and told them what Zorth had just told me.

THE XANUE

We drove about five miles down the logging road and there were no Deer to be seen. Suddenly, a very large Deer about the size of an Elk, ran from my left side, across the road in front of me, and up the hill to my right side. It was all black in color and had a big white spot on it's right rear hip. I've never seen a Deer like that in my entire life. That got our attention. That was most definitely a sign. More importantly, it was a confirmation to myself and the others that Zorth was actually speaking to me.

We drove for another two miles and came to the bottom of the logging road. While sitting at the stop sign, pondering if I should turn left or right, Zorth told me via Mind Speak to take a right turn. I turned right and drove for a little way. Then Zorth told me to stop and take a left on to another logging road. I said, "How do I know it's you rather than simply my own thoughts inside my head? Is it me or you who really wants me to turn left here on to that logging road?"

Zorth responded, "You didn't tell yourself to stop and turn left. I told you to take a left. Also, I'm the one who told you that Deer will be your sign. Turn left and keep an eye out for the Deer."

As directed by Zorth, I turned left on to the logging road. Jacqui and Brian continued to follow me. After driving about a mile on the logging road, a very large Deer, the size of an Elk, ran from my left side, across the road in front of me, and up the hill to my right side. It was all black in color and had a big white spot on it's right rear hip. It was the exact same Deer that we had seen about three miles behind us on the other logging road.

We continued driving on the logging road, following Zorth's lead, in order to find a backup base camp so I could still bring my group of friends on an expedition after the conference was over at the end of April. As we progressed along the logging road, normal looking Deer started showing up on the road. We drove for a couple more miles and saw a whole lot more normal looking Deer. Finally, we reached the location where Zorth wanted us to go to.

I said, "How do I know this is you telling me that this is the area that you want us to go to versus me simply entertaining my own

Chapter 13: The Xanue Ambassador

thoughts and ideas inside my own head? Can I keep driving up the logging road just in case there's another spot that we can camp at?"

Zorth responded, "Go ahead and continue driving up the road. You won't get any farther than one hundred yards up around the corner before you run into snow and are forced to turn around and come back down to this area where I would like you and your friends to camp."

With Zorth's permission and encouragement, I drove up around the corner on the logging road. I made it about one hundred yards before the snow on the road forced us to turn around. We headed back down to the location where Zorth had originally told me to stop because this was our backup camping site. Jacqui, Brian, and I checked out the location and found it to be an excellent backup site.

As we were leaving the backup site to head back down the logging road, I zeroed out my odometer. While we were driving back down the logging road, we continued to see more Deer. I glanced at my odometer and wondered how far the backup base camp site was from the main road. Suddenly, Zorth responded, "Approximately 4.5 miles." Sure enough, when I had reached the stop sign and looked back down at my odometer, it was exactly 4.5 miles from the backup base camp site to the stop sign.

Finally, by the time we had reached the stop sign, we had counted a total of twenty-seven Deer. Now, I want you to think about this for a moment. Zorth said, "Deer will be your sign." Then we went on to see a total of twenty-seven Deer. Do you know how many logging roads I had driven on for decades before that moment in time? I have driven on thousands of miles of logging roads. I consider myself blessed if I get to see one Deer. Really blessed if I see two or three Deer. However, twenty-seven Deer is off the charts. Even you don't know anyone who's ever seen twenty-seven Deer along a ten mile stretch of logging roads.

At the end of April, Cynthia and I brought our friends from the conference down to southern Oregon to our backup SOIA location. We had a great time together. We were all visited at night while we were sleeping in the rain. Some younger Xanue managed to make it under Cynthia's and my tarp and were patting me on the head with their little hands while saying, "Matt! Matt! Matt!" Then an older male Xanue, standing about fifteen feet away, grumbled something in a low, deep bass, guttural sound, and the two young ones sighed and left our cots.

However, the coolest thing that happened was when Chris was visited at night. He had some major kidney issues and positioned his cot about fifty feet away from the rest of us. During the night, the Xanue visited Chris and worked on his body. They folded his tarp and put it on the ground at the base of his cot. They also left him a pile of fresh Manzanita berries on the ground in the shape of a heart. They were local berries, out of season, that could be used for kidney problems. The crazy thing was that it was the end of April, there was still snow on the ground, and there were no flowers or berries to be found as of yet. It was too early in the year. Afterwards, Chris was tested by a medical clinic in association with a prestigious university on the east coast. His kidney functioning had improved and flabbergasted the medical staff.

By the summer of 2017, Cynthia and I had decided to leave the people, traffic, and crime behind and move from Puyallup to the area of Chehalis, Washington. As I continued to learn how to differentiate between my own thoughts and Zorth's speaking to me in my mind, he told me that because of our role in the EXODUS, whenever we found our new home, he would have a family of Xanue there waiting for us. Well, we found our new home up on a mountain top about fifteen miles west of Chehalis, Washington. We are surrounded by ten acres of trees which are surrounded by about half a million acres of Weyerhaeuser Timber property.

On the day of the house inspection, before we solidified the purchase of the home, Grady and I walked through the woods on a trail. Grady found a freshly woven asterisk which means "welcome." Then a minute later, we both saw Kontue stand up, turn around, and walk down the trail to the bottom where the wetlands are located. Grady looked at me and said, "Dad, did you see that?"

Chapter 13: The Xanue Ambassador

I responded, "I sure did, son. Zorth told me that he would have a family waiting here for us when we found our new home. It looks like this is going to be our new home." Afterwards, we were asked to take pictures. I managed to snap a picture of Kontue holding his youngest child by a tree on the backside of our new home.

Kontue is the head clan leader for the families in our local area. He and his wife, Sayreah, moved twelve miles to live on our property. Since that time during the summer of 2017, we've had seven other families move on to our property or near our property. We have nonstop interaction with the Xanue. It's totally amazing. I'll share a little bit more about this later.

As I continued to learn how to differentiate between my own thoughts and Zorth's communications with me via Mind Speak, I was driving home from work one night in the dark. Please keep in mind that my commute home from work is not on a three or four lane highway. Nope. My commute home from work is through farm land and mountains which consist of lots of curvy roads without any guardrails. Sometimes, for the entire hour, I'm the only vehicle on the road.

Anyway, while driving home in the dark, Zorth told me to slow down and keep an eye out for Deer. He went on to say, "First, you will see a female Deer cross the road in front of you. When you see that Deer, you must stop your truck as fast as possible because a male Deer will come down the hill on your left side and stand in front of your truck. He will have big antlers. If you don't stop right away, you will hit him. He will roll over the top of your hood, through your windshield, his antlers will gouge your neck, and you will bleed out and die."

Okay. It doesn't take a rocket scientist to figure out that was Zorth sending me a Mind Speak message. I don't drive through the curvy mountain roads thinking about my throat being gouged by a Deer crashing through my windshield. When I drive, I'm thinking about Cynthia, Grady, my friends, politics, Hawaii, the Oregon Ducks, or the Seattle Seahawks. Nope. I'm not thinking about a male Deer with large antlers killing me. That was most definitely Zorth and not me.

THE XANUE

No less than one mile up the dark, curvy, mountain road, did a female Deer walk across the road in front of my truck. I immediately slammed on my brakes and brought my truck to an immediate stop. I felt sorry for Zeus and Mr. Butters. They had been lying in their doggy bed on the back seat and I had managed to slam them into the backside of the right, front passenger seat. I looked up quickly and there he was – a beautiful male Deer with very large antlers. He was standing in the middle of the road just looking at me. I managed to stop about two or three feet away from him. After about thirty seconds, he turned his head and walked across the road, down the hill, and out of site to catch up with his female companion.

Although I've had many opportunities over the past four years to learn how to differentiate between my own thoughts and Zorth's communications, here's one last really good example. For about a month, I was experiencing repetitive dreams. Sometimes, I would dream that I was standing on a beach. Suddenly, a one-hundred-foot tsunami wave was coming toward the beach. In my dream, I would attempt to run away from the wave unsuccessfully. On other nights, I would dream about hiking through a canyon. Suddenly, a wall of water caused by a flashflood was coming right for me. In my dream, I would attempt to run away from the wall of water unsuccessfully.

Near the end of the month of my repetitive, deadly, aquatic dreaming, I was standing on the beach again. I saw the one-hundred-foot-high tsunami coming right for me. Then I heard Zorth's voice, "Don't turn and run. Stay the course. Go straight into the water." I had this dream three nights in a row where Zorth was telling me to not turn and run, stay the course, and go straight into the one-hundred-foot-high wall of water.

Shortly thereafter, one night, during the winter of 2017-18, I was driving home from work in the dark. It had been raining heavily all day long. As I was driving through the farm land on the curvy roads, I hit a straight stretch where I could increase my speed to fifty miles per hour. Please keep in mind that I'm driving on dark country roads

Chapter 13: The Xanue Ambassador

without any street lights and it's still pouring down rain. My wipers are going as fast as possible so I could see what was in front of me.

Suddenly, while driving approximately fifty miles per hour in the dark and rainy night, I hit a lot of water that had flooded on to the road. All I could see was a big tsunami wall of water in front of me that was continuously spraying over the top of the cab of my truck. Immediately, I heard Zorth say, "Don't turn. Stay the course. Go straight into the water." So I took my foot off of the gas pedal, stayed the course, and went straight into the water. The wall of water lasted for about ten seconds which seemed like ten minutes. I thought that I might be driving into a river.

When my truck came to a complete stop on the other side of the water, I opened up my door, stepped outside, and surveyed the road and adjacent land. Sure enough, the endless pouring rain raised the water level enough to flood on to the road and created the pond that I just drove through at fifty miles per hour in the dark. It occurred to me that if I had attempted to turn my truck, I would most likely have rolled it over, got myself severely injured, and possibly drowned. I was thankful to be able to hear Zorth's voice and to respond to it accordingly. For some reason, he wants to keep me around.

During the Fall of 2018, I was camping up at SOIA with Grady and a friend of his. We had a grand time together. We did some hiking, enjoyed the nearby sites, and experienced some awesome night sits with shimmering images, heavy footed walking, and Orbs. On the last night, I took my Sony Digital Recorder and laid it on my cot to record all night long. Silly me forgot to bring my Bionic Ear Parabolic Microphone Dish with me.

After I returned home to the State of Washington, I listened to the one night of audio recording. In the middle of the night, I could hear several Xanue moving around. Then I heard Zorth say, "Hail to my son." Since Zorth and I have a 24/7 open com with one another, I immediately asked him, "Did something special happen for Mogdue or Tukwa?"

Zorth responded, "I was talking about you. Hail to my son was for you." Hopefully, at this point in time, you can hear the brakes come to a screeching stop inside my head. I responded, "Wait a minute. You're a funny guy. You and my mom never did the 'wild thing' so what are you talking about?"

Zorth chuckled and said, "No. I've adopted you as my son. That's why I said hail to my son. We had an adoption ceremony while you were sleeping."

My mind immediately jumped to the old saying between arguing boys in grade school while I was growing up: "My dad is bigger than your dad so you better leave me alone." Because of my sense of humor, I intend to have a whole lot of fun with the fact that I've been adopted by Zorth. I'm officially a Xanue now. At six feet and nine inches in height, I've already been accused of being a Bigfoot throughout my entire life. Now it's official. Although, truth be told, I'm a pretty small Bigfoot (Xanue).

Learning how to listen to Zorth's voice has saved my life twice. Also, it has led to ongoing learning and sharing about the Xanue with other people. Zorth has also encouraged Cynthia and I to share the Xanue interactions and experiences on our property with other people. Therefore, we established Camp Xanue.

Every summer, we host weekend "Night Sits and Sleep Overs" for approximately thirty-five people to attend. The out of State or out of country guests show up on Friday while the local west coast guests arrive on Saturday morning. Everyone stays until it's time to depart on Monday around one o'clock. The motto is: "Camp Xanue – Where connections are made." This statement is so true. Not only will you make enjoyable connections with a bunch of human friends, you'll also make connections with the Xanue too. Once you get on the Xanue radar, your locals usually step up to interact with you upon your return home.

During people's stay at Camp Xanue, they have had visuals of flesh and blood Xanue, shimmering images, shadow figures, Orbs, flashing lights, etc. Also, people have had the Xanue visit with them while

Chapter 13: The Xanue Ambassador

they're dreaming. Not to mention the fact that some people have had miraculous healings including from cancer, kidney stones, heart issues, paralysis from strokes, and many other problems. Zorth, or should I say Dad, attends the weekend events along with some of the other members of the Council of Twelve. Don't forget that we have a total of eight families that have moved into the area as well. Finally, Kontue and Sayreah, come out and visit with everyone and offer hugs. While hugging attendees, the rest of us have witnessed them disappearing because of Kontue's and Sayreah's high vibrational frequency. It's mind blowing to say the least.

If you're flying in from out of State or out of the country, it's best to fly into the Portland International Airport (PDX). It's a smaller airport compared to the Seattle International Airport (SEA). There's less people and traffic to contend with too. Finally, the drive from Portland is closer and prettier than the drive from Seattle.

I would not be doing my job as the Xanue Ambassador ("The 13") if I didn't remind you regarding the fact that the closer you get to God, Jesus, the Xanue, and other humans (i.e., "Do These Two Things"), the more you're going to anger the Xuxiko and get yourself placed on their radar too. No worries. The Xuxiko are a bunch of toothless demons (i.e., Fallen Angels) who like to bully and intimidate people. They thrive off of negativity and fear. Therefore, do not feed them negativity and fear.

Instead, I mock them and laugh at them. I rebuke them in the name of Jesus Christ. On top of that, we all can call on God's Holy Spirit to surround us with His protection. Finally, we also have the Xanue to protect us if we have a friendship with our locals. There are plenty of people who walk close with God, Jesus, and who are also friends with the Xanue. They can testify to the fact that the Xanue are happy campers when we are connected with God, others, ourselves, and the planet that was given to us to be good stewards of. Nevertheless, there's really nothing to be afraid of when it comes to toothless bullies.

Up to this point, with everything written and stated in this book, hopefully you now have a much better understanding of who the

Xanue are, where they're from, and why they're here. Also, hopefully you have a much better understanding regarding the role of "The 13" and how and why I was asked to take on this position. Although plenty of believers can communicate with their local Xanue, there is only one Xanue Ambassador. There is only one individual who speaks for Zorth and the Council of Twelve.

For the record, the Xanue Council of Twelve consists of two members from each habitable continent on the Earth. There are no Xanue living on Antarctica. They can visit there but they don't live there. The two members from each habitable continent are selected by their tribes. Their tribes consist of clans. Their clans consist of family groups. As previously stated, Kontue is the local clan leader for the family groups living on our property.

Once a Xanue is elected to the Council of Twelve, they maintain that position until they resign or pass away. The average Xanue lives a life span of two-hundred-twenty years. They can live as long as three-hundred years. Very rarely, some Xanue will live as long as four-hundred-years. In a nutshell, their lifespan is about three times longer than the human lifespan. At present (2020), Zorth is one-hundred-seventy-eight-years old. Kontue is one-hundred-fifty-eight-years old. Both will outlive me and you. According to Zorth, when they die, when we die, we all go back to God in our Orb form (i.e., Our soul).

I look forward to hopefully enjoying a long life with Cynthia, with my family, and with my friends. In spite of my imperfections and wild and crazy sense of humor, I intend to take my role seriously as the Xanue Ambassador. I hope to speak boldly and confidently regarding the information that Zorth and the Council of Twelve would like me to share with you in my books, via social media, at Camp Xanue, at our annual Xanue University Conferences, and via media interviews. With all of the above stated, with a humble spirit, I will proceed with the next section of this book.

Oh, one last thing, please don't forget that the title of Xanue Ambassador ("The 13") was given to me by the Xanue Council of Twelve. Also, the title of "Doctor of Psychology" was given to me by

Chapter 13: The Xanue Ambassador

George Fox University and confirmed by the State of Washington. However, rather than call me the Ambassador, "The 13," Dr. Johnson, or Dr. Matt, I would prefer it if you would just simply continue to please call me by my first name - Matt. Matt works for me. Please remember, I'm not your guru. I'm not your cult leader. I'm just a kind person with a good heart and an open mind passing on information that I'm being asked to share with everyone. That's it. Nothing more and nothing less. Just plain old simple me – Matt.

PART 3
QUESTIONS & ANSWERS WITH ZORTH, THE LEADER OF THE XANUE COUNCIL OF TWELVE

CHAPTER 14
THE UNIVERSAL LANGUAGE

I'm going to be completely honest with you, this whole Xanue Ambassador gig sounds crazy to me too. Yup. Trust me, I don't want to be putting myself out there as some crazy loon or as someone who's striving to be some stupid cult leader. Just a public service reminder, I've made it clear on several occasions that I'm not your guru, I'm not your cult leader, and I don't want your money or Earthly possessions. I'm simply just Matt who happens to be a Licensed Clinical Psychologist. I'm not writing this book as a psychologist. Technically speaking, the Xanue thingamajig is simply my hobby or side interest or leisurely passion. I'm merely stating what my training is and what I do professionally when I'm working to make a living, Monday through Friday. During my non-work hours, I enjoy spending time with Cynthia, my family, and friends which happen to include the Xanue.

I can assure you that I do not make a living with this Xanue stuff. I'm not even trying to do so. It's impossible to do so. Rather, as my passionate hobby, I just happen to love sharing with others about what I'm learning from my friends, the Xanue. More specifically, I love sharing with others, as the Xanue Ambassador ("The 13") what I'm learning from Zorth, and the Council of Twelve.

This section of my book is going to be the most challenging part to write. Mainly because I'm going to be reading the questions and Zorth, if he chooses to do so, will be answering the questions. How does this all work? Good question. Mind Speak or telepathy is the quick answer to your question.

THE XANUE

All I know is that ever since the morning after the EXODUS was completed, and I accepted Zorth's and the Xanue Council of Twelve's request to become their Ambassador ("The 13"), Zorth's mind and my mind have had a 24/7 open com link. It's kind of like the "Bat Phone" between Batman and Commissioner Gordon. However, in this case, it's the "Matt Phone" between me and Zorth and the phone is never hung up. In other words, Zorth is aware at all times what I'm thinking, saying, and doing. He's more thorough and aware than Santa Claus happens to be. Zorth knows when I am sleeping. He knows when I'm awake. He knows when I've been good or bad so, okay, okay, so you get the picture now, right?

Does this feel like an invasion of privacy? No. Does Zorth control my mind and make me say or do things? No. Does he ever interfere with my private or professional life? No. Does he ever pipe up and throw in his two-cents-worth? Yes, in my private life but never in my professional life. For example, when Cynthia and I are talking, he will occasionally interject his wisdom, but more often than not, he will interject some humor. He often sides with Cynthia if we have a disagreement. By the way, Zorth loves Cynthia and thinks she's the best daughter-in-law in the world.

I can't begin to tell you how many people have asked me to ask Zorth if he and the Xanue would do this for them or do that for them. They also ask me if I talk with him all of the time every day. No. The truth of the matter is that days or weeks may go by without Zorth and I exchanging any kind of communication. Why? Because we both have our lives to live and daily responsibilities to manage.

I try to educate others, regarding my relationship with Zorth, that he is not a genie in a lamp that I rub and, therefore, have three wishes to make. This is an ignorant and disrespectful approach to interacting with the Xanue. Rather than treat them like they're genies in a lamp, we should respectfully approach them as friends and ask them for their input or help if they have the time, ability, and willingness to do so. Please keep in mind that sometimes our friends simply don't have the time, ability, or willingness to help us.

Chapter 14: The Universal Language

Sometimes, they're busy with their own lives and what they're doing in their own world.

The other thing I try to educate people about, regarding my relationship with Zorth, is the fact that he's the head of the Council of Twelve. That pretty much makes him the president of the planet. Now, please think this through for a moment. Let's pretend that your good friends with the individual who has become elected to the office of the President of the United States (POTUS). You know them really well. You have their cellphone number and email address. If you have a clear head on your shoulders and any respect for your friend's position of responsibility, you are not going to be bothering them on a daily basis. It simply would not be the right thing to do.

Instead, you would wait quietly to hear from them if and when they have an opportunity to say "hello" to you. Maybe, just maybe, you might send him or her an occasional text message encouraging them and letting them know that you're praying for them. However, you most certainly wouldn't be taking advantage of your friendship while they're engaged in fulfilling their daily responsibilities of governing our nation, right? If you just answered "yes" instead, then you lack serious manners and respect.

In the same way, although I'm honored to have been asked to be the Xanue Ambassador ("The 13") and the adopted son of Zorth (i.e., "Hail to my son" in the previous chapter), I try not to pester him. Instead, I try to be encouraging and simply let him know that I'm in his corner if he ever needs me for anything. Zorth does likewise with me because he knows that I have a personal and professional life too. However, it's always good to know that we have a 24/7 open com just in case we need to say something to one another.

I've been asked numerous times about how does Mind Speak actually work. Well, it's most definitely telepathic in nature. It's the communication of thoughts – not spoken words. Mutually consensual thought insertion. I've learned overtime that we're all gifted differently. Some people simply are not hardwired in their brains for telepathic communication while others most definitely are. When we pray to

THE XANUE

God and Jesus or when we communicate telepathically with another species, we are communicating via the Universal Language.

The Universal Language is the language that everyone can understand in the entire universe. In other words, every created species can understand the language of the mind – Universal Language. It isn't until our thoughts are rolled out onto our tongues and projected out of our mouths into actual spoken language that we start running into geographical challenges and language barriers. Simply put, we don't all speak Chinese, Russian, German, Spanish, Portuguese, Italian, Japanese, Inupiat, Farsi, or God's chosen language – English. Relax! Just kidding. Nevertheless, when we are communicating with God, Jesus, and other species, everyone understands Mind Speak because it's the Universal Language of the mind.

Over the years, I've seen some people improve their ability to engage in Mind Speak with the Xanue. Others, no matter how hard they try, just don't seem to be able to do so. It's okay. The Xanue communicate with us in many different ways besides Mind Speak. They communicate with Steve Bachmann by pushing on his body after he asks "yes" or "no" questions. They communicate with others via glyphs, gifts, or audible sounds. Although I don't want anyone to give up trying to communicate with their local Xanue families, I also don't want anyone beating themselves up inside because they are gifted differently. If you're patient, you and your local Xanue family will figure it out, regarding how to communicate with one another.

With everything said, I'm going to honestly share with you that writing the remainder of this section in my book is going to be overwhelming for me. The reason is because when I allow Zorth to speak through me over a prolonged period of time, it's very physically and emotionally draining on my body.

Last year, after a lengthy period of Zorth answering several questions for attendees at SOIA, we began our journey home the following morning. As we were driving down the mountain, I had to stop and get out of the truck because I was dizzy, weak, and emotionally overwhelmed. I leaned over the back of my truck and balled like a baby. The guys were supportive and comforting. I had to have my good friend, Joel, drive us back home to the State of Washington.

Anyway, I haven't done any prolonged linked up communication with Zorth for over a year. Therefore, I'm a little gun shy. Nevertheless, I'm going to do it because I know that Zorth and the Council of Twelve have information that they want to share through me and with the rest of you. I'll be sitting upstairs in the quiet recreation room, with the door shut, and free from distraction from our two dogs and three cats. Cynthia will be close by if I need any assistance at all. Also, I know that Zorth will tell me to take breaks when I need to do so. It will be interesting to see which questions he chooses to answer and which questions he chooses to pass by. Wish me luck. Here we go.

CHAPTER 15

Q&A WITH ZORTH

COUNCIL OF TWELVE QUESTIONS:

1. **How did Zorth become a member of the Council of Twelve?** Members of the Council of Twelve serve in their positions for a lifetime. There are two members from each of the six habitable continents with trees on the Earth. After much discussion and prayer, I was selected from the tribe in my region. Tribes consist of clans. Clans consists of family groups. Jakut, my good friend, was selected by his tribe in the eastern region of North America. He lives in upstate New York in the Finger Lakes region.
2. **How did Zorth become the leader of the Council of Twelve?** The Xanue Council of Twelve are entrusted with the responsibility and authority to name their own leader. All twelve members talk, pray, and vote together. No one can vote for themselves. This process is repeated as many times as needed until there is a majority of seven or more votes. Once the decision is made, there is total loyalty and submission bestowed by all Xanue worldwide upon the Xanue Council of Twelve and to their elected leader. My position is not of that of king, president, or dictator. I simply serve as the leader of the Xanue Council of Twelve. If and when we are divided in a decision, I have the final deciding vote. However, we strive for unanimous decisions. Then I become the spokesman for the Xanue Council of Twelve and deliver the message to our

people. I also communicate on behalf of the Xanue Council of Twelve directly to our selected Ambassador – The 13. I speak to no one else because Matt is our only Ambassador.
3. **Is there patriarchal-only leadership within the Xanue?** The Xanue do not view the world in the same way as humans do. Although our leadership consists of elected males, the female Xanue serve in all other capacities as the males do. We do not see things in terms of patriarchal or matriarchal. Both genders are happy to serve in their positions. Everyone is viewed and treated as equals.
4. **When the Council of Twelve shut down SOIA because of government interference, what were they doing in the area?** Our old meeting grounds at SOIA were near the Oregon Caves National Park. Some of government workers were watching Matt's YouTube videos online. As a result, they began to survey Matt and his friends when they were at SOIA. They were also exploring the region in Matt's absence. They also began the process of expanding the park boundaries so they could eventually control the area where SOIA was located. They were attempting to find the three portals in the area. As a result, the Xanue Council of Twelve decided that it was time to relocate our meeting grounds.
5. **Where did the Council of Twelve move their new meeting place to? Is it to the new place where you live now?** The Xanue Council of Twelve chose to relocate our meeting grounds to the State of Washington where I now reside with my family.
6. **How did "Patty" respond when the Council of Twelve asked her to allow Patterson and Gimlin to film her?** Enrith, who humans refer to as "Patty," was honored to be asked to be the subject of the Patterson and Gimlin film. It was an honor for her because she knew that the film would eventually make it possible for the EXODUS to happen.
7. **I heard that Gimlin was pointing a rifle at "Patty" while Patterson was filming her. Was "Patty" in any danger?** We

are Beings of Light. We cannot be killed by humans. Besides, we know that humans with negative intentions are coming before they even know that we are there. However, the Treykon, who look like us but are smaller, uglier, and menacing can be killed by human weapons because they are only flesh and blood beings. The Treykon are not Beings of Light.

8. **Patterson and Gimlin filmed "Patty" fifty-three years ago. Is she still alive? If yes, how is she doing and where is she living?** Enrith is alive and well. She is living in northern California. She is enjoying life with her family and friends.

THE XANUE AMBASSADOR ("THE 13") QUESTIONS:

9. **Please explain how you and the Council of Twelve decided to select Dr. Matt as your Ambassador?** God has gifted some of us with the ability to see into the future in a limited manner. We are only able to see what God wants us to see. Based on insights, discussions, and prayer, we focused our attention on a few individuals who had the potential of helping us to achieve our goal of the EXODUS. We had to spread our eggs out into several potential baskets because someone might be scared and quit, grow tired and quit, not make the progress that we were hoping for in a timely manner, or die before they completed the process. These individuals needed to be kind, good-hearted, open-minded, committed, passionate, intelligent, willing to learn and grow, and be a good communicator. Matt was simply the first one to complete the process. Although he is far from perfect, his heart is in the right place. We agreed unanimously, based on all of the criteria, that he was the right choice for the Ambassador – The 13. Therefore, when appropriate, Matt shares with others what I ask him to share on behalf of the Xanue Council of Twelve.

THE XANUE

10. **Will there be a 'replacement' someday for Dr. Matt and Cynthia?** As I just answered, God has gifted some of us the ability to see into the future in a limited manner. At present, God has not shown us the answer to this question. For now, Matt will serve as the Ambassador for me and the Xanue Council of Twelve until he dies or decides to resign his position. We speak only through him. As that time nears, the Xanue Council of Twelve has the confidence that God will reveal his plans for the future.
11. **Does Zorth speak to any other humans besides the Xanue Ambassador ("The 13")?** As I have stated, I am the elected leader of the Xanue Council of Twelve and I speak only through the Xanue Ambassador – The 13. Anyone else who claims that I am speaking through them is mistaken or a fraud.
12. **Matt and Cynthia seem like a really good couple and team to help make the EXODUS happen as well as the subsequent Camp Xanue events. Did the Xanue help to bring them together?** Like all humans, Matt and Cynthia have free will. Ultimately, the decision to enter a relationship and maintain it is up to them. However, we are able to see into the future in a limited capacity. We may have had something to do with them crossing paths in the lobby of the hotel on the morning of their thirtieth high school reunion. The rest was up to them. Personally, I'm happy for my adopted son and his wife – my daughter-in-law. They make a great couple.

EXODUS QUESTIONS:

13. **The Xanue who arrived during the EXODUS, do most live in the Pacific Northwest now or do they live all over the world?** The 23,542 Xanue who came to the Earth from our dying home world, minus the three elders who died within an hour or less of arrival, were given a period of time to adjust to their new

world. Then they were dispersed to all six habitable continents. They are all happy and adjusting well.

14. **Is the Exodus now a 'memorial holiday' for all Xanue?** We celebrate the Exodus as many times as possible by traveling to the part of the Earth that enjoys the full eclipse of the sun. Attendance is optional. The eclipsing sun represents our dying sun and home world. When the sun becomes visible again, it represents our new world and new sun that we are enjoying today. We thank God for this new lease on life.

15. **How is the Xanue 'great reveal' going worldwide?** It's only been three years since Matt courageously shared about the 'great reveal' at their conference. The Xanue Council of Twelve is pleased with the constant spreading and growth of the 'reveal' worldwide. The numbers appear to be increasing, slowly but surely. Our only desire is to help reconnect humans back with God, one another, and to be better stewards of the Earth that God gave all of us to tend.

16. **Approximately how many Xanue are there worldwide?** How many trees are there worldwide? There are more Xanue than humans on the Earth. Fortunately, we don't have to rely on vegetables, fruits, nuts, dairy, and meat to survive. There would be no food left on the Earth for humans or the Xanue. Instead, we obtain our sustenance from the trees during the day. As Beings of light [Orbs], we go into the trees during the day. We soak up the energy from the sun and the nutrients in the ground through the roots. This is our primary source of our sustenance.

17. **Regarding the three older Xanue who died within an hour or less of their arrival to the Earth via the EXODUS, what happened to them? In other words, do the Xanue bury the dead?** We are Beings of Light [Orbs]. We can shapeshift in and out of our flesh and blood bodies. When we reach the age of passing, our time is up and we go back to be with God. We do not bury our dead because there is no body to bury.

However, the Treykon bury their dead because they're flesh and blood beings.

18. **The Xanue who traveled to the Earth must be excited about the reunification with their family and friends. What is the biggest difference between the two worlds that they notice and speak of the most?** The 23,542 souls that immigrated to the Earth during the EXODUS, minus our three friends who passed within an hour or less upon their arrival, speak of the humans with great inquisitiveness and passion. On our home world, there were no humans, roads, buildings, planes, boats, and the like. There was just the Xanue, lots of trees, and the wildlife. The new arrivals are fascinated by the humans and their technology. More importantly, they are beyond grateful for what Matt, Cynthia, Mike, Steve, and Grady did to help make the EXODUS possible. Therefore, they appear to be extra excited and motivated to help humans reconnect with God, each other, themselves, and with the Earth.

FORMER PLANET QUESTIONS:

19. **Was the dying planet that you escaped from really just the Earth billions of years in our future?** No. Our home world is in another galaxy far away from the Milky Way galaxy.
20. **Can the former Xanue planet be seen from the Earth or is it in another galaxy?** No. Our former planet is way beyond the humans' ability to see it at this time.
21. **Do the Xanue live on other planets besides living on the Earth?** Although we have visited many other worlds, the Earth is our home world. Matter of fact, we have been here longer than the human race has been here.

22. **What is the state of the former Xanue world?** Uninhabitable.
23. **Would you please describe your home world in the height of it's marvelous beauty?** Our home world, in the height of its beauty, was filled with trees, oceans, mammals, birds, and fish. The size of our planet was about a third larger than the Earth. Although everything was different, it was as close to the Earth as many other planets could get.
24. **Do Xanue ever visit your home world?** No. It is dead.
25. **Are there any other sentient beings still on your home world?** No. It is dead.
26. **Is the Xanue's former home planet in our galaxy?** No. Our home world is in a galaxy far away from the Milky Way galaxy.
27. **What is the Xanue's name for their home planet?** Xanue. Planet Xanue.
28. **What happened that made their home planet eventually uninhabitable?** Over a long period of time, our sun slowly burned out and left our planet uninhabitable.
29. **How did the Xanue find the Earth?** We sent out scouts via portals that were built by an ancient race billions of years ago.
30. **How long ago did the Xanue first settle here?** We first settled the Earth during the last period of the dinosaurs.
31. **Are there Xanue on other planets in our galaxy?** Although we can visit other planets, the Earth is our home.
32. **Do you know what caused your planet to die? Was it just the natural cycle of the planet, just as our Earth is progressing through at this time?** Our planet eventually died because our sun slowly but surely burned out. No sun, no life.
33. **Where is your former planet located in relationship to the Milky Way Galaxy?** Our sun is located in another galaxy way beyond the human race's ability to see it with their technology. The universe is vast and exists in many dimensions. Think in terms of all the grains of sand on a beach multiplied by trillions. God is infinite. God is great.

THE XANUE

XANUE FAMILY QUESTIONS:

34. **What is the average number of children that Xanue families have?** That choice depends upon the mated couple. Sometimes there are none born. At the most, there are three or four born to a couple.
35. **Are the baby Xanue born in Orb form or physical form?** They can be born in Orb form or physical form. The choice is the mother's decision.
36. **Who teaches the baby Xanue to cloak?** No one. Our natural vibrational frequency is higher than that of humans. Therefore, we exist outside the humans' visual field of range which makes it appear like we can cloak. Dogs and cats can see us. Some humans can see our shimmering images. Also, cameras can capture our images which tend to be blurry because of our high vibrational frequency.
37. **What is the average length of a Xanue pregnancy?** The answer to this question depends upon which way the mother chooses to deliver her baby. If she chooses to deliver in physical form, mainly for the experience, the gestation period is about eight months. If she chooses to deliver in Orb form, the gestation period is approximately twelve months.
38. **Do Clans consist of Father/Mother-In-Laws, Grandparents, etc.?** Yes. Our family structures are very similar to that of humans. However, please keep in mind that we are all connected to one another. Therefore, we are all one people and one family.
39. **I'd like to know more about the individuals who came over during the EXODUS but passed away within an hour or less of their arrival? Were those three buried here?** No. We are Beings of Light [Orbs] who can shapeshift into flesh and blood. When our bodies die, we return to God in our Orb form. We do not bury bodies because there are no bodies left behind to bury.

Chapter 15: Q&A with Zorth

40. **Do the Xanue live on the Hawaiian Islands?** We are in the trees and the trees are everywhere, including on the Hawaiian Islands. However, we are not in every tree.
41. **Is there any divorce among the Xanue? Any single Xanue?** We are much different than the human race because we never fell in the Garden of Eden. We experience no conflict. We don't have divorces. We find this to be sad for humans. All Xanue are single until they choose a mate for life. Some choose to never mate. My spouse died prematurely a while ago. I am single. I will never choose to mate again. I love her and miss her.
42. **How do Xanue choose their spouses?** What one knows, we all know. When we are ready to look for a mate for life, everyone knows and God directs our paths. When we find a compatible mate for life, there is no question. We all know.
43. **Do Xanue celebrate yearly birthdays?** We are very different than the human race when it comes to this matter. Unlike humans, we do not celebrate one's birth on an annual basis. We are all connected and feel the joy and blessing of everyone's existence on a daily basis – not just once a year. It is a great reinforcing experience of community, love, and acceptance.
44. **When young Xanue become adults, are there customs for the young leaving home, finding spouses?** We Xanue have the freedom to pursue a mate for life when we feel like we are ready to do so. Not all choose to pursue a mate for life. We have no right way or wrong way to pursue a mate for life. However, everyone knows when the choice is made and are loving and supportive.
45. **Like humans, do the Xanue practice "marriage" or something similar?** Yes. Some of us choose mates for life. There are no formal ceremonies. We simply know when the choice is made and rejoice in the decision.
46. **Many encounters report there being an authority figure monitoring the adolescent males in the woods while they appear to be going through to rite of passage or training.**

233

Are Xanue young adults required to stay in their physical form for a set period to potentially interact with humans, hunt small animals, and survive while being supervised by an adult? Yes. We are guardians of the forest and protect all who dwell within. There are many responsibilities that our young ones need to learn, male and female. They have many tasks to learn and follow through on in both their Orb form and physical form. The majority of our daily sustenance is obtained while dwelling in the trees during the day light. However, rarely, we will eat of the physical Earth too. We occasionally enjoy consuming fruit, vegetables, and nuts. Rarely, we will consume birds, small rodents, and fish. We do not eat large mammals. However, we may occasionally harvest one for our pets such as the Coyotes, Cougars, or Wolves. The Treykon are the ones who eat large mammals.

47. **What are the family structured activities for the Xanue during the day time and at night time?** We teach our young ones to balance both work and leisure together. We teach them how to tend to the trees and other vegetation. We teach them to tend to the animals, birds, reptiles, fish, and insects. Finally, we teach them about the social and cultural responsibilities of being a Xanue, which includes some play at times. Although what one knows, we all know, there's no substitute for hands on training and experience.

48. **We spend available time on what we call hobbies to pass the time or for personal enjoyment. It can be building or creating things for ourselves or for others. Do the Xanue also have hobbies? Example please.** We enjoy landscaping, making structures, wood and plant art, singing, and play together.

49. **Do you possess material items as we do?** Because we never fell in the Garden of Eden, we are not locked into our flesh and blood bodies like humans are. Therefore, we do not need to possess items because everything we need is available in nature. Besides, Orbs don't have pockets. That's Xanue humor.

Chapter 15: Q&A with Zorth

RELATIONSHIP QUESTIONS:

50. **How can humans be better friends with the Xanue?** It is actually pretty simple. If a kind person, with a good heart, and an open mind reaches out to us, we will reach back to them. However, many humans immediately assume that they are kind, have a good heart, and are open minded. Some are and some aren't. Honest self-reflection is necessary. Also, patience and persistence is needed. Finally, if you try to reach out to us while surrounding yourself with others who are negative, self-centered, and closed minded, it doesn't matter where you are personally, we will not reach back to you. Please surround yourself with positivity and love.

51. **Will our two species ever live in harmony?** We are already living in harmony. Most humans don't believe in us and we have been avoiding most humans. However, God is now directing us to begin the process of slowly but surely bringing our two worlds together. This will take some time. God is the Creator of all things, visible and invisible, and Christ really does hold all things together. He is the God Particle. With that said, there is no way that a kind person, with a good heart, and an open mind can interact with us without accepting the fact that everything else unseen exists too, including God, Christ, Angels, Xuxiko, and everything else. Believing is seeing.

52. **Will more humans begin to believe and accept the existence of the Xanue?** Unfortunately, no. Not all humans are kind, have a good heart, or are open minded. The human race was negatively affected by the fall of man in the Garden of Eden. Humans have to intentionally choose to be loving.

53. **How do we learn the names of our local Xanue families?** It is our custom to share our names with those we choose to interact with when we believe that the relationship has developed to the point of sharing such an honor. Depending on the human's

THE XANUE

ability or lack thereof, we will speak our name out loud to them or share it in a mind speak. Humans call it telepathy.

54. **Is there anything that we humans can do to expedite and improve our interactions with the Xanue?** Yes, engage in a daily assessment of yourself. Are you a better person today than you were yesterday? Is what you're about to say or do displaying your love for God, your neighbor, yourself, and the Earth? Screen what books you read, what music you listen to, and what shows you watch at home or in your movie theaters.

55. **What can I focus on to improve the possibility of interacting with the Xanue rather than just observe and analyze their existence?** Self-reflection. Are you truly a kind person to everyone? Do you have a good heart? Are you open minded? Do you surround yourself with others who are also positive?

56. **When I travel for work, my husband and I stay in hotels. Sometimes, I sense that at least one person is in the room with us. Is this person from the family near our home or a local Xanue near the hotel?** Most of the time, we tend to be what you humans call "homebodies." It's not that we won't ever travel far from home because some of us have the responsibility to do so. However, in most cases, you're encountering a local Xanue in the area of your temporary dwelling.

57. **I have a connection with my local Xanue family. They healed my broken kneecap last summer. Sometimes they're in my bedroom but they won't Mind Speak with me. What can I do to encourage them to talk or Mind Speak with me?** More often than not, if you're not experiencing mind speak with a Xanue that you have a relationship with, it's not because they won't mind speak with you. Rather, more often than not, it's because you can't mind speak with them. Everyone is gifted differently. A good example is that Matt can mind speak with the Xanue fairly easily. On the other hand, Steve Bachmann needs to ask questions and his local Xanue answer him by

pushing or tapping on him one time for 'yes' and they do not do anything for a 'no' answer.

58. **Is there a way to increase the open-mindedness of humans?** Humans are raised differently around the Earth. Once they learn what they've been taught as children, it's hard to move them from their way of seeing the world to any other possible point of view. In order to increase the open-mindedness of humans, parents must start by raising their children at an early age that anything is possible and that there are many points of view – not just one. Then when it comes time to learn the truth as things really are, they will be open-minded enough to accept the truth.

59. **Are the Xanue willing to help train humans to use their third eye?** We have been able to help some humans to learn how to use their third eye. However, to be honest, many humans just don't want to learn or are too stubborn.

60. **What is the best way to help spread the word that things are changing in the Bigfoot world and that the Xanue want to interact with humans in their natural form?** Live your truth and tell others of your interactions with us. Let them know that the Xanue are fellow children of God and that we simply want to help humanity to live better and happier lives.

61. **Can the Xanue train humans to develop the ability to sense or read other humans to see which individuals would be good to spread the word to?** If the human you're trying to reach is mean, negative, rude, or arrogant, walk away. Don't waste your time. If they are kind, loving, and open minded, then they're worth your time to communicate with.

62. **What is the best or easiest way for humans to communicate with the Xanue?** You don't have to come out into the forest or mountains to find us. We are in the trees and the trees are everywhere. However, we are not in every tree. Therefore, go out into your backyards or to a nearby park, sit in the dark, play us some music, and attempt to talk with us with your

mouths and with your minds. We value patience, persistence, and effort.

63. **Do the Xanue use sign language?** No.
64. **Can the Xanue teach their language to humans? If yes, is it close to any human language?** There are so many aspects to our language that it would be impossible for a human to learn it all. However, if you record at night like Matt has taught others to do, you will find a pattern of our use of language and be able to identify some of our words. Most people don't realize this but we've been here on the Earth longer than humanity. Therefore, we have observed your development and we know all of your spoken languages. We can speak all human languages.
65. **Why do some people have bad experiences with Sasquatch?** First of all, most people don't know that there's a difference between the Xanue and the Treykon. People will almost always have bad experiences with the Treykon. If humans run into the Treykon out in the forest, they will kill the human, eat the human, and disperse their bones. On the other hand, if a human has a bad experience with the Xanue, it's because we perceived the human to be negative and we guide them out of the forest and out of our home. Do you want a negative person in your home? Although we intimidate humans in order to get them to leave our homes, we never kill humans.
66. **Why do many children have wonderful playful experiences with the Xanue?** Most human children are kind, loving, innocent, playful, and open-minded. Therefore, they're much easier to interact with. However, as they age, they begin to learn how they're supposed to see the world and the doors to their innocent and accepting minds are closed off. It's very sad to see.
67. **Does Zorth want all of us to contribute to helping to teach the Xanue children or just "The 13?"** "The 13" has the responsibility to try and open the eyes and ears of humanity regarding our existence and to try and teach you how to interact with us.

However, Matt, is just a man. Therefore, he's not omnipresent like God. As a result, we would appreciate all of the help and effort we can get to have humans interact with our children by talking to them, reading to them, singing to them, and playing with them. Matt can't do it all.

68. **Do the Xanue ever get tired of us asking them to appear, heal us, or to please interact with us? Sometimes I feel like I may be over doing it with all of my requests.** Although we will do nothing outside of the will of God, you have not because you ask not. Therefore, please ask. You might hear yes, no, or wait awhile.

69. **Can you tell me the names of the Xanue who live on my property?** The names of the Xanue who are living on your property will be revealed to you when they're ready to do so. You must earn their trust, respect, and friendship over time. Be patient, persistent, and committed.

70. **Why are there less Xanue on my property than there were a few years ago?** Some Xanue choose an area and stay there throughout their lives. Other Xanue, enjoy moving around and experiencing new parts of the Earth that they have never seen before. Many humans are the same way too.

71. **How do I know whether or not my local Xanue family likes me?** You must exercise patience, persistence, and commitment over an extended period of time. Show them trust while losing your fear. Sit in the dark and talk with them. Sleep outside under the stars. Show them that you do not fear them.

72. **I've been trying to connect with the Xanue for several months without any obvious signs that they're responding to my reaching out to them? Should I keep going or give up? Does this mean that they don't like me?** How long did it take Matt to connect with us? How many miles did he drive every month roundtrip to visit with us? How much money did he spend to make it possible? Although Matt put forth the time, effort, and money to reach out to us, his goal was to

help shorten the time that it would take you to connect with us by teaching you what to do. Are you following his protocol? Are you demonstrating the same level of patience, persistence, and commitment that he demonstrated? We are waiting to see where your heart is truly directed.

73. **Do the Xanue shapeshift into other living forms such as Blue Jays, Crows, or Grackles? If yes, can they visit humans repetitively in these forms?** Yes and yes. We can shapeshift into anything we want to such as birds, mammals, reptiles, humans, etc. However, we prefer to remain in the primary form that God designated us to be in.
74. **Do the Xanue mate for life?** Yes. We do not divorce.
75. **What can I do for the Xanue?** If we need something from you, we will most definitely ask for your assistance.
76. **What can we do in our lives to help make things easier for the Xanue (i.e. Service projects, doing good always to everyone)?** Our goal is to help humanity reconnect with God, one another, and to be good stewards of the Earth that was given to all of us to tend to. Therefore, love everyone to the best of your ability. Recycle. Plant trees. Love God's creatures.
77. **What things do we humans do that most hinder progress in our relationship with Xanue?** Hatred, negativity, and fear hinders the development of having a relationship with us. However, the Xuxiko feed off of hatred, negativity, and fear.
78. **Will we ever know any of the names of Xanue we interact with?** You will know our names when we want you to know our names. You must earn our trust and friendship first.
79. **If we move to a new location will the Xanue who live there interact with us, or do we have to 'start over'?** What one knows, we all know. Therefore, if you know us in one location, the locals will know you in your new location. However, just like when humans move to a new location, you're still going to have to put forth effort to get to know your new Xanue neighbors too.

Chapter 15: Q&A with Zorth

80. **Do Xanue have anything similar to our sports?** We enjoy playing and experiencing fun and laughter together. We have no formalized sports. We are not competitive. We are cooperative.
81. **Sometimes I speak out loud to Xanue, sometimes just in my mind. Do you prefer one more than the other?** We prefer both. More importantly, we prefer patience, persistence, and commitment. We prefer to see your heart move in a consistent positive direction over time.
82. **Do Xanue have any material possessions that are special to them?** We possess nothing because all things are available to us in the wild. We have not pockets or shelves.
83. **Xanue never seem to be in a hurry – is that true?** We live a mellow and peaceful lifestyle. We are not in a hurry. The best things happen when time is allowed to pass without worry. We trust God's will.
84. **It is an easy thing to convince humans of your existence. Why do you not use that ability (showing yourselves) very often?** Quite the contrary, it is not any easy thing to convince humans that we exist. The human race has about a third of individuals who are open minded enough to accept the truth immediately for what it is. Then they have another third that have to think through things for quite a while before they will finally allow themselves to accept the truth. Not to throw my adopted son, Matt, under the bus but he's our chosen Ambassador – The 13 and yet he continues to struggle with accepting the truth at times. He struggles with his Christian faith and whether or not we are demons or are the Nephilim or some other evil entity trying to trick him and you into believing a lie. As you have read earlier in the book, and as you'll read later in the multiple testimonials, we are anything but an evil entity. We truly are just another species created by God and we are your fellow brothers and sisters. In spite of all of the positive interactions over the past twenty-years, Matt still struggles from time to time because of all of the hammering

that he receives from the final third of the human population that will never accept the truth. Matt has a good heart. He truly is a faithful failure who maintains his focus on the right path. Finally, there's no greater example of the representation of the truth than the Son of God – Jesus Christ. Although he walked on water, changed water into wine, caused the blind to see, healed the sick, helped the death to hear, fed over five-thousand people with a few fish and loaves of bread, and raised the dead, the human race still chose not to believe and crucified him. So, no, it's not easy to convince the human race that we exist even if we reveal ourselves to them daily in the flesh and blood form that we can shapeshift into. Therefore, we choose to go about it in the manner that we are using. We prefer to reach out to the open-minded third of the human race. We will let them speak up on our behalf to the adjacent third who will eventually be convinced over time.

85. **Have there been or is there any rogue Xanue on Earth at all?** Unlike the human race, we are not a fallen species. We have no rogue Xanue. If you see something that resembles a Bigfoot and it is menacing and deadly, you are witnessing a Treykon. They are a vile and malevolent species. They will kill humans, large mammals, and they are the ones who are connected with UFOs – NOT the Xanue.

86. **Do the Xanue experience human emotions of jealousy, fear?** No. We are a content and peaceful species. However, we do experience frustration when negative humans wonder into our territory and we won't hesitate to intimidate them in order to get them out of our homes. With that said, we have never injured or killed a human being. We are simply protecting our homes just like humans protect their homes. You wouldn't want negative humans in your home either.

87. **Have the Xanue ever experienced war or fighting between clans?** No. Once again, humans are a fallen species. Therefore, they are disconnected from God, one another, and the Earth

Chapter 15: Q&A with Zorth

that God gave them to tend to. Because of the disconnectedness, humans lie, steal, fight, rape, murder, and go to war. On the other hand, we never fell in the Garden of Eden. We passed the test and remain connected with God, one another, and the Earth. Humans need to stop projecting the attributes of their fallen nature on to our species.

INTERACTION QUESTIONS:

88. **I've been wanting to get involved with positive interaction groups in my area (Butte/Bozeman MT). Are there any available? How would I go about finding them?** We are in the trees and the trees are everywhere. However, we are not in every single tree. The Council of Twelve, as well as myself, have been encouraging Matt to educate humans that you do not need to go deep into the wilderness to find us. All you really have to do is go do "night sits" and "sleep overs" in your own backyard. Simply follow Matt's instructions of no lights, sing, play musical instruments, and start talking with your local Xanue. Please forgive us but we are very careful and usually take our time in reaching back to humans in order to interact with them. You have to earn our trust and friendship through your patience and persistence. As some of you humans say, "Rome was not built in a day."

89. **I don't mean to complain but it seems like I've been trying to do what Matt teaches. For the past two months, I've been going out into my backyard at night, sitting in the dark, playing music, and talking to the trees with my mouth and my mind. The end result – absolutely nothing. What am I doing wrong?** The locals in your area know you better than any of the other Xanue. In many situations, the Xanue are evaluating humans to see if they are kind, have a good heart, and are truly open minded. Then, the Xanue are also assessing

for fear versus trust. Do you fear them or trust them. Finally, they are assessing for commitment, patience, and persistence. Please remember that the individual you're citing as your example and teacher, Matt, was willing to drive one-thousand-miles roundtrip once or twice a month, from Washington to southern Oregon. He would spend five-hundred or more dollars per trip on gas, food, camping supplies, and gifting bowl supplies. Out of a total of his first sixteen years Bigfooting in the mountains, he spent a total of four-years with his boots on the ground in the forest trying to connect with the Xanue. Finally, while at the Southern Oregon Habituation Area (SOHA), he left food out for four years. We didn't begin to take his food until year number five. Matt passed the test. To be fair to all the other humans, we certainly don't expect them to do exactly what Matt did. What would be the point in doing that? With that said, we might expect a little bit more commitment than just sitting in your backyard for a couple of months.

90. **What kind of gifts are most appropriate to give to the Xanue?** First of all, no gifts are ever required. As I've said before, we don't have pockets, drawers, or shelves to store things in. We are not in need of holding on to things. With that said, we are most definitely interested in your heart and motivations. Therefore, we understand that a gift from the heart has a special meaning. As Matt has shared on many occasions, if we so desire, we can obtain vegetables, fruits, nuts, and meat from the natural environment. However, bread products are our favorite because we can't pick bread from trees or bushes. We like peanut butter and jelly sandwiches. We like cookies, donuts, cake, rolls, bagels, and Cinnabon rolls. With that said, it doesn't mean that we are always going to take what you give us. If we don't take it, please don't be disappointed. We have our reasons. Just know that we value the heart behind the act.

91. **Will I ever see any Xanue in my home or on my property, and will I ever have any contact with them?** That depends

Chapter 15: Q&A with Zorth

on your locals and whether or not they perceive you as being a kind person with a good heart and an open mind. One or two out of the three requirements are not good enough. Therefore, you must do some serious self-reflection and clean house if necessary. Once you have yourself prepared, then they're going to be watching you for patience and persistence regarding your reaching out to them. Finally, fear repels them. Your local Xanue do not want you to be afraid of them. They will keep their distance from you if you're afraid of them.

92. **Would it be possible for a human to learn your language?**
Humans can learn some of our language but it would be impossible for them to learn all of our language because we communicate with other Xanue on multifaceted levels. For example, through listening to thousands of hours of recorded audio, Matt has been able to correctly identify some of our spoken words in what he likes to call "Squatchinese." He has correctly identified that the word "Hick" means an acknowledgment to what an individual just heard. "Hick" is like a human's use of "okay," "uh huh," "right," "gotcha," or "I understand." If anyone was to record us at night and listen to thousands of hours of our talking and singing, they could begin to do likewise. However, with that said, we also communicate via whistling, clicking, tree pops, imitating animals and birds, mind speak, screams, growling, and the use of all human languages on the Earth. In short, I don't believe that any one human has the ability to master all of what I have just stated above.

93. **Do you ever intervene in human events, such as preventing a crime, saving a life in an accident, putting out a fire, etc.?**
We are a people of faith in God through Jesus Christ. Our hearts, minds, eyes, and ears are always open to fulfilling God's purposes on the Earth. If and when He asks us to do something on His behalf, we gladly respond. For an example, as Matt has previously shared in this book, we prevented him from dying in a car accident by stalling his engine just as the speeding car

was driving down Fairview Ave. As per God's will, we removed the very large blood clot from his left leg so he could continue to live, help us with the EXODUS, and to be our Ambassador. As you have seen via the testimonial videos and as you'll read in the testimonials in the back of this book, God has directed us to heal others too. Finally, we are assisting the 'White Hats'.

94. **Do Xanue ever respond against those humans who try to capture or kill them?** No humans can ever capture or kill us. Can you capture and kill light? However, we do find it somewhat humorous and entertaining when humans think that they can try to capture and kill us. Eventually, knowing where their hearts and minds are at, we simply guide them out of the forest and away from our homes.

95. **How much influence do Xanue have in altering our minds or the way we think?** Although we do have the ability to subtly alter the thinking path of a human, we seldom ever do so. Normally, our communication is much more direct. However, in the case of needing the right individuals in place, working together, to help make the EXODUS occur in June of 2016, God permitted us to work behind the scenes much earlier in time in order to bring Matt, Cynthia, Mike, Steve, and Grady together. When we do so, it's only for positive reasons and only with God's permission. We never use these abilities for nefarious reasons.

96. **Will our Xanue clan let us know of things we should or should not do?** Once a solid friendship has been established with your local Xanue family and clan, they will most certainly attempt to guide you down a much more positive path in life. It's our goal to help you be connected with God, Christ, your neighbor, yourself, and to be better stewards of the Earth. Matt will tell you that we continually and patiently work on him to be more positive, don't let the trolls suck him into pointless debates, and to back away from his political postings on Facebook. In short, Matt is a very passionate soul and can

Chapter 15: Q&A with Zorth

be very stubborn at times. Yet, his heart is most definitely in the right place and he eventually follows our guidance sooner or later. In that same manner, we try to influence others too.

97. **If I'm in the forest where there might be some Xanue, and I'm in need of help, will they assist me if I reach out to them?** This is a hard question to answer because there are so many variables involved. First, we will not do anything outside of the will of God. Therefore, we need His okay. Then, we tend to be subtle on some occasions or not so subtle during other occasions. For example, we most definitely were involved in keeping three-year-old Casey Hathaway alive for three days while he was lost in the woods in North Carolina. It was not a bear.

98. **I hear that Bigfoot finds a human before the human sees the Bigfoot. Then the Bigfoot throws rocks or screams to scare the human away. How will humans ever understand or want to get to know the Bigfoot if they treat humans this way?** As I have stated previously, we know whether or not a human is kind, has a good heart, and an open mind. Humans are not very good at self-reflection and often think they're doing just fine when the truth of the matter is that they're negative, mean spirited, self-centered, arrogant, and fearful. Humans prefer to not have negative friends or family in their homes. Neither do we. However, I have said on numerous occasions, and Matt continues to repeat it over and over during his teachings, "If a kind person, with a good heart, and an open mind reaches out to us, we will reach back to them." If we guide a human out of the forest, it's because of their negativity or it's because they're walking into a dangerous situation with a bear, cougar, wolves, or Treykon and we're simply trying to keep them safe.

99. **Do we have to be in a particular place or just in a particular frame of mind in order to make contact?** If a kind person with a good heart and an open mind reaches out to us, we will reach back to them. Engage in self-reflection. Also, if you come outside in an attempt to engage us, don't bring your negative,

angry, closed minded friends or family members with you. We expect you to prove yourself via patience and persistence. You must earn our trust and friendship. Matt has done a very good job of repeatedly teaching the proper protocol for developing a relationship with the Xanue.

100. **We have heard and read stories of how Bigfoot rescued someone who was in danger, does Bigfoot interfere in human history as far as taking out bad people?** We never take out bad people. We don't kill humans. However, if a bad human is about to encounter death, we certainly won't intervene unless God directs us to do so. Most times, God does not direct us to do so. However, He has directed us to assist the 'White Hats'.

101. **Is there a song, a book, other art, or literature that us humans can look at or reference that was written or created by the Xanue?** No. We have no such need to do so. However, if you pay attention while you're out in the forest, you will see our art [tree structures and glyphs] and you will hear us singing in the distance.

102. **Do you whisper to humans in the scientific world to help them develop systems and processes that will help humankind?** We most certainly whispered into Steve Bachmann's ears hoping to influence him to build his electromagnetic pulsating device which ultimately helped to keep the portal open during the EXODUS. However, with that said, we are not a mechanical people. We have no need to build cars for transportation, skyscrapers, airplanes, homes, etc. Instead, we are a natural people. We have everything that we need in the forest.

103. **Were the Xanue present at any particular historic event in the history of the United States? In the history of the world?** We are always present. However, we are merely watching. On some occasions, we may pray to God to ask His permission to intervene. However, on most occasions, we're merely watching, observing, and waiting to hear God to ask us to intervene if He so desires. However, He has directed us to assist the 'White Hats'.

Chapter 15: Q&A with Zorth

104. **Do you visit people to give them lucid dreams?** We have the ability to communicate with humans while they are sleeping. We will only do so if something really important needs to be communicated to a human.
105. **Is there any popular landmark on Earth that was created by your people that was credited to humans?** The "Xs" that we construct in the forest are often credited to humans or winds or snow. Humans, Treykon, and other Aliens worked together to create many of the old large structures on the Earth.
106. **Did you help ancient humans or Natives build their homes or dig out caves for their dwellings?** No.
107. **Do you have any favorite games you love to play with each other, such as making sounds of animals or birds?** We most definitely do have a playful prankster side to us. Especially, during our younger years. The rules are simple: Have fun and don't physically hurt anyone or anything. For example, we just made a bouncing ball noise on the floor next to Matt's chair while I had him answering this question. Yet, there's no bouncing rubber ball.
108. **Have the Xanue ever helped raise human children or helped a family in need?** We have never raised a human child. However, we've been by their side helping to keep them safe and out of trouble, if and when God asks us to do so.
109. **Why are so many humans afraid of the Xanue?** To be quite honest, as a species, humans are afraid of most things that are new to them or that they don't understand. Therefore, many engage in what humans call a "Fight or Flight" response. The simple truth is that we exist outside of what humans are taught to be true and real. As a result, they fight or flight. However, if someone is willing to face their fears and embrace something outside of the worldview that they were taught to believe, then they end up learning that they have no need to fear the Xanue.
110. **Do the Xanue prefer day or night?** We enjoy the nighttime the best because we are mostly free to do our thing without

THE XANUE

outside interference from humans. However, we also enjoy the daytime too because we can watch the humans and interact with them. Our predicament is that we need to go into the trees during the daylight hours to partake of the energy from the sun and the nutrients in the ground through the roots of the trees. The good news is that we don't have to go into the trees every day, or if we do go into the trees during the day, we don't have to be there for the entire day to charge ourselves up. In short, we get to enjoy the best of both worlds, if we want to.

111. **Do the Xanue swim for pleasure?** Yes. We enjoy the water when we shapeshift into our flesh and blood predesignated form that God gave us.

112. **Do the Xanue ever hike and explore the forest just for fun or pleasure the way humans do?** We are the keepers of the forest and we protect all who dwell within. Therefore, we know the forest, as you humans might say, like the back of our hand. We most certainly enjoy living on and tending to God's green Earth.

113. **Do the Xanue play practical jokes on each other like humans do to each other?** Yes. Especially among our youth.

114. **Do the Xanue play practical jokes on humans, then laugh at their reactions?** Yes. Especially among our youth. The older we get, the more proper we become. However, the Xanue adults still have a sense of humor.

115. **I've heard of Native American stories where people have gone on to have husbands with the Forest People, is this true?** No. This is most certainly not true. The Xanue do not interbreed with humans. However, interbreeding has occasionally occurred between humans and the Treykon.

116. **Can humans learn to mind speak with animals?** Some humans do already. However, not everyone's brain is wired in the same manner. Everyone is gifted differently. [Please read 1 Corinthians 12:1-31].

117. **How does an individual determine if the Xanue are in an area and get their attention?** Please look for signs such as

foot tracks, tree structures, glyphs, large "X's," visuals, tree pops, voices talking, whistles, Orbs, or shimmering images. As Matt has been teaching on the behalf of the Xanue Council of Twelve, it takes a whole lot of time, patience, and persistence.

118. **How does an individual welcome the Xanue into their home in a suburban area?** Truth be told, many Xanue youth are inside most homes to simply observe and learn. Occasionally, they will playfully prank their hosts and are often misidentified as ghosts.

119. **What should we expect from the Xanue while interacting with them?** Kindness, love, encouragement to be a better person, medical scans and possible healings, mind speak, visions, pranks, observation, and joy.

120. **Where do the Xanue live?** We are in the trees and the trees are everywhere. However, we are not in every tree. So I ask you, where are the trees? Do you have trees in your backyard? Do you have trees in a park near your home? Are there trees in Central Park in New York City? You don't have to go deep into the wilderness to find us because we can simply be living in your backyard too.

121. **There seems to be a lot on interaction stories between humans and the Xanue in the USA, Canada, and England. Are the Xanue interacting with other humans around the world too?** Yes, we interact with humans around the world. Simply look at historic human works of art and you will occasionally see us in the pictures. Also, study human myths and legends and you will find many stories from all over the Earth where the humans believe in and interact with "Tree Spirits." That's us!

122. **Are "Night Sits" and "Sleeping Outside" the only way to be able to interact with the Xanue?** Although "Night Sits" and "Sleeping Outside" is not the only way to be able to interact with us, it is most certainly the best way. We are looking for a show of commitment, patience, persistence, and baby steps

of trust building with us. Many humans, including Matt, are afraid of the dark. However, Matt showed us his commitment, courage, and trust when he started doing "Night Sits" and "Sleep Overs" up on the mountain top at the Southern Oregon Habituation Area (SOHA) when he started coming alone. He showed us that he did not fear us by doing what he did. He faced his fears and it paid off. Are you willing to face your fears?

123. **Was there ever a time when the Xanue and humans lived as friends and cultured contact and communication?** Yes. We still do to this very day. That's what this book is all about.

124. **There have been many stories of healing, help and gifts from the Xanue. As with humans, are there also Xanue individuals who are malevolent or otherwise not kind or otherwise dangerous?** The human race often projects its own point of view, including their malevolent, dangerous, and nefarious behaviors, on to other species – especially the Xanue. However, we did not fall in the Garden of Eden like the human race did. We are connected with God, one another, and the Earth. We live and walk by faith in God and Jesus Christ. We are a kind, loving, gentle, caring, and joyful species. We do not hate, rape, steal, lie, murder, or go to war like the disconnected humans do.

125. **Do you reach out to those of us who are easy to communicate with, even when we've never gone out looking for you but have always known of your existence?** Most of the time, we wait for a kind person, with a good heart, and an open mind to reach out to us first. However, occasionally, we will initiate the pursuit of developing a relationship with a human.

126. **Are you able to hear thoughts from anyone or only those that you are directly connected to in a "mind speak session" that you initiated?** We are able to read the minds of all humans. We don't need to initiate a two-way communication session to know what humans are thinking and feeling.

Chapter 15: Q&A with Zorth

127. **Can you mind-speak from a great distance?** Yes. For example, Matt and I have an open line of communication. I know everything that he is thinking and feeling. He can ask me a question at any time and I will answer him. No matter where I'm at on the Earth, we can communicate via mind speak from afar.

128. **Are all Xanue peaceful if they encounter a human?** We are always a peaceful species. However, we won't hesitate to use intimidation to guide a negative human, Treykon, or Xuxiko out of our homes because they are never welcome there. That does not mean that we are not peaceful. We are simply preserving the peacefulness of our homes by guiding negativity away from us.

129. **If we need to cut down some trees on our property due to rotting, wind, or fire danger, is it okay with the Xanue? Are we cutting down someone's home?** You may proceed with managing the vegetation on your property, including the trees. We also manage trees in the forest when they are dying and become a danger to others. There are plenty of other trees for us to dwell in during the day.

130. **What can I do as a person who loves the Xanue, with all of my heart, to help your people?** If and when we are in need of help, we reach out to the appropriate individuals who we think will do the best job. In the meantime, please simply focus on being a better human being. Every day, you need to try a little harder than the day before to love God with all your heart, soul, strength, and mind, and also love your neighbor as yourself. You need to be a good steward of the Earth. Finally, you can reach out to us, connect with us, communicate with us, come out in your backyard and sit with us, play music for us, and tell stories or read books to our young ones. We also like it when humans read from the Bible to us. We prefer New Testament readings.

131. **I am certain we have a Xanue family here in our home. We have had a lot of activity since reading Matt's book last year.**

THE XANUE

We've had several episodes of deep, guttural growling in the house, witnessed by my husband and I, and today our 12-year-old son. We are wondering if the growling from the Xanue is just their way of saying hello and making their presence known, or coming from a place of anger? It is a bit startling when it happens. Your local Xanue are simply letting you know that they're there inside your home. They're saying "hello" to your family. Many people experience this from the Xanue. One thing I appreciate about Matt is his sense of humor. He usually asks people, "Did they hurt you or kill you?" The answer is obviously always "No." Growling doesn't always come from a place of anger. I have watched Matt play with his dogs and they growl at him from a space of playfulness or just to get his attention. My voice is deep and growly but I'm not angry.

132. **How does one learn the meaning of the glyphs from the Xanue?** The "X's" are the mark of the Xanue. We chose it as our representative symbol to let other entities know that this is our territory. We took the "X" from the Greeks because it is the CHI and represents Christ. The woven asterisks (*) found in the forests represents "Welcome" for humans from the Xanue. The "Ys" represent our desire to merge our two worlds together. A circle of rocks around an object represents the fact that we are surrounding you with our presence and love. Finally, "Teepee" structures represent an area where we can be found nearby inside the trees. Your local Xanue families will let you know what they mean by the glyphs they leave for you.

133. **Is there a way to learn, written, or through mind pictures or speak? This would greatly enhance the messages from the Xanue.** Mind speak utilizes the universal language that all created species in the universe understand. The universal language is used when humans pray to God. It is also used between all species. As I've already addressed, our language style that Matt refers to as "Squatchinese" is too complex for humans to learn. Mind speak is the best means of communication with us.

134. **How would one know that the glyph seen, is from the Xanue, in a known Xanue area, or feeling their presence etc.?** As you mature in your interactions with us, there will be no doubt in your mind that it was us who left the glyph for you. You will feel our presence and see other physical signs in the area as well.

135. **Can we enhance our use of our Pineal Gland (third eye to broaden our views) with help from the Xanue?** We do not enhance the third eye in humans. That process is between the God who gifts us all and the human who desires to grow. We are not all gifted in the same way. Yet, we are all equally important in the eyes of God.

136. **What is the easiest way for a human to tell if the Xanue are in or control an area? A feeling or signs?** The first thing to look for is one or more large "X" signs. Also, look for snapped trees and footprints in the ground. Listen with your ears and heart. If we are there, you will most likely sense our presence. You will get that feeling, like many humans talk about, of being watched.

137. **Do the Xanue keep people safe while they're camping in the woods?** It depends upon the circumstances, the people involved, and the will of God. Every situation is different. The most important thing for humans to do is be completely prepared for their hiking, camping, and hunting trips so they're not caught in a situation that they can't handle themselves.

138. **Is it annoying when people traipse through the woods whooping and tree knocking trying to communicate with you?** We think it's funny and entertaining. That's when we possibly enjoy playing some tricks on the humans such as tossing pinecones or small rocks near their feet, making vocal noises, pushing a tree over, or walking around them so they can hear our footsteps but they can't see us. Most importantly, we appreciate the time and effort that they are demonstrating to reach out to us. If they remain patient and persistent, we will reach back to them.

139. **What is the method of contact you would prefer?** Simply go outside in your backyard, play us some music, sing songs to us, and talk to us with your mouths and your minds. Demonstrate patience and persistence over time. We will reach back to you.

140. **If the Xanue people want to help us become closer to God and understand them, why do they scare us by their appearance and noises?** Yes, it is our goal to help humans to grow closer to God and to your fellow man. The real question is why do you choose to be scared by our noises and appearance. We have no intention of scaring humans unless we are trying to guide one or more negative humans away from our homes in the wilderness. Matt has been open about his first encounter with me on the mountain above the Oregon Caves National Monument Park. When you watch his early media interviews, he is very tearful and afraid. Later on, he owned his emotional responses and declared that I did nothing to make him so afraid. All I did was to observe his family and to make sure that he saw me uncloak and then cloak again. It took Matt a long time to own his emotional response to the situation. Ever since Matt successfully processed his own thoughts and feelings about the event, he is no longer afraid of our appearance or noises because he knows that we are not threatening or dangerous. He knows that we are simply different than him and that doesn't make us scary.

XANUE GUARDIAN QUESTIONS:

141. **Once the Xanue know us, are they able to locate us wherever we are through some natural 'homing signal'?** What one Xanue knows, we all know. Every living being possesses a unique energy signature similar to fingerprints. Once we have established a relationship with a human and we recognize their energy signature, then all Xanue know their energy signature. There's no homing signal involved in locating a human. Rather,

Chapter 15: Q&A with Zorth

there are simply Xanue almost everywhere and we recognize the human who passes us by. Then, because of the fact that what one Xanue knows, we all know, we are all aware of where Matt is at all times.

142. **What are the responsibilities of a Guardian?** First, I would like to let humans know that not everyone has a Xanue Guardian. Matter of fact, most humans don't have a Xanue Guardian. With that said, Xanue Guardians are assigned to a relatively small number of humans on Earth who have helped our people in a significant monumental way, such as the EXODUS. Humans are also assigned Guardians when God asks us to do so. Finally, because of our gift to see somewhat into the future in a limited manner, if we believe that a young human will grow up and eventually do something significant to help the Xanue in a significant monumental way, we will go out of our way to keep that human safe and protected just like we did with Matt during his lifetime.

143. **Are there part time Guardians?** Guardians usually do their guarding in the home area of where the human lives. However, during the Spring Vacation Break of 2019, Matt took his son, Grady, to Boston, Philadelphia, and New York City. During that time, the locals in the area gladly stepped up to provide protection while Matt was in the New England States. Ceska enjoyed the time off.

144. **Is 'Guardian Training' for younger Xanue or for more older Xanue?** The Xanue who desire to grow up and become Guardians are usually trained to become one during their adolescent years. Not everyone passes the test.

145. **When a human receives a Guardian, is it always for 'life' and are there changes in who the Guardian is?** Once again, not every human is assigned a Guardian. Matter of fact, most humans do not have a Guardian. In order to be assigned a Guardian, the human has to have done something very important to help out our people or they must be seen as having great potential to

THE XANUE

help our people in the future. Under these circumstances, when a human is actually assigned a Guardian, it is usually for life. There can be changes in Guardians based on many possible circumstances. For example, my nephew, Ceska, was assigned as Matt's Guardian in SOHA. My nephew, Onx, was assigned as Matt's Guardian during the temporary location between SOHA and SOIA. Then my son, Mogedue, was assigned as Matt's Guardian at SOIA. Finally, Ceska stepped up to the plate and enthusiastically accepted the role of Guardian for Life for Matt at his home in Chehalis, Washington. There are a total of eight families living on Matt's and Cynthia's property and they gladly help Ceska keep the Xuxiko and bad people away.

146. **Do humans always know when they have a Guardian?** If a human has a Guardian, they will know with one-hundred percent confidence.

147. **Can a human apply for a Guardian?** No. Once again, Guardians are assigned to a human based upon their potential of contributing to the benefit and welfare of the Xanue people. Also, they're given a Guardian for life if they have actually done something beneficial for the Xanue people. With that said, if a human has befriended a local Xanue family, although they won't be assigned a Guardian for life, it certainly doesn't mean that the local Xanue family won't be keeping watch over them.

148. **I heard that Matt and Cynthia have anywhere from one to six Guardians in their bedroom per night. Why so many?** Matt and Cynthia are on the Xuxiko radar and near the top of their hate list. Matt and Cynthia are responsible for education about the Xanue via books, camps, and conferences. Therefore, the Xuxiko are constantly looking for ways to intimidate them, persuade them to go down a different path, or to end their relationship. Therefore, Matt and Cynthia are on the top of our grateful list and protection list. We will do anything to keep them moving along safely down a positive path in the right direction.

Chapter 15: Q&A with Zorth

ORB QUESTIONS:

149. **What do the different colors of the Orbs mean?** The different color of Orbs represents the roles and status within the Xanue community.

150. **Does the color of the Orb have any significance?** Yes, they do have significance. They help the Xanue to know who they're dealing with and who to go to for certain forms of help, assistance, guidance, or protection. For example, the majority of the Xanue are white Orbs. Green Orbs are in charge of managing the forest. Yellow Orbs are our spiritual leaders. The blue Orbs are our healers. The red Orbs are our protectors from the Xuxiko. Finally, orange Orbs represent leaders in the Xanue community such as heads of clans, heads of tribes, and members of the Xanue Council of Twelve.

151. **What is the purpose of Orbs?** The purpose of Orbs is that they are the souls of all created beings in the universe. God is light. We are all created in God's image. We are light. We are all energy. The various created species that chose to obey God in the Garden of Eden eventually left and went to their new worlds that were created for them. Because they did no sin or rebel against God in the Garden of Eden, they were able to live as God intended them to live. They were able to freely exist in both Orb form or shapeshift into their predesignated flesh and blood form. However, because the human race rebelled against God and ate from the Tree of the Knowledge of Good and Evil, their Orbs were stuck inside their flesh and blood bodies. All humans have an Orb inside their body. You are the Orb. That is your soul. You are not a human having an spiritual experience. Instead, you are a spiritual being having a human experience. When we all die, our Orbs [souls] all go back to God.

152. **Are there different kinds of Orbs?** Yes and no. Yes, there are different colors of Orbs which I just explained in a previous

question. No, every Orb is a soul created by God. When we die, all Orbs return to God.

PHYSICAL BODY QUESTIONS:

153. **Do you know what the tingling sensation is that I get on my right shoulder blade area?** While we are in energy form, we may touch humans to conduct a medical assessment, or try to heal them, or simply just to say 'hello' to them. When we touch a human, they usually feel tingling energy at the point of contact.
154. **Is the brain of the Xanue split like the human brain?** Our brains are one. There is no split. A split brain is the sign of a fallen species. The split is intended by God to put a damper on all of the brain potential that the human species was created with before the fall. Many humans say that they're only using ten or fifteen percent of their brain capacity. They are correct. As they grow in faith, God helps them to utilize more of their brain to accomplish great things as well as to perform miracles of faith. God has put a damper on the human brain by splitting it as to minimize their destructive tendencies.
155. **I know we have two bands of light around our body so I'm wondering if the Xanue do as well?** Interesting. You think that it's a fact that you have two bands of light around your body and, therefore, you are wondering if we do too? The truth of the matter is that you're concluding that your assumptions are truth. Yet, they fall far from the truth. The truth is that you are light and those aren't bands. All light inside and around your body of flesh and blood is you and your energy. You are not like Saturn with rings or bands of light around you. You simply are light. All of the light, both inside and outside your body. Given the perspective I just shared with you, all created Beings of Light are the same. So, yes, we do too.

156. **What is the total population of the Xanue on the Earth?** How many trees are there on the Earth? We're in the trees and the trees are everywhere. Although we do not occupy every tree on the Earth, there are certainly more Xanue on the Earth than humans.

157. **When you raise your frequency, do you hear your bands of light spinning faster?** As I previously stated, the light that is observed comes from within. We are all Beings of Light. Light does not make sound. However, we do feel the differences in our vibrational frequencies. Since we vibrate at a higher or faster frequency than humans do, we often find ourselves lowering our vibrational frequency so that humans can see us in our flesh and blood bodies. When we are vibrating at our natural vibrational frequency, we exist outside the human's visual field of range.

158. **Can the Xanue shapeshift into inanimate objects like a stump?** No. We cannot shapeshift into inanimate objects. However, we can pass through inanimate objects such as stumps, doors, windows, walls, and metal. All we have to do is adjust our vibrational frequency to match the vibrational frequency of the inanimate object and then we can pass right through it. With that said, if the stump that you're asking about is alive, we can go inside the stump. Regarding shapeshifting in general, we can shapeshift into birds, reptiles, mammals, and insects. Humans are considered mammals.

159. **When the Xanue give birth, are they born in an Orb form or in a physical body form?** The answer to your question depends on which way the Xanue mother decides to give birth. She can give birth to her child in Orb form or physical form. Although the Orb form of gestation and birth takes longer, it is much less complicated than giving physical birth. The Xanue mothers who choose to give birth physically, want to experience the physical or tactile moment with their newborn child. If the Xanue mother chooses the option of giving physical birth, the complications

include remaining in her physical form waiting for the birth to occur, during the birth, and after the birth. Her Xanue husband is then responsible for protecting her while she's in a prolonged state of physical form, providing her with food, water, and other comforts. If there are already other older children in the family, they will help their father take care of their mother.

160. **As Beings of Light, why did you choose to take on such large, hairy, seemingly lumbering bodies?** God creates all sentient Beings of Light on the planet called Eden. We are all Orbs. When God creates a new species, He is the one who chooses what our flesh and blood forms will look like. God is very creative and has designed many different physical forms for Orbs to shapeshift into. The differences between the physical forms subtly change along an infinite continuum of possibilities. There are other sentient Beings of Light in the universe that look exactly like humans or almost like humans. Likewise, there are other forms that look similar to the Xanue such as the Treykon. However, they tend to be shorter, uglier, and more menacing looking in their appearance.

161. **As the Xanue children age, are they required to stay in their physical form for an extended period of time so that they can reach out to us?** The Xanue children are given the freedom to shapeshift between their Orb form and flesh and blood form. They spend a lot of time inside of human dwellings and learn from the things they see in drawers, cabinets, shelves, and inside of cars. They also enjoy observing the humans interact when they return home from work or school. The Xanue adults are mostly the ones who reach out to humans.

162. **In what form do you procreate?** The Xanue can procreate in either the Orb form or in our flesh and blood form. Procreation in our Orb form is very loving and spiritual. Procreating in our physical form is more tactile and sensual. Most Xanue parents will try both ways just for the experience.

Chapter 15: Q&A with Zorth

163. **Are female Xanue able to go into the trees while they're pregnant?** The female Xanue have a choice as to whether or not they want to deliver their baby in Orb form or physical form. If they choose to deliver in the physical form, then they must remain in their physical form and, therefore, will not be able to go back inside the tree until after delivery.
164. **How long does the Xanue pregnancy last?** The answer to this question depends on whether or not the Xanue mother chooses to give birth in Orb form or physical form. The gestation period for a physical pregnancy is approximately eight months. The gestation period in Orb form last approximately twelve months.
165. **At what age are the Xanue children able to go into the trees?** Immediately and with plenty of supervision from their family members.
166. **Do the Xanue have the ability to use infrasound? If yes, when do they use it?** Yes. We use it for many purposes such as intimidating negative humans to leave our homes in the forest; to cause humans to fall asleep; as one of our many tools for healing; and to alter the paths of animals in the forest.
167. **Do the Xanue have eye glow?** Yes. The fact that we are Beings of Light allows our energy to glow through our eyes. Also, thank you for using the correct terminology. Our eyes glow. Our eyes do not shine.
168. **Is the US government aware of the Xanue?** The U.S. government is aware of our existence. They are frustrated because they can't capture us or control us. They are constantly monitoring any and all of Matt's online communications. They intruded into the Southern Oregon Interaction Area (SOIA) which is why we chose to shut it down and relocate the meeting area for the Council of Twelve. Matt has agreed not to post online where it is located.
169. **Do the Xanue have a spoken language?** Yes. As I've previously stated, our way of communicating is very complex. Although

humans can learn the meaning of some of our words, they cannot ever learn how to communicate in the manner that we speak with one another.

170. **Do the Xanue have an odor all of the time or do they use it on selective occasions?** We do not have an odor all of the time. We do use odors on selective occasions such as to let humans know that we are in the area; to say 'hello' to our human friends who return to our homes for interaction; and not all of our odors stink. Our female Xanue like to emit very strong and lovely smelling floral odors such as your Hawaiian Leis.

171. **What is the purpose of the X's erected by the Xanue?** The small and large "X's" that we erect in the forest simply convey a message to other entities that we live in the area. This is our territory. Those entities who are our friends will confidently approach us for visitation time and fellowship. Those entities who are not our friends will know to avoid our territory. We chose the "X" to represent our people because it is also the Greek symbol for CHI – The Christ.

172. **What is the purpose of the asterisks made by the Xanue?** The woven asterisk simply means welcome. It is a similar gesture like some humans do when they leave a 'welcome mat' on their front porch.

173. **What is the purpose of the Y's erected by the Xanue?** The "Y" represents our desire and goal to help merge our two worlds together. Although it will take a long time to accomplish our goal, we feel confident that it will eventually happen.

174. **How does one know the difference between the Xanue and the Treykon?** We are Beings of Light and can shapeshift back and forth between our Orb form and our flesh and blood form. We are somewhat human in appearance. We are kind, gentle, caring, loving, benevolent, healers, and we walk by faith in God and Jesus Christ. We never harm humans. On the other hand, the Treykon, like the human race, fell in the Garden of Eden. As a result, they're locked into their flesh and blood

bodies. They are shorter than the Xanue. They stand anywhere between six to eight feet in height. Occasionally, some Treykon can grow as tall as nine or ten feet. This is rare. They are uglier, menacing, and malevolent. They tend to hide deeper into the forest in order to avoid humans because, in the past, they lost several skirmishes with the human race. If a lone hiker, camper, or hunter accidentally stumbles across their lair, they will kill the human, eat the human, and scatter their bones. We don't eat large mammals. The Treykon eat large mammals. My next point, I am very adamant about: We are not involved with UFOs in any way. However, the Treykon are involved with UFO activity. We love humans. The Treykon hate and despise the human race.

175. **Do the Xanue spend much time in physical form during the day besides when the female is pregnant?** Although we Xanue are one, we are also separate individuals with the freedom to make our own choices within the cultural constructs of our people. Therefore, the answer to your question depends on which Xanue you are asking. The spectrum of choices is wide. Some Xanue prefer to spend more of their time in Orb form. Other Xanue prefer to mix it up evenly. Finally, some Xanue enjoy spending more of their time in their flesh and blood form. The fact that we did not fall in the Garden of Eden provides us with the freedom to be ourselves and enjoy life in both forms. God is good.

176. **Do the Xanue speak when in physical form?** We speak with each other mainly through mind speak, regardless of what form we are in. Yes, we speak while we are in our physical form. If you haven't already done so, you need to listen to Matt's audio recordings of our spoken language.

177. **Have the Xanue ever abducted any humans?** No. We do not abduct humans. The Xanue are a gentle, kind, compassionate, and loving people. However, the Treykon do abduct humans. Usually, for nefarious reasons and sometimes for mating.

178. **Do the Xanue ever protect humans?** Yes. We have protected humans in many ways. Most of the time, our protection is not even noticed by the humans that we have protected. Other times, our helping of humans is noticed and documented as in the case of the three-year-old boy, Casey Hathaway, in North Carolina. We are not Bears. However, to a three-year-old human, the concept of a Bear was the only thing that he could come up with to describe his experience.

179. **Will we humans ever be able to fellowship and talk with the Xanue face to face?** The Xanue want the human race to learn how to interact with us in our natural form. We continue to occasionally show ourselves to humans while we are in our flesh and blood form. Matt and I talk with one another quite frequently. Although Matt and his friends have seen me in my shimmering image form on several occasions, Matt – The 13, has only seen me once in my flesh and blood form.

180. **Will we ever be able to see Xanue in your 'natural spirit form'?** Many humans have seen us in our 'natural spirit form" when we appear as Orbs. We are all Beings of Light. The Orb form is our 'natural spirit form' and it's your 'natural spirit form' too.

181. **Are Xanue paranormal abilities all present at birth or are some learned?** For the purpose of clarification, what you humans refer to as 'paranormal' abilities are simply 'normal abilities' for all sentient Beings of Light who never fell in the Garden of Eden. The 'natural abilities' of the faithful who believe in God and who chose not to rebel against Him were also exhibited by Jesus Christ, himself, during the last three years of his life and Earthly ministry. As Jesus once said to humans, "If you have the faith the size of a mustard seed, you can do what I do and more." Believing is seeing.

182. **Can Xanue remain underwater for long periods of time without breathing?** When we are in our Orb form, we do not have a need to breath oxygen. Light has no lungs and does not

Chapter 15: Q&A with Zorth

breathe. However, when we are in our flesh and blood form, we have to hold our breath while we are underwater. Since our lungs are larger than human lungs, we can hold our breath underwater for a very long time.

183. **Do Xanue ever have disabilities like deafness, blindness, injuries that don't heal?** There are similarities and major differences between humans and the Xanue. Many of the problems that you cited are the result of the humans being a fallen species. Because we did not fall in the Garden of Eden, we are spared from experiencing birth defects, disabilities, deafness, and blindness. On the other hand, while we are in our flesh and blood form, we can experience intestinal issues due to eating certain foods. For example, some of our Xanue children experienced upset stomachs after eating the peanut butter and raspberry sandwiches that Matt left for them at SOHA. Therefore, we shut the Xanue children down from eating from the gifting bowls until we figured out what was happening. It turned out that some of our Xanue children are allergic to peanuts. Now they know to leave the peanut butter and jelly sandwiches alone. Finally, although we do not experience birth defects or disabilities, some Xanue are vulnerable to allergic responses to the environment. Fortunately, our Xanue who are gifted as healers are able to remedy most problems.

184. **Are there peoples who live longer than Xanue?** Prior to the great flood, some humans lived longer than the Xanue. However, the environment of the Earth changed drastically afterwards and apparently shortened the lifespan of humans. Today, the average Xanue lives to be about two-hundred-twenty-years old. Some Xanue pass on before then and return home to God. Other Xanue have lived to around three-hundred-years of age. In short, our life span is about three times that of the average human lifespan.

185. **Can you please explain what the different colors of eyeshine represent?** As I previously stated, our eyes do not shine.

Eye shine occurs when you're in the woods at night and shine a flashlight on an animal such as a cougar, deer, bear, raccoon, or coyote. Their eyes will shine because they are reflecting the light. On the other hand, without any light being directed at us, you will see the glowing of the energy from within us coming our through our eyes. When we are in our flesh and blood form, you will most likely see our eyes glowing in the color of white. However, when we are in our natural form, vibrating at a higher frequency, you will see our shimmering image form accompanied by a faint red glow of energy coming out from within our bodies. Once again, our eyes do not shine. Instead, our eyes glow from the energy coming from within our bodies.

186. **Do Xanue prefer sunny days, cloudy days, rain, etc.?** When we are in our Orb form, the weather does not affect us. That's why we are able to endure the harsh environments of the northern hemisphere during the winter months or the hot summers of the desert regions. However, when we are in our flesh and blood physical form, we are effected by the environment and need to take precautions just like all other flesh and blood creatures. Nevertheless, we like all kinds of weather because we are simply grateful that God created us and has given us the gift of life to enjoy.

187. **What is your favorite Earth food?** The Xanue are able to access most Earthly foods from the natural environment just like humans can. Although we enjoy fruit, vegetables, nuts, birds, fish, and small rodents, most of us enjoy bread products the most. We cannot access bread products in the natural environment. We enjoy donuts, sweet Hawaiian bread, Cinnabon rolls, bagels, peanut butter and jelly sandwiches, cheese bread, cookies, cakes, and other bread products. Matter of fact, some of our younger Xanue will sneak and consume some bread products while they're inside of human homes exploring their environment.

Chapter 15: Q&A with Zorth

188. **Why don't we ever find Bigfoot bones in the forest?** When a Xanue dies, our Orb form returns home to be with God. We leave no bodies behind. On the other hand, the Treykon are stuck in their flesh and blood bodies just like the fallen human species. Therefore, when the Treykon die, they do leave behind bodies to be disposed of through burial.
189. **Does your conception and birth take place in a fashion similar to humans?** Yes. If the Xanue female decides to deliver while she's in her flesh and blood form, then the fashion is similar to humans.
190. **Do you experience pain while in your physical body?** Yes. When we are in our physical flesh and blood form, we experience just about everything that humans experience, including pain, fatigue, temperature changes, tactile sensations, hunger, thirst, and many other things.
191. **Do you age? Do you mark years as we do? How old are some of the elders?** As I have previously stated, we do age and our bodies do eventually die. Then our Orb form returns home to be with God, just like all sentient species do. Our average life span is about three times that of the human race. I am one-hundred- eighty-six-years old. Most of the Xanue Elders on the Council of Twelve are right around my age. Some are a decade older and some are about a decade younger.
192. **We humans see you as muscular and hairy people. What keeps you protected against the elements during winter?** During the winter months, most Xanue will remain in the Orb form because temperatures do not effect light. We do not experience heat or cold in our Orb form. Also, some Xanue will choose to migrate during the winter months to warmer climates if they wish to spend more time in their flesh and blood bodies. Contrary to some human theories, the Xanue do not migrate to follow the mammal food sources such as Elk or Deer. Rather, some Xanue migrate simply to stay warmer while in their flesh and blood bodies or because they prefer to

THE XANUE

soak in the energy of the sun in deciduous trees as opposed to conifer trees.

193. **Do you have the same skeletal structure as a human?** No. God is very creative and has designed many different skeletal structures and body types that exist throughout the Universe.

194. **Do you have more bones or fewer bones?** We are a much larger species than the human race. Therefore, God chose to use more bones to support our flesh and blood bodies.

195. **Do you have the same physiological processes as humans do, such as, eating, digestion, excretion, thirst, hunger, sleepiness?** Yes. We experience the same physiological processes that humans do while we are in our flesh and blood form.

196. **I am wondering how the Xanue deal with cold temperatures and snow. Do they migrate or simply stay in the trees?** While we are in our Orb form, we do not experience temperatures. Some Xanue like where they live in the northern hemisphere and simply choose to spend most of their time in Orb form during the harsh winter months. Other Xanue, who enjoy being in their flesh and blood form more often, will migrate to warmer climates during the harsh winter months. When they migrate, it's not to follow the mammal food supply because we don't eat large mammals. Instead, they're migrating to find trees that will sustain them until they can return to their homes in the spring, summer, and fall months.

197. **What happens to the Xanue's physical bodies when they die?** God created all sentient Beings of Light with the ability to shapeshift back and forth between our Orb form and flesh and blood form. It takes more energy to remain in our flesh and blood form. Therefore, when some sentient Beings of Light decided to rebel against God's simple test in the Garden of Eden, they were locked into their flesh and blood form which utilizes more energy and remains constant all the way through to death. Because the human's Orb form returns home to God after death, there is no more energy or life force to sustain the

Chapter 15: Q&A with Zorth

human body so it decays. On the other hand, the Xanue are not permanently locked into our flesh and blood bodies and, therefore, we expend much less energy than humans do to maintain the flesh and blood body. When our body has aged to the point of death, our Orb form simply returns home to God and we leave no body behind.

198. **Since the Xanue are able to appear in different energy forms, do their physical bodies simply cease to exist when they die?** Exactly!

199. **How do you think the climate changing will impact the Xanue people?** The Earth's climate has always been changing ever since God first created it. This is true for all habitable planets that God has created. Climate changing is nothing new. Therefore, we simply shapeshift back and forth between our Orb form and flesh and blood form. Sometimes, some Xanue will simply migrate to another part of the Earth.

200. **As Beings of Light, does our weather, hot or cold affect you as it does us?** Weather does not affect light. However, if we are in our flesh and blood form, then our bodies can be affected by the environmental temperatures. We simply adapt by shapeshifting back into our Orb form or migrate to a warmer climate during the winter months. All Xanue choose to handle their adaptation to the changing weather conditions differently.

VISUAL QUESTIONS:

201. **The Xanue are around me all of the time. I live with one. They make sounds, heal me, but they never let me see them in full body form. Why won't the Xanue let me see them?** As I have previously shared, the Xanue want the humans to learn to interact with us and see us in our natural form. We naturally vibrate at a higher frequency than humans do which takes us outside your visual field of range. It doesn't mean that you can't

THE XANUE

see us. You simply need to work on training your eyes to see us in our shimmering image form. Also, you need to work on sensing our presence when we are with you. You don't need to see us in our flesh and blood form. Believing is seeing.

202. **Do the Xanue all look alike?** No. We vary in appearance just like humans do.

ABILITY QUESTIONS:

203. **Do you have abilities that humans have forgotten how to use in order for you to communicate with us? If yes, can humans get these abilities back?** We have normal abilities that humans have been prevented from using due to the fall of man in the Garden of Eden. God has put a damper on the human brain by splitting it. However, humans can regain some of the natural abilities that God created all sentient Beings of Light to experience simply by walking by faith, belief, and obedience to God and Jesus Christ. Then humans can do what Jesus did and more simply because of faith. This includes being about to communicate more clearly via mind speak. Believing is seeing.

204. **Since your capabilities are on a higher level than humans, would it be true that your emotions or feelings are on a higher level also?** Yes. The Xanue are one people. We are all connected with God, with one another, and with the Earth. What one Xanue knows, we all know. What one Xanue feels, we all feel.

205. **Can the Xanue travel to other planets in other solar systems, and if so, where are they?** Yes. The twenty-five- percent of the Xanue population that has the ability to manipulate portals can travel to other planets as long as they have the approval of the Xanue Council of Twelve. We send out ambassadors to make contact with other sentient Beings of Light who did not fall in

Chapter 15: Q&A with Zorth

the Garden of Eden. We tend to avoid fallen species because of their impure hearts, motives, and behaviors. It takes great patience to interact with a fallen species who lack a belief and faith in their Creator. They tend to worship the created rather than the Creator and they think they can become Gods.

206. **Do the Xanue have hobbies?** The Xanue people have varying interests as well as likes and dislikes. All Xanue spend their leisurely time in different ways just like humans do.

207. **Do the Xanue make their own music?** Yes. We have many songs that the Xanue people sing. However, our music is different than that of the humans. We sing a capella and the lyrics usually last in a couple of sentences or a paragraph at the most. We enjoy listening to most of the music made by humans, as long as it's positive. Occasionally, we will come into your homes and listen to your music. For example, we enter the home of Matt and Cynthia to watch American Idol, The Masked Singers, and The Voice. The music made by humans is beautiful and soothing to our ears.

208. **Do Xanue have 'perfect memory'?** Yes. We do. That's the advantage of being one connected people without split brains.

209. **Do you see colors that we don't?** We see colors that humans don't see. Also, we see images that humans don't see. However, we don't see everything that God can see.

210. **Is your sight and hearing far superior to ours?** Yes.

211. **Is your range of sound and smell far greater than ours?** Yes.

212. **Do Xanue ever alter our sight, hearing, brain, etc. to help us see, hear, or understand them better?** At times, yes. However, it depends on the human that we are working with. Everyone is wired differently in their brains. Some humans are easy to work with and other humans are very difficult to work with.

213. **Can Xanue see through solid objects?** We have the ability to see energy signatures through solid objects such as the walls of a home or office building. That is how we are able to keep tabs on the whereabouts of certain humans – both good and bad.

214. **Do Xanue understand the laws of physics that govern your paranormal/supernatural abilities?** As I previously shared, our abilities only appear to be 'paranormal' or 'supernatural' to humans. However, they are simply 'normal' or 'natural' abilities to us. This is the way God created all of us to be. However, with the fall of man in the Garden of Eden, the human brain was split, and humans were locked into their physical bodies. All sentient Beings of Light, who did not fall in the Garden of Eden, possess these 'normal' and 'natural' abilities. As a result, we have the simple ability to manipulate quantum physics just like Jesus did during his three-year Earthly ministry. Some humans that have the faith the size of a mustard seed are also able to do so, just as Jesus promised.

215. **Are Xanue able to read in any language that they are able to speak?** Yes. Throughout human history, we have been watching and observing. We are able to read and speak all human languages, both ancient and modern. We are also able to read and speak all alien languages who have spent time dwelling on the Earth.

216. **Xanue seem to love music. Do you have any kind of organized way to learn music and perform it for others? Do you have musical instruments?** We sing together several times a day. We sing in praise to God. We sing of the blessings God has bestowed upon the Xanue. We express our joy and gratitude through a capella music. We do not have instruments. That is why we also enjoy listening to human music because of your different genres and use of instruments. We love positive human music and avoid negative and angry human music.

217. **Have you heard any of the 'music of heaven'? If so, what is it like?** No. Heaven is reserved for those who have passed on. We have not heard the heavenly choirs. Though I am certain that it is beyond anything that any of us can imagine. I look forward to hearing it one day.

218. **Do Xanue practice 'morphing' into different forms 'for fun' or is there a greater purpose/reason to 'morph'?** Our younger Xanue will practice morphing and even sometimes have some fun while doing so. It is very interesting to see how their humor comes through when they are playing around and having fun. They've created some very interesting blends of physical species from the Earth. They are not permitted to shapeshift into such creative images within the presence of humans. We do not want to scare humans. Finally, as adult Xanue, we will morph into other organic creatures for a variety of reasons in an attempt to communicate with or guide humans down a particular path along their journey in life.

219. **Can the Xanue alter weather events to any degree?** Yes, but only if it's within God's will for us to do so. While staying at the Southern Oregon Interaction Area (SOIA) during the fall of 2018, on two occasions during the same night, Matt actually silenced the harsh winds simply by commanding them to stop within his mind. This confirmed for other Xanue that Matt was the proper choice as the Ambassador to the Xanue Council of Twelve. As I have stated previously, Jesus clearly taught that if humans had the faith the size of a mustard seed, then they can do what he did and more. In this situation, Matt merely exercised his faith in Christ. Also, he wanted to sleep without the harsh winds blowing on him and his friends all night long. Matt is no saint but he is a faithful failure.

220. **Since the Xanue know all the languages on this planet, do they know how to read and write our language as well?** Yes.

221. **Do you read, or write, or simply communicate telepathically?** Amongst ourselves, we communicate mostly via mind speak. We have no need to write anything down because all of our history is stored in our collective memory. We are one people.

222. **Can you speak any human language you desire?** Yes. We can speak and read all ancient and modern human languages.

THE XANUE

SEEING INTO THE FUTURE QUESTIONS:

223. **Did the Xanue know in advance that the eruption at Mt. St. Helens was going to happen? Were any Xanue injured?** Yes, we knew about the impending eruption of Mt. St. Helens and were able to move our people to areas far away from the blast zone. No Xanue were injured. However, there were humans and Treykon killed in the explosion.

224. **Where do you think the human race will be in 100 years' time?** We are only permitted to see into the future by around fifty- years at the most. Usually less than that amount of time. We are not permitted to see all things or speak of all things. God has His plans. Even Jesus, the Son of God, said that he nor the angels know the day and hour of the return of the Son of God. Only the Father knows. With that said, we hope to have as much positive influence as possible on the human race between now and then.

225. **Can you travel forward in time?** We have access to portals that can take us to anywhere on the Earth, the universe, and time. However, we can only use the time travel portal to go into the future if God permits us to do so. We can go back into the past but we are not allowed to influence the past. We can only learn from the past or the future and try to influence the present.

226. **Since the Xanue were here on the Earth before mankind, did they know ahead of time that we would also end up on this planet too?** We did not know that the human race was coming until God informed us of their fall in the Garden of Eden. He assigned to us the responsibility of trying to influence humans to reconnect with God, one another, and the Earth. We are our brother's keeper. We are all children of God.

227. **At 58 years old, would a person live to see humanity restored to its loving, peaceful, roots?** No. Humanity has never experienced life as God intended it to be because of the fall of man in the Garden of Eden. There is no history of man with loving

and peaceful roots. Man has only known conflict, competition, divisiveness, and dominion. Humans have never been one because of the fall. Humans will never experience God's intended love and peace until they reconnect with Him, one another, and the Earth through faith in Jesus Christ. Humans cannot and will not accomplish this on their own without faith.

228. **Will the second coming of Jesus Christ happen anytime soon?** In your Bible, Jesus clearly stated that no one knows the day or hour, including himself. Jesus clearly stated that only the Father knows when that time will come. With that said, I am pleased that you asked that question because it indicates that your focus is in the right place. Unfortunately, there are people who don't even believe that Jesus came the first time. They will be greatly caught off guard when he returns in the clouds for the entire world to see.

WHAT ONE KNOWS, THEY ALL KNOW QUESTIONS:

229. **When a Xanue uploads the memories of one human, do all of the Xanue species gain that knowledge?** Yes, what one Xanue knows, we all know. We are one people. We are all connected.

230. **Since the Xanue have been on the Earth for millions of years, is the long history of the Earth also uploaded to all of the Xanue?** Yes. We have all of the history that we have experienced stored within our collective memory.

231. **Do the Xanue people attend any type of schooling or conferences where they teach one another?** We do not have formal training as humans do. We are all connected so our children learn as they grow older. They gain knowledge from the collective memory of the Xanue people as well as from personal instruction, guidance, and observation.

232. **Do the Xanue children go to school?** No. We have no educational institutions.

233. **Is the history of your people all contained in your collective memory or by some other means?** All history that we have experienced or observed has been stored in our collective memory.

234. **If "what one knows, they all know" - How is it that 75% of them don't know how to manipulate the portal?** As I've heard Matt say, "Everyone knows how a basketball is dunked in a game. Just because everyone knows how a basketball is dunked does not give everyone the ability to dunk a basketball." In the same way, it appears that approximately twenty-five percent of the Xanue people are born with the ability to manipulate the portals. They can only take themselves through the portal. That is why we needed the assistance to help us with the EXODUS. The electromagnetic pulsating device built by Steve Bachmann allowed us to have the necessary energy to create a shunt that could hold the portal open on both ends and allow the rest of our family and friends to come through the portal to Earth. At present, it still appears that only about twenty-five percent of the Xanue people are born with the ability to manipulate the portals. Although we are one people, we are gifted in many different ways. Knowledge does not guarantee ability.

235. **Is there anything private or personal among the Xanue?** Yes. "What one knows, we all know" simply implies a collective access to the memory archives among our people. Although we are one people, we most certainly do have our private moments with our mate, family, and friends.

SPIRITUAL QUESTIONS:

236. **How do the Xanue tie into God (i.e., Do they have a spiritual purpose)?** All created sentient Beings of Light have been created to 'tie into God' or be connected with God and to have

Chapter 15: Q&A with Zorth

a spiritual purpose. However, every newly created species does not pass the test in the Garden of Eden. If a created species fails the test in the Garden of Eden, they become disconnected from God and from one another. On the Earth, we are cohabitating with the human race. God has asked us to assist Him in the process of helping the human race to reconnect with Him via faith in Jesus Christ, as well as to reconnect with one another, and the Earth that God has given to us to be good stewards of. We are doing our best to accomplish this goal one human at a time. We could use the help of enlightened humans to spread the word.

237. **I was pretty excited about the Xanue until Matt interjected all of this God and Jesus crap into the equation. Can't we just get to know the Xanue and interact with them without having to buy into all of this fairy-tale God and Jesus stuff?**
We Xanue have a sense of humor. We won't hesitate to chuckle or laugh when something provokes us to do so. Your question is one of those moments. You do realize that there are a lot of humans who think that your belief in the Xanue is a fairy-tale story, right? You talk about our existence and the opportunity to interact with us as a fact – not a fairy-tale. Yet other humans mock you when you speak with such confidence and boldness. Don't you realize that you're doing the exact same thing to humans who believe in the existence of God and Jesus Christ as if it's a matter of fact – not a fairy-tale? More importantly, don't you realize that you're doing the exact same thing to us – the Xanue. We don't just simply believe that God and Jesus Christ exist, we know for a fact that they exist. However, you want to believe and interact with us as a matter of fact while rejecting the fact that we are telling you the complete truth. In short, if you want to get to know us and interact with us, then you must accept the complete package. The complete package is that God, Jesus, the Holy Spirit, Xanue, humans, Satan, and the Xuxiko all exist. You don't get to pick and choose who you

want to exist and who you don't want to exist. That's not the way it works.

238. **Does only one Creator exist who has created everything or is everyone creating their own reality?** There is only one God. He is the Alpha and the Omega – The beginning and the end. There is only one reality created by God. With that said, you most certainly have some influence on your life and destiny based on your free will choices. Not everything that sounds spiritual is sound.

239. **Can the Xanue see our aura?** We can see the energy signature of all humans, including that light that shines from within that you refer to as an aura.

240. **Do the Xanue people reincarnate? If yes, do they come back to where they died or do they go to other planets and what forms do they take on?** When any sentient Being of Light dies, we all go back to God. What God decides to do at that moment in time is up to Him. God's plans and purposes are not always easy to understand until He reveals his purpose to each individual at that moment in time. God is good.

241. **When the Xanue die, where do they go?** When all sentient Beings of Light die, including the Xanue, we all go back to God.

242. **After the Xanue die, do they continue to learn and grow spiritually and to what end?** After all sentient Beings of Light die, we all go back to God. At that point in time, He determines what each individuals path will be.

243. **After the Xanue die, do they eventually become Gods?** There is only one God. He is the Alpha and the Omega – The beginning and the end. There were not Gods before Him and there will be none after Him. Not everything that sounds spiritual is sound.

244. **The Xanue obviously are around and observe the misbehaviors of human children. How do you stop any negative influence of human children on the Xanue children?** Human

Chapter 15: Q&A with Zorth

children exhibit negative misbehaviors because of your species disconnectedness from God and one another. Good parenting helps some human families to raise more appropriate children. The fact that our species is one, connected with God and one another, prevents our children from mimicking such negativity.

245. **How do you protect the Xanue children from the evil in this world?** The unity of being one connected people combined with our daily walk of faith in God and Jesus Christ prevents our children from choosing evil over love.

246. **Was the Earth chosen by the Xanue to immigrate to due to human's compassion for other species?** When we realized that our home world's sun was slowly burning out, with God's permission, we sent scouts through portals to explore and find a planet for our people to colonize. When the scouts returned and reported to the Council of Twelve, after much prayer and discussion, we decided to send the twenty-five-percent of our population who could manipulate the portals to colonize the Earth. We arrived during the last period of the dinosaurs. There were no humans on the Earth during the time of our arrival. We were here first. God chose to send your Adam and Eve through the portal to the Earth because of our compassion for other species.

247. **What name do they give their most important holiday – the solar eclipse?** The Xanue view the solar eclipse as a symbolic representation of our old sun burning out leading to the slow death of our former home world and then living under a new sun on our new home world – the Earth. This is our most sacred holiday. We refer to it as "The Great Rebirth" of the Xanue people. We are grateful to God for the opportunity that He provided regarding our relocation to Earth and for the EXODUS.

248. **What does Zorth say are the most important things that Xanue families want as far as the type of interactions with us?** The Xanue people live in the natural environment.

Therefore, it is special to us when humans take the time and make the effort to come outside and visit with us. As I have previously stated, we enjoy it when you talk with us with your mouth or in your mind. We enjoy your singing, whistling tunes, playing instruments, or playing music to us with your electronic gadgets. Whether or not we choose to take anything, we appreciate the heart and attitude behind your gift giving to us. Most important of all, we enjoy the fellowship of humans who are trying hard every day to reconnect with God, their neighbor, and to be better stewards of the Earth that God has given us to tend.

249. **What does Sayreah mean when she said, "Agathos. Oh come, you should be positive about living with us?" Was that just for Matt ("The 13") and Cynthia or for all of us?** Our people are very positive and full of joy. We are grateful every day to God and Jesus Christ for how they provide for us. We are not a fallen species. We are connected. We experience never ending love and encouragement. Therefore, we sometimes have difficulty understanding the negativity that humans struggle with on a daily basis. Until recently, Matt constantly struggled with whether or not we Xanue are who we say we are or if we are demons attempting to deceive him and use him to trick other people into going down the wrong path. He was getting hammered everyday online by other humans who were accusing him of being deceived, a cult leader, and negatively influencing other people against God. That night, outside by the fire pit area in their backyard, Matt and Cynthia were talking about this very issue. Cynthia reminded Matt about all of the people whose lives have changed for the positive, including reconnecting with God and their neighbor. She reminded him about all of the love and healings. She encouraged him to see the positive rather than the negative. As they were inside the house, Sayreah felt compelled to speak into the Bionic Parabolic Microphone Dish and encourage Matt to be positive.

Chapter 15: Q&A with Zorth

So, to answer your question, the message was primarily for Matt. However, in general, it applies equally well to all other humans who want to live with the Xanue people as family and friends.

250. **If I build a fence around my yard to keep the Coyotes and Deer out, so we can sleep more soundly and safely on our cots at night, will this hinder the Xanue in any way?** No. Fences do not hinder our ability to approach you or access you. Neither to the walls and doors of a house. All we have to do is match the vibrational frequency of the fence, walls, or door and we can walk right through it.

251. **How can someone who is disabled, and cannot even go out on my porch, interact with the Xanue?** We can come inside homes to visit people. As in all of the other situations previously addressed, we want to see commitment over time displayed via patience and persistence. Some humans say that they want to get to know us but they don't put in much effort to convince us otherwise. For example, between the time Matt and his family encountered me up on the mountain above the Oregon Caves National Monument Park on July 1, 2000 and the EXODUS in June of 2016, he had spent a total of four-years with boots on the ground in the forest attempting to earn our trust and friendship. He drove one-thousand miles, roundtrip, once or twice a month, for several years to spend time with us. Yet, some people who have learned from him via his lectures, videos, or books want what they want and they want it now. They're impatient. They give up after a few days, weeks, or months. Patience and persistence is a must if you're desiring to earn our trust and friendship. Fear repels us and trust compels us. Simply continue to reach out to us and we will reach back to you.

252. **What can I do for the Xanue that would be of benefit to them?** If we have need of anything from you, we will ask you. Until that point in time, we simply want to help you reconnect

with God, your neighbor, and the Earth. Live a life of faith, hope, and love. Be who God originally intended you to be.

253. **Would it be possible for the Xanue to teach me about God and help me get a closer relationship with Him?** You humans can be silly sometimes. You have everything you need to learn about God and how to grow closer to Him. Simply, read your Bible – especially the New Testament. Also, fellowship with like- minded believers. Even Matt and Cynthia are finally going back to church to fellowship with others. This is the first time that Matt has seriously plugged himself into a church for the past eighteen years. A log burns brighter with other logs. It doesn't burn so bright all by itself. Finally, Matt did a very good job of simplifying the message of the gospel of Jesus Christ: Love God with all your heart, soul, strength, and mind; and love your neighbor as yourself. If you do these two things, you fulfill all of the Laws. It's not complicated. I love it when Matt tells others to use the KISS method – Keep It Simple Silly.

254. **Do the Xanue come from a different soul family/race or are the Xanue an original soul family?** We are an original soul family. We do not come from another race.

255. **Do the Xanue have full soul memory or have they retained their full memory?** We are not a fallen species. Therefore, we are one. As a result, we have a collective memory that holds a vast amount of historical, cultural, intellectual, emotional, and spiritual memories. This information also includes human history. We don't need to go to a library or sit down in front of a computer to access the above information. We simply have access to it at any time we wish to know something. The collective memory is available and accessible to all Xanue.

256. **Is there any advice you could give me for personal improvement?** Keep it simple silly. Every day, ask yourself is what I'm about to do or say an act of love towards God, my neighbor, myself, or the Earth? Simply try to be a little better today than

Chapter 15: Q&A with Zorth

you were yesterday. Live your life for others rather than for yourself. Let others see the love of God and Jesus Christ shine through you everyday life. Let your light shine.

257. **Have the Xanue ever seen Hell?** We are not a fallen species. Only those who reject God and Jesus Christ end up seeing Hell.

258. **Do Xanue ever have confrontations with Satan himself?** We have only experienced confrontations with Satan's demons – the Xuxiko. Unlike God, Satan is not omnipresent. Therefore, he needs to manage his time well and where he chooses to raise Hell.

259. **Do Xanue interact with angels?** On occasion, we have worked with God's angels to accomplish tasks for fulfilling His purposes. We consider it a great honor when we are asked to help in any form or manner. We are helping the 'White Hats'.

260. **Can Xanue sense when a human is close to the end of their life?** Yes. A human's life-force energy begins to dampen and they're no longer able to channel enough energy to keep their bodies going. They conserve their Orb energy and eventually let go of their bodies.

261. **Are there other peoples in the universe who have not fallen From God's grace?** Yes. God has created many sentient Beings of Light in the Garden of Eden. God continues to create sentient Beings of Light in the Garden of Eden. The Universe is vast and consists of many dimensions. About two-thirds manage to pass the test. About one-third fail the test. No one falls from God's grace. Instead, they fall out of fellowship or connectedness with God because of their rebellious choice to eat from the Tree of the Knowledge of Good and Evil. In spite of the disconnectedness, God's grace abounds. He has made a way back to fellowship and connectedness with Him via faith in Jesus Christ.

262. **Can Xanue still fellowship with loved ones who have died?** There is a veil between life and death. On occasion, God allows paths to cross. There is always a reason for when and why He permits it to happen. This is not a routine occurrence.

263. **Xanue seem to be contented, happy people overall – is that true?** We are not a fallen species. We are one Xanue people. We are connected with one another and with God. We live in the love and the joy of the Lord every day. We have much to be grateful for, especially after the EXODUS.
264. **Will you be in Heaven with us?** When the bodies of all sentient Beings of Light die, all of our souls all go back to God. At that time, He decides what is in store for each individual.
265. **Do you ever get temporarily overwhelmed by all the evil and sin and suffering taking place on Earth and perhaps around the Universe?** We are not a fallen species. Therefore, we live by faith, hope, and the love of God. We are continually connected with Him and one another. It is difficult at times to see evil, sin, and suffering on the Earth because of the choices that the humans have made and continue to make on a daily basis. We count it a privilege and honor when God gives us tasks to fulfill that might help the human race move closer to Him.
266. **It seems the Xanue would be an extension of the Holy Spirit's work in our lives – is that true?** We are certainly given tasks to complete on occasion by God's Holy Spirit and enjoy doing so when asked.
267. **Are the Xanue the Nephilim?** No. We are the Xanue. We are sentient Beings of Light who were created in the Garden of Eden just like all other sentient Beings of Light. We came from a different planet before we colonized the Earth. We do not mate with any other species than our own. We are not the byproduct of two other species mating. However, the Treykon have mated with humans before the great conflict between them and man and some still do today.
268. **Will mankind ever be able to show the same love to one another and have the same kind of bond with one another that the Xanue do for each other?** Yes. If a human is willing to reconnect with God, their neighbor, themselves, and with the Earth, then the love of Christ will dwell within them.

269. **If you die here on Earth, do you return to your interdimensional state?** When any sentient Being of Light dies, their soul or Orb returns to God. This truth applies to all sentient Beings of Life in the Universe and all of the multiple dimensions found within. We all return home to God.

270. **Besides faith in God, can you offer any advice for humans to be serene or have complete peace of mind?** Live in the present. Don't regret yesterday and don't fear tomorrow. Live for others and not for yourself. Love God, love your neighbor, love yourself, and take care of the Earth. Be grateful for everything and always forgive.

271. **Did you visit with Jesus and/or His disciples during his boyhood or during His three-year ministry?** Personally, I was not alive at that time. That was over two-thousand-years ago and I'm not quite two-hundred-years-old. However, the Xanue who were alive at the time can attest to the existence of Jesus Christ, his Earthly ministry and miracles, as well as his death on the cross and resurrection from the dead. We were quiet observers and witnesses to the work of Jesus Christ as he strove to reconcile humans with God. We were in the trees. God is good.

272. **Do animals have spirits?** Some do and some don't.

273. **Do the Xanue believe that the ultimate sin is the taking of a life?** The ultimate sin is not the taking of a life. Many of God's faithful failures have taken lives. Even God has taken lives. The ultimate sin is the blasphemy of God's Holy Spirit – the rejection of the power and conviction of the Holy Spirit. God can and will forgive anything that a human has said or done, including the taking of a life. However, He will not forgive the rejection of His Holy Spirit. The blasphemy of the Holy Spirit, which is the rejection of the Holy Spirit's power, voice, and conviction of sin.

274. **Did the Xanue have contact with Old and New Testament figures such as Adam and Eve, Noah, Abraham, Moses, Elijah, David, Jesus, etc. through the will of God?** We are in

THE XANUE

the trees and the trees are everywhere. Our existence is found in the Old Testament when the writers referred to the trees as singing or clapping their hands. That was us. We never interfered in God's plans. However, we joyfully participated in any task that He gave us to help fulfill his plans. God is good.

275. **Xanue rites of religion or worship. Most humans believe in some form of a creator who made all things, and with a purpose to fulfill. Most beliefs followed by humans have traditions and ordinances associated with them (i.e., Prayer, rituals, etc.) to honor God. Do the Xanue use similar ordinances such as baptism and sacraments, and do you use formal worship traditions to honor God?** When a race of fallen sentient Beings of Light attempt to reconnect with God on their own, regardless of the planet they live on, they routinely develop rites of religion or worship, traditions, and ordinances to honor their perception of God. However, when you're connected with God, none of the above are necessary because you're simply in a relationship with Him. You don't need to do any of the above to be in a relationship with your spouse, family, or friends, do you? No. Instead, you simply interact with them in a day to day relationship. You spend time with them. You talk with them. You laugh with them. You love them and they love you. It's simply a connection – a loving relationship. God does not want your piety. God simply wants your heart, soul, mind, love, and friendship.

276. **The Xanue were here on Earth long before Jesus Christ was here and the old Hebrew texts were discovered. What is the reason for clan leaders having old Hebrew names such as Zachariah, Isaac, Samuel, etc.?** Not all clan leaders have what you refer to as old Hebrew names. Please remember, although the Xanue are one people, we consist of many individuals with regional differences and customs around the Earth. Individuality is also very much a part of who we are. Therefore, in some regions of the Earth, some Xanue have

adopted the names of which you talk about. However, in other regions of the Earth, they will adopt local names or draw from many Xanue names that exist as well. I can guarantee you that none of the Old Testament Hebrew names ever consisted of Zorth. I was named after my great, great, great, grandfather. When a Xanue names one of their children after a human, it is an honor to do so.

277. **When I pray to Jesus, do the Xanue also hear me and reach out if I am asking Jesus instead of asking the Xanue directly?** Always pray to God or Jesus. Never pray to the Xanue. We are not gods. We are fellow children of God. We are your brothers and sisters. Therefore, you pray to God but you talk with us. There's a major difference between the two approaches to communication. With that said, there are times when we hear what a human is praying about. We never intervene in any situation unless God directs us to do so. We consider it a privilege and honor if and when God seeks our assistance as His faithful servants. God is good.

278. **Since you are Beings of Light and without sin, where do you spend Christmas? Is it in heaven or on Earth?** Unless God makes special arrangements, no one goes back home to be with Him until after our bodies die. Therefore, we spend Christmas on the Earth. Now with that said, the meaning of Christmas is different for us than it is for humans. Because we did not fall in the Garden of Eden, we have no need for atonement to reconcile ourselves to God through the blood of Christ like the human race is in need of. From our initial creation in the Garden of Eden, we simply fellowship with God and His only begotten Son, Jesus Christ, as a glorious routine daily matter – the way it was meant to be from the get go. However, throughout the entire Universe and its multiple dimensions, Jesus has and continues to take steps to help atone for the sins of the various fallen sentient Beings of Light. Jesus, the carpenter on Earth, is a different figure on a different planet,

THE XANUE

helping to right the wrongs and reconcile that particular species back into a relationship with God. As Matt has shared earlier in this book about Jesus Christ, "All things were created through Him, by Him, and for Him. All things visible and invisible. Christ holds all things together. Jesus is the firstborn among many." He is the God Particle.

279. **What awaits us after death?** When our bodies die, our souls or Orbs go back home to God. At that point in time, God determines what happens next for us on an individual basis.

HEALING QUESTIONS:

280. **Do you have to have permission from the person before you heal them?** No. However, we do have to have permission from God before we heal a human. In 2012, Matt did not know that he had a major blood clot between his left groin and left knee. While he was sleeping in the Southern Oregon Habituation Area (SOHA), we conducted a routine medical scan and discovered the deadly medical problem. We prayed to God and asked Him if we could remove the large blood clot. We wanted to save Matt from an unexpected and early death because we knew that he had a very good chance of helping the Xanue complete the EXODUS. Fortunately, God concurred and gave us permission to remove the large and deadly blood clot. Matt had no idea that we had done so until about three years later when he saw a Cardiovascular Surgeon about his nonstop swollen elephant leg. The doctor was blown away by the obvious miracle because absolutely no one lives through what Matt had in his leg. However, with that said, many people ask us for a healing and we will proceed as long as it's in God's will.

281. **Do you have to have permission from God before you heal anyone?** Yes. We always have to have permission from God to

Chapter 15: Q&A with Zorth

heal anyone. The difficult thing for some individuals to accept is the fact that God answers prayer with yes, no, or wait awhile. Also, God can heal through direct divine intervention, through the hands of a physician, through medical treatment, through medication, through the hands of the Xanue, or through death. More often than not, many sentient Beings of Light receive their healing through the process of death. When we die, our souls or Orbs return home to God. At that time, we are given new bodies and we are, therefore, healed. God has his ways and purposes for everything. God is good.

282. **When the Xanue perform healings, do you use natural laws or do you heal through faith and God uses you as an instrument of His healing?** We are very aware of the natural laws of healing. However, more often than not, we will heal through our faith in Jesus Christ, the Son of God. Jesus told his disciples that if they had faith the size of a mustard seed, they could do what he did and more. Well, we have a lot of faith in Him.

283. **Can healing abilities be given to us, through our Xanue friends?** God dispenses gifts to everyone as He sees fit, including the gift of healing. There are human faith healers.

284. **I've been healthy most of my life. However, can the Xanue conduct a medical scan to tell me whether or not I should go in for a medical checkup with my physician?** We conduct medical scans on a routine basis. If we find something, we ask God if we can intervene. On other occasions, humans ask us to conduct medical scans or they already know what their medical problem is and they ask us to heal them. Once again, all healing will only proceed if we have God's permission to do so. In the meantime, I recommend that you develop the habit of scheduling routine medical visits with your human physician.

285. **I understand that the Xanue live in trees as Orbs during the day. Could you please clarify "the process" a human can do

by sitting up against a tree to focus on healing for themselves by the Xanue? Humans are funny at times. They believe that certain routines have to be developed and acted upon in order to achieve a desired goal. Yes, we are Orbs and we dwell in the trees during the day to take in the sun's energy through the tree and the nutrients from the roots. Truth be told, you don't need to sit up against a tree in some predetermined process in order to get healed. All you have to do is talk with us and ask for a healing. Night time works best for us because we are busy during the day acquiring our sustenance. Also, not mandatory, it works better for us if you're sleeping on a cot or a hammock because then it's easier to access your entire body. However, we have been known to conduct healing sessions while humans are sleeping in their beds inside their homes.

286. **Do the Xanue know about the natural herbal remedies all around us that could be used for cures to help individuals who may be ignorant or unwilling to do the steps needed to interact with the Xanue?** We know about every possible natural herbal remedies on the Earth that humans know and then some. However, we prefer to use our loving energy to heal humans rather than natural remedies. It's faster, cleaner, and more direct. If humans are into learning more about how to utilize natural herbal remedies to help improve their health, they have many sources of information to learn from. In the case of Chris Pettross, who visited the Southern Oregon Interaction Area in April of 2017, we worked on his kidneys and then left a pile of Manzanita Berries for him on the ground by his sleeping cot in the shape of a heart. These berries will help to improve his kidney functioning if he chooses to consume them.

287. **Do Xanue heal other species of people or animals also?** We will attempt to heal anyone who needs our help as long as God permits us to do so. This includes mammals, birds, fish, reptiles, and plant life.

Chapter 15: Q&A with Zorth

288. **Are Xanue specialists in healing certain body systems or 'all systems' in general?** Xanue healers have different skill sets and levels of expertise when it comes to healing. The younger Xanue are trained by the elders. If necessary, we will assemble a team of Xanue to work on an individual who needs our help. At times, it can look like a human medical team in an operating room.
289. **Can Xanue lower a person's blood pressure on a permanent basis?** If God permits us to do so – yes.
290. **Are there any limits to Xanue healing our health problems?** Occasionally, we have tried our best to heal someone without achieving the desired results. In those rare situations, the only one who can heal the individual is God. At that point in time, God will heal now or through the process of death.
291. **Did the Xanue help to heal Dr. Dan Reilley after his motorcycle accident in Iowa?** I personally sent two of our best Xanue healers to be with Dr. Dan while he was recovering in the hospital in Iowa. The two healers paid attention to the physicians' work and then supplemented their medical interventions with our expertise. This is why Dr. Dan recovered so quickly and thoroughly.
292. **Can anyone call on the Xanue people for help and healing?** Yes. Anyone can ask us for help and healing. If God permits us to do so, we will do our best to intervene. We usually accomplish our desired goals when we attempt to heal someone. You have not because you ask not.
293. **Have you shown anyone how to cure diseases that plague mankind? Cancer? Leukemia? Diabetes? Things of that nature?** That is not our role while interacting with humans. We are not here to teach them how to heal. Our role is to help humans reconnect with God, one another, themselves, and with the Earth. We are also permitted to heal and save lives when God permits us to do so.

294. **When you use people's bodies to teach your young how to heal, do you ever use that same person's body after your young have learned?** Sometimes we will use the same person's body to teach our young one's how to follow up with necessary medical procedures and for monitoring for long-term care and maintenance. For example, we have our healers constantly following up with Matt and his left leg just to make sure that no more blood clots develop. We also help to maintain his prostate health and intestinal health. We have even removed cancer from his body. At present, we're not allowed to touch his back.

295. **Before you heal our pets, must you ask God first if it is his will to do so?** We are one people. We are connected with God. We always seek His will in everything that we do, including healing human pets or animals in the forest.

296. **Could you explain how the Xanue do their healing? Can we learn how to simulate it? Many people suffer. Energy, Frequency and Vibration are involved in their healing process. Why can't we take advantage of this wonderful gift they have? They claim that they wish to help those who are open minded and people of faith. I would never abuse such a discovery, and would use it to benefit mankind while giving the glory to God.** It is not up to the Xanue to teach humans how we go about using our gifts of healing. Like the human race, God has gifted everyone in different ways. I believe Matt has referred to 1 Corinthians 12 and how this chapter explains the gifting process and what the gifts happen to be. Matt has a human friend, Diana Frost, who has a healing ministry and travels around the USA and other countries to heal many people. Therefore, you are asking for the gift of healing which is not for the Xanue to give to you. Instead, I strongly suggest that you read 1 Corinthians 12 and pray to God to consider giving you the gift of healing. However, please be prepared for the possibility that He may gift you with something other than the gift of healing. God is good.

Chapter 15: Q&A with Zorth

GLOBAL STEWARDSHIP QUESTIONS:

297. **What do we need to do to save our planet for all, including the Xanue?** You can do your small part right where you are. Recycle and reduce your carbon footprint. Also, join volunteer groups that work on improving the health of the Earth, such as cleaning up garbage or planting trees. Regarding this question, I'm more concerned about the future for humans on the Earth. We will be okay. As long as the Earth has trees and the sun continues to shine, the Xanue people will live on.

298. **What are some of the Xanue's daily responsibilities?** The Xanue are guardians of the forest and we protect all who dwell within. This includes both plant life and wildlife. There are over three-trillion-trees on the Earth along with other plant life, birds, mammals, fish, and insects. On top of these caretaking responsibilities, we teach our young, befriend humans, and monitor the human race, including their governments. All of the above keeps us very busy.

299. **Is there any area of planet Earth that you do not inhabit?** We live on all six habitable continents. We do not live in Antarctica. However, we do travel to Antarctica in order to monitor what humans are doing there. They are finding some very interesting things that they are choosing not to share with humanity. They ignorantly fear that civilization will collapse if humans knew that other ancient aliens have visited the Earth in the past. That is nonsense. The Xanue are from a different world, yet humans are interacting with us without any difficulties.

300. **Can you tell us or do you know how old the Earth really is?** The Earth is billions of years old. A day is a thousand years unto the Lord and a thousand years is a day. The Xanue find it humorous that humans constantly argue over evolution versus creationism. The truth of the matter is that God spoke life into existence – the Big Bang. Then He's been working behind the

scenes regarding creationism and micro-evolution. Evolution and creationism is not an either/or scenario. Rather, it's a both/and scenario.

301. **What is your main focus or purpose out there?** We are guardians of the forest and we protect all who dwell within. We are the caretakers of the Earth. That is our primary purpose and our main focus. However, our secondary focus is to help mankind reconnect with God, their neighbor, themselves, and with the Earth.

TECHNOLOGY QUESTIONS:

302. **Do humans have technical capabilities far above what the government tells the masses?** Yes.
303. **Have humans traveled to other planets? Frequently? For how long?** Yes. Humans have traveled to other planets but not of their own doing. They have been and still are abducted by various alien species and are being used as research subjects, slaves, entertainment, and food. As I have adamantly said before, and I'll say it again, we are not involved with UFOs. The Treykon are involved with UFOs. Any species that has to travel from planet to planet inside an artificial environment is a fallen species. As a result of being a fallen species, they are prone to behaving in malevolent, self-centered, and uncaring ways.
304. **What can humans do to survive?** Humans, like most species, have a built in survival instinct which many seem to be obsessed about. The obvious answer is to live a healthy lifestyle and avoid dangerous people, places, and things. However, its more enlightened to be asking, "What can we do to be closer to God?" or "What can I do to show my neighbor that God loves them and so do I?" In other words, what does it matter if you survive anything if you are not loving God or your neighbor as

Chapter 15: Q&A with Zorth

yourself? What is the point of surviving without God? What's the point of dying without God?

305. **Since the technological species on your former planet created the portals and placed them on numerous planets, can portals be destroyed?** Yes. Portals can be moved around or destroyed. However, I'm unaware of anywhere in our collective memory of a portal actually being destroyed. They are considered neutral instruments of travel and are freely used by all sentient Beings of Light.

306. **How many portals have been placed on planets around the universe?** This is an impossible question to answer because there are numerous planets all over the universe, including in all of the multiple dimensions. Only God knows the answer to that question.

307. **How do you know where the portals go?** Every portal has what I would describe as an energy signature map or sign. You only know where that particular portal has the capacity to send you to. Once you arrive at the new destination, likewise, you're able to read where that portal has the capacity to send you to next. Along the way, it is assumed that we are keeping track of where we came from and where we are going so we know how to find our way back. In short, you have to be good at keeping track of directions and making a memory map in your mind.

308. **Do you know what's on the other end of the portal before you go through it?** Yes. Please read the previous question.

309. **Can echolocation be used to help identify where any of the Xanue are located?** No. We are sentient Beings of Light.

310. **Study of the DNA Sasquatch Genome project, has been studied as well, and the results are: It is a human hybrid species, the mtDNA (female or mother side) is human and the nuDNA (father or male side) is unknown. When you hear someone mention contamination, all tests are done with robotics, and if it is contaminated we would know by the**

THE XANUE

genetic test results. All testers DNA are in the GENBANK. Would the Xanue agree with this and feel it is correct? The Xanue have no interest in the DNA Treykon Genome Project. If you're implying that the Xanue have mated with humans, we are offended. Xanue only mate with Xanue. However, the Treykon have mated with humans, both past and present.

311. **Do you see us humans as primitive compared to your knowledge and experience in the universe?** The Xanue are one people. We are not a fallen species. We have existed for millions of years. Our collective memory is vast and covers much territory and species. The human race is a fallen species and are disconnected. They have only existed for thousands of years. We consider ourselves to be their fellow children of God. We are not here to be better than humans. We are here to help the humans.

312. **Do the Xanue ever utilize fire?** No. We have no need to have a heat source. The Treykon will utilize fire on occasion.

ENERGY QUESTIONS:

313. **Can the Xanue see electrical energy?** Yes. We see the energy in everything around us. We see energy in all living things as well as in all mechanical creations. Everything has vibrational frequencies and energy. If only you could see what we can see. It is very beautiful.

314. **Does it take more energy, or is it harder, to change to physical form from your Orb form?** Changing from our Orb form to physical form does require energy in order to maintain our physical form. Over time, it can become draining which is why we have to go back into the trees during the day to essentially charge ourselves back up.

315. **Do the Xanue always go back to the same tree to recharge or do they move around to different ones?** Although the

Xanue are one people, we are also uniquely different. This includes likes, dislikes, and preferences. Therefore, some Xanue prefer to go back to the same tree and others don't mind switching around. I personally prefer to switch around in order to enjoy the different charging experiences. Not every tree is the same.

316. **Are electromagnetic fields from various sources all usable to Xanue (i.e., Generator, alternator, transformer, Tesla coil, AC or DC motors, etc.)?** Yes. We can utilize the energy from mechanical devices and power pole lines. However, they're more along the lines of what you humans would call a strong drink that holds a lot of punch in a small shot. Our young Xanue will experiment around with partaking of such energy but grow to realize that a nice and prolonged charging within the trees is much more soothing to the soul. Oh, and the young ones also have fun quickly consuming the energy out of your flashlights and cameras just to watch you humans standing around in the dark wondering what just happened to your fully charged batteries. Like I said before, we can be pranksters.

317. **Do Xanue have 'favorite' trees?** Some do and some don't. I prefer to switch trees.

318. **Does it take more energy to cloak?** When we are cloaked or in our shimmering image form, we are actually in our natural state of existence. So the answer to your question is no. However, if we should choose to slow down our vibrational frequency so you can see us in our full flesh and blood physical form, then the answer is yes. It takes more energy to slow down our vibrational frequency than it does to remain in our normal higher or faster vibrational frequency.

319. **Do the Xanue use the trees in the winter when they lose their leaves? If so how is that different then when the trees do have leaves on them?** When deciduous trees lose their leaves and go dormant for the winter, we will either switch over to

conifer trees or simply migrate to other geographical locations to rest inside trees in order to obtain energy from the sun.

PORTAL QUESTIONS:

320. **Is there a portal in the Bermuda Triangle?** The largest portal on the planet exists inside, what humans refer to as, the Bermuda Triangle. It is very powerful and is avoided by the Xanue people. This is the only portal on Earth where we have lost some Xanue who were never able to return from where they went to. It is wise for humans to do the same.
321. **Can humans travel through portals?** It depends on which portals you are talking about. Yes, there are some portals that humans can travel through because they are short portals. It's like walking from one room directly into another room. However, there are many more portals that are long portals. The human body cannot withstand travel through the long portals unless they are accompanied by the protection of a sentient Being of Light such as a Xanue or angel. They can also travel through long portals if they are in an artificial environment within a strong and sturdy vehicle of travel. This is how many aliens from other worlds travel to Earth.
322. **Are there portals near all the Xanue clans?** No.
323. **Are portals movable to another location?** Some can be moved. Most are stationary.
324. **Are peoples from other worlds using the portals on Earth?** Yes. As I just stated, sentient Beings of Light can travel through portals. Also, fallen species can travel through portals inside a traveling craft with an artificial environment. You call them UFOs.
325. **Can you travel back in time through the time portal? If so, does that mean that all that ever existed, still exists, somewhere?** In your world, you view time as linear – past,

present, and future. That is the only way that a fallen species is able to perceive time. It's one of the consequences of the fall of man. On the other hand, God, Jesus, the Angels, and other created species that did not fall in the Garden of Eden view time as circular. Everything exists all at once. There is no past, present, or future. However, there is one very clear rule to obey. No one is to interfere with the free will choice of another regardless of what plain we exist in. Only God is allowed to make such decisions and interventions.

326. **Do the Xanue experience or perform time travel?** Yes.
327. **Can humans travel through portals by themselves?** Yes, but only through short portals – not long portals.
328. **Are the missing people purposefully being taken through portals or is it an accidental crossing? If yes, where do the people go?** Some humans disappear in the wilderness because they're lost, get injured, or are consumed by animals or Treykon. Other humans accidentally walk through portals or they are abducted and taken through portals. Finally, some humans are abducted by aliens and flown away in UFOs. Sometimes, the Treykon will abduct humans and give them to the aliens in exchange for food, drink, and natural herbal medications from their home world. The exchange of a human for these products is the closest that a Treykon will ever come to experiencing their home world ever again. This keeps the Treykon willing to interact with the aliens inside the UFOs.
329. **Can we back up to get out of the portal?** Only if you have just walked through a short portal.
330. **Can a human go through the time travel portal safely and return?** Some humans have accidentally walked through a time travel portal. Unfortunately, they did not return.

THE XANUE

XANUE TRAVEL QUESTIONS:

331. **Would you please describe the various forms of travel that the Xanue utilize?** The Xanue are able to travel via walking, running, using short-portals, long-portals, and flying as Orbs. Our maximum speed while flying on the Earth as Orbs is approximately 3,000 miles per hour. Therefore, it takes us about eight and a half hours to fly around the Earth in our Orb form.

332. **Are you allowed to roam the universe and enjoy God's wonders of creation?** Yes. We are allowed to travel freely throughout the universe while utilizing portals. However, we are one people and accountable to one another. Therefore, travel beyond the Earth, among the Xanue, must have purpose and preapproval.

333. **When you use the portals, do you travel at the speed of light?** Portal travel is actually much faster than the speed of light. Portals are shortcuts and utilize the folding of space to get from one location to another location.

334. **Do Xanue 'fly' for fun sometimes?** Yes. Our children practice a lot and even take touring trips together.

335. **Do Xanue ever travel with us in our daily activities?** Yes. We will hitch rides in cars, trains, planes, and ships. We enjoy the human modes of transportation and seeing how they interact with one another while traveling.

336. **Can the Xanue go from different areas of the US whenever they want to?** Yes. Travel on the Earth is not restricted. However, our young are expected to ask for and receive permission before traveling abroad.

DIMENSIONAL QUESTIONS:

337. **Do the Xanue teleport to other locations?** As previously stated, the Xanue walk, run, use short-portals, use long-portals,

Chapter 15: Q&A with Zorth

or fly around as Orbs. We also use human transportation such as hitching rides in cars, trains, planes, and ships.

338. **Would the Xanue really be in trees in a city park?** We are in the trees and the trees are everywhere. However, we are not in every tree. For example, we are in the trees in Central Park in New York City. When Matt took Grady to New York City in March of 2019, we sent two Guardians to be with them, including staying in their hotel room during the night. We are usually in the trees in your backyard too.

339. **Is the dimension that they go to in the "infrared" (i.e., the dimension above this one)?** Yes. Matter of fact, while sitting in Serenity Meadow, Matt is actually able to see us in the infrared dimension in the area behind the woodpile. Also, Maynard Schweigert has taken some pictures capturing the infrared glow behind the woodpile. We appreciate Maynard's diligence and documentation.

340. **Is the "infrared" dimension still on the Earth?** Yes.

341. **Are there burial places in the other dimension?** We have no burial places. We do not bury our dead. When we die, our Orbs return home to God. Our bodies simply disappear.

342. **Are all Orbs the Xanue?** No. All Orbs are not the Xanue. All heavenly beings can be Orbs. All created sentient Beings of Light that never fell in the Garden of Eden can be Orbs. Also, the Xuxiko can be Orbs. Humans fell in the Garden of Eden. Therefore, their Orbs are locked into their flesh and blood bodies. However, every once in a while, the Orb of a human is able to leave their body for various reasons. Given the entire human population of the Earth, this is an exception to the rule rather than the norm. For example, Matt's Orb was able to leave his body to go help his friend, Kevin, in Grants Pass, Oregon. This does not happen often.

343. **Are the Xanue great ascended Masters that only made it to the light level plane?** The Xanue are the Xanue.

344. **How many dimensions are there?** Infinite. God is good.

345. **Can we 'see' into your dimension?** Yes. As I previously stated, Matt is able to see into our dimension while sitting in the Serenity Meadow.
346. **When we see you, are you in our dimension?** Yes.

TREYKON QUESTIONS:

347. **Are the Treykon the only Bigfoots that have been killed?** The Xanue are the Bigfoot, Sasquatch, etc. The Treykon are the Treykon. With that said, the Xanue are not a fallen species. Therefore, we can shapeshift from our Orb form to our flesh and blood form and back to our Orb form. We can also see into the future in a limited capacity. Finally, we can read the minds of humans. We know that humans are coming before they know they're coming. Can a bullet kill light? On the other hand, the Treykon are a fallen species. They are locked into their flesh and blood form. They cannot shapeshift into their Orb form. Therefore, the Treykon can be killed. Matter of fact, in the past human history, the Treykon have been documented as having skirmishes with human warriors such as your Vikings or North American Indians. After losing many skirmishes with humans, the Treykon retreated into the forest far away from humans for their own safety.
348. **Are the Treykon the Bigfoots who abduct people?** The Xanue are the Bigfoot and the Sasquatch. The Treykon are the Treykon. The Treykon have and will abduct humans. They will occasionally breed with female humans. Mostly, they kill and eat the humans or they give them to aliens in UFO's.
349. **Why do the Treykon and Xanue look so much alike?** God is the Creator of all life. There are many planets and species throughout the universe and its multiple dimensions. The Earth is not the only planet with species that look like humans. In a similar manner, God has created many species that look

nearly like one another, including the Xanue and the Treykon. We are taller and more human looking. The Treykon tend to be a foot or two shorter, uglier, and more menacing looking.

350. **Do the Treykon use infrasound for zapping?** No.
351. **Do the Treykon ever work with the Xuxiko?** The Xuxiko may take the liberty of possessing a Treykon in order to use its body for a particular task. However, when it comes to cooperation, the Treykon will work with the aliens who fly the UFOs.
352. **Do the Treykon ever venture into human populated areas? If yes, why?** Normally, the Treykon will stay deep in the forest, far away from human populations. If a lone hiker, hunter, or camper stumbles across their location, they will kill the human, eat them, and scatter their bones. Occasionally, the Treykon will send a small party of two or three hunters to the outskirts of a human rural area in order to obtain food such as a pig, sheep, or cow. Finally, under rare circumstances when the Treykon are low on their own species for breeding, they will abduct a human male or female in order to produce offspring.
353. **Do the Treykon have eye glow?** No. However, their eyes will shine if you point a flashlight in their direction.
354. **Can the Treykon use Mind Speak?** No.
355. **Can the Treykon use fire?** They have used fire on occasion. However, after burning down a couple of forests, they are very shy to use it on a regular basis.
356. **Do the Treykon live underground?** The Treykon live wherever they can find shelter, including underground and in caves.
357. **Is the US government aware of the Treykon?** Yes. The government has Treykon bodies from the Columbus Day Storm and the Mt. St. Helens disaster.
358. **Do the Treykon have any paranormal abilities like the Xanue?** No. The Treykon are a fallen species.
359. **Do the Treykon have a spoken language?** The Treykon do have their own language. However, after having lived among humans for quite some time, they also know how to use many

of the words of the local human population. Matter of fact, Matt has an audio recording of a Treykon at the Southern Oregon Interaction Area (SOIA) that says, "Human," with a lot of disdain in its voice. Fortunately, we were at SOIA in high numbers to keep Matt and his friends safe.

360. **Do the Treykon ever try to befriend humans?** No. The Treykon hate humans. Historically, the Treykon have lost many skirmishes with humans and they try to avoid them at all costs.

361. **Do the Treykon ever try to breed with humans?** As I have said before, the Treykon will occasionally abduct human females for the purpose of breeding to obtain more children. In very rare circumstances, the Treykon will abduct a male for breeding purposes if they're shy on fertile males. Such was the case of your Albert Osterman. However, he got away before they could give the breeding process a try. He was fortunate because after a successful breeding between a male human and a female Treykon, they will kill and eat the human male. On the other hand, they keep the female human around to produce a few babies before they kill and eat her.

362. **I remember you saying the females cannot be in the trees while with child and for a period after giving birth as well as the baby Xanue, and are protected to the max during this time. My question is: In the PNW on Columbus Day 1962 a female Sasquatch was found under a tree and a later autopsy showed she was also pregnant. This was a highly talked about event. Would the Xanue know if this was a Treykon?** You are correct. If the female Xanue chooses to deliver her baby in her flesh and blood form, then she cannot go back inside the tree in her Orb form without losing her baby. Therefore, she is highly protected by all the other Xanue in the area. However, to answer your question, the female body that they found during the Columbus Day Storm was a Treykon and not a Xanue. Your government still has the female Treykon body.

Chapter 15: Q&A with Zorth

363. **I heard this story about a native woman who had a child with a sasquatch male. Is this possible, or maybe in the future?** The Bigfoot and Sasquatch are the Xanue. The Treykon are the Treykon. Yes, the Treykon have mated with female humans. The Xanue only mate with Xanue.

364. **How many missing persons can we attribute to the Treykon?** Humans go missing in the forest because they get lost; they get injured and can't get themselves back to civilization; they die of natural causes; they are killed by predators and consumed; they are killed by sociopathic humans; they are accidentally killed by another hunter and are buried to cover up the mistake; they stumble into portals; or they are captured, killed, and eaten by the Treykon. Finally, some are abducted by aliens.

365. **Are all Treykon dangerous and should be avoided?** Although there are a few nice Treykon, they are the exception to the rule. Never trust a Treykon because they will deceive you and literally knife you in the back and eat you.

366. **Are there Treykon who are friendly and show good will toward humans?** Only on rare occasions. The problem is that they're hard to distinguish from the majority of the Treykon who will deceive you, kill you, and eat you.

367. **If we are in the forest and encounter an upright, hairy, bipedal, humanoid, how can we tell whether or not it's a Xanue or a Treykon?** The Xanue tend to look more human and have a kind and gentle appearance. The Treykon are uglier, don't look very human, and are menacing looking. I've heard you humans describe it as a resting bitch face. They always look angry and upset. Now, with that said, we are not a fallen species and therefore, we have what you humans would call paranormal abilities. Although, our abilities are normal to us. We can mind speak, cloak, and shapeshift. The Treykon are a fallen species and are not able to do such things. Finally, statistically speaking, where are you most likely to find the majority of the Xanue during the daylight hours?

THE XANUE

368. **Where do the Treykon live?** The Treykon live deep in the wilderness, far away from humans. They will live in caves, underground, or build temporary shelters.

XUXIKO QUESTIONS:

369. **When the Xanue and the Xuxiko fight, are any of them wounded or killed?** No one is wounded or killed. It's more like weakened or sidelined. When the Xanue and Xuxiko engage in a skirmish, it's usually to protect an individual or a territory. For example, we have struggled with the Xuxiko to remove them from Matt's and Cynthia's bedroom at night. No one was injured or died.

370. **How often do the Xanue and Xuxiko fight with one another?** If we're considering around the entire Earth, the answer is daily.

371. **When the Xanue and Xuxiko fight, do the Xanue women participate?** The human way is not the Xanue way. The Xanue way is not the human way. The Xanue males are responsible for the protection of others – Not the Xanue females. Among your race, some humans consider this sexist. Among the Xanue, it's simply the right thing to do and it is appreciated by all.

372. **Do angels support the Xanue during these skirmishes?** Occasionally, God will send us some reinforcements during our skirmishes with the Xuxiko. However, we are fairly capable of handling the Xuxiko on our own because of our faith in God's only begotten Son, Jesus.

373. **Do the Xanue know ahead of time about the Xuxiko attacks?** The Xuxiko are very prideful and will occasionally announce their plans ahead of time as an act of intimidation. However, we never fear them and face them head on when they arrive.

374. **Are the Xuxiko among us all of the time?** There are always Xuxiko located on the Earthly plane. They're constantly doing the work of Satan. They continually seek to discourage humans,

Chapter 15: Q&A with Zorth

distract them away from God, and sow seeds of anger, hatred, lust, jealousy, strife, envy, murder, lying, stealing, and war among the humans. Misery loves company.

375. **How does one know whether or not they have a guardian?** Xanue Guardians for life are only assigned to humans who are perceived as having the potential of accomplishing important things in the future or for those humans who have accomplished important things such as the EXODUS. Most humans don't have a Xanue Guardian. Now with that said, if you are friends with your local Xanue family and clan, it's not like they're not going to help their friends out in a time of need.

376. **My question for Zorth concerns an incident I had several years ago on the Current River in the Missouri Ozarks. I paddled out of the main river around a little fork bend from a side stream to take a break. When I got into the calm water by the woods, looking around at such a beautiful place I was inexplicably overcome with an overpowering sense of fear and dread! I just told my wife we couldn't stay there and immediately got back out in the main river and headed down stream. As soon as I was back out on the river the dread and fear left like nothing ever happened. Was this caused by the Xanue or the Xuxiko?** Although the Xanue will intimidate some humans to leave their territories, the specific incident that you're referring to involved the Xuxiko. It was good that you left. They were about to perform a ritual sacrifice. Much goes on in the forest that most humans are clueless about.

OTHER ENTITIES QUESTIONS:

377. **Does the Dogman exist? If yes, what is it?** The Dogman species does exist. They are sentient Beings of Light that never fell in the Garden of Eden. They are able to do everything we can do because of their faith in God and Jesus. They are benevolent

beings. Matter of fact, one appeared to Mike Kincaid while he was sleeping on his cot at the Southern Oregon Habituation Area (SOHA). Mike had a very pleasant experience with the Dogman.

378. **Do I need to worry about the Dogman?** No. They are a benevolent species. Humans are always quick to judge a book by its cover. Any species that does not look like them generates fear within.

379. **Is the Loch Ness Monster a dinosaur that comes in and out of a time-travel Portal or are they an interdimensional species that travel through a Universal Portal?** The Loch Ness Monster is simply a dinosaur that comes in and out through a time-travel portal.

380. **Who are the Treykon and where are they from?** The Treykon were brought to the Earth a long time ago, way before Adam and Eve arrived, by an ancient alien race. They used the Treykon to mine the Earth. When they were done, they left the Treykon behind without any means of returning to their home world. The Treykon are a fallen species and are locked into their flesh and blood bodies. They look similar to the Xanue but they're about a foot or two shorter, uglier, and menacing. They live deep in the wilderness and avoid humans as much as possible.

381. **Can the Treykon cloak?** No. The Treykon are a fallen species. They are locked into their flesh and blood bodies. They do not possess what you humans refer to as paranormal abilities.

382. **How many other types of Beings call the Earth home?** The only thing that I feel comfortable saying is that there are many, but most of them exist in other dimensions on the Earth. Also, the Earth is visited frequently by extraterrestrial life forms.

383. **What other species are humans in contact with?** Human governments around the world are in contact with several extraterrestrial life forms. Mainly the more powerful countries such as the USA, Russia, and China. Some of these species are trying to help humans on the Earth while others sow seeds of mistrust and dominion.

Chapter 15: Q&A with Zorth

384. **Is there a rule or set of universal laws that one kind of species cannot eliminate another species?** Yes. However, not all species play by the rules including humans.
385. **Are technological and non-technological beings living on all habitable planets?** I am not God and I'm not privy to all the things that God knows. Therefore, I cannot speak for 'all habitable planets'. However, I can say that I'm aware of some other habitable planets where technological and non-technological beings are living.
386. **Do the people who put the portals around the Universe still exist?** Yes. However, they do not exist in one place. Instead, they are spread throughout the universe as a scattered people who have transitioned into the cultures of other civilizations. Matter of fact, their present day descendants aren't even aware of the magnificent history of their ancestors. The knowledge has been lost among their people.
387. **If the people who installed portals around the Universe still exist, do they still come to this planet?** The descendants of the builders of the intergalactic portals are spread throughout the universe. None of their descendants live on the Earth.
388. **Do the Xanue know who or what the Dogman, Mothman, and Reptile like cryptids are, and where they come from?** Yes. I have already discussed the Dogman. The Mothman is an interdimensional being. The Reptilians come from another world.
389. **Do other cryptid beings exist? Little people, Mothman, Lochness Monster, Dog Man, etc.? If so, what are they and do they relate with the forest people at all?** Many cryptid beings exist. We prefer to interact only with unfallen species. The fallen human race is the only exception to this rule because of God's directives to us to help them.
390. **Can you tell us what planet UFOs and aliens come from? I Know there are more than just the ten planets currently recognized by us here on Earth.** God has created an infinite

number of habitable planets in the universe and its multiple dimensions. UFOs come from planets with fallen species who need to travel inside a craft with an artificial environment to support life while traveling between worlds. On the other hand, sentient Beings of Light that did not fall in the Garden of Eden can travel without the assistance of a spacecraft with an artificial environment. Those of us who can simply travel through the short-portals and long-portals.

391. **Do any species of aliens mean to harm us humans on the Earth? If so, who are they and what do they look like?** No. However, some aliens are working with humans to harm other humans as in the case of your Coronavirus pandemic crisis. This is an attempt to thin out the human population and to move in the direction of a one-world government. Unfortunately, not all humans who appear to be good actors are good actors. This problem runs deep among the human race and is a worldwide coup – not just a national coup. We are helping the 'White Hats'.

392. **Do the Xanue communicate with other entities and or Aliens here on Earth?** We prefer to limit our communications with other species who have not fallen. Once again, the human race is an exception to the rule because of God's directives to have us help them reconnect with Him, one another, themselves, and the Earth. God is good.

393. **Are there other entities that present as Orbs?** Yes. Heavenly Beings present as Orbs. Other created sentient Beings of Light that have not fallen present as Orbs. Also, the Xuxiko present as Orbs. Finally, Satan can present himself as an Orb.

394. **Who built the Megalith/Cyclopean structures here on Earth?** The structures were built by ancient aliens with the assistance of their slaves, the Treykon. Also, humans were also occasionally used as slave labor too.

395. **Some people have reported seeing upright, hairy, bipedal humanoids walking on and off of UFOs. Are the Xanue involved with UFOs?** Ever since the EXODUS occurred in

Chapter 15: Q&A with Zorth

June of 2016, I have adamantly declared through Matt – The 13, our Ambassador to the Xanue Council of Twelve, that the Xanue have absolutely nothing to do with UFOs. Once again, fallen species have to travel in crafts with artificial environments to get from one planet to another. They are locked into their flesh and blood bodies and, therefore, cannot travel in their Orb form which is stuck inside their bodies. The Treykon are also a fallen species and they are locked into their flesh and blood bodies. It is the Treykon who are seen interacting with the occupants of UFOs. The Xanue avoid fallen species. The only exception is the human race because of God's directive for us to be involved with them. God wants us to help them reconnect with Him, their neighbor, themselves, and the Earth.

396. **I have read articles and watched videos which claim that the evolution of the human species was accelerated millions of years ago through genetic manipulation by one or more ET species. Is there any truth to these claims?** No. There is absolutely no truth to those false theories. Please keep in mind that we came to the Earth during the last period of the dinosaurs. We were here before God sent Adam and Eve to the Earth. No one has altered the DNA of the human race. They are the same today as they were when they first arrived on the Earth. By the way, the Xanue and the humans were not the only species sent to inhabit the Earth. There were other humanoid species too but they did not adapt very well. They eventually died off. Theories are theories and truth is truth.

397. **Are there other Beings on Earth besides the three we know about, and how many? If so, are they mostly good or bad?** There are more species on the Earth than you or other humans know about. Also, many come and go from the Earth as visitors. Regarding whether or not they're "good" or "bad," I prefer to use the terms "unfallen" or "fallen" instead. Therefore, to answer your question, it is about an even split between the two.

THE XANUE

The "unfallen" travel through the portals in their Orb form. The "fallen" travel to the Earth in crafts with artificial environments.

398. **Do other beings masquerade as Xanue, - large, hairy, red eye glow? If true, how can we tell it is NOT the Xanue? I need to know who I can trust!** The Xuxiko can masquerade themselves as pretty much anything, including Angels of Light. With that said, they can't contain their evil for very long. Most beings, when they're around the Xuxiko, can sense their evil presence right away, in spite of how they masquerade themselves.

399. **Zorth, how many creatures have you encountered during your stay on Earth and what should we do to avoid them.** Please allow me to answer your question with a question: "How many creatures have you encountered during your stay on Earth and what have you done to avoid them?' There's your answer. You have nothing to fear but fear itself.

400. **Zorth, over the five years, the Xanue have revealed an awful lot about themselves to humanity (i.e., Portals, Mind Speak, Cloaking, Reading through Memories, Healing, Reconnection of Humanity with God, Neighbors, Self, and the Earth, etc.). What's next?** You're asking the question as if all of the above has been accomplished and there's something new to do. Well, truth be told, we have just started this journey of helping humans to reconnect with God, their neighbor, themselves, and the Earth. We would like you to hop on board the "Woo-Woo Train," as Matt calls it, and help us accomplish this task first. Then, down the road, we will talk about what is next.

PART 4
MULTIPLE EYEWITNESS TESTIMONIALS

CHAPTER 16
Multiple Eyewitness Testimonials

Eyewitness testimony is a legal term. It refers to an account given by people of an event they have witnessed. For example, they may be required to give a description at a trial of a robbery or a road accident someone has seen. This includes identification of perpetrators, details of the crime scene, etc. (SimplyPsychology.com).

When it comes to the Bigfoot Forest People (AKA, The Xanue) phenomena, eyewitness testimonies are greatly relied upon as important data to support or back up the circumstantial evidence. Just look at various Bigfoot investigation websites on the internet. They will list numerous eyewitness sightings, classify them, and then supplement the reports with a Bigfoot investigator who has gone into the area afterwards to confirm the reported sighting through the collection of circumstantial evidence (i.e., Footprints, handprints, hair samples, etc.). In short, a solid and credible eyewitness combined with circumstantial evidence is a hard case to refute. Over the past five decades, the kingdom of Bigfootdom has been built, brick by brick, upon this simple truth: Eyewitness testimonies plus circumstantial evidence.

Just a reminder, this is exactly why my family's encounter on July 1, 2000, stood out like a sore thumb. An entire family experienced an encounter, a psychologist saw the Bigfoot Forest Person, and a National Park Ranger found circumstantial evidence two days later. The credibility of my family, my credentials as a psychologist, and the confirmation of Ranger John Roth was very hard to dispute.

That's why the media was all over my family's encounter like a cat on catnip.

Now, I'm smart enough to realize that the testimonies from multiple witnesses far surpasses the testimonies of the few or the one. Therefore, when I began to conduct my research in the Southern Oregon Research Area (SORA), which eventually changed to the Southern Oregon Habituation Area (SOHA), I knew that my individual testimony of the results that I was starting to glean from my research approach was not going to be enough to appease the skeptics. In other words, anyone can go out into the forest and make all kinds of claims, but if they're the only one experiencing those events, then it's easy for the masses to write them off as crazy or a hoaxer. Therefore, over a twenty-year period of time, I managed to bring over five-hundred witnesses with me to SORA, SOHA, WAHA, SOIA, and Camp Xanue. Either we're all crazy or we're all liars or we're all telling the truth.

Likewise, if you want to establish credibility as a Bigfoot Forest People researcher, it's not enough to go out there by yourself, experience them, and then come back and report your data. Once again, you can be written off as crazy or a hoaxer. However, when you go to the great lengths to document your research as I have done, and I still do, utilizing multiple eyewitness testimonies, then it's harder for others to blow off your results.

I brought people out with me who are psychiatrists, mental health counselors, nurses, teachers, principals, attorneys, janitors, hairstylists, policemen, businessmen, avid hunters, military personnel, engineers, grocers, artists, investigators, computer technicians, pastors, music DJ's, financial planners, TV personalities, etc. Most have testified publicly about their experiences with me up in the mountains via my YouTube.com channel. Just go to YouTube.com, type in "Team Squatchin USA," and you'll come across over three-hundred-fifty videos to watch and learn from. Many of those videos include eyewitness testimonies from SOHA, SOIA, and Camp Xanue.

I would like to share with you how I went about screening individuals to join me in my research area. It's very important that you

Chapter 16: Multiple Eyewitness Testimonials

don't just bring anyone along with you. First things first, do not bring anyone along with you who reeks of negativity. If they're dark on the inside, constantly treat others rudely and disrespectfully, and all they care about is themselves, I guarantee you that the Bigfoot Forest People will spot them a mile away and have nothing to do with them. They don't like 'A-Holes.'

In a couple of cases over the years, I've had people ask me to provide them with some consultation in order to assist them in improving the possibility of success in their research area. I always have them openly and honestly tell me about their research team members. Then if necessary, I'll hone in on an individual team member who is coming across to me as a potential 'A-Hole.' If my suspicions are confirmed, I'll tell them to cut the 'A-Hole' off of their team. Those who listen to me and have followed through with my advice started to see improvement in interactions almost immediately. Those who ignored my advice continued to experience very little, if anything at all, in their research areas.

In one case in the Midwest, a gentleman who ignored my advice at first because the guy that I identified as the proverbial 'A-Hole' on his team was his best friend, eventually cut his best friend off of his research team. As a result, he noticed an increase in visuals and interactions almost immediately. I don't care if the 'A-Hole' on your research team is your best friend or spouse, either they change their ways or you cut them from the team if you want to experience results. Serious Bigfooting is not about going out into the woods to have a fun time with your friends. Rather, it's about doing anything and everything to increase the likelihood of experiencing increased sightings and interactions. If you have to cut someone from the team, then cut them from the team. You can spend fun times with them doing other things besides Bigfooting with them (i.e., Bowling, fishing, sports events, etc.).

Next, I screen for people to accompany me to my research area who are (1) kind, with (2) good hearts, and (3) open minds. They also have to be teachable and willing to submit to my protocol. If you have established a successful protocol in your research area and are experiencing the Bigfoot Forest People multiple times, why would you risk bringing someone out with you who thinks they know it all and who's un-teachable? They will set your research success backwards.

A couple of years ago, I had to withdraw my offer to bring a well-known figure in Bigfootdom with me to SOHA. I had been pestered by others for years to bring this gentleman to SOHA with me. However, when it came time for me to vet him like I do everyone else who comes to SOHA with me, this person became offended. They thought that they should be able to come to SOHA simply because of who they were and their status in the kingdom of Bigfootdom. I was left with no other choice but to inform this person that they weren't going to be able to come along. He most definitely did not have a teachable spirit about him. Many people know that this gentleman is polite but arrogant. Unfortunately, he doesn't know as much as he thinks he knows.

The next thing that I would do when it came to inviting potential eyewitnesses to SOHA, I would have them sign a nondisclosure agreement (NDA). Contrary to the rumors that the TROLLS in Bigfootdom were spreading, the NDA did not prevent anyone from talking about their experiences in SOHA. Why on God's green Earth would I invite multiple witnesses to SOHA and then prohibit them from talking about their experiences while being there with me? That doesn't make any sense at all. Instead, the NDA encouraged them to talk about their experiences at SOHA. The only thing that the NDA prohibited anyone from doing was (1) not to tell anyone else where SOHA was located, and (2) never go back to SOHA unless they were coming back as my guest. Oh yes, plus I got their first-born child. Muhahahahahaha! That's the way cult leaders roll.

I always explained my protocol to my potential guests and told them that they would follow it to the letter of the law or I would escort them off the mountain and that they would never be welcomed back. This included no alcohol or drugs, peeing and pooping only in the identified areas, smoking in the designated spaces, no fires or lights, and absolutely no freaking out allowed. I always had to chuckle when individuals would respond to me with, "Freak out about what?" I

Chapter 16: Multiple Eyewitness Testimonials

would tell them about all of the potential things that they could see or experience while in SOHA, including waking up in the middle of the night to a Bigfoot Forest Person right next to their cot.

As I just said, they were told that they could not freak out. I would tell them that they were to act like they were a Navy Seal and that they were as strong as steel. Almost everyone who comes with me is totally scared to death on their first night to my research area. It's kind of cute. When they wake up the next morning, I'll look at them and ask them if they're alive? Naturally, they respond to me with a "Yes" and ask me why. I just remind them that the Bigfoot Forest People surrounded us last night and that it's important data to note that absolutely no one woke up dead in the morning. They get my point and manage to relax much more during their second and third nights to my research area.

Finally, I require my attendees to speak out about their experiences when they come to my research area. Multiple witness testimonies, that all see, experience, and say the same things over and over again, provide some serious credibility to my research methods and results. Their eyewitness testimony is especially compelling when combined with circumstantial evidence. Most of my multiple eyewitnesses have been willing to give their testimonies via my YouTube videos (please watch them in order from the oldest video first to the newest video last). Afterwards, they have talked with their family and friends about what they experienced in SOHA, SOIA, or at Camp Xanue as well as participated in group discussions via my "Team Squatchin USA" Facebook Group page. Finally, several of them have provided written testimonies which you can read at the end of this book.

However, every once in a while, I'll run into individuals who hesitate to testify publicly, out of fear of retaliation from others. In other words, the kingdom of Bigfootdom can be very political and there are people out there who, don't want to hear the truth, nor do they want others validating the truth that I am sharing with the world. For example, initially, Ron Morehead and his fiancé, Keri Campbell, didn't want to testify publicly about coming to my research area nor share what they experienced in SOIA. Ron is well known and connected in Bigfootdom and he feared that some individuals might shun him or get on his case for hanging out with me and verifying my research results. Eventually, he spoke up and even submitted a write up for my first Bigfoot book. Thank you very much, Ron and Keri.

Another example would be my third child, Micah. He came to my SOIA research area with me twice during the 2016 research season and was totally blown away. He told me that it turned out that his dad wasn't crazy after all. I needed to hear my son say that. Nevertheless, he wanted me to delay any public mentioning of his coming to my research area because he needed some time to process everything before he was willing to go public with his experiences.

Finally, I brought a world renowned Cryptozoologist to SOHA in 2014 with me and he was so overwhelmed by what he experienced that he didn't want to tell anyone anything for fear of public ridicule. The first two nights, he and his friend were overwhelmed by the amount of Bigfoot activity, visuals, and vocals around the perimeter of the SOHA base camp. Then if that wasn't enough, the last two nights were spent dealing with a portal that they accidentally opened up along with the two guardians who were doing their best to keep us away from the portal.

In conclusion, there's absolutely nothing wrong with you going out into your own area and keeping your experiences private. In that case, you're not trying to share your data with others nor are you trying to educate the world. Keep on Squatchin in privacy. On the other hand, if your goal is to share your data with others and you want to help educate the world about the Bigfoot Forest People phenomena, you're going to need to collect circumstantial evidence and you're going to need to supplement it with a whole lot of credible eyewitness testimonies. There's truth to be found in a multitude of eyewitnesses, especially when combined with a whole lot of circumstantial evidence. The skeptics can doubt or disbelieve you but they're much less likely to successfully deny information provided by a whole bunch of credible eyewitnesses.

Chapter 16: Multiple Eyewitness Testimonials

With all of that said, I would strongly encourage you to read the following thirty eyewitness testimonials submitted by people from all walks of life who have been with me to SOHA, SOIA, and Camp Xanue. It is absolutely amazing to read through all of the stories. You'll see that everyone has unique, personal experiences. While at the same time, there are a lot of overlapping, similar experiences too. The thirty eyewitness written testimonials are guaranteed to blow your mind.

Steve Bachmann

(Buckley, Washington)

Hello to everyone reading this book! Almost four years have passed since the time of the Xanue EXODUS from June 25th through the 28th of 2016. Looking back at the three days that I participated in the EXODUS, I have come a long way in the world of the Xanue. In fact, they have taken me so far down the Rabbit Hole, it has given me a front seat view of who these people really are. But having said that, I do not claim to have all of the answers nor the scientific evidence to prove how they do the things they do. Yes, they are a people with special abilities and a devotion to God Almighty.

First of all, I would like to put my association with the Xanue into perspective. After June 26, 2016, I had no idea how my life was going to change because I had taken an electromagnetic pulsating device to the Southern Oregon Interaction Area (SOIA). The machine became a source that the Xanue could use to keep a portal open which allowed the rest of their people (23,542 souls) to abandoned their dying planet and live here on the Earth. However, what I did not know is that we have evil here on the Earth – the Xuxiko.

The Xuxiko did not like what I had done. Matt had warned me about this. However, it just seemed like a story until they attacked me – twice. You may be wondering why didn't the Xanue stop it. Well, they did stop it. They caught them in the act both times and saved me. Since the attack, the Xanue have increased their protection around me at all times.

I am very aware of the Xanue's physical presence during the day as there are three Xanue Orbs with me at all times. They never leave me unattended. At night, when I go to sleep, I am much more vulnerable to attack. Therefore, they always have extra Xanue Orbs on me and around me while I sleep. I have counted up to eight to ten Orbs with me during the night. You might be wondering how I can get to sleep with all of this activity? Well, I have actually gotten used to it and I don't mind them being with me at all. Yes, it's pretty crazy stuff but I've come to accept it as a fact of life.

While I'm working, they seem to not interact with me unless I ask them to. They do this to help keep my life normal as possible. Sometimes people will ask me where the three Orbs are who are protecting me. Well, I have two that are attached to my body. I can feel them when they move around. The third one is a female Xanue Orb named Shenka. She protects my head and interacts with me when I ask her to.

The interactions with Shenka are incredibly physical as she will answer questions with a 'yes' or 'no'. It's not mind speak. Rather, she pushes or squeezes the side of my head to answer 'yes' or does nothing to answer 'no'. Other individuals experience mind speak with the Xanue and it sometimes seems hard to believe. However, I did have a mind speak with a male one year after the EXODUS. Utilizing mind speak, he told me just how thankful they all were for me bringing the electro-magnetic pulsating device up to the mountains at the Southern Oregon Interaction Area (SOIA). He was grateful that I helped to save his fellow Xanue brothers and sisters. It was such a shock to me. I could hardly believe what I was hearing. He proceeded to say the same thing over again three times. I'm sure that he repeated it three times so that it would sink in that I was actually being mind spoken to and not imagining something. The voice was clear, loud, and in perfect English. By the way, mind speak is really cool and I hope to experience it on a regular basis someday. It has been indicated to me that it will happen someday. For now, the physical aspect of interaction and communication is just fine.

The abilities that the Xanue have in which I have witnessed or experienced are numerous. I have no idea how they do it. I have witnessed and experienced the following: Orbs have gone right through my body without me experiencing any pain. Healing that seems to be more like a procedure, but not like our modern medical doctors – It's almost magic like. Higher states of consciousness that allow for astroprojection and total ascension from my body. In order to prove that the Orbs were the Bigfoot, Sasquatch, Xanue, they have shapeshifted in front of me so that I could see them and touch his hairy arm. They did this about six months after the EXODUS. These Orbs visit me every night and interact with me because they know that I do not fear them. I constantly tell them that they are my trusted friends and that I love them very much. Please keep in mind that as I explain this to all of you who are reading this book, I'm merely scratching the surface of explanation. It is impossible to explain the deep and personal relationship that I have with the Xanue.

There are many people out there who are in many different places regarding their experiences with the Xanue. There are readers of books, YouTube researchers, campers who listen for knocks and screams, people who enjoy the social activity of conferences, people who gift food, and the serious researchers who are scouring the forest floor looking for tracks. Most researchers are of the mindset that Bigfoot is an allusive flesh and blood giant mountain ape or a Wildman of the forest. This mindset is very wrong. Myself, I'm very distant from all of this but I do agree that people have the right to do and have fun as they wish.

There was a time when I felt strongly that I should go to my local woods and find a Xanue family that I could get to know and socialize with. However, I was stopped by the Xanue with a very powerful mind speak that said, "Steve, do not come looking for us because we will come to you." To date, the Xanue have lived up to their word and the bond between us is stronger than ever.

I would like to talk a little bit about the Xanue who came through the portal. During the first two years after the EXODUS, the Xanue orbs came and interacted with me every single night. There was never just one. Several of them would come visit and cozy up to me while giving me energy kisses, as I refer to them. Some people refer to it as getting zapped. They gave me soft energy kisses letting me know that they were grateful for what Matt, Mike, and I had done for them.

THE XANUE

Stop and think about it for a moment. It must be nice to escape a dying planet and come to the Earth where they can live a healthy life. 23,542 Xanue lives were saved. If you've done your homework and read Matt's first Bigfoot book or watched his four-part video series about "The Great Reveal," then you'll know that these individuals did not have the energy and ability to manipulate the portals to get through on their own. They needed assistance. We helped them. Pretty simple.

Two weeks before writing this testimonial for Matt's second Bigfoot (Xanue) book, I had the most extraordinary Xanue Orb visits that I've ever had. This particular Orb responded to everything that I said. If I asked a question that required a 'yes' or 'no' response, it would tap, tap, tap on my leg for 'yes' and do absolutely nothing for a 'no' response. I asked the Orb, "Did you come through the portal when I brought the electromagnetic pulsating device up to the mountain at SOIA?" The orb gave me a 'yes' response. I said, "I'm incredibly happy that you made it here." The Orb immediately responded with an energy kiss. I asked if the Orb was a female and I received no response. I asked the orb if it was a male and I received a tap, tap, tap response. The entire conversation went on for thirty-minutes. I finished by telling him that I loved him and that I hoped he lives a long life. He responded with another energy kiss.

Let me tell you, the interesting thing now in my life is that I have totally adapted to the Xanue living and interacting with me. It's a normal thing to have the Xanue tugging on my foot or arm just to wake me up in the middle of the night to say 'hello' and give me a soft energy kiss. This is so personal and private and nothing short of amazing. I wonder how many people will read this book and be thinking, "Boy, this guy is whacked out." Well, if that's the way you're thinking, don't bother thinking again because you're the one who's missing out on interacting with God's wonderful children. Imagine your most trusted brother, sister, mom, dad, or friend in the whole wide world – a person who you know that always tells the truth because you know this person all too well. That's who I have always been. The people who know me know that I'm telling the God's honest truth.

Steve Bachmann

Many other people have experienced what I've experienced with the Xanue. However, it seems like one person to the next has a slightly different experience. Many people have told me about their interactions with the Xanue and about their trouble dealing with their own fears. I'm here to tell you that the Xanue, who are children of God, will not hurt you. Matter of fact, if you ever have the opportunity to interact with the Xanue, I strongly encourage you to speak honestly from your heart and they will help you.

I have been asked many times how did you get used to this way of life. My answer is that I had no choice because it was a matter of circumstances. If I was to live after the EXODUS, then I needed to be heavily protected by the Xanue. There were 23,542 Xanue who were very happy that they were allowed to escape their dying world. As a result, many of them are very happy to help keep me safe. It's a little overwhelming at times. I would like to express my deepest gratitude for the Xanue helping to keep me safe and for doing their upmost to help keep my life fairly normal while they're doing so. I'm sure that it's no easy job keeping a human safe 24/7.

The other thing that I would like to shed some light on is social media. The social media platforms provide a place to tell the world of your Xanue experiences. I like to read about other peoples' experiences with the Xanue and how exactly the interactions occur. Healings are my favorite stories. I was recently asked why I don't share about my personal experiences on the social media platforms. Well, because I don't want to feel like I'm competing with others. The experiences that I'm having are never ending and to be honest, I can't keep up with it all.

A man once wrote me and said that if you do not write a book and share about your Xanue experiences, then history will be lost forever. At this point in time, I don't feel the need to write a book. However, I must admit that this is far from being over and it really feels like the journey is just beginning. What I mean by this is that a lot that they have taught me has left me at a cross road. Until the Xanue take me down that road, I will not write a book without these personal experiences being fulfilled first. These experiences are tied to meditation and higher consciousness that include the Xanue. There is so much to be explored.

I leave you now with a ton of unanswered questions or disbelief. Yes, I know the rest of you totally get it based upon your own experiences with the Xanue. I was very lucky to be in the right place at the right time. I went from a novice YouTube Bigfooter to a full blown Xanue family member.

If there's one thing that I want to leave readers to remember, it's this: If you want a true friendship with the Xanue, please follow Dr. Matthew A. Johnson's guided information provided in his books or Google the four-part YouTube video series, "The Great Reveal." Read his book, "BIGFOOT: A Fifty-Year Journey Come Full Circle." Watch hundreds of his YouTube videos by starting with the oldest one and working your way up to the newest videos.

At the time of the EXODUS in June of 2016, Dr. Matthew A. Johnson had sixteen-years of research under his belt. The first ten years started off with the "Old School" philosophy. When he changed his perspective and approach to interacting with the Bigfoot Forest People, they began to mind speak with him and shared with him who they really are, where they're from, and why they're here. Matt brought me in and in one month, he shared with me everything that he had to offer about the Xanue. Then in one night, yes, just one night, my world was shaken to the core. I became, along with Matt and Mike, a family member of these GREAT CREATURES OF GOD.

Cindy Barger

(Royal City, Washington)

I don't really know where to begin, but here goes. We have watched the "Finding Bigfoot" shows on TV. We wondered about why they were always going out at night to look for Bigfoot when many of their witnesses would state that they had their Bigfoot encounters during the day. Nevertheless, we watched the "Finding Bigfoot" TV program anyway and waited for them to find that big hairy being. My interest in this TV series lessened and I didn't really give it another thought.

My husband, Stuart, didn't give up. He kept researching and found Dr. Matthew A. Johnson ("Dr. J."). He started telling me about what "Dr. J's" experience and research revealed. He pre-purchased "Dr. J's" book. Also, he anxiously waited for the four-part video series, "The Great Reveal," to be posted on "Dr. J's" Team Squatchin USA YouTube channel. Honestly, I only halfway listened to this and watched "The Great Reveal" video series with doubt on my mind. Stuart always said he wanted to go to Oregon to "Dr. J's" interaction area. However, this simply was not to be due to my cancer battle in 2017. I had five surgeries. Two of those surgeries were lifesaving emergencies.

Then in 2018, Stuart repeatedly mentioned how "Dr. J." was going to host night sit and sleep over weekends on his property. Stuart wanted to go. I kind of kept listening but I wasn't overly interested. However, Stuart wanted this so bad that without his prior knowledge, I contacted "Dr. J.," to see if we could attend the September 2018 night sit weekend. So, to prepare, I read "Dr. J's" book: "BIGFOOT: A Fifty-Year Journey Come Full Circle." I also re-watched the four-part video series, "The Great Reveal." Reading "Dr. J's" book and watching the four-part video series is required to attend the Camp Xanue weekend events at their property. As I stated in my first introductory video, I was there for Stuart.

In September of 2018, during the first night sit and sleep over weekend, I met many wonderful people from all over the US and Canada. "Dr. J." and Cynthia were so welcoming. When you step on their property, you feel nothing but love, respect, and welcomed. Anyway, during that weekend, I listened intently to what "Dr. J." had to say. However, I didn't really have a lot of interaction that weekend. I thought that I might have seen some twinkling lights in the trees. However, I was so unsure so I chose not to mention it.

While we were beginning the night sit on the second night, I did hear a very large howl. However, another night sit guest kept howling back. When "Dr. J." walked up, he asked her to stop. I did not get to hear the large howl again that night. Again, I questioned what I really heard that night. In spite of some of the possible interactions, I remained a skeptic during my first night sit and sleep over weekend. I questioned all that I saw and heard but I could not deny the testimonials I heard of others' interactions. I enjoyed listening to others telling their stories.

In 2018, I had gone through radiation treatment. I also took chemo pills. Finally, I utilized natural medication to help fight my cancer battle. In September of 2018, when we attended our first night sit, I was still very weak. Stuart did not allow me to walk too far down into "Dr. J's" property. After I returned home, things began to happen that I cannot deny. One night, I was sound asleep and I felt my arms and legs suddenly be moved. On another night, I woke up to my puppy barking and I saw a shadowy figure standing in my bedroom door. As time passed, I continued to get movement in my sleep, tingling sensation in my body prior to sleep, and most important of all, my health began to improve.

Fast forward to June of 2019. My son, Matt, and my husband, Stuart, attended the June night sit and sleep over weekend event at Camp Xanue. My son wanted to ask Zorth about me through "Dr.

J." However, Zorth answered my son's question before he could ask it. The answer was, "There are two Xanue with your Mom. They are not quite done. They are still working on her." So, I started talking to my friends here with me, although I did not know their names.

In July of 2019, Stuart and I attended the night sit and sleep over weekend event at Camp Xanue. On Friday night, we were sitting in Serenity Meadow. Above and behind us, up high, there was a couple pops of strobe light. Twice, later that night, I said I would really like to see that again. Each time I asked, it happened.

On Saturday night, while Stuart and I were visiting the woodpile, I thanked the Xanue for sending help to me. I let them know that I had a scan coming up in two weeks and that I would really appreciate it if I could have a clear scan with a reduction in tumors or have my tumors be gone. Afterwards, we continued with the amazing night sit. While we were sitting there with the others, "Dr. J." said that Kontue was over to the right. Stuart walked over to visit him. As Stuart was over there, I thought my eyes were going crazy. I kept seeing my husband fade in and out. Then from behind me I heard others ask, "Is Stuart's head disappearing?" I leaned over and asked "Dr. J.," "Am I seeing things or does Stuart keep fading in and out?" He looked and saw it too. Eventually, others took their turn and walked over to visit with Kontue and his wife, Sayreah. Any light-colored clothing or grey or white hair would disappear. This was due to Kontue's and Sayreah's higher vibrational frequency which was partially or fully cloaking the people that they were hugging.

Later that night, I asked Stuart if he would go over so I could see him disappear again. He went over and he was hugged by Kontue. Once again, Stuart was cloaked and disappeared. Two weeks later, I had my scan and bloodwork done. My tumor markers in my bloodwork came back normal and the tumors were almost non-existent in my scan. A prior scan in October of 2018 showed they had been shrinking but not like this. I was officially in remission. Since then, all my scans and bloodwork have continued to be normal and clear. I have another scan in two days on December 24, 2019. I feel this scan will be clear as well.

THE XANUE

I also want to mention at this point that I did not take any chemo of any sort in 2019, yet my cancer went into remission.

Back tracking just a bit. After my son, Matt, was told there were two Xanue with me, I would talk to them and kept asking them for a name. After months of this, I grew impatient and began calling my friends "Fred." Well, one day, I was driving and I was just thinking of my friends at home and kept referring to them as "Fred." Then I heard, "No! Tobias." I decided to mentally argue and kept thinking, "No! Fred." Then, he became very insistent, "No! Tobias." I responded, "Okay. Now I know you are Tobias." That is not the only time I have heard Tobias speak. One morning, my dog would not stop barking. He barked on and on and on. Eventually, I said "I don't know what has got you going and barking so much this morning but you need to settle down." Then I heard Tobias say, "He is barking at me." I replied, "I know but he needs to settle down."

Since attending the night sit and sleep over weekend events at Camp Xanue, I have now seen dark figures in my home. I have also seen Orbs in my home. I have even taken a picture of a shimmering dark figure in the corner of my dining room. The same location that my dog barks at every night. My son, Matt, has visited and has seen shimmering images in my home. I have gone on early morning trips and I have had large Orbs pop or flash at me outside of my car as if to say, "We are here with you." I honestly do not mention this to many individuals because most people are still too skeptical. However, I do tell my hubby and son these experiences.

Whether or not my improved health is due to God's will, the help of the Xanue, or because of my natural medication, I am still here. I am thankful for every breath I take. I do not attribute my improved health to any of the modern medication. I am here to state that I believe that the Xanue are with us. They are Beings of Light. I cannot continue to deny the things I have seen and heard myself.

Putting myself and my health aside, I must mention the outright miracle I saw happen with my own eyes. I saw a miracle happen to a fellow night sit and sleep over attendee at Camp Xanue in August of

2019. When I first met Ruth, she could not walk far due to several strokes. She relied greatly on her husband for support. The next day, I saw her running and jumping. It was a true miracle! The rest of the story is her story to tell.

I am thankful for my husband, Stuart, for leading me down this "Rabbit Hole." The doubters will continue to doubt until they witness an interaction for themselves. I am thankful for all the connections I have made at Camp Xanue. Not only have I made new friends; I have new family. Thank you, "Dr. J." and Cynthia, for opening your home and allowing these connections to be made. Not only between the weekend attendees, but with the Xanue and for the interactions with them we witnessed.

Andrea Billups
(Bowling Green, Kentucky)

A person smarter than I once told me that the Forest People will ultimately give you what they think you're ready for, understanding perhaps better than we do that our capacity to understand them and their gifts — differs from person to person. I still believe this is true. They respond and contact as you are ready. They know your intentions. This is, as weird as it might sound, a part of their special gifts. They can see through people and their motives. That's what I now have come to believe.

For years, I knew I was on some sort of journey. I'm still not certain what drew me to all of it. But not until my visits to Oregon and Washington State, confronting the truth of their existence alongside Dr. Matthew A. Johnson (Dr. J.), did I fully embrace what was happening to me and what continues to happen.

Not long after my return from the Southern Oregon Habituation Area (SOHA), they made themselves known in a big way. It was, I think, their way of ensuring that what I saw was indeed real and they would not be bound by geography. One day, while meditating in the forest near my home, I said in my mind: "If you are real, show yourself." I knew beyond all doubt from my experiences with Dr. J that they were real, but things had happened to me back home in Michigan that suggested they remained close.

Nothing happened immediately. So I got up from the pine fur carpet where I'd been sitting, off trail, and turned around to hike back out. I was at least a mile from the trailhead and alone, midday. I took several steps and then a flash of red caught my eye to the left. The color was significant because it stood in stark contrast to the green of the pine stand that infused this area of my woods. Something was running like a jet. Moving so fast that my mind wasn't processing. But what I saw was red fur, hair, billowing in the propulsion. Something was up and then dropped down and disappeared over an embankment. It happened in the blink of an eye and it was initially just too much to process.

Your mind drifts — a fox. A flying squirrel. No. What I saw moving so fast was at eye level and then dropped. I never saw a face. I think perhaps I saw a shoulder and arm, but that was it. The whole thing happened so fast and my heart was racing. Strangely, I walked toward it. I got back on the trail, walking about twenty yards, and then it hit me. I was alone. I had no protection — did I need it? It was that "oh, my gosh?" moment. What did I just see?

Overcome with fear, I took off running. Up and over the trails, across a marsh, into dense hardwoods, where I finally had to stop because I could not breathe. I sat down on a log to catch my breath. My head was spinning. Then the unthinkable happened. I look across the woods, perhaps fifty yards away. I watched as a log was dropped out of the top of a tree. Not end on end. Dropped horizontally and smashing to the forest floor in a giant crash.

Was something trying to get my attention? Was I being followed out? It was so shattering that I got up and began running again, never stopping until I got to the trail head. Whatever had happened, whatever the rationale, I knew I was not alone that day. Something was responding to my demand to "show yourself." Something surely did.

And that would be only the start of weirder, odder things to come in my woods. My space here is limited so let me share a couple of anecdotes. This past Christmas, I returned to Michigan for a visit. We sold our home there in 2018. I am now a professor of journalism, teaching in Kentucky. I entered my woods with the only two people I've ever taken there — my friends Timothy Collins and Jim Silsby. About four years' prior, all of us had met up and visited my Angel tree area where I'd gifted and had my interactions. At that time, we left a hand-crafted grass doll in the crook of this broken tree, at least seven feet up and hidden. A few weeks passed and then poof! The doll had been removed.

Four years passed. We returned right after Christmas 2019. We hiked into the area about mid-afternoon and to our great shock, the same grass doll was returned, at the base and inside the hollowed part of the tree. We were, to say the least, stunned. But ponder it — a doll left years back by us all, was returned to us the only day we'd been out there in the past two years. It was in good shape. Although the doll was weathered, it was still very dry and intact. We thanked our Forest People and felt like we'd just received the greatest acknowledgement ever. The pictures I took on my phone while we were out there confirmed, as I knew, that we were not alone.

My interactions continue. From Michigan to Florida, where I taught for a time, to Kentucky. Recently, Dr. Daniel Reilly, who wrote this book's forward, visited me at my home in Bowling Green, Kentucky. We went for a chilly night sit together. We followed our protocol — no lights save a red light for the trail so we wouldn't stumble. We hiked down a trail and sat down quietly. About twenty minutes later, the energy shifted and the forest floor lit up in the most unusual way — it was luminescent. White lights began to shine and pop. Then, as I felt vibration under my feet, the howls and screams began. Later, the requisite wood knock and then a sighting of the Orbs. We knew from the start that our friends were with us. The interaction on a dark night, deep in Mammoth Caves National Park, was so loving.

I believe that if they know you — and your heart and intentions — they will always be with you. I have moved a lot and everywhere I go things happen. Gifts, glyphs, signs that are often subtle but unmistakable. I know they want to reach out to me and I appreciate having them around. Yes, I've received and continue to get the mind speak that others have shared about. It's a beautiful reassurance. Shocking but amazing.

I hope to always continue on this journey down the rabbit hole. I am glad my earliest connections to SOHA, SOIA and Dr. J have opened up this path. I would not have believed any of this was possible ten years ago. My mind has been opened and I am learning and embracing. I feel lucky and I thank them.

Brittany Bosen

(Salt Lake City, Utah)

My father introduced me to Matthew's book and his online YouTube videos. My father has been really interested in this sort of thing for many years and he has kept me well informed with most of his findings. I accompanied my father to Matt and Cynthia's home for a weekend at Camp Xanue in September of 2018. It was a very memorable experience, and I intend to return for as many visits as possible in the future. Not only was the company good, and the food delicious, but the hospitality of Matt and Cynthia was amazing.

I am more of a shy person when placed in a large group of strangers, but Matt and Cynthia made me feel very comfortable and very welcomed. They both went above and beyond to make sure it was a great experience – not only for me, but for everyone in attendance. It takes a special kind of person to be able to open up their home to so many strangers, and so frequently. Matt and Cynthia will always hold a special place in my heart for the kindness they have shown me.

I was able to stay overnight on their property for three nights in a row. The first night was rainy and cold, but I was determined to be outside sleeping on a cot, covered in a tarp, to experience the weekend in its fullest. That first night was the most memorable night of the weekend for me. After sitting up until about midnight with my father and two other CIA guests, I felt that I should make my way back to my cot to be by myself. We were on the far side of the property further down the trail than anyone else. It was a chilly night, so I was wearing multiple layers, had a heavy sleeping bag, two blankets, and then had a heavy tarp over the top of all of it. About ten minutes after I got settled in the cot under the tarp, I heard unusually heavy footsteps approach

THE XANUE

the side of my cot. The end of the tarp lifted, was put back down, but there were no footsteps walking away. I did not have a sense of fear, or uneasiness. I felt a strong sense of peace, but it had definitely got my blood pumping. I was wide awake. Then I heard my father walk up the trail and go to bed in his cot that was about five feet away from mine.

I fell asleep and was having one of the most vivid dreams I've ever had. I can still tell you exactly what was happening when all of a sudden I was wide awake. The tarp was still covering me. It was raining lightly. I laid there listening to the raindrops hitting against the plastic. All of a sudden, I heard what sounded like children's footsteps running up the trail towards me. It sounded like there were maybe three different younger Xanue racing each other. I could hear them giggling as they ran right up to the edge of my cot. I then heard them turn around and run away. They ran back up to the cot, and then once again ran away while giggling the entire time. It was almost as if they were playing a game with each other.

Then I heard just one pair of feet run right up to the very edge of my cot. I could sense the Little One standing right next to me. I couldn't help but smile, and wish that I could take the tarp off and see them. I heard the Little One move, and I felt him touch the small of my back. It was as if there was no barrier between the Little One and myself. As soon as I felt the hand on my back, energy started moving within me – possibly coming from the Little One itself. It felt like ripples all over my entire body, starting from where the hand was resting. This went on for possibly two to three minutes. Then I heard a pair of very large heavy feet walk up the trail. When that Xanue reached my cot I heard it give a low rumbling growl, then the Little One walked away with the bigger one. Not once did I feel unsafe or threatened. In fact, I felt very peaceful the entire time. I felt very honored that I was able to have such a personal experience with a Little One.

The next morning, when my father woke up, I asked him how his night went and if he had heard or experienced anything. All he had to report was that he slept very well considering it had been raining. I found this interesting, because I honestly believe that the Xanue can customize the experience for each individual to whatever is best for that person – no matter the surroundings, or if there are other people present.

Later, that same day, a majority of the group was able to go on a hike, led by Matt, around his and Cynthia's property. He showed us all sorts of structures in the trees, gifting stumps, and we even came across a couple of Xanue footprints in the mud. The feeling and the energy on their property is amazing and beautiful. It's such a positive, warm, and welcoming environment that no wonder so many people want to go back again.

The remaining two nights, I moved my cot down to the very end of the trail so I could be by myself. Throughout both nights, I could hear the Xanue walking around me and making loud whooping calls. I could feel them and I could smell them. The smell was so strong that it was almost as if one of them was in the sleeping bag with me.

After I returned back home to Utah, I was able to better understand what was going on around me. Things that I had already been experiencing, I now felt very strongly that they are tied to the Xanue. These experiences started to increase significantly, and I am so glad that they have. Things that some people might view as coincidence, or just an unexplainable event or accident, I know that there is more to it. We aren't alone. The Xanue want to make contact and want us to be aware of them. They will come to you if you are a kind person, have good heart, and an open mind.

Ruth Cameron
(Phoenix, Arizona)

I'd like to share my story and my wonderful experience with the Xanue. First of all, I want to tell you just a little bit about myself and how all this ties in together. I am a preacher's kid (PK). My dad was in the ministry for over sixty-years before he died. I was raised knowing God's word and faith, but I lost it when I had my strokes. I've suffered three strokes. The first two strokes were not your typical symptoms that we've all learned to recognize. Unfortunately, they went untreated because of that. After losing most of the use and control of my right leg and some in my arm and hand, the third stroke left me having to learn how to walk again. I could barely walk. I got chiropractic adjustments but nothing worked.

It wasn't until the evening that my husband was in the room and noticed my face started to droop. Also, my right arm began to tingle and go numb. My husband, David, just grabbed me and said, "We're going now!" Fortunately, there was an Urgent Care less than a mile from us. After the CAT Scan, they could see the two previous lesions on my brain and the larger most recent one. They transferred me to the hospital immediately.

After about a week in the hospital, I went into rehab for about a month before I was released. All of this caused me to fall into a very deep depression and I just didn't want to live anymore. One night, I had a very vivid dream or vision of my deceased parents.

I was with my mom and dad in heaven. I was so happy because I was back to my old self again. I was feeling whole again. I was so happy and I wanted to stay but my dad told me, "You have to go back." I said, "No! I don't want to go back. Please don't make me go back. I want to stay here with you and mom." Then my dad said, "You can't stay. There is a lot you still need to see and experience." We spoke without actually talking. I could hear what they were saying but their lips weren't moving. I just felt so much love and I didn't want to leave.

I ended up coming back and I was angry. I was so angry because when I awoke, I wasn't healed. I was upset because I couldn't do a lot of simple things like dressing myself or getting up from a chair. I couldn't even be trusted to hold and watch my great grandchild that I had looked so forward to doing so. That angered me even more. I couldn't even ride my bike with the grandkids. They urged me to try one day. However, after a few tries, I would just fall over and I would land hard on the ground. I tried a few more times but I couldn't stay up on it. I just cried and cried.

I became so depressed. I kept telling David, "Just let me die! Just let me die!" I even prayed and asked God, "Just let me die!" I felt alienated from my loved ones because they treated me differently. I was no longer invited on things that required physical action and that just deepened my depression further.

Early in the year of 2019, David told me about Dr. Matthew A. Johnson and the Xanue. My first thought was that my husband had lost his mind. It all seemed to be way too much. My husband brought me into this because he was always interested in Bigfoot. When he found Dr. Johnson, he was so intrigued by what Dr. Johnson called the Xanue - The Bigfoot Forest People. David jumped at an open invitation to visit Camp Xanue in Chehalis, Washington. In the summer of 2019, he took the trip with our two grandsons, Armani & AJ. Upon their return home to Arizona, they all shared their experiences with me and I couldn't believe it. My grandsons confirmed all that my husband was telling the family of what he had experienced. With Armani's and A.J.s experiences, I believed something was going on there.

I was really shocked that this could actually be true. Society tells us that these sorts of things can't possibly be real. What David was telling me sounded like a fairy tale story. Well, there was one more event at Camp Xanue coming up in two months and David asked me if I wanted to go. I initially said, "No!" However, my grandson, Armani, said to me, "Grandma, you have to go. There's so much love there. You have to go see it." I still wasn't sure though and knew that getting any kind of healing was out of the question. David reassured me that the Xanue can heal. He also told me that while he was at the wood pile on his first trip, he told the Xanue that he wasn't concerned about any healing for himself. Instead, he asked them to take a look at his wife who had recently suffered from strokes. I was in doubt of healing from these "forest people" because I knew only God could do this. I fully didn't understand. I did pray and asked God, "If this is of You, then You will let me know."

About a month before the trip to Camp Xanue, we had stayed in the mountains of northern Arizona. I needed to get out of the city. I was really hitting rock bottom. My sister offered me her cabin and I jumped at it. There was something about that trip and being in the forest that put me back in touch with nature and God. I hadn't necessarily cared and forgot the true beauty of nature. God showed me and gave me a new appreciation of the forest and nature. I suddenly was so ready to now go on this trip to the State of Washington. I know now that God had a plan for me and was preparing me for this. Let me tell you, I am a big city girl and camping of any kind was not my cup of tea. Sleeping on a cot in the woods was something I would NEVER do!!! I knew God had heard my prayers.

When we arrived at Camp Xanue, I saw the hills and the terrain. The Johnson's home is on a mountain top and it slopes down the south side of the mountain to the wetlands below. It scared me right away because I knew I wouldn't survive walking through that terrain on their property. I also didn't really care to socialize as I saw others who were already there. I tried hard to put on a smile. I said to myself, "What am I doing here? I can't do this." My doubts and fears were returning again. My husband said, "I'll help you. Just take your time."

I was worried because I had forgotten to pack my braces that I usually wore. I struggled everywhere I walked. I had to hold tightly on to my husband's arm as I walked in the house and around the property. I was so embarrassed for my husband. He stayed with me the whole time. David constantly reassured me that everything was going to be ok.

I mentioned to Cynthia, Dr. Johnson's wife, that I had forgotten my braces. She said that she happened to have some braces that might work. I was so relieved. They helped me so much. I thought, "At least it will be a bit less challenging." However, I still felt like I was being a burden to David but I tried not to show it so much. Everyone at Camp Xanue was so helpful. I couldn't believe the love all around that I was receiving from complete strangers. I was making connections with others. Something wonderful was happening, but I wasn't sure exactly what it was yet.

My husband, David, showed me around Camp Xanue. We picked our spot in the forest where we were going to sleep each night. Sleeping in a very dark forest on cots was something I would never even have considered in the past. However, now I wasn't afraid in the least. I didn't know why yet but I wasn't afraid. I actually felt very safe and peaceful.

During our first "night sit" in Serenity Meadow, David and I walked together to the Wood Pile. Every night, the Xanue gather behind the woodpile for everyone to come and greet. While there, I introduced myself and held out my hands. I said, "I'm not afraid. It's okay to touch me if you want to." I watched as my fingers and hands began to tingle. Little bluish lights danced on them. My right hand is partially numb and tingles from my stroke. At first, I wasn't sure if what I was feeling was from my stroke or from the Xanue touching me. I looked past the wood pile and into the dark forest. I thanked the Xanue. As I did this, I could see a light back in the forest. I said aloud, "I can see you back there." My husband was being touched as well. We looked at each other smiling when we both heard loud heavy footsteps just a few feet away. Clearly there were three steps just a few feet to right of us. I said to David, "Did you hear that?" He said, "Yes." We both said 'hello' to whoever passed by.

After a while, we decided to go to our cots in the forest and go to sleep. I awoke later in the night to a light in a large tree in front of me. I blinked and rubbed my eyes and thought it would surely be gone when I reopened them. The light was still there. It wasn't on the tree. Rather, the light was within the tree. It gave me a feeling of peace and calmness.

After our first night sit, Dr. Johnson was speaking to the group in the morning. While he was talking, I felt my father's presence. I felt that God was talking through Dr. Johnson. He was sharing with us how the Xanue were healers through faith in Jesus Christ. When he tied the Xanue, God, Jesus and the Holy Spirit all together, I suddenly felt so much love and began to cry. His words of love and faith, were the same words I heard all my life from my dad. Dr. Johnson was sharing with us that the Xanue were giving the credit for any healing to God, Jesus, and the Holy Spirit.

He told us that the Xanue will only heal with God's permission. Being the daughter of a Pastor, I truly felt something special. After the group discussion and testimonials from the previous night's events, I began talking to Cynthia just outside the house. I confessed to her that I had anger from my strokes. I'd never told anyone of this except my husband and sister. I was surprised that I spoke of this to her. I told Cynthia of the anger and told her right there, "I'm releasing my anger. I'm letting it go." I suddenly felt something come over me. I felt like I was being renewed - a rebirth.

It was about then that my husband, David, came up the hill to help me. He grabbed my arm but I pushed him away and told him, "No! I can do this!" I removed my braces and started walking faster and faster. I began yelling, "Look, I'm walking without my limp!" I was so excited. I wanted Cynthia to be the first one that I told about my healing. I went looking for Cynthia and handed her the braces that she had lent to me. I told her, "I don't need these anymore." I took her to one of the hills and I ran for her several times. I couldn't help but do a little hop every now and then to show that I was healed. I told my husband that I was so glad that I came. I walked all of the way down the very long and very steep trail to the wetlands on the property. On the way back up the hill, my husband would say, "Slow down!" I beat him to the top of the hill. This trail is no easy hike. On the first day, before my healing, we walked down the hill only a little ways before I had to stop and turn back. I just couldn't do it. Now, it was easy peasy.

I went to Camp Xanue expecting only cold nights in the forest and being uncomfortable with strangers. I found loving hosts, loving Xanue, and wonderful people from all over country. We even had a special visitor from England. The love at the Johnson's property, and the love I felt from the Xanue, left me with no doubt of what I had experienced. I feel like my old self again!! I am able to run, carry my great grandkids in my arms, and play with my grandchildren. I praise God for using Dr. Johnson and Cynthia. I am thankful for all they shared with us. I am grateful to my husband, David, for taking me to Camp Xanue. I'm thankful that my two grandsons encouraged me to attend Camp Xanue. Finally, I thank the Xanue for embracing me. Today I am happy, grateful, and enjoying life again! God's love is amazing!

Mike Collier
(Green Bay, Wisconsin)

I would first like to start off by thanking Dr. Matthew A. Johnson ("Dr. J.") and his wife, Cynthia, for their unbelievable hospitality. I would also like to thank them for their very well run events that I was allowed to attend.

I met both of them at their wonderful home and property just west of Chehalis, Washington. My impression of "Dr. J." and Cynthia was really amazing. They were nothing like I had read or heard about. They were way better than the people I saw in the four-part video series, "The Great Reveal." However, I do understand why. Cynthia is a very heart felt lady and an AWESOME host. She shared her home and everything was just AMAZING to me. Thank You Again! The point is you are better in person than any videos. I suggest that people shouldn't judge until you meet the individuals in person.

During the June Camp Xanue weekend event, I wanted to learn what I needed to be doing or trying for more results on my own. I was definitely touched twice on my right ear lobe, during the sitting part of the event. During the September Camp Xanue weekend event, I felt a pretty constant presence on my left again, during the sitting portion. I think it was caught on a special camera used during this event.

I've learned that I must pay more or different attention. I must also add some music to my own research efforts. Hopefully, I've learned much more about the Xanue, and I'll be able to interact with them in time. I also hope to tell the difference between Xanue and Treykon.

"Dr. J." and Cynthia are VERY caring, gracious, kind, and loving people. They're Christian Believers! I had heard things about the two of them, good and bad, from different people. As someone who needs to know for himself, I read your book along with over 190 other Bigfoot books in the past five years. Also, I have attended thirty BFRO expeditions and four times that of my own throughout the US and Canada. I've spent over forty-seven thousand dollars and have traveled over ninety-seven thousand miles.

I saw a testimony of someone I had met, Faydra Romero, while on expedition in Arizona. You can watch her amazing testimonial on "Dr. J's" Team Squatchin USA YouTube channel. I am friends with her on Facebook. Her testimony really piqued my interest to learn more about what "Dr. J.," Cynthia, and the Xanue were all about. So that is when I wanted to attend the 2018 June Camp Xanue weekend event. I came to learn for myself.

I think that the "Old school," flesh and blood, Squatchers (like I once was) have a very hard time stepping outside of their own thought processes. I am one that is more willing and able to think about the paranormal abilities of the Bigfoot Forest People.

Timothy Collins
(Madison Heights, Michigan)

Dr. Matthew A. Johnson's clan is more open than my clan. Yet, we both have had similar experiences over the years. The Forest People are nurturing, caring, and loving. They have healed me several times. I asked why they would heal and watch over me. They responded, "You are an Elder. It's what we do and your nature demands it!" I asked my Clan why did you choose me? They said, "We did not choose you. You chose us."

My experiences increased rapidly after I reached out to the Forest people by asking for a closer relationship. Andrea, Jim, and I went for a winter walkabout. My first ever. We asked the Forest People to leave us some tracks to find and they didn't disappoint. We got some video and stills. I did a white sage ceremony, we played my singing bowls, and said a few prayers. It was perfect weather and good snow. It doesn't get much better than that. The prints measured six inches across the heal and over seventeen inches in length with a forty-eight-inch stride. There were two walking, one behind the other, to make it look like a twenty-four-inch human stride. The inline stride was forty-eight-inches. That was a cool and fun walkabout.

We shot a video and took few photos to share with others. As an afterthought, this was hands down the very best example of a track way that I have ever experienced. The longest with the most prints, with two individuals clearly defined mid-tarsal break, and the longest stride. We had to take pause and thank the Forest People for filling our request to leave us tracks to find. We were gifted without question. That was cool and a fun walkabout.

THE XANUE

Another encounter, I had an interacting dream with the Forest People's children the other night. I had a dream or what seemed like interacting within a dream but felt so real just the same. I woke up with two Forest People children wanting to play. They were all over me so to speak. They were in and around my bed pulling on the covers and hanging on me. It made me smile. One seemed like a three-year-old and the other was perhaps five or six-years old. I gave them hugs. I observed, for their size, that they were quite solid, muscular, and their hair was on the thick side all over. The younger one seemed to be a female. One had his head on my chest. I stroked his head and touched his ear. It seemed long and laid flat with a similar shape to a human. They were laughing and giggling like kids do. They wanted me to get up, pulling on the covers and my arm, but I was tired and smiling. They were so cute. This went on for some time. I did sit on the edge of the bed, half asleep. The red glow from the LP heaters gave off a soft light, just enough to see. It seemed like I fell back to sleep while they tried to get me up. I'm not sure I wasn't totally awake. It seemed like they were there for about twenty minutes wanting to play. Finally, I did wake with the blanket oddly wrapped on me.

I got up to go to the bathroom. I came back straightened out the sheets and fell back asleep again. I'm not sure if it was a dream or if they were actually here with me. It all seemed very real. Also I'll add that at times, I wasn't sure where I was. It's like being in two places at the same time with similar surroundings in my peripheral vision but not identical. It was just odd. Sort of like dream, time, space, reality, and 3D time space reality.

I received this confirmation from one of my interpreters about the experience: "I got a bit of mind speak or at least was shown something. Essentially what I'm hearing is that two young Forest People are a part of your clan there. They were allowed to come and visit with you because they have been watching you and were curious. The clan there explained that you were their great elder, a leader with them. They allowed these two (they say boys) to come in and get close to you, to see what you are like as a human. They said that they didn't want you to be scared so they let you feel it in dream scape. But they acknowledge you were touching two of the small boys in the clan. They said there are many more children who are around. They said it was important for their young generation to know who you are and they also said for you to listen for them at all times when things are quiet."

Then I had this happen the next day. I have had only a few open shows and this is one of them as follows. I just got two more full visuals (open shows) while changing the #2 Trail Cam SD Card. I saw a youngster, black hair, about six-foot-tall, on the thin side, big chest, maybe about two-hundred pounds. It appeared for a second walking up the hill and then it vanished. I got a similar visual changing the #3 SD Card Trail Cam. He let me see him again just for a second and then he disappeared near the road.

When I got back to the cabin I got the impression that was one of Somhe's boys. Somhe is my guardian. I want to thank him for showing himself to me. I don't know his name but that's the impression I got. I said, "Thank you for your bravery and letting me see you. Can I get a name so I can acknowledge him properly?" One of my interpreters said: "His name is Mandilla. I now have twenty-six names of persons in my Clan.

I have been touched a few times by the forest People over the years. The most unusual touch was on a camping trip with Dr. Matthew A. Johnson. It was high up on the mountains in southern Oregon. It was rainy and cold that night. I was snug in my sleeping bag. It was perhaps around 2 or 3 am when I was touched on my right leg a bit above the kneecap. It felt like three large finger tips the size of quarters touching my quadriceps. Then I had what felt like electricity surging from the three points of contact for a second or two. I wasn't expecting that. All was quiet again with a five-minute pause. I'm not sure when the rain had stopped.

The Forest People came back again and touched my toes this time. One at a time, they touched all ten toes. It was so odd. I was surprised but not alarmed. In the morning, we talked about our experiences. I think it was later on that second night that we had to have a camp fire going because it was so cold. Normally, we don't have camp fires. We all had folding chairs huddled around the campfire. I had my hands in my pockets. With the chill in the air, looking at the fire and flames, I clearly heard my name called, "Tim." It was a female voice like a youngster or teenager perhaps. I turned and looked for who called. No one was looking in my direction. I asked Andrea if she had called my name and she responded, "No." I turned to my left and asked Cynthia if she had called my name and she shook her head no. That was my first mind speak. I smiled and looked back at the fire. Then unexpectedly, I felt arms wrap around me from behind and give me a gentle but firm hug. I looked for the arms around my arms and saw nothing. I turned my head and no one was behind me. It felt like a person's arms about my size that gave an affectionate hug to me. I think it was the same youngster that called my name.

The Forest People do everything with purpose. They connect us with others. There are never any accidents. Up to this point in time, that I know of, Dr. Matthew A. Johnson has the largest documentation and recorded experiences with the Forest People in current history. My special thanks to Matt and Cynthia for asking me to be part of their Bigfoot conference as a speaker and for allowing me to accompany them to one of their interaction areas in southern Oregon. It was truly amazing.

Andrew Cunningham
(Torrance, California)

CAMP XANUE (Chehalis, Washington)

August 23, 2019: I arrived from Portland airport and met up with Dr. Horne and Amy both from Alabama. The ride from Portland to Chehalis was really uneventful. During this time, I got to know these two ladies. Upon our arrival to Camp Xanue, I immediately set up my cot in the woods about one-hundred yards from the top of the hill where the night-sits are held.

At about 9 pm, the twenty or so of us in attendance met up at the night-sit area. I witnessed some small Orbs and some color lights flashing in the forest. I went to bed around midnight. I didn't hear or experience anything that night while sleeping in my cot.

August 24, 2019: Night two was different. Again, we met up at the night-sit area around 9 pm. This time, there were about forty people in attendance. I decided that I would accompany, Howie, Mike, Christine, and Teresa down the hill from the meadow. We were about two-hundred-fifty yards from the night sit area. It was a good idea. We saw several shimmering images, heard a few coyotes howling, and saw some Orbs. It was amazing. On the way back, around 11:30 pm, I stopped off at my cot and went to bed. I set my Snore-Lab app to record the evening and in the morning, after listening to the tape in the morning, there was someone/something walking around my cot at 1:39 am. There were five distinct footsteps. Pretty amazing!

August 25, 2019: Sunday night, I saw an apparition of red color in the bushes at the top of the night-sit area. It was probably four feet by six feet. The apparition just hung back about two-feet in the bushes. I witnessed it with a young lady named Christine. It was truly awesome to experience this and to have someone see it with me too.

August 26, 2019: On Monday, we left at 11 am for Grants Pass Oregon. Whew! Six hours in a car with two ladies at a time. Regina and Amy from Alabama, and Amanda from England took turns riding with "Dr. J." Time flew by. We arrived in time to see Howie and Mike arrive at the Black Bear Diner. After we all had introductions, we went inside for our dinner.

The Southern Oregon Interaction Area (SOIA): The first night at SOIA, we arrived in pitch blackness. Howie and Mike experienced a Xanue in the bushes upon arrival. We set up our cots. We saw lots of orbs and a few 'outlines' of some of the Xanue, but for the most part, it was quiet.

August 27, 2019: During the second night at SOIA, it went off! There were lights, Orbs, silhouettes of Xanue, and branches breaking. We all went into the forest to see if we could experience the Xanue. I felt an energy when I went into the forest for about five minutes. The hair on my arms and back of neck stood up. Although I didn't see anything, it felt like there was an energy in the area where I was standing. However, the real story of the night was when Amy (Alabama-2nd timer) went into the forest. At first, I could hear her talking, and then she was crying and sobbing. Then again, silence. Ten minutes later, Amy was crying and sobbing again. "Dr. J." asked someone to go into the forest and retrieve her. No one budged, so I decided to go and bring her back to the seating area. Boy, that was interesting.

First of all, it was very dark. It was so dark that you could not make out anything until you were about five feet away from something or somebody. I walked in and I heard Amy crying. I walked up behind her and asked her if she was ok. Her only response was sobbing. I reached out and wrapped my arms around her to turn her around to head out of the woods and back to the seating area. However, she couldn't move. I felt engulfed with energy. I was shocked with this energy that enveloped both of us. We were kind of "stuck" together. Again, I felt the hair on my arms and back of the neck stir. I knew that there was some energy that was present that I could not comprehend. Something was definitely happening in here. After about two minutes of holding Amy up, I asked her she was ready to leave. She said "yes." When I let go of her, she began to collapse. I grabbed her before she hit the ground. We proceeded to leave the forest area. It took almost two minutes to get her back to her chair. That was an experience I'll never forget. After I went to bed that night, I didn't hear or feel anything. I slept very good and I didn't snore very much.

August 28, 2019: The third night at SOIA was quiet. I saw some orbs and a few glowing eyes, but nothing more. We all retired earlier than we normally did, awoke in the morning, packed up the truck, bid farewell, and drove to the airport in Medford, OR to catch an afternoon flight. It was an amazing time at Camp Xanue and SOIA. Many thanks to "Dr. J." and Cynthia for opening up their home and for opening me up to this great adventure.

Bill Cunningham-Corso
(Redondo Beach, California)

After a year or more of watching internet based media about Bigfoot – from my comfortable home in Redondo Beach, California, Dr. Matthew A. Johnson, his story – and antics – caught my attention.

Both he and his group told about repetitive and predictable interactions with the Bigfoot Forest People, as they are called. Matt showed many artifacts proving these interactions. He spent many years in the woods, sleeping out in the open on a cot. His reports, mirrored many of what I would call the "credible" reports. I had read, listened to, and sometimes watched other credible reports on the internet, mostly on various YouTube videos. What I liked about Matt was the fact that he appeared to me to be honest and credible. He deflected the various criticisms with respect and humor.

My brother, Andy, and I traveled together and we took on Bigfoot as a hobby together. During the summer of 2018, we went to visit Matt at his home in the State of Washington. We met his fiancé then, wife now, Cynthia Kreitzberg. We also met several other people, some in the same situation as my brother and me. Some of these people already knew Matt and Cynthia. Some of them were already experienced "Bigfooters."

We slept outside in the woods, adjacent to their house, and participated in some outdoor, nighttime activities. These activities are best described as "Bigfoot Stargazing." We all sat in an open meadow at night. There were no campfires and no lights. We talked, listened, played music, sang songs, and awaited Bigfoot interaction. Some people saw what they referred to as Light Orbs. I did not. Some people, including my brother felt a "presence" in the adjacent woods. I did not.

THE XANUE

Some explained that they were more attuned and that others needed to learn and adapt their senses. We took some daylight hikes and observed some large footprints. Also, we found some branch and stick formations that, in Bigfoot World, are known to be similar to those found around the globe - presumably set by Bigfoot Forest People.

A couple of months later, we made a second trip with a much smaller group. I believe that there were six of us. We drove deep into the forest in the mountains in southern Oregon, many miles up a very rough terrain logging road. We thought the rental car would bottom out or fall off of a cliff. The trees were scratching the car on both sides. There was dust everywhere. We finally made it to a plateau. We made a camp in a small level patch that measured about a half-acre. The area was totally solid woods – not a person or campground in site. There were the same activities but this time, I did in fact see and hear some unexplainable things. I think we stayed two nights. There were four "incidents" that were, what I would call, authentic. They could not be caused by anyone in our group – as everyone was present and the setting and terrain itself made it impossible to fabricate or conceal any illusions or tricks of any kind.

The first incident occurred when one of our party was facing the dark forest at night and was talking while addressing the Forest People. In fact, we all heard a loud crashing, footfall, perhaps thirty-yards into the woods. The crashing and footfall seemed to be in direct response to his out loud remarks.

The second incident was a visual sighting. Not of a Bigfoot but of some kind of glitchy light patch that passed by our food and supply table. We all saw it and were VERY surprised. There was no mistaking that something passed along the table. It did not seem totally physical. Some of the party thought they saw an image walking past the table. Whatever it was, it was very real. It was not made up, not a trick of any light, and it just appeared and disappeared.

The third incident was early in the morning, just after midnight. Everyone was asleep by then. We were all sleeping on cots. We were all within ten to twenty feet from one another. It was absolutely freezing outside. I heard the loudest crash you can imagine. It was like someone fell out of their cot into the bushes. I assumed it was my brother, Andy, since the sound came from his direction. I yelled to him and asked if he was ok. No reply. I shined my flashlight on him and he was still on his cot. Everyone else were on their sleeping cots too. Yes, this could have been a bear. It would have been a big one but it was nowhere to be seen.

The fourth incident happened around 3:30 am. I awoke and I was staring up at the stars – the most abundant display I have ever seen. I heard loud wood knocks. I think there were six of them in a row and they grew progressively louder. Deep into the forest, perhaps one-hundred-yards away, possibly two-hundred-yards away - the way sound travels in the still of night. It was otherwise, absolutely totally silent. These were spaced evenly and sounded clearly intentional to me. The best way I can describe it is like what a giant woodpecker might sound like. Like a fifteen-hundred-pound woodpecker! They also sounded like they were high up in the trees – not on the ground, but that may have been the way the sound traveled. Yes, the sounds could have been made by a person. However, this is so ridiculously unlikely. Deep in the woods, maybe twenty-degrees outside, no one anywhere around us, barely walkable terrain, no camping sites around, and all of us accounted for, and the depth of the sound – so deep and loud. I do not think these were done by a prankster, that's for sure.

Can I say I saw Bigfoot? No. Can I weigh in on the debate that these creatures are like mammals or like metaphysical beings like Dr. Matthew A. Johnson believes? No. What I can say is that my experience with Matt was a very positive one. He was credible, truthful, and honest with me. He is kind, respectful, and everything he did and said struck me as authentic and truthful. I did in fact experience some unexplainable phenomena when in his and his groups' company. The Bigfoot or Forest People's friends and advocates, people like Dr. Matthew A. Johnson and his group are good people. There are many others across the nation too – and they all tell similar tales. I hope maybe someday; I will be able to say YES to the question: "Have you seen Bigfoot?" It might be more than meets the eyes.

Karen Davies-Johnson
(Bristol, England)

Firstly, I shall start by thanking Dr. Matthew A. Johnson ("Dr. J.") for giving me a voice to share my experiences with you all. Thank you, Big Man. Secondly, I would like to thank my Xanue Friends who reached out to this funny human and changed my Life. Literally! This friendship - what me and the Xanue have, I guess only a few can speak of and experience. I hope at some point in your lives, you can also share your life with such amazing beings.

I'm Karen from southwest England. It all started for me near the end of Spring of 2019. A good friend of mine found a beautiful Woodland walk. He showed me the map and within two days, I was there hiking with my husband, Jason. The time was approximately 8:30 pm. It was at dusk. While we were walking up this creek, to the left of us was a waterfall. To the right, a deep old forest. For some reason, I was just drawn to it.

We headed that way. Then I noticed a huge "X" set back off the stone path. Of course, I had to go check out such a massive structure. Also, I had watched some of "Dr. J's" YouTube videos a few months before, which I found by pure accident, or did I? "Dr. J." shared that "X" marks the spot of the Xanue. By now, the time was closer to 9 pm. So it was very dull and even darker within the woods.

I was just in awe of this structure. Part of me couldn't wait to approach it and touch it. The other half of me was nervous. In the back of my mind, I knew I had nothing to fear. While standing there, Jason was ahead and shouted to me that he will wait for me by the car. I put my thumb up and stood there alone. I went to take a step forward up the bank and I smelled one of the most beautiful floral scents I have ever smelled in my life. Being a florist myself, for the past fourteen years, I didn't recognize the smell. It was exotic. A few sniffs later, the unique floral smell was gone.

I thought, "Hmmm? Weird!" I continued to the "X" structure. As I approached it. I took a picture. As I snapped the picture, I was growled at. It was very deep and throaty and came from above me. I froze solid. I was too scared to turn around. Jason was shouting at a distance from me. I didn't want to shout back at him. I closed my eyes and said in my mind, "I am so sorry if I have caused any disrespect. I won't be here long. I don't want anything from you but just to say that I know you exist. I reach out the hand of friendship." I took a deep breath in and turned around, opened my eyes, and nothing was there.

I then invited him, her, or them to come to my home and check me out. I finally left, explained what happened to my husband, Jason, and he totally believed me. After twenty-years of knowing me, he knows I have no reason to lie. I've gained nothing from actually telling Jason what I experienced that evening.

After a few days passed, I was sitting in bed one evening. My dogs were barking and they kept going to the back door. I kept letting them outside. Nothing was ever there. It baffled me at the time. Later that evening, I kept getting a name in my head – "Carlson." The next morning, I got in contact with Gordon Dodds who explained many things to me. He confirmed that it was the Xanue who were checking me out. I then found out that Carlson was the Xanue who growled at me. He is the Clan leader. I also learned that the female Xanue give off a floral smell to humans. I knew I wasn't mad!

I then started visiting the spot quite regularly. I wanted them to get used to me. I played a few songs which mean a lot to me. I played Hymns as well. I would just sit there and talk to them. I also left them odd food gifts such as cakes, pretzels, muffins, and even a homemade Apple and Cinnamon Crumble. A few evenings later, I heard, "Hi, I'm Zana! It was me who wafted that smell under your nose." This communication was via mind speak. I asked Zana, "Why me?" She said, "We could tell you have an open mind and a great heart. We wish to be friends with you." That was it.

Again, I was taken back by what was happening to me. I started to notice little things around my home. Rocks were left on my bedroom window seal. Several twigs and sticks were left at my backdoor and were made into the shape of Norse symbols. One meant "friendship" and the other was "knowledge."

Even personal items of mine were misplaced. My glasses seem to be a favorite. However, when I ask them, they return them to me. Zana became a nightly visitor to me. We had several mind speaking moments. I asked questions and Zana asked questions. According to Zana, we became sisters. I was asked if I could learn to be more patient. I said that I would try. I thought, "Maybe I was asking too many questions." I had many other Xanue come to visit my home too. They wanted to speak to me.

One day, while walking in the forest, I was introduced to Abel. He told me that he was Carlson's son. That is how our Friendship started and it grew from there. Since meeting Carlson and Zana, which are father and daughter, many Xanue have reached out to me. I know of three clans now. Carlson is my first clan. Abel is the second clan. My third clan is Gideon and his is a smaller clan. It took Gideon a little while to learn how to mind speak. During our first mind speak conversation, he thanked me for my time and asked to read my memories. I agreed. I must say, even though I value and love all my Xanue friends, Zana and Gideon are my best friends. They rarely leave my side. They have warned me so many times of situations, mostly before getting in the car.

For example, one Friday evening I was in my car. While I was putting the key into the ignition, I had a vision of a man running in front of my car. Gideon said, "two hands on the wheel and slow down on your way home." Where I had to drive was a long fifty-mile-per-hour road. The road is not lit up very well. What happened while I was driving home? A man ran across the road on a blind bend. It was pitch dark and if I was driving at the fifty-mile-per-hour speed limit,

I would have most likely killed him. But because of the warning that Gideon gave me, I was watching for him and managed to miss him. I was ever so grateful of that.

I have had my memories read several times. The Xanue have taken me to different landscapes and places. They have healed me. I had permanent sciatica for roughly five years. It's gone now. I had colon problems. It's gone now. I had hip and knee problems. They're gone now. They love prayer. They love open peaceful hearts and kind, selfless people.

I have to say that the most special thing that has happened to me is that I practically have a clan right on my doorstep. I literally put on my wellies, and within ten-minutes, I am there. There's a lane to walk up with open fields and a woodland all the way through. I clean it up. I've placed bird feeders and boxes up. It's beautiful now. The Xanue have thanked me so many times. Even when I'm doubting myself and the efforts I am putting into cleaning up this area, I receive mind speak saying, "Please don't give up on our home. We need you." They confirm this by occasionally allowing me to find a massive footprint. My shoe size is a 5 UK.

Their track was like - OMG! It was double and more my size. At a guess, I would say it was a UK 12. There were toe indentations and the works. I was as giddy as a school girl. I actually fell to my knees and said, "Thank you! Thank you!" It was their confirmation that they were there and they know of me. They see me.

You know the story, right? If one knows you then they all know you. I've found this to be true. While I was on a weekend break, I took some pictures of a few Xanue peeping out at me in the woodland lane by a beach. In so many other woodland places, I hear wood knocks. I've had invisible feet stomp around me. I've been sitting down by a tree and heard a Xanue walking toward me with heavy bipedal steps although I couldn't see it. I've had little twigs chucked at me. I've had so many things happen to me. Its beyond amazing.

I feel so lazy. How did these "Beings of Light" change my life? As a result, I love more. I spend more time in nature. I value nature more. I'm more relaxed and more open-minded. I'm more at peace. The Xanue even comforted me when I lost my Nan (grandmother). In July 2019. I was totally heart broken. I drove out to Carlson's spot and sat there and cried and cried. I felt such love and understanding. Two deer walked out of the bush right towards me. They didn't fright or run off. They just looked at me so calmly. I knew that this was the Xanue. They have the power to morph into anything.

That evening I was so sad I just went to bed. I heard, "She's elevated. We will all elevate one day." I asked, "You go to heaven too?" He replied, "Of course. We all go back into God's garden." They even brought Nan to see me on my birthday. She looked amazing. She was fresh faced and happy. Nan said, "I will wait for you when it's your turn. Come on my girl, snap out of this. I am happy." I've never cried over her as much as I used too because now I know that she is happy.

Wow!!! What a gift!!! How can I ever repay that gift? It was purely to ease my broken heart. Even when I'm at work, sometimes Zana sends others who wish to learn to mind speak my way. I had a lovely male shimmer in the corner of one of the offices that I work in. He said, "Hi, I'm James. I'm named after one of Jesus' apostles." I actually had to go home and Google "Jesus' Apostles" and bam! There was James' name! My Xanue friends all seem to have some kind of Hebrew name. This amazes me. In fact, they have amazed me many, many times.

If you wish to have such connections, then do what "Dr. J." says because it works. The music, the gifting bowls, the time, and the mind speak. It one-hundred-percent works. It's become a family matter now. My daughter has seen them in her bedroom watching over her. My husband knows of them and we speak of them like extended family members. Even during Christmas, while watching the midnight Mass on the TV, they were so happy! The energy in my living room was excellent! I could feel so strongly that the hairs on my arms were standing on end. Every now and then, I do have to remind them that when they get too close to my TV, it either goes off or loses signal.

The Xanue no longer go around my back garden now as it sets my dogs off and the neighbor's dogs too. Too funny! I have spoken to

Carlson, Zana, and Gideon and they know I am writing this for "Dr. J's" book. I asked if they wanted to forward a message to humans. They said "yes." Carlson said, "The trees are our heart beats. Their roots run deep and spread like love." Zana said, "We are the music in the trees." Finally, Gideon said, "The path we choose can lead only into the light of life. Trust in the Lord."

I am so close to Gideon and his clan that they have given me a clan name – "Sisi." I am very honored. I've heard them with my very own ears. They have such gentle voices. I've heard them singing, "Sisi," with such angelic sounding voices. It's beautiful. I could type on and on about how I've been blessed because I am being blessed. I feel so lucky. This journey has introduced me to such fantastic people from all around the world as well. What more can this Brit ask for?

Hope you enjoyed my experiences. Even more so, I hope you get your own experiences. God Bless you. Love, Karen ("Sisi"), Carlson, Zana, Abel, Zel, Dolby, James, Edward, Andrew, Zena, Zella, Oberon, Neku, and many, many more Xanue from the UK.

Jacqui Davis, MS, LPC
(Grants Pass, Oregon)

Experiences at SOIA after the Exodus: I have been to the Southern Oregon Interaction Area (SOIA) with Dr. Matthew A. Johnson ("Dr. J.") over the past few years. I live near SOIA in the southern Oregon area. There have been many Sasquatch sightings in this area over the years, but I did not have the privilege to meet any of them until Matt introduced me to the Xanue several years ago at SOIA.

Each time I have been to SOIA, the experiences have been very different, with different Team Squatchin members. All of the experiences have been profound. My first experience was very personal and welcoming by the Xanue people and is documented in Matt's first book. I have two trips in particular that stand out at SOIA. One trip with Matt present, and one trip with the Team Squatchin members only. Matt was not able to make this trip.

The trip to SOIA without "Dr. J." consisted of myself, a psychiatrist, a computer programmer, and a psychic. All individuals were experienced members who were very familiar with the protocols requested by the Xanue and taught to us by "Dr. J." Dr. Johnson gave us permission to go without him this trip, so be assured he was not there to give us his magic Kool-Aid!

Although we go to SOIA with no expectations, something always happens there. However, one of the Team Squatchin members, our computer programmer, really wanted some tangible contact with the Xanue.

The four of us set up our chairs in a row, near the 12 o'clock position, on the base camp time grid. As it got dark, we sang, played music, told jokes, and had a rollicking good time. We spoke out into the woods greeting the Xanue and asked permission for contact. As it got darker, we had the experience of seeing in the trees and bushes around us: eye shine, twinkling lights, and shadows going between the trees.

As the night progressed, it seemed that the Xanue came in closer to observe us. We felt we were being watched but we were not nervous as they are loving, gentle beings. All of a sudden, about three-feet to the right of our group, right in the bushes to the side of our chairs, there were definite footsteps, breaking branches, and we all heard a stomp, stomp, stomp, as something large walked right beside our chairs. All of us heard it! Then the Xanue walked in front of our chairs, from our right to our left, and then he walked back into the woods. It was very dark by this time but a large shadow was seen definitely moving. We also observed several small Xanue, possibly children, watching us from the bushes close by. They are very curious but are always protected by their parents or their older adolescent Xanue siblings. Most of us felt it was a large adolescent who walked in front of us, probably doing this on a dare from other young Xanue.

On another trip to SOIA, during the Fall, 2019, there were several Team Squatchin members in attendance, including "Dr. J." On the second night, in the 12 o'clock position on the perimeter of the base camp time grid, an unusually friendly small buck came into the circle and looked at us. I gave it a little popcorn, which he loved, and he kept coming back around the camp all night. He was absolutely fearless. We all felt it was a pet of a small Xanue.

We set up our chairs in the dark and placed the food table behind us with cookies, fruit, and more popcorn on it. Then we began to sing and talk to the Xanue people. It seemed quiet this trip and we spent much time reminiscing, laughing, watching that young deer, who kept watching us! All of a sudden, we heard footsteps running behind us. Then we heard someone playing with the food on the table behind us. No one saw the deer at this time. We heard munching on the cookies. When we went over to check on it, the cookies were mostly eaten, the fruit was rearranged in a pattern. No one was seen but we felt it was the small Xanue children. Later that night, we heard more munching. This time, the deer had returned to finish up the popcorn. The little ones liked the sweets. I am really glad they liked my oatmeal cookies!

Gordon Dodds

(Basingstoke, England)

My first interest in Bigfoot started when I was a teenager. I saw a newspaper article in 1967. It told a story about two cowboys, Patterson and Gimlin, who had caught a creature on a movie camera as it walked across a creek bed at Bluff Creek, California. The creature had turned to look at them while it was walking away. The article included a picture of the creature. Now that famous picture of the 'look back' the creature gave is blazed on many tee shirts, hats, and coffee mugs.

After that, there was little about Bigfoot until Sky TV started putting out more documentaries and the internet was also getting established. This led me to take up my interest in Bigfoot again. I started to catch up with what research was going on. I watched lots of videos and read lots of stories online. Eventually, I came across a story of man and his family and their Bigfoot encounter at the Oregon Caves. The man spoke with so much emotion and credibility that I was intrigued. I wanted to know more about his research. Of course, that man was Dr. Matthew A. Johnson. He's also known as "Dr. J." or Matt. I started to follow his research and emailed him to discuss aspects of his activities.

I was very interested in his explanation of the Xanue and more so when he told about the Exodus. His book came out at that time: "BIGFOOT: A Fifty-Year Journey Come Full Circle." I was one of the first to order a copy! The healing power of the Xanue was of interest as I have a long-term leg injury. I asked if I could come visit the Southern Oregon Interaction Area (SOIA) from England and I was delighted that Matt said "yes." I had also contacted the other two EXODUS team members - Steve Bachmann and Mike Kincaid. When I told them that I was coming over, they both reorganized their weekend so they could join me and Matt at SOIA.

In August of 2017, I flew from England all the way over to the Rogue Valley International Airport in Medford, Oregon. I joined the EXODUS team and Lieutenant Colonel Kevin Jones, Retired US Army Special Forces, on a trip to SOIA. We had four mind blowing days on the mountain with the Xanue. What I saw and experienced was all unbelievable. I saw the Xanue in all forms: Solid form, silhouette form, shimmering image form, white hot glowing outline form, and also as flashes of lights and in Orb form. There were shimmering images around me every night. I had the special close company of Ceska, Zorth's nephew, in shimmering image form. He was my temporary guardian for my time at SOIA. I also had some healing of my bad leg.

After asking for healing, I lay in bed in anticipation with the sheets pulled up over my head. The other attendees were experienced outdoor campers and all of them snored their heads off. It wasn't long before I heard two sets of heavy footsteps walk down either side of my sleeping cot towards my feet. I felt the blankets being lifted and a slight touching of my feet. At that point, a wave of what seemed like an electric current moved quickly from my feet through my legs to my stomach. This made me have a sharp intake of breath. My response must have startled my visitors because they zapped me out and to sleep. The next thing I knew, I was waking up at 4:30 am in the morning! This happened again for the next two nights. However, as soon as I got into bed, they zapped me straight away so I would not be startled. Just as before, I woke up at about 4:00 am each time without any memory whatsoever of what happened. I had some healing but I needed more!

On one occasion, Zorth came to the edge of the camp at night. He was a huge shimmering image standing about ten feet tall. Matt asked me to approach him. Then he asked me to put my arms out toward Zorth. As I did, I got a mild electric shock up each arm reaching my elbows. I said, "Hello" and "Thank you" to Zorth. It was awesome!

I had extended my stay in southern Oregon by one day so that I could be there for the eclipse on August 21, 2017. This was the first eclipse that Oregon had in approximately thirty-six years. It was a significant event for the Xanue. The eclipse represented the rebirth of the sun and their new life on the Earth. It was a joy and honour to be with them, on their mountain, during the eclipse.

Of all the events and experiences in SOIA, there was one which I can say now, was the most significant for me. One night, I asked Matt if I could do anything to help or interact with the Xanue in the UK. Matt said he would speak to Zorth. The next day, after coming back from one of our day trips, Matt laid down on his sleeping cot for his usual thirty-minute power nap. I sat down to do some email and Facebook stuff. No sooner had Matt laid down for his nap, he got up again. He told me that Zorth asked him to get up to speak to me. Zorth had told Matt that I could be a teacher for the Xanue in the UK. Also, when I went home, a family would be waiting for me. I asked where to go and I was told to go to 'where you had seen the black panther'! Well, ten-years earlier, while walking in the woods near my home, I had seen a black panther. I told people but no one believed me! Zorth said that it was not a black panther but a Xanue shape shifting in order to attract my attention. I was blown away!

I returned to the UK thinking that meeting the Xanue family would be the end of my experience but little did I realize it was the start of something else. I went into the woods and met the Xanue clan. The clan leader is named Ison. I had some great interaction with them. Now, I have a constant companion, Zameath, who is the clan leader's son. When I go out, he is with me in shimmering image form. While golfing or at the dentist office, he and his sister, Zara, are often there.

I linked up with another UK researcher, Paul Glover. We have managed to have some awesome experiences together. He interacts with a clan near him. His clan leader is named, Zac. We have found two other clans near me. Their clan leaders' names are Isaac and Nyala. We have had some unbelievable group meetings with all four clans.

There are usually about sixty Xanue present. More significantly, we have had two meetings with the clan leaders in the UK all present – a total of five-hundred-fifty clan leaders. At one meeting, Zorth and the Council of Twelve also came over! My local clan leader, Ison, is on the Council of Twelve and looks out after Europe.

The most awesome and humbling experience was when I asked Ison if I could meet 'Patty' from the 1967 Patterson and Gimlin film. She is the most famous Xanue on the planet. I was told that she is still alive and is one-hundred-fifty years old. Her Xanue name is Enrith. I was blown away when she came over to meet Paul and me. We saw her in her smoky grey form. She engaged in mind speak with Paul. She also gave us the 'electric handshake' when we put our arms out. She has since then been back to see us about five times. She brought her son with her on one occasion. She also has a daughter.

There are so many other stories of interaction that both Paul and I have had with the Xanue in the UK. Way too many stories to tell in a short testimony. Sufficient to say, the Xanue are part of our lives now and we are honoured and privileged to have them as our friends and companions. We now spend time working with Ison to help researchers in the UK and Europe to meet and interact with their local clans.

Paul Glover
(Swindon, England)

Dr. Matthew A. Johnson is crazy, delusional, a hoaxer, and a liar. He is making all of this up in order to gain publicity. Back in 2015, that is the conclusion that I had come to. On his Team Squatchin USA Facebook group, I had, like many other people, questioned his integrity publicly. I was subsequently kicked out of the group. The stories coming from SOHA were just too farfetched for me to accept as being true. Yet, I had noticed that Adam Davies had remained silent for a long period of time before coming clean. Almost one year after Adam visited SOHA, he finally admitted that there were some strange incidents that did actually take place there. His admission backed up Matt's claims (although with different opinions). Listening to the podcast of "Binnal of America" on the 4th October, 2015, left me very, very confused. This whole Bigfoot theory had now been turned on its head and if we are going to progress with the subject, we should all have a bit more of an open mind.

It was also at that point, I started to consider the weird stuff that I had personally witnessed here in the forests of the United Kingdom while looking for the forest people for myself. I had recorded stuff that I could not explain. Yet, all those years (50 years at that!) it was there already and recorded in the one-minute footage of the Patterson/Gimlin film. Due to the painstaking efforts of M.K. Davis, he had, unaware of the significance, opened up Pandora's Box to the strange element of 'woo' of Bigfootology. Yet, here was Matt with the lid right open staring inside of it and no one was prepared to listen to him.

My journey? I remember clearly when I saw for the first time a picture of the Bigfoot which was nick-named, "Patty." I was about eleven years old and we were on holiday in France. My Dad had brought along a book, written by Arthur C Clarke, about the world's mysteries. The book had a color image of frame 352. My head was full of awe that such creatures roamed the Earth. However, my fascination grew towards studying Dinosaurs as I grew older. I went to Plymouth University to study Geology. This led to me discovering a new species of marine reptile – an Aigalosaur. The Aigalosaur is the earliest marine ancestor to the T-Rex's of the oceans – the mighty Mosasaurs.

I had not forgotten about "Patty" and my interest had never faded. It was just in hibernation mode. For a lot of people, they are unaware of their first encounter - sounds in the forest, distinctive smells, brief glimpses of shadows, sighting of large black cats even. Yet, we are TOTALLY unaware. For me, it was when I was in my early 20's, I took my then girlfriend to a secluded forest lane to talk and listen to music. Well away from any human contact, after some time had passed, I saw a large human figure standing twenty-feet away behind the car. My thoughts were that it was some kind of weirdo in the forest. I reversed the car back and shone the headlights into the forest. Nothing was there. I thought nothing about it for 20 years. After all, this was the UK and not Northern California. I now consider that my first encounter.

It was when I was around thirty-nine-years old, I saw Dr. Jeff Meldrum's book, shortly after being published – "Sasquatch: Legend Meets Science." The front cover picture was enough to demand my attention. Therefore, I purchased a copy from Amazon and I read his book with keen interest. The evidence, and scientific evidence at that, leading to the idea that frame 352 of the Patterson/Gimlin film was most likely real and the Forest People do exist. I wanted to go to the USA and go and take a look for myself. That's when the "Finding Bigfoot" series first hit TV. It was crazy, exciting, scary, and fascinating all rolled up into one package. However, it was such a shame it was all happening on the other side of the Pond or was it?

I did some of my own research about reports in the UK. I bought Nick Redfern's books (which alluded to a green man spiritual element). For fun, myself, my future wife, and my daughter went to a nearby forest and took a daytime look for ourselves. That is when the penny dropped. We were coming across structures that are seen across the USA and Canada associated with Sasquatch behavior. Now, we were seeing them here within a few miles of my own home! My quest for answers now had a secure hold on me. Every chance I had, I ventured into the forest. Yet, little did I know, I was being watched all the time. I had trail cameras failing, fresh tree breaks, new tree arches, and trees pushed across paths - just like in North America. The more times I visited, the more times I found things.

I then felt a pull to a different part of the forest that I would never have picked. That's where my Bigfoot journey exploded. The forest people in the UK use ground sticks. Something not explored very much in the USA or Canada. Glyphs, tree arches, and t-pee structures. At this location, there were ground sticks everywhere. I would guesstimate over one-thousand in a concentrated area. This was their home that they had drawn me to. My contact with them was starting to take on a new meaning.

My first contact was a stick broken off from a tree branch ten feet above my head (with an almighty crack), on a still summers day, and it was thrown at an angle right in front of my feet. My reaction was, "I am dead!" I said some nice words and carried on. Only about 50 feet away, did I turn my back and looked behind me. Nothing was there! I left food, gifts, and then went home to calm my heart down. I returned a few days afterwards with the understanding that they meant me no harm. This was all good during the daytime. However, what I really wanted to do was to do night time visits. At this time, I was too scared to entertain that idea knowing there are eight to ten-foot-tall Forest People snapping trees like matchsticks out there.

Therefore, I started by using overnight recording equipment. I got a friend to visit too. He secretly labelled me as mad. That was soon revised following our first night time contact. This recording is on YouTube. You can clearly hear bipedal footsteps and a crystal clear strong wood knock. Also, you can hear a lot more hidden sounds, I have been told that even I cannot make out – like bic clicks!

THE XANUE

While I was in the middle of a forest at night, in absolute darkness, and just using my hearing as senses, the experience was my second heart-stopping adrenaline rush. Lights on and we cleared out, yet we came back. My journey only got better from then on. A lot happened. We gained all sorts of evidence that science demands. Yet, the likes of Dr. Bryan Skyes and others, whom I approached, did not want to know about our experiences and the evidence that we were finding. Although they were only forty-miles away, behind a desk in Oxford, they had no interest.

It was during those early days, while doing night time visits, that we started to witness light anomalies in the forest. When more than one person sees the same lights, you know it is not your eyes playing tricks with you. These light anomalies were Orbs, sometimes very bright, just shooting through the trees. I can go on for ages talking about all the strangeness we had. So I came to the conclusion that they mean us no harm. We decided to ditch the electronics and methods of trickery and let them approach us and that's what they did. Not only did they approach us in the woods, but they also visited us at home. How did they do this? Well, my TV would switch on at 2:22 am every time they visited. At first, I thought that the TV had an issue but it didn't. The visits often occurred with lucid dreams about world events – most that had not yet happened. I had heard about mind speak so I tried to explore this and sure enough they were speaking back to me.

Just for the record, it should be noted that I understood that I was a 'sensitive'. Following a ghost hunt, ten years earlier, I was able, via meditation, to obtain the name and age of a girl who had died at Southsea Castle on the English Southern Coastline in the 1800's. She was the daughter of the lighthouse keeper. She had fallen down a water well. I used the same techniques to make contact with the Forest People. Although I was confused at first, I was getting messages back.

I shared my experiences within a private Facebook group. I was having a real hard time coming to terms with who the Forest people were. I was fully aware of Matthew's SOHA/SOIA by now. I was also aware of Adam Davies and John Carson's testimonials. I was now sure that I had been wrong about Matt and I took more of a keen interest in his experiences. My own contact with the Forest People was getting more intense. This is when my contact with Gordon Dodds happened. He was a fellow Brit who had been to SOIA and had confirmed things. When Gordon returned, he was looking for open minded people to contact in order to open the doors to the Woo in the UK. I instantly got in touch with him. Others took a more negative view of him. Enough said on that subject as that negativity still reigns supreme here in the UK.

My mind had already been blown by what I was dealing with. But now, I was climbing inside of Pandora's Box, the box that Matt had unleashed. My teaming up with Gordon was the start of an historical journey. It is now that I have to say, that it is only through personal experience, that my sense of reality was blown away. Our trips to the forest were experiences that I will cherish for the rest of my life. I started to see my very first cloaked sasquatch standing right in front of me. My eyesight isn't great so it took me time to adjust to seeing them. They can help from time to time by going from a shimmering screen of glass to a smoky outline. They were there, not just one, but many. Red eye glow at low heights and yellow eye glow at 8 to 9 feet tall.

Can my journey get any more surreal? Yes. My mind speak was getting stronger and I could happily receive communication during the daytime... but was best at bedtime just before falling asleep. Gordon had been told by Matt that he will have a guardian upon his return to the UK – and there he was – standing in front of me – his name Zameath. Gordon could not mind-speak with them, but he could see them much better than me... so together we had the ability to have awesome night time experiences.

I would like to add that around this time, I had an overwhelming sense of guilt. In the past, I doubted Matt and had publicly questioned his integrity on his Facebook channel. I had to put the record straight. I openly apologized for my ignorance a couple of years ago. I was happy that he cordially accepted my apology and our friendship increased to a new level from that point onwards.

THE XANUE

Today, I have the utmost respect for Matt. When the whole world told him that he was mad, delusional, and a liar, he continued to carry on beating his drum. That was a testament to the faith he had in his own journey. That was the cross he chose to bear. Knowing the Bigfoot world on both sides of the pond, to endure the ridicule and abuse, he needed to have a strong personality to take it and persevere. That's why the Xanue chose Matt. That's why I stand firmly by Matt and the messages he and the Forest People are trying to broadcast to us.

Now I would like to get back to the adventures that Gordon and myself have had here, in the sleepy English Countryside. My mind-speak had improved because of the contact I now had with Zameath and the clan that Gordon was involved with. It was great! I now sensed the difference between mind-speak and my own thoughts going on inside of my head. I could also start to understand who was giving me the mind-speak. Names had already come from my own contacts at the woods I go to. My contact was Zach. I was later told I had my own guardian, named Sol. With the contact we had with Gordon's clan, we got to know the eight-foot tall clan leader there, named Ison. It turns out that Ison is one of the members of the Council of Twelve. Mind blown? Nowhere near yet.

As we were making an effort to travel miles to each other's location, Gordon had a request to ask towards the Xanue. We wanted to know the name, the Xanue name, of Patty. Gordon asked me to ask my contacts. On the 25th February, 2018, I was given the name Enrith from Zach. I asked and asked again for confirmation and each time I was given the same name back again. This name was later confirmed with Steve Bachmann and his Xanue contact and also with Matt through Zorth. To be honored with now knowing Enrith's Xanue name, Gordon dared to ask if Enrith would come to the UK and meet us at one of our joint visits. Because of the nature of this request, it took a few days before we had confirmation that not only will this event happen, but also, beyond our wildest dreams, each clan leader from the UK will attend this historical event.

On the 15th March, 2018, I had arrived late due to new roadworks on the motorway. We continued with the way we had proposed at Gordon's location. We were met at the car by Zameath. Walking down the wooded paths, we were greeted by a host of others. There were lines of shimmering shapes. We then proceeded to our spot. I remember looking up at the clear sky with Orion clearly rising above the horizon. It was a beautiful night.

We then set up for the evening and I started to mind speak with my contacts. I was told there were over 500 clan leaders here from all around the UK. Were they all here? I was getting all sorts of ramblings going through my mind. We were seeing yellow eye glow and seeing the odd shimmering images. Then down to business, Enrith had been wandering the forest and was just about to arrive.

For this historic event, I took a small dicta-phone to record our words. Gordon spoke out first. He had a speech prepared. He spoke from the heart. He talked openly with Enrith and the clan leaders. It was well received. I then gave my own speech, in recognition of my own personal journey leading up to this point. I offered my hand out to her and I received an electrical handshake in return. We asked if Enrith would show us more of herself just to confirm it was her. She responded by going a smoky grey. It brings a lump to my throat just thinking about this. I do understand just how far from our reality this appears to be. I get that. Alas, the truth will always be the truth and Gordon and myself were there to witness this.

We got messages and had a long chat about all manner of things. The significance of our event was the reason why all the clan members from around the UK had arrived. There were also other members of the Council of Twelve there too. Am I and Gordon making this up? It is not in our interests to put our names out there only to be ridiculed. But hey, like Matt, we will keep beating that drum. Also, just for the record, Matt was asked afterwards if this had happened. Zorth confirmed with him that this event took place. So, as hard as it is to accept, we are now aware of Patty's real name. That is something to celebrate.

As you can imagine, our visits didn't stop. Many more visits occurred at both my own and Gordon's study sites. Plus, new visits that were encountered following this. I am sure Gordon has more words to say about this. Again, Enrith continued to attend the different meetings we had. She even attended with her family and other clan members from Bluff Creek, California.

We had only managed two overnight sleepovers in the year of 2018. One sleepover was a bit of a wash out. The second sleepover was awesome for myself. Twice during the night, I felt my spirit leaving my body, being held and pulled from my body, by my forest contact – Zach. He then spun me around at high speed before he carried me off into the clouds. While high in the sky, he took me on a tour around the planet at a supersonic speed. There is so much more I can say. However, these are personal experiences which I can provide no evidence for. My journey still continues.

In summary I just need to underline that sometimes you need to experience things before your sense of reality is blown away. This is where we are now with regards to understanding the Bigfoot Forest People – the Xanue.

As for my acknowledgement to the work that Matt has done to date, I was once one of those ignorant, flesh and blood, missing link, ancestral primate researchers. I was ignorant to a much bigger picture. Matt has shown the way. He is spot on. The Forest People, the Xanue, are indeed Beings of Light and inter-dimensional travelers. They can change their energy vibration so they can be seen and disappear – be seen on thermal cameras and also as Orbs of light. We have a lot to learn from the Xanue. So, those individuals who constantly demand a physical body as the ultimate form of evidence, you're going to have to wait. Get out from behind your computer screens. Put the hours in so you too can experience the things I have. Learn from what Matt has been saying and show the respect to the people of the forest. We are on the cusp of a turning point in mankind's history. Please remember the lessons from Galileo before passing negative comments.

Howie Gordon

(Anchorage, Alaska)

2018 Night Sit at the Chehalis Interaction Area (CIA)

Night One: Friday Night, on July 20, 2018, was our first night sit. We sat in the chairs at the 12 o'clock position at the Serenity Meadow for about an hour. We then got in our cots which were also in the meadow. The stars were visible but there were no Orbs or sounds of footfall. This trip involved twenty people or more. In my opinion, the excess of people, with their background noise, prevented unique sounds and activity from being heard.

Night Two: Saturday Night, on July 21, 2018, Mike, Pete, Cindy, Stu, Joel and I moved the night sit area down the mountain near where Cindy, from Spokane WA, slept the night before. Within a few minutes, we saw an Orb light show that took place for about a half an hour or so. I felt a pressure shift when an Orb moved right into where we were sitting. I had the sense of a Bigfoot, cloaked and in Orb form, pretty much stepping right into the area very close to us. There was a lull for a bit until we saw some more Orbs again later on. After the light show, Pete, Mike and I slept in the Serenity Meadow area at the top of the mountain. That ended up being uneventful.

Night Three: Sunday Night, on July 22, 2018, Mike, Pete, Cindy, Stu and I once again had a night sit; down the mountain near where Cindy has been sleeping on her cot. We saw a few Orbs here and there but things mostly were relatively quiet. After an hour and a half or so of the night sit, we decided to go back to our cots and go to sleep.

THE XANUE

After Pete and Stuart Hill had an encounter of seeing several sets of eye glow in the bushes and trees near the trail that leads to the backside of the garage, near the top of Serenity Meadow, he decided to go sleep in the house on the couch with the cats. Pete had a rough time with cat hair as well as the cats jumping around the couch.

Mike and I moved our cots down the path and away from Serenity Meadow. We went down the 3 o'clock trail about one-hundred yards into the forest near the end of the path. It was around midnight or so and we decided to go to bed. We sat there on our cots with bugs buzzing by our ears as well as landing on our face and head. It was really annoying the crap out of us. I admittedly was a little scared being so far away from Serenity Meadow. This was the furthest I have ever been away from "Dr. J" on a night sit and sleep over. I kept thinking that a bear or a mountain lion could be moving through this path. Also, Mike and I heard a pack of coyote's bellowing at the bottom of the mountain. Mike reassured me that we shouldn't be afraid of the coyote's coming anywhere near us.

It was dead silent almost the entire time. I fell asleep several times and I would instinctively nod off and on while trying to stay awake. Mike said that I didn't voice my thoughts of maybe calling it quits and dragging our cot's back to the Serenity Meadow in the dead of night or going back to the house and sleeping on the couch with Pete. Nevertheless, I seriously thought about doing that. Nothing was going on and the bugs were continuing to antagonize us.

Around 3 am, I had passed out but Mike was still wide-awake. Mike reached over to shake me and said, "Howie! Howie!" I woke up to footfall (bi-pedal walking). Mike said that he heard about ten steps coming from something a lot heavier than us. I heard three to four steps while I was trying to wake up. The steps were walking straight towards us. They stopped about twenty-five feet or so in front of us.

Immediately, I saw green and red Orbs twenty-five feet or so in front of us. I said to Mike, "They are here." I said, "Hello, my friends." In less than a minute, I felt the Forest People energizing my left leg with their medical scan, light energy massages, and tagging. Bipedal walking was taking place all around us. Mike and I both agreed on the fact that we heard the snorting sound of clearing one's throat and a type of breathing as our Forest Friends walked around.

I could see Orbs at my feet, at Mike's feet, above both of our cots, as well as in the middle of our cots which were less than two-feet apart. I verbally, as well as mentally, asked on several occasions, "My friend Mike has been hearing my stories for years about my encounters with the Forest People. He would like to see a sign of your kindness, peacefulness and incredible existence." I also asked for a larger and more illuminated Orb or some type of massaging, grabbing, or electrical stimulation for Mike. Mike voiced the same requests as well for over the two-hour time span that the Forest People visited us.

Mike asked if they were still massaging me. I said, "I can't feel it right now." But within minutes or seconds, they would be back at it with even stronger doses of light energy stimulation that included now both legs. They worked on more than three-quarters of the way up my right leg and all the way up my left leg. They also worked on my lower back where I had some broken vertebrae from before.

I thought that when the Forest People were done working on me, and possibly before that, they would jump over to Mike and start to medically scan and or heal his left shoulder or other parts of his body. Before these events, Mike said that he was a little nervous about being so far out into the woods. However, when the Forest People arrived, he felt a certain sense of calm and peace as his heart rate slowed down with fear of the outdoors slowly disappearing.

I noticed the same feeling over the years. I never slept better than after the Forest People would vanish back into the darkness of night. Twice, I felt during the time span that the Forest People were present with what seemed like a cool raindrop landing on my right cheek. Stu from Edgewood, WA had these same sensations during his July 2018 CIA Trip. I continued to have a lull here and there, or maybe just lower doses of energy that at times I couldn't sense, with healing hands returning to work on me. Mike repeatedly asked me what was going on while we continued to reach out, verbally and mentally, to our Forest Friends, asking them to show Mike what they are capable of doing.

I wish the story could have ended the way Mike and I had hoped too. However, the Forest People just wouldn't reach back to Mike. He continually reached out to them over the course of three nights. Hopefully, they will show up at a future time to visit Mike. Around 5 am, we started to hear the birds chirping as well as seeing the sun starting to come up. On that note, the Forest People retreated back into the woods to re-charge for the day. Hopefully, the Forest People visit me in Alaska as well as pay a visit to Mike in Florida.

The Southern Oregon Interaction Area (SOIA), Monday, 8-26-19, at SOIA - Night 1: We arrived at the Southern Oregon Interaction Area (SOIA) at around 9 pm in pitch darkness. One minute after our arrival, Mike and I went to take a pee at the 6 o'clock base camp grid location. We turned our cell phone lights on as we got to the edge of the bushes. "Dr. J." has been very clear about the fact that this is a "No! No!" while Bigfooting. He has told us to always point our flashlights toward the ground if we turn them on and never point them towards the bushes or trees. Well, an eight-foot-tall something (i.e., a cloaked or an invisible Bigfoot) went running backwards from us. It created footfall sounds while displacing all of the grass, brush and trees. Mike and I back peddled as well. Apparently, we scared this creature due to our cell phone flash lights startling him about three to four feet into the tree line. A few minutes later, some pebbles landed on Andy's cot. The Bigfoot we scared earlier at the 6 o'clock base camp grid position was still at the edge of our basecamp. He appeared to be welcoming us to SOIA with a little bit of light rock throwing. A while later, around 4 am, about twenty-five feet away from my cot, I was hearing branches being crushed due to some light foot fall. It wasn't super-plentiful but I did see some Orbs in the tree line during the night.

Tuesday, 8-27-19, at SOIA - Night 2: Like so many times before at SOIA, there were a lot of Orbs surrounding the entire base camp. I was standing up and felt some light zapping at about a fifteen-percent level on my hips. I also felt it on my hand when I held it out while sitting on the night sit chairs in the middle of the base camp. I asked the Forest People to shake my hand and they were sending energy into the palm of my hand, once again, at about a fifteen-percent level. I occasionally thought of the Treykon. They're scary and bad creatures that look like Bigfoot. However, they're somewhat smaller and menacing looking. But I felt reassured with all of the Orbs and many Xanue/Bigfoot Forest People around to protect us.

Amy and Andy had intense levels of scanning and zapping walking out to the twelve o'clock position. Mike had some light concentrations of energy in the same location. After I got in the cot for the night, I pretty much fell asleep without incident.

Wednesday, 8-28-19, at SOIA - Night 3: A little bit before total darkness, I saw this black or brown energy roughly knee high about forty to fifty yards up the path in the 9 o'clock base camp grid position. Then I realized this was a shimmering image. It was ghostly or like a partially cloaked "Predator" from the Schwarzenegger movie. There were one or two Xanue standing there. I told everyone else. All seven were seeing the same thing that I was seeing. The images stood there for 5-10 minutes before I no longer could see them in the darkness.

While I was seeing Orbs in the trees, I began to fall asleep in my chair in the middle of base camp. We all went to bed around the same time. Within thirty-minutes or so of lying down in my cot, I started to feel my cot shake a little bit. It was at about a twenty-five-percent level as compared to a hundred-percent level in 2016. I also felt that some medical scanning was occurring. I felt the highest concentration, about a thirty-percent level, in my left leg for three or four minutes. I was talking to Amy, who's cot was right next to me, and she said that she could see Orbs under my cot.

I could see green Orbs above me similar to when I saw them above Mike and I in Chehalis WA last year (i.e., The Chehalis Interaction Area = CIA). The Xanue only scanned me for a short time, then they left for thirty minutes or so. Then they continued with the same process again for another five minutes or so. This repeated again. When they left after another half an hour or so, they returned for a final third time and scanned me for another three to four minutes.

That night, I saw some shooting stars and a few more Orbs but I didn't hear a lot of walking around or any branch crunching either. Other SOIA guests who were with us made it difficult to hear clearly due to their snoring. This background snoring noise made it difficult to hear, listen for, and discern any footfall sounds.

This was "The LAST NIGHT EVER IN SOIA" because the Xanue are moving out of the area due to government intrusion. In doing so, the Xanue are allowing the Treykon to move into the area. The Xanue will now be based near the Chehalis Interaction Area (CIA), otherwise known as Camp Xanue.

STUART HILL

(EDGEWOOD, WASHINGTON)

1980: I didn't think "Bigfoot" existed in the early part of 1980. But things have a way of changing. I considered myself a 'Regular Joe' and thought it was maybe a story, maybe not. The change started on a hunting trip in the Southside of the Olympics with my buddies six months after high school. We had a spot picked out, behind a locked gate, to make sure we were not crowded in on by others. Scouting the area for months ahead of time, we were sure it would be a good hunt. After arriving and setting up camp, we prepped for the next day. It was all good or so we thought.

When hunting the next day, my partner and I noticed there was no new sign of animals and that it was way too quiet. When we got back to camp for dinner, the other two hunters got the same vibe from the same area as we had covered. We purposely cris-crossed our routes to make sure we had not missed anything.

After dark is when we were scared out of camp by 'something'. A large branch or tree being broken, heavy footfalls of the two-legged variety, and a long extremely loud scream that still brings me chills to this day. The smell was like a festering city dump almost under your nose. The branch sounded like a 4x4 being snapped like a twig. The footfalls were definitely the two-legged gait and covered a huge amount of ground in almost no time. These very heavy steps were not fast, but they covered a one-hundred-eighty-degree circle of camp far faster than any man. Then lastly, that scream or howl that lasted about fifteen seconds and was so forceful it shook my guts. Needless to say, we high-tailed it out of there and never to return. We left some equipment at the site. Afterwards, we didn't talk about it much. The

THE XANUE

other three members of the party quit hunting or camping. They sold all their equipment as well. It seems that I was the only one to return to the woods. However, I had no contact with them since that night.

1986: After a short stint in the military, I returned to camping. I was now a family man. My old 1944 Jeep is what really got me back into the woods. It was a good way for the family to enjoy the outdoors. Soon I began hunting again. However, I never really forgot what happened and I was still not speaking of the incident to anyone.

1993: On another hunting trip, this time with the trusty old '44 to ride in, we ascended a long grade of old logging road on the eastside of the Cascades. Stopping at a good vantage point, we dismounted our trusty steeds for some glassing time. It was a snow covered valley populated by fifty-foot tall firs that looked promising. After about 10 minutes of seriously glassing for elk, or signs of them, the four of us heard a large tree fall. None of us had ever heard anything like that before. It was conveniently located just out of sight. There was not a wind or breeze.

1994-1997: Later, by myself, while hunting in other spots, I would hear slight noises and get that 'feeling' that I was being watched. By now, I had enough experience in the woods to know that this 'feeling' was not a cougar or bear. I had been stalked by a cougar and run into bears and this is NOT the same, period. My hair is standing up as I write this.

1998: My next exposure was at an old mill pond near Mt. St. Helens. I had scouted the area and brought my bow without a sidearm due to regulations. Strangely, there was no new animal signs as I entered the area. Just like the day we hunted elk in the first part of my written testimonial. That's when I noticed a slight rustle above and behind me about forty-feet. There was a forty-foot tall pile of dirt from the making of the pond that was covered with forty to fifty-year-old re-growth. I blew it off to rain falling from the trees since it had just stopped raining. But there it was again. This time, there weren't any breezes. I figured if it's a cougar, I will move as fast as possible and turn towards it when it comes after me. So I move twenty yards at a run, stopped, and turned to only hear what sounds like two footsteps of something stopping. Whatever it was, it remained hidden just over the top of the hill. Here comes that 'feeling' of being watched again. I repeat the run and stop procedure two more times, only to get the same results. I watched the area where the noises came from intently, as I slowly made my way out of the area. Nothing was to be seen or smelled on this trip.

2003: By this time, I had tried to study at the local library. I wanted to soak up all the information I could get or borrow or coax out of people, especially Native Americans. After some other life events, I went back to college where, of course, you have to write papers and speak on the subject matter. The professor said "pick something unusual to write about." Well, you don't need to tell me twice! Living in Washington State my entire life, I have obviously heard the stories. So you guessed it, my subject paper was "Bigfoot!" I loved this opportunity as it gave me a huge, deep, library network to use for six months of intense research. You should have seen the faces in that class as my subject came to life right in front of them with slides, graphs, Native American legends, and sighting maps. After this, my family was well aware of my experiences and understood better than most people, even if they lived in the Northwest.

On a family mushroom picking trip by Mt. St. Hellens, my daughter and I got slightly separated from the main picking force. We were on a lower plateau with sparse trees and lots of mushrooms. We could occasionally see the main party through the trees. The road was uphill from us, opposite from the thick trees to the south. About half way through the area, my daughter suddenly stops, stands fully upright and says, "Dad?" All you parents know that tone. The one tone that says, "I don't know what's up, what's going on, or what should I do all in the same word." The 'feeling' had been with me since we had started picking on that field away from the others. In my own way, I just wanted her to experience it. Experience is the best teacher to me. This time the 'feeling' was like, "Hey! What are you guys doing?" I told her, "It's ok. They're just watching us. You know. They're just checking out what we're doing. They're curious." I told her, "Just keep your eyes open. Maybe you'll see something. We will just keep picking our way back to the group."

At this point of my life, I absolutely knew between my research and experience that not a single person, scientific or self-researcher, had explained what was going on in the woods to my satisfaction. There was something more to it. There was no convincing me that the information seen by me to date that could explain the situations or my experiences fully. Let's just say I could "FEEL" it.

2017: I attended the Paranormal conference with alien witnesses and investigators. However, the reason I attended the conference was because it also had "Bigfoot Researchers" who were presenting too. I enjoyed the alien/UFO presentations. I could tell these encounters had really happened by their personal emotion and stage presence. I will say that it didn't take me much effort to discern between the outside investigators and the individuals who actually experienced what they spoke of. Then came the part I attended for, the good stuff as far as I was concerned, the Bigfoot researchers.

For the most part, all of the speakers presented solid cases of research and logging many hours in the field. Then this little guy, all 6'9" of him, spoke. Almost immediately, his honesty and the integrity of his scientific research struck me as truth. I thought, maybe this Dr. Johnson guy was on to something here. The more he spoke, at times with extreme passion and emotion, the more he spoke like he was with me in the woods. It was like he had been with me for all those past hunting trips. The trips that I like to call my "What the heck is/was that" experiences in the woods. During his moving presentation, he hit all the things I had experienced in the woods. Yes, every last one of them. With the new information and confirmation of what had happened during his research, and to me in the woods, I had to meet this guy. Just as I had been thinking for years and could not prove, he had come to the same conclusion as myself. However, he put together the proof I had been looking for all these years. These "Bigfoot" are a type of being. They are not an ape or anything else. The dominoes were finally looking like a line and are ready to topple for me.

After his speech, I eagerly went to meet him after I had first met with all of the other great researchers. I knew I would be spending most of my time with this Dr. Johnson guy, so I saved that stop for last. After introductions, and purchasing his new book: "BIGFOOT: A Fifty-Year Journey Come Full Circle," I had to ask for my own positive proof. Thankfully, his fiancée and now wife, Cynthia Krietzberg, told me where I could go to find some signs of what I was looking for while he was busy chatting with others. Amazingly, it was quite local. I felt this would be a huge step in the right direction for me and was very hopeful.

After arriving at the location, I asked the Xanue for a sign. Just as Cynthia and "Dr. J." had suggested, I was looking for anything that would give me the confirmation I had sought for so long. It all fell into place just as if it were planned for us to find. A broken and leaf stripped stalk that seemed to point the way, like a flag, was the first item. Then sign after sign, just as Cynthia had said to look for. But still I doubted a bit, even though all the signs were present. I thought to myself, "For a big guy you sure are subtle with your clues."

Then I asked if the Xanue would please show me a definite sign that would remove all doubt. After asking, for some reason I cut across the trails that went through the area. I ended up stopping between the trails where the forest duff was quite thick. There, standing in a spot of sunshine, where I was surveying the area for a sign, I got the feeling I needed to look down. To my amazement, between my feet in the heavy duff, was a distinct foot print! It was half again as long as my size 10.5 W and half again wider. The track was one full inch deep in the duff. I couldn't believe my eyes for a minute. I took a picture with my phone and then tried to make a print in the forest floor myself. There was no way I could come even sort of close to making an impression that deep in the duff that day. The Xanue were probably laughing at me while they were watching me jumping up and down in the forest trying to make a track in the duff! Elated, I thanked them for the proof I needed. As I left the area, I could 'feel' their presence and could almost hear them thank me for my interest and our visit.

This experience left no doubt in my mind that I must attend "The Great Reveal" that Dr. Johnson was putting on near the end of April in Bremerton, Washington. If you see the pictures of the stage at the event, I was just off camera on the left of the seating area. If you read his first book: "BIGFOOT: A Fifty-Year Journey Come Full Circle," you will know what I experienced that night. To say the least, the information in the presentation blew my mind. It took me a full three months to get my mind out of the spin cycle. Nevertheless, it all made sense to me. Everything fit into what I had experienced in the past. Dr. Johnson's information gave me a whole lot more to look forward to.

January 13, 2018: This was Cynthia's and "Dr. J's" first night sit and sleep over event. Nothing was going to get me to miss this event! After the introductions and information session, we picked out our night sit spots and cot spots for the night. We set up per protocol and didn't have to wait long for things to start happening. Alex sat left of me and he sang a love song. Almost immediately, his song attracted two Orbs. They were above him and behind his head. They were about three feet away from him. One Orb was red and the other Orb was orange. They floated there until he finished singing and faded away when he was done. While they were there, I asked for and received group confirmation on the sighting. The Orbs were there for at least fifteen to twenty seconds.

Minutes later, we heard a large rock that was tossed into the water on the far side of the wetland at our 6 o'clock position. Then a bit after that, we smelled a sweet fragrant flower-like perfume wafting through the area which lasted about fifteen seconds. All of the attendees confirmed smelling the sweet floral aroma. A bit later, I heard what I originally thought to be a mosquito buzzing. However, it was only January. There are no flowers or bugs in January. The metallic ring I was hearing was stationary and about six feet away. It was above my head and the others could hear it too. It was like a tuning fork noise without being struck.

Next up were the two white Orbs. They were the size of softballs. They were about twenty-five feet away in the tall vine maple at our

12 o'clock position. They appeared gradually and left the same way too. Except these Orbs came and went three different times and they showed up in different positions each time. Then the entire vine maple, all forty feet of it, became back lit three separate times. Between each set of Orb's appearing, the tree looked like there was a light behind it! There were also some movement noises by the tree but not definitive in any way.

After all these happenings, there was a large metallic sound to the 2:30 position. The sound seemed like it was about thirty-feet up in the trees. Between all these sights and sounds, we could hear when Matt would play music for the Xanue as he worked his way from group to group. Additionally, we could hear singing by others and flute playing by Cynthia. At this time, I think everyone in the group was a bit saturated with all the happenings since the sit started. We talked quietly about the experiences we had just witnessed and decided it was time to pack it in for the night. We had been there a little over two hours.

As we stood up to leave, we thanked the Xanue for the evening's entertainment. It was at that moment in time that we noticed the far side of the wetland. We all asked each other if they saw it too. There were hundreds of tiny lights, of many colors, floating in the trees! The discussion centered around how subtle the signs and lights were. All of us agreed that sometimes you had to ask yourself if you were seeing what you thought you were seeing. We were all stunned at the site. We soaked up the view for several minutes before leaving the night sit area.

On another date, I witnessed eye glow of a small entity within ten feet of our group. During our night sit, it moved slowly around the trees and stump in front of the group. Accompanying that entity were thirty to fifty pin tip sized lights moving through the trees a few at a time. These lights were similar to the ones seen in the trees on the far side of the wetland previously. Then looking to my right, I noticed numerous silhouettes moving in the trees across the trail about fifty to eighty feet away. These experiences happened numerous times during this night sit.

THE XANUE

After moving back to the Serenity Meadow, I was talking with another participant by the trail that leads to the backside of the garage. As I was talking, he looked past me into the brush about eight feet behind me. Then he said, "You need to turn around." He had to say this three times and he was getting more insistent with each utterance. The last time, he was quite direct. Well I finally got it and I'm glad I did. I wondered as I turned around, "What is he seeing? What's going on?" Well, to be honest, I was pretty surprised when I saw not one but six sets of glowing eyes! These glowing eyes ranged from about two feet off the ground to at least eight feet off of the ground. They seemed to be standing in a group, similar to the way I would see a family at a zoo checking out an interesting exhibit. Their eyes glowed red, not defined like we see, but blurry red and brightest in the center. I wouldn't say the sight intimidated me as much as catching me off guard. After all, I thought the experiences were done for the night. I'm glad that I was wrong. All I could do, after quickly picking my jaw up off the ground, was to say out loud to them, "Hello. I hope you're doing well. Thanks for coming!" Then they faded away leaving us in awe. The other gentleman refused to sleep outside after that. He slept inside Cynthia's and "Dr. J's" home on the couch.

During one-night sit, I decided to sit with Matt by the fire pit. Soon after dark, with no campfire or lights, closely following protocol, Matt played some music from MP3 player. This night was like a trading of friendly deeds now that I think back on it. Matt would play a couple tunes and then we would see or hear something in return. What I witnessed that night was true communication without talking. Matt and I were standing together. As he finished playing a few songs, he directed my gaze to the far right side next to the corner of the wood shed. There was a set of red glowing eyes from a younger member of the Xanue group. His eyes were just a little higher off the ground than mine. I'm 5'10".

During that night, I saw more than I can remember. So I'll start with the white Orb, about the size of a softball. It moved along the ground on the left of the trail towards us. It stopped about fifteen feet away from us. The Orb remained there for at least twenty minutes. Also, the fifteen or more Xanue silhouettes I saw that night were amazing. They were moving on the trail about fifty feet away from us. Then the fog-like mist that came afterwards, moved slowly on the left side of the trail. It stayed for about twenty minutes. There wasn't any rain, wind, or other weather going on at the time. When the fog was there, we observed two sets of glowing eyes for a moment behind the fog. After that, we were treated to the sounds of a frog croaking. This frog however was about fifty feet away and thirty feet up in the trees! At first, it was a pretty good impersonation. However, the impersonation of a frog quickly degraded to a humorous version which gave us all a good laugh! That's about it for the sights and sounds, as if that's not enough.

Now on to the healing portion of my experiences. During my visits to the Chehalis Interaction Area (CIA), also known as Camp Xanue, I always feel a deep sense of comfort, caring, and peace of mind along with a big welcome tossed in. When I arrive, I greet Matt and Cynthia and move into the trees shortly thereafter to talk to the Xanue. I greet them the same way as I do anyone else. That's when I feel a huge sense of 'good' emotional power greeting me.

At this point, I need to explain the 'feeling' I get when I'm at Camp Xanue. During my first visit, we took the tour of the grounds. On this tour, I was first in line behind Matt. As we turned left, down off the main trail, I got this cool kind of electric feeling that made my hair on my arms stand up. This occurred on the same trail where we had previously seen the softball-sized Orb for about fifteen minutes. At that same time, another attendee took a picture from behind us as we were rounding the corner. The picture captured the entire group plus, as we discovered later, a cloaked Xanue in the trees about fifteen feet away from all of us. He was just checking us out. Ever since my first visit to the property, I have had this feeling many times. It seems that the closer they are, the stronger the feeling. It starts at the top of my head and runs down my back, arms, and finishes under my feet. At times, there is a very strong, good, emotional wave that comes with it. The feeling is so strong sometimes that I can't talk for a brief period. Please see my testimonials on "Dr. J's" YouTube channel. It took me awhile after that to put two and two together regarding the feeling and what was going on. Since then I talk with them, or like right now writing about them, I get the 'feeling'. Some of the other feelings I get during a night sit are; comfort, safety, well-being, and caring or love. I have to say it was strange at first but have come to like it and appreciate it in ways I never thought that I would.

During my first visit, I was a bit nervous about sleeping outside with only a cot and tarp. I use a Bi-Pap machine when I am at home and the doctors tell me the next step is a respirator. I have camped, hunted, and fished staying out all night before but not like this. During this visit, my knees were pretty painful as was my back because I had been over doing it at work. When I retired for the night, I had asked the Xanue to see if they could do something for the pain. So, I had no machine for breathing and my back hates cots. I wasn't too sure how it was going to go. However, once I laid down with the tarp on top for a misting rain, I felt very relaxed and fell asleep quickly. During the night, I woke up to find my tarp edge down at my knees. I pulled it back up and I fell right to sleep again, this time to be woken up by my tarp rustling to my left near another attendees' cot. I thought that maybe she just had to use the restroom so I drifted off quickly back to sleep. Again, I was woken up a short time later. There was too much rustling of a tarp at the same cot. This time, I rolled over to see what was up. I could see that she's up and putting the tarp on her sleeping bag.

The next morning, we talked about what went on during the night. We took turns talking about sights, sounds, etc. After a while, we were talking in a group and put the clues together. I slept like a rock. I never sleep that good at home without my machine! Numerous folks had to pull their tarps back on top of their bags during the night. The lady who slept next to me had to get up to fix her tarp. She had noticed that the tarp was laid out just as if someone had pulled it off her in an orderly fashion. She found it perfectly flat with one edge at the foot of her cot. I was woken up by her fixing it and not by it being removed. On top of that, there was no pain in my knees and back like there was when I went to sleep. That never happens. So why today?

During another night sit and sleep over event at Camp Xanue, I could not stay awake at all while sitting in the chairs in the Serenity Meadow. I have worked graveyard and all kinds of crazy long shifts and I have no problems staying awake. But this night, I couldn't stay awake no matter how I tried. My back was seriously hurting on this night due to a lower back incident a few weeks before. I was on steroids and ibuprofen in an attempt to try to get things back in order. Again, I asked for any assistance the Xanue might be able to provide for me. I could barely walk the property during the day. I woke a few hours later. It felt like my kidneys were literally on fire! I hurried to the restroom for relief. This happened three more times that night. Each time was a little less painful. This made me worry about kidney stones. But my back felt better, not good, but better.

I have had the good fortune of having a healthy body other than my back to this point in my life. I went to my doctor's office to see what's going on. After an MRI, Ultra sound, and blood tests, all is good under the hood, so to speak. The only anomaly found is a one-sixteenth fatty deposit in one kidney. A little physical therapy and my back is as good as it's going to get for my age. Again I did not need the Bi-Pap machine. So I have to ask myself, why did they find nothing? Curious.

The "little guy" (Matt), as I jokingly refer to him, has been right on the money with everything he told me I would experience or see. He has not guaranteed anything and I can't blame him with the way the world is today. Matt has always said that a kind person with a good heart and an open mind who is willing to experience the Xanue interactions will be amazed. I'm here to tell you that I never thought that I would experience these being's in this way. I am blown away and I love it! Cynthia and Matt's generosity, having me to their place, is above and beyond expectations. One thing that rings true, Matt always asks his attendees, "Did you wake up dead this morning? No? Then what are you afraid of?"

THE XANUE

Just a little side note: While working on my truck engine one day, a piston spring clip got away from me in a big way. I looked for it for four hours. I called the part store for another only to find out that those are specialty clips. They can only be ordered by the set and delivery is two weeks out. In desperation to find my missing clip, and because I needed my truck in two days, I reached out to the Xanue. Closing my eyes, clearing my head, shutting off all noise around me, I asked them to guide me in the direction of the missing clip. It was like being nudged by a big pillow of air. I turned or moved in the direction that I felt I was being guided in. I repeated the process numerous times. Success! I found the missing clip twenty-five feet away from me. It was under the center of the truck in the gravel driveway! Thank you Xanue!

Regina Horne, D.V.M.
(Daphne, Alabama)

I am a veterinarian practicing on the gulf coast. I had a peaceful childhood growing up on a small farm in central Alabama. I left all of that behind at age eighteen for college and the city life. Later, I became the owner of a business with a hectic work schedule. As a child, I roamed the woods on one hundred acres within the boundaries of a national forest. I greatly missed being able to do that.

In 2015, I was clicking through TV channels when I stopped on a show with people walking in the dark woods banging on trees with baseball bats. The sound they made brought back memories of playing in one particular section of woods near my home. I remember thinking as a little girl while hearing that sound many times, "What good does it do to chop the tree just once?" When I was about eight years old, I saw a silhouette of what I thought was a man during one moonlit night in my bedroom window. However, it was way too tall and wide to be human. My parents told me that I imagined it, but I knew better.

That TV show that I was watching was called "Finding Bigfoot." I watched all of the reruns and could not wait for the next new episode to air. The information that I was getting from their town hall meetings, and the memories they brought back, started me on my own quest to find Bigfoot. I started reading every book I could get my hands on covering all aspects of Sasquatch, from ape to paranormal; from bad to good; scary creature to gentle giant.

Since I have slowly learned over the years to always trust my gut instincts, I quickly came to believe that the Bigfoot Forest People had been around me all along while I was growing up. I often roamed those

THE XANUE

woods alone as a little girl, picking flowers or just exploring. I believe that on one occasion, they even protected me from something by using infrasound to make me run at full speed all the way back home for no apparent reason. They had never hurt me with thousands of chances to have done so. From all of this reading and watching YouTube videos, I began to lean toward the gentle giant side as the truth. There had to be something else altogether happening with the scary side. Now I have come to know that there exists the Good (Xanue), the Bad (Xuxiko), and the Ugly (Treykon).

In late 2017, I came across Team Squatchin USA and Dr. Matthew A. Johnson (Dr. J.) on YouTube. The story of his own quest to find Bigfoot struck a chord in me. My gut instincts were again helping me and telling me that this man was right. Even after watching his four-part video series, "The Great Reveal," I was thinking, "Wow, this is a little out there" and yet I still believed him. His description of all things Xanue helped to explain all the mystery surrounding the Sasquatch. I thought, "Ok, if I really want to find Bigfoot, and this man says that Bigfoot is in his back yard - come and meet them; well, any genuine Bigfoot hunter would have to go." That is, as long as that hunter is a kind person with a good heart and open mind.

I planned to go visit Dr. J in 2018, but due to illness and surgery, I had to postpone until 2019. I invited an open-minded employee, Amy, to travel with me to the Camp Xanue weekend in June. I did not witness as much on that first trip as I had hoped, but the testimonies of some of the other campers made me believe even more that the Xanue are real. I did see twinkling lights in the dark woods that I could not explain.

After that trip, I did not think that I would go back to the State of Washington; however, when the July camp videos came out about some people becoming invisible when being hugged by the Xanue, I knew that I had to return. So Amy and I went back to Camp Xanue in August 2019. I saw more lights, Orbs, and flashes than I saw during my June visit. I experienced tingling from head to toe when I was hugged by Sayreah, the mother in the Xanue family at Matt's home. I also witnessed, firsthand, the healing that another camper, Ruth, received.

The people who come to these camps are good, kind people from all walks of life who quickly become friends. The Xanue make you want to be a better human.

Matt also invited Amy and me to stay after the camp weekend and go to the Southern Oregon Interaction Area (SOIA) with a small group for the last time ever. He told us that Zorth was shutting down SOIA due to government intrusion. I certainly could not pass up that offer. I thought, "Awesome, we'll be in the Xanue's home and surely I will see one there." I did get scared when Matt said the Treykon had moved into SOIA when the Xanue moved out, but I trusted that we would be protected.

When our group of seven humans arrived at SOIA, it was already night in the dark woods - way, way out in the logging woods of southern Oregon. After we sat up camp and turned off the truck headlights, I began to see foggy shapes of all different heights moving around the perimeter of the camp like people moving and mingling at a party. I asked Matt if that was the Xanue, and he said, "Yes." He had already told us that there would be fifty-six Treykon in the area, but there were two-hundred-thirty-eight Xanue surrounding and protecting us. I do not camp in the woods and have always been afraid of the dark woods at night. It is saying something for me to be at peace with sleeping all night in the woods with Treykon nearby. My seeing those foggy images moving about gave me the confidence to sleep soundly.

Over the next few nights at SOIA, I experienced so much - lights, orbs, and glowing trees. There was definitely no electricity there to light up any electronic equipment. I also saw twinkles. My fingers were tingling and disappearing whenever the Xanue touched my hands. I began to learn how to see their shimmering images when they are cloaked standing nearby. I had one great wish to ask of Zorth during this whole trip, which was to get to meet and have interactions with the Xanue back at home where I grew up. At the end of our SOIA trip, Matt told me that Zorth said I would have a family waiting for me when I got back home. He said that some are still there who remember me as a little girl. The Xanue live to be two-hundred to three hundred years old. Words cannot express how happy that made me. I now think of these Xanue as family since some grew up with me, and some older ones watched me grow up. They are my family and I love them.

I returned home from the State of Washington and immediately went to visit my mother for that Labor Day weekend. We walked around her property and talked to the trees, but everything remained peaceful and quiet. I took many photos of the woods at her home just like I had done at Camp Xanue and at SOIA. On Labor Day morning, I was startled awake by a loud female voice right next to my ear saying, "HELLO!" However, there was no one in the room with me. That let me know they are here.

Since that time, I have since been finding tree structures at mom's home - X's, asterisks, tree breaks, bent saplings and woven branches in the woods. A few weeks after that first Hello, I sat down to review my photos. One photo of a large tree structure with an area of shadows in the pine trees behind it caught my attention. I zoomed in several times to find the face of my first Xanue at home. This face looks just like a very big man with a lot of hair. They are not apes!!! I had been standing only thirty-feet from where he was but had not seen him.

Matt has explained that the human retina cannot see them when their frequency is sped up (cloaked), but animals and cameras can see them in that form. Once I found this face, I went back through all of my photos on my iPhone, zooming in and finding many other Xanue. That first face, a small boy in a tree, and a family group under an oak tree are some of the most "uncloaked" and easy-to-see pictures that I have. But they continue allowing me to take their photos in different levels of "cloaking" and poses. This Xanue clan is HUGE!

I also found that I have a photo of a Treykon in the woods from my SOIA trip. Also, I have some Xanue in a photo of Matt and myself on top of the Council of Twelve hill. To date, in my immediate family, I have told my two sisters, one niece, and of course my mother. They believe me because I am a normal, honest person, and because of my photos. One sister and her daughter have participated in night-sit concerts in the woods behind mom's house for hours playing music for the Xanue. The Xanue have let us know they are there by loud owl hoots, coyote, and not-so-coyote howls, and some big Orbs that flash right across the tree tops - they are beautiful! I have also seen some of the shimmering images and twinkling lights around us as we sit in the dark.

I now have photos of Xanue at my veterinary hospital and at another farm that I own in a different part of the state. I have seen smaller Orbs moving about randomly on my hospital security cameras at night. They visit my sister at her home, too. I have tried to choose wisely who I tell and show the photos because the Xanue want to meet good, kind people. By the way, you will NEVER find them by banging trees in the woods! Maybe a Treykon or a Xuxiko, but not a Xanue. You must change your attitude.

All of the people whom I have told are very interested, especially when I show the photos; however, half of these same people then go back to their regular lives without wanting to further their knowledge of the Xanue and open up their worlds any larger. I cannot comprehend this, but to each his own. I guess it is just too overwhelming for some and they are so caught up in their small worldly human existence to let in anything bigger (pun intended). If you want to know Bigfoot, you have only to open your heart and let them come to you.

Traveling to experience the Xanue with Dr. J. will greatly speed things up for you. Then you can go back home, sit under the trees and ask them to come. They will. They will help you to become a better person. Even if you cannot go to the State of Washington, read Dr. J's books and watch his YouTube videos. Think about the Xanue and talk to them. They want to get to know good humans, and help us to love our neighbors and the Earth more. They are a people. They deserve our respect. They are good, kind, and wise. They are our brothers and our sisters.

Cindy Johnson
(Spokane Valley, Washington)

I first met Dr. Matthew A. Johnson ("Dr. J.") at a "Meet and Greet" at a little airport in Puyallup, Washington. I had heard about these monthly get-togethers online while researching Sasquatch videos on the internet. I was living in Spokane, Washington at the time and was going to be visiting a friend in Olympia at the same time as this meeting. Matt was even larger in life than he was in the videos and he had a personality to match. We chatted throughout dinner and then he gave a presentation that included the fact that the Sasquatch were not a big, dumb, giant mountain ape and described them as being a people with intelligence, raising families, and limiting their interactions with humans.

My experience with the Sasquatch up to this point was an encounter on the east side of Mt. Saint Helens in Washington. A friend and I were camping in a very remote area when we both heard a whooping and howling call from three different directions. At first the calls were at least a mile from us, but they were quickly converging on our campsite. Neither of us recognized the call as being any animal we had previously heard. By the time they were approximately 100 yards from us we jumped up and ran to lock ourselves in the truck. It was raining so hard it was difficult to see anything around us let alone the trail we followed to get to where we were. We ended up sleeping inside my truck that night. In the morning we did not see any tracks or indications that anything had approached our camp. We stopped and visited with a camp host a few miles up the road and he told us that he and several of the campers also heard the calls.

"Dr. J." invited me to attend his upcoming conference in Bremerton, WA in the spring of that year. I attended that conference and remained in contact with Matt and his fiancée (now his wife), Cynthia Kreitzberg. I spent one weekend with Cynthia at her home in Puyallup where we explored the green belt behind her house.

My interactions with the Xanue began slowly. I had just moved into a house I had purchased in the fall of 2015. It was situated on the corner of two very busy streets. The first few days when I went to bed, someone would walk along the outside wall of my bedroom and knock on the wall. It was always three knocks. Then I would hear an occasional loud "Whoop." When it finally dawned on me it might be them and not the guy that lived in my basement, I began to hear other things inside my house. I would hear children running in the hallway, laughing and giggling, whispers, cupboard doors opening and closing. I spoke to them and told them that I enjoyed having them in my home and that they were welcome to look at and touch whatever they wanted to.

One day, after I had just finished painting two walls in my dining room and hallway, I noticed little dirty fingerprints on both walls where they met on the corner. The night before, I had heard children running around the house after I had gone to bed. Well, apparently, as they ran from the kitchen through the door to the dining room and they continued around the corner into the hallway, they would put their hands onto the wall in order to swing around the corner faster. The fingerprints were about twenty-five to thirty inches from the floor and quite dirty. I texted Matt to tell him what I found and he asked if I had taken pictures but that never even crossed my mind. I had already washed the walls.

It was about this time that I began experiencing their healing powers. The first time it happened, I thought I was having a stroke while we were having an earthquake. I was laying on the couch watching TV when I suddenly felt that sensation I get just as the anesthesia begins to take effect and the out of body sensation as it begins to wear off. At the same time the couch was literally vibrating so violently that I thought we were having an earthquake. But I looked up and the lamps weren't moving, the curtains were still and no lights were flickering. The scary thing was, I couldn't move a muscle! Not my eyes, nor my mouth. I was completely paralyzed! I didn't know what was happening. I honestly thought I had had a stroke.

A few days later it happened again. I was laying on the couch. I got that anesthetized sensation and was again paralyzed while at the same time my body was literally vibrating so heavily that the couch was actually moving. Then I remembered something that Matt had mentioned when I was visiting them. He said that when the Xanue worked on his arm, his arm began to vibrate. It was like the Xanue were raising our vibration frequency in order to closer match us up to their frequency. I continue to experience this healing process whenever the Xanue choose to work on me. Many times I will wake up because of the elevated vibrational frequency and I know that the Xanue have been helping me heal.

One night I noticed a huge shadowy figure standing at the foot of my bed and I began speaking to "it." As I was talking, I accidentally "fluffed." I immediately apologized and explained that it was considered rude to pass gas in the presence of another. Almost instantly, I got a whiff of the most putrid odor and I laughed and said, "That's okay, you don't need to show me that you do it too!" They definitely have a sense of humor!

In the spring of the 2016, Matt invited me to attend a weekend in Oregon at the Southern Oregon Interaction Area (SOIA). I was recuperating from bilateral knee replacement and I wasn't able to attend but he would later share the results of those weekends with me via the phone.

I believe it was a Tuesday night in June of 2016 that I phoned Matt, just minutes after he returned home from the epic experience of the Exodus of the Xanue people from their dying planet. Matt answered the phone and I could immediately tell that something was different about him. He was exhausted, his voice was extremely emotional, and I could tell he was on the verge of tears. He said something epic had happened that would change the worlds view of the Xanue people but that he was told that he could not share everything that had happened until April of 2017. I had to wait almost an entire year to hear the fantastic experience that Matt, Steve Bachmann, and Mike Kincaid were privileged to be a part of.

In May, I went to Olympia to help my friend LeAnn do some remodeling on her home. The first night I slept in the basement bedroom and was awaken at 3:00 am by someone zipping and unzipping my suitcase. It was too dark to see anything, but I could hear rustling under the bed and could sense movement around the room. I could hear someone moving my clothes around in my suitcase. I felt no sense of fear or anxiety.

Days later, I moved to an upstairs bedroom. Again, at 3:00 am, I was awakened by who I thought was my friend LeAnn on her hands and knees next to my cot and she was reaching for something just out of my sight. I said "LeAnn, what are you looking for? Oh, you aren't LeAnn you silly girl!" It wasn't LeAnn. It was what looked like a six or seven-year-old little girl with a big smile on her face and she was trying to reach something ahead of her. When she saw me looking at her, she got a big grin on her face and she "twinkled" out. She went all bright and shimmery and pixilated out as she disappeared!

About a year later, I again saw her as she climbed up on my bed and crawled over the top of me and down to the floor on the other side of the bed. Then she crawled around to the foot of the bed, all the while with her head above the bed and grinning at me. Then she again "twinkled" out! What had awakened me prior to her climbing on the bed was who I think may have been her younger brother. I felt something or someone in my room and opened my eyes to see a very small, hairy arm and little dark fingers holding a used piece of red dental floss. He was dangling it in my face and bobbing it up and down. I don't know why I thought he was a boy, he just felt like he was male. When I realized that the floss was used and not new, I said, "Oh honey that's yucky. You don't want to play with that!" I then reached up and took the floss from his fingers. As I held it, someone took it from me.

Later that same night I woke up and saw a large dark figure standing next to my bed. It was only there a few seconds before it disappeared. Again, I did not feel alarmed or afraid.

It was about this time that I began having health problems. I had a pretty good-sized bunion on my left foot. I went to a friend who was a podiatrist and he fixed it for me. Just before he was going to take the stitches out, I dropped a huge roll of plastic wrap on my toe and split the whole thing open again. I got that fixed and had a cast put on it to help protect it. The day I was to get the cast off, I was using a knee scooter and the wheel got stuck in a seam in the road as I was crossing to go into the doctor's office to get the cast off. The scooter stopped but I didn't! I broke the toe again. For some unknown reason, I began falling frequently and started breaking bones. After nine falls and repeated visits to my doctor friend, I was too embarrassed to let him see all the damage I was causing.

I fell a total of seventeen times up until that December. By then, I was in excruciating pain constantly. I knew my foot was in bad shape. I had had both knees replaced at Virginia Mason Hospital in Seattle and I felt impressed that I needed to go see a doctor there. I took all my x-rays and showed the orthopedic surgeon the films. He couldn't believe I was able to walk into his office with the amount of damage I had done to my foot. He said the only thing that could be done was to amputate.

I asked him if we could try to save it and he said there were only two hospitals in the United States that would even think about trying to save my foot. Virginia Mason Hospital in Seattle happened to be one of them. Even with that, he said that there was only a five percent chance of it being successful. At best I would be able to use the foot but I would be in constant pain. The surgery was performed. It took two surgeons six and a half hours to remove countless bone fragments and to try and stabilize the foot and toes. When I woke up, I had six screws and four rods holding my foot together. I had to be completely off it for what turned out to be nearly sixteen weeks.

During my recuperation I stayed with my friend, LeAnn. Night after night, I knew that the Xanue were there working on my foot. I

THE XANUE

could sense them in the room. Several times, I could hear them walking around the house. At the end of twelve weeks, I returned to have the foot looked at. The surgeon came in, after looking at the final x-rays, and he wanted to know what I had done for that foot to heal the way it did. He said that it was a bonafide miraculous healing! There was no way that foot could have healed like that on its own. So, I told him about the Xanue. Would you believe that he didn't even "bat an eye!" He said that there was no way that foot could have healed that well without some sort of miracle. Something, other than the work he and his colleague performed, had stepped in and healed that foot.

At the end of sixteen weeks, I went back and saw another colleague of his for my right foot. She first wanted to know what I did "differently" to get my left foot to heal like it did. She also said it was a miracle. When I told her about the Xanue healing, she admitted that it had to have been something or someone out of the norm to cause that foot to heal so well. According to two orthopedic surgeons, and with plenty of x-rays to prove it, my foot's healing was a "walking miracle!" Thank you Xanue!

After another extended stay in Olympia, upon returning home, I went to bed hoping for a good night sleep. I was worried that I might accidentally hurt my recently reconstructed foot by my restless leg movement. Therefore, I positioned myself in the center of my king-sized bed. Normally I would sleep on the right side of the bed, closest to the bathroom. As I laid on my right side, I wondered if the Xanue were still at my house because I had been gone for about six weeks. I asked out loud, "Are you guys still here?" Immediately, I felt a huge warm hand placed on my back and it gently pushed me across the bed to the spot I would normally have been laying in. The hand was so large, it reached from the small of my back to the base of my neck. I could feel all five huge warm fingers. They moved me as if I were an infant! So gentle! I was thrilled to know they were there with me.

Days later, again while I was lying in bed, I hear what sounded like someone at my front door. I jumped out of bed and hurried into the hallway. I felt a whoosh as though someone had been in the hallway and fled when I opened the door. I hesitated and then apologize for startling them. I returned to my bed where I found a small stuffed animal that had been placed on top of my pillow. The toy had been at the foot of my bed on top of a dog crate.

On another occasion, I heard something or someone at the front of the house. I got up and checked the front door and found no one was there. Upon returning to bed, I started thinking, "What if it was burglars or maybe a prowler. Should I be afraid? Should I call 911? What if it wasn't the Xanue?" So now I was starting to scare myself. I then asked out loud, "Was that you guys?" Immediately, a thumb and forefinger pinched my nose three times and someone whispered, "Yep, yep, yep," in my left ear! Another time, I watched as two huge arms crept under my covers from the bottom of my bed and reached up to my feet and gave them a tickle. Some people ask me if I ever get scared when these things happen? The answer is "no" because the Xanue exude kindness and love. It is all so natural that I really have never been startled by them.

When Matt and Cynthia decided to start hosting Camp Xanue night sit and sleep over weekend events at their home, I suggested that I would be happy to come over and cook the meals for the attendees. That way, they wouldn't have to drive all the way back to town to eat. I have cooked for large groups since I started cooking at the age of thirteen. During those summer weeks, I experienced numerous interactions with the Xanue.

At first, I only heard vocals and footsteps in the woods. One night, after we conducted a night-sit, I returned to my cot. It was situated deep in the woods away from all the other campers. I had just laid down when I heard voices coming down the trail towards my cot. My first thought was it must be two of the guys coming down to make sure I had made it to my cot okay. I tried to identify who they were by their voices. I suddenly realized that they were not speaking English. Their words were spoken rapidly and were interspersed with clicks, chirps, and whistles. I sat up on my cot and watched them as they continued down the trail leading them to my cot.

THE XANUE

As they got nearer to my cot, they began to fade out or rather "pixelate out." It was like they were suddenly formed by thousands of pinpricks of light. They began to fade out and I could see through them to the forest behind them. I could still hear them speaking and I heard their footsteps stop at the head of my cot but they had disappeared! They spoke a few more words then they stopped speaking. I then thanked them for coming to see me. I asked if they were healers, would they please work on my legs and feet. I then got back in bed and immediately fell asleep. Later that same night, I woke to a super bright dome made up of countless pinpoints of light. My first thought was, "Wow, the stars are really bright!" But as I continued to look around me, I realized that the lights were beneath the canopy of the trees. They formed a huge dome that continued to the ground and surrounded my cot. It was brilliant and breath-taking to witness.

In August of 2018, I was getting ready for another Camp Xanue weekend event at Matt and Cynthia's home. Both my mother and father were attending with me. We arrived on Wednesday in order to give me time to do all the shopping and preparation prior to campers arriving. Mom was staying in the spare bedroom at the house and dad and I were set up in the Serenity Meadow. Dad was up by the parking lot and my cot was set up in the middle of the field, about forty-feet from dad. Both mom and dad went to bed early. I stayed up till around 11:30 pm until I was ready to go to bed. It was fairly light out so I could easily walk to my cot without a flashlight. I sleep on a cot made with sheets and a blanket because I don't like being tied up in a sleeping bag. I usually tuck the blankets under the mattress sponge so my feet stay warm.

I had just laid down and I was beginning my prayers. Suddenly, I felt someone pull the blankets out and roll them up to my knees. I immediately sat up, and without opening my eyes, I started excitedly jabbering about how excited I was because I was fully awake and they were actually here. There was no way that it could be my imagination. Nobody could convince me that I was making this all up. Finally, I took a breath and asked if it was alright if I opened my eyes to see them.

Cindy Johnson

During that fast, crazy, and excited rant, I hadn't yet opened my eyes! As I jabbered on, I began to hear two men start chuckling. They continued to chuckle until I finally stopped and asked them if I could open my eyes. I could tell one gentleman was kneeling at the foot of my cot and he had laid both his hands on my shins. I immediately knew they were there to work on my feet and legs. His hands were huge. The width of his hands went from my ankle all the way to just below my knees. I could feel the warmth coming from them.

The other gentleman was kneeling by my left side and he had his hands resting on my abdomen. I knew that he would be acting as the anesthesiologist. The gentleman at the foot of my bed answered my question with, "No, not just yet." I then began another request stating that I wouldn't be afraid of what they looked like. I had seen all kinds of movies with weird looking characters and it wouldn't matter if they had three heads and were purple with pink dots because nothing ever scares me. Again, both men continued chuckling. The one at the foot of the cot stated, "Well, we might not look exactly like you think we are going to look." I again assured him that nothing ever phases me and that I wouldn't be startled or shocked.

Then I noticed that there were three little kids running, back and forth, from my cot up to my dad's cot. When I stopped talking the three kids stood next to me and started stroking my arm with their little hands. They then worked their way up to my head where they began pulling their fingers through my hair and fluffing it up in the air. It then occurred to me that they were touching me so perhaps it would be alright for me to touch them! So, I asked if I could touch them and the gentleman on my left stated, "Yes, you can touch me!"

I reached my hands up, still with my eyes closed, and was able to feel the top of his head and down the side of his head. As I felt across his face, I could tell that he had a big smile on his face and no facial hair. I felt his right shoulder and down his arm and all the way to his hands which were laying on my abdomen. By this time my dad had heard me talking to someone and he sat up and looked down the hill to see who I was talking to. He didn't see anyone with me. However, when

THE XANUE

I reached up to feel the gentleman's head, dad said he saw two sets of arms reaching up. It was as though someone was guiding my hands to the man's head. Again, I asked if I could please open my eyes so that I could tell my disbelieving brother that I had actually seen them with my own eyes. At that, the gentleman at the end of the cot let out a big sigh and said, "Cindy, just be patient!" With that, I laid back down feeling thrilled because they knew my name and I immediately fell asleep.

The next morning, I woke up feeling like a million dollars and on cloud nine and I couldn't wait to tell everyone that arrived what had happened! It was an incredible experience! I had actually had a conversation with the Xanue! Out load, in English, wide awake and face to face. I could never doubt it! It happened! To this day that still thrills me to my core! And again, throughout the conversation I knew they loved me unconditionally. That feeling is overwhelmingly present whenever they are around.

Because these experiences are so precious to me, I am careful who I share them with. When Matt began asking for those of us who have been interacting with the Xanue to share these events with others through his upcoming book, I hesitated to share my written word because I know there will be people who will scoff and claim it's all a bunch of fanatics and mass hysteria. But as Matt's deadline for our submissions to be accepted grew closer, I began to wonder if I should tell my story. The Xanue haven't made their presence in my home known for many months. I have often wondered if they had moved on. Several of the attendees to Matt's campouts have been videotaping orbs in their homes. I tried doing the same thing but I've never seen anything remotely looking like an Orb.

So, I decided to ask the Xanue if they wanted me to write up my experiences so they could be submitted for the book. I talked to them. I didn't know if they were even around but I had to try, nevertheless. I asked them to show themselves to me in Orb form if they wanted me to give Matt my story. I was videotaping in my dining room. When I turned on my camera, the Orbs were flying everywhere! They were zipping around so fast, it was hard to see them. I asked them if they would slow down and get bigger so I could get a good picture. Just then, one blue Orb flew right in front of my camera and I was able to get a beautiful picture of it. So that's why my testimonial is available for your reading pleasure and to give you more "food for thought."

This journey continues to enlighten me and thrill me. It is humbling to know that the Xanue are very aware of who I am and my desire to learn more about them. I hope you too can come to know the Xanue people and accept them as our brothers and sisters. I am blessed to have them in my life. I hope someday my family will come to know that what I have experienced is real. It's been an amazing life-changing thrill to be a part of this incredible experience.

Joel Kaminskas
(Rainier, Washington)

I first met Dr. Matthew A. Johnson ("Dr. J.") in September of 2016 at the Triad theater in Yelm, Washington. Several weeks prior, a friend of mine, the late great Robert Quinn, was having dinner at my house and said he had recruited the world's foremost Bigfoot researcher to speak at the aforementioned location. Being curious about Bigfoot for nearly my entire life, I had agreed to go to the Triad and hear what Dr. Johnson had to say.

Shortly after arriving at the theater, "Dr. J." appeared on stage - all 6'9" of him. I don't remember his exact introduction into the lecture but recall he exuded much confidence and was a fairly comical speaker. While I didn't exactly agree with everything he said, I recall him using the word "cloak" or "cloaking" as a capability of the Bigfoot Forest People. That was the moment that everything instantly fell into place for me regarding this subject. The Bigfoot Forest People have the ability to go beyond the visual range of a human by raising their vibrational frequency. It all made sense! After an evening of great learning, it became apparent to me that I wanted to take my experience to the next level. My friend Robert and I decided that we wanted to befriend "Dr. J." and hopefully have the opportunity to be invited to visit the Southern Oregon Interaction Area (SOIA).

Several months later, as chance would have it, "Dr. J." again spoke at the Triad Theater in Yelm, Washington. Robert informed me that there would be a VIP dinner in honor of "Dr. J." and Cynthia. He asked if we could host it at our home in Rainier Washington. After emphatically agreeing my wife, Nancy and I hosted the VIP dinner in

June of 2017. "Dr. J." and a few others spoke at the dinner and it was a lot of fun.

After most of the guests had departed, we did a short night sit in my backyard at about midnight. This was the first time that I had ever done a night sit. There were just six of us: "Dr. J.," Cynthia, Robert, Kevin, Samara, and myself. Not knowing what to expect and certainly not expecting anything in my backyard, both "Dr. J." and Samara, who is very psychically gifted, said that they had felt and seen the Bigfoot Forest People very close to where we were sitting. Robert and I, being new at this, did not know what to look for. However, I did notice some twinkly white and blue lights in the nearby bushes. About an hour or so into the night sit, it felt like nothing was going on. I asked if "Dr. J." and Samara still felt the Bigfoot were around. As soon as I finished my sentence, something crashed into our rear metal gate at the rear portion of our acreage with a fairly loud bang. "There's your answer!," Samara said while chuckling. Wow! I thought that was pretty cool!

"Dr. J." and Cynthia stayed over that night at our home. The following morning, while having breakfast, "Dr. J." invited us to attend his next trip to SOIA. The trip was just only a few days away, near the end of June. Much to my chagrin, I had a previous engagement and I could not make it. However, my wife, Nancy, was able to go and she had amazing experiences there. I would have to wait until August which was his next available trip that had some spots available. In the meantime, "Dr. J." told me to sit out at night in my backyard and just talk to the trees and see if I could get any interaction. I did so for nearly the whole summer. I sat outside in my backyard for three to four nights each week.

I did have one very unusual experience but it was during the daytime. I had set up a cot underneath our 12 o'clock tree in our backyard. I decided to take a nap at about two in the afternoon. Yes, I laid down there near some taller yellow grass which was a little over two-feet tall and about fifteen-feet away from me. I heard something walking in that grass. I got up off my cot to check it out. Much to my amazement, I could see foot prints "in real time" walking right in front of me but there was no entity to be seen making those prints. I watched three or four steps with foot prints being made right in front of me! It was beyond the beyond! SOIA was just a few short weeks away and I could not wait to go!

Dr. Johnson arrived at my house during the last week of August of 2017 to pick up Robert Quinn; Eva, our chiropractor; and my wife, Nancy, and myself. We were all excited to go to SOIA. After a very eventful trip driving down to southern Oregon, we arrived at our campsite. It was a little bit late in the evening, around 8:30 pm. It was getting dark. We had to unpack quickly and get our camp set up.

"Dr. J.," Robert, and I immediately went to the back of the truck to remove our sleeping cots and baggage. While I was looking at the ground, I immediately noticed that a rock had scooted in front of my line of vision. It came from the direction of the bed of the pickup truck. "Dr. J." and Robert were standing there, unloading the truck, and I asked if they tossed a rock my way. They both said, "No!" However, "Dr. J." followed up my question by saying that the Bigfoot usually throw in a rock or a pinecone upon arriving at his interaction area! How cool! We hadn't been there but only thirty-seconds and the fun had already started!

To be honest, this first night at SOIA would be my first time ever doing any real Squatchin. Well, at least it wasn't in my backyard. I was super excited, but also somewhat nervous, about having to sleep out in the open under the stars, in the middle of nowhere, eight-miles up on the logging road, at a five-thousand-foot elevation. Fun and exciting but still a little unnerving.

After setting up our camp, we began our night sit. We all heard tree pops. They were hollow and tinny in nature and sounded like they were coming from the tops of trees. Shortly after we heard the tree pops, we noticed that the tippy tops of many of the trees were being lit up with a soft white light. They kind of looked like a flashbulb was hitting them from an old Kodak camera. We all witnessed this for several minutes and determined it was coming from our 3 o'clock position. This was in the same direction as a portal that "Dr. J." had spoken of before.

THE XANUE

After a long day of travel and a long night sit in which we experience some additional phenomena, it was time for bed. Everyone hit their sleeping bags at once. Then, almost like "synchronized swimmers," the snoring commenced! Earlier that evening, "Dr. J." told the Bigfoot Forest People that it was okay to come up and touch us and scan our bodies while we were sleeping. I don't remember saying "yes" to that. But I didn't say "no" either. Now, I had to sleep with that thought in mind. Shortly after I was in my sleeping bag, and everyone else fell asleep rather quickly, I heard someone walking through our camp. I figured it was one of our members just going to the bathroom. However, when I asked in the morning, a few others said they heard the same bipedal walking but nobody actually got out of their cot! Needless to say, I was unable to sleep after that. I felt it was my duty to protect everyone who was snoring from I'm not sure what. Anyhow, after the sun rose, I did manage an hour or so of sleep to be prepared for the next day.

We left the mountain to go to grab some lunch and supplies for the following evening. During the trip off the mountain, "Dr. J." told us that Zorth had come in to camp the previous evening. Well, we all thought how could we miss a ten-foot tall Bigfoot? "Dr. J." explained that Zorth was cloaked and that he was in his shimmering body. He told us to look in the head area for two dim red eyes and kind of swirling energy below that. Wow! I had seen that kind of energy swirling around in my backyard at night but I thought that that was what my eyes just did at night! The second night at SOIA could not come fast enough for me.

Upon returning to SOIA later that evening, we again arranged our chairs in a half-moon position. We began our second night sit. Almost immediately, shimmering images begin to appear. I could see the dim red around their eyes. The rest of the group was starting to see the energy of the shimmering images as well. Some of the Xanue were seven or eight feet off the ground. Another one was a good ten feet off of the ground. Matt explained that the tall one was Zorth and that the other two individuals that were slightly shorter where his sons, Mogdue and Tukequa.

Joel Kaminskas

It was an amazing sight as you could see all of the shimmering images move. We could also see the eyes that were attached to their heads. They were standing fifteen to twenty-feet away. They seemed to be as interested in us as we were in them. Words cannot accurately describe the experience. It was all at once - spiritual, mesmerizing, exhilarating and fascinating. It was not one bit intimidating or scary. I remember while having this interaction, I looked in the direction of where our sleeping cots were located. I saw a literal sea of red eyes all around our sleeping cots. Some were tall and in the bushes and others were low and seemed to be on the ground. It was a sight that I will never forget. I still didn't get any sleep that night either.

On day three, "Dr. J.," Nancy, Eva, and myself went off the mountain to go out to dinner. Robert decided to stay at the camp for the day. After dinner, we returned to camp a bit late with "Dr. J's" son, Grady. It was close to 10 pm and already dark. We had probably left Robert a bit too long up on the mountain by himself. As we pulled into camp, the headlights hit Robert. He looked a little bit gaunt. He relayed to us, that for the past hour, he was inundated with a bunch of little Forest People running all around him in the bushes close by. He told them that he was not afraid but that his body had a defense mechanism which made it look like he was freaking out a little. After talking with them, he thought that the elders had the children calm down a little bit so as to make Robert feel more comfortable. Robert then went on to explain that one of the adult Xanue came into camp and started breathing very heavily, which stopped after a few moments. He then heard what he described as two rocks clacking together for several beats about one-hundred-feet or so away from him. It was shortly thereafter that the rest of us arrived back to SOIA.

The third and final night that we sat out in the SOIA base camp was probably the most amazing. After Robert described his encounter with the younger Xanue, we all had small shimmering images come up to each and every one of us. They were three to five feet tall with a little dim red eyes. There were several of them and they came very close to us. They were only a foot or two away. They seemed very intrigued by us. We put our hands out for them to touch with their energy. We all felt little tingles of energy from them. It was just amazing!

As the third night sit ended, we all headed for our sleeping bags. I decided to try to get some sleep since I made it through the first two nights without dying. I was so tired and no longer cared if I got "touched." I fell into a deep sleep and woke up at exactly 5:20 am. It was the end of August and the light had just cracked but it was still pretty dark. I picked up my phone to check the time then put it back in my boot and tried to get some more sleep. As soon as I closed my eyes again, I heard a very loud vocalization which sounded like "EEEEEEEEEEEEE!!!" I decided I did not hear it and tried to go back to sleep. Then, three seconds later, it happened again: "EEEEEEEEEEEE!!!" No sooner did the vocalization end that I heard four or five of the largest bipedal footsteps I could possibly imagine! I felt the vibration in my sleeping cot. Whatever made those footsteps, most definitely had urgency. It was moving at a quick pace. I can only describe the sound as Clydesdale Horse walking on two legs. It totally blew my mind!

I sat up immediately and put my glasses on. "Dr. J." was already sitting up on his sleeping cot and he was pointing toward the logging road where his truck was parked. He said, "Did you see that?" "No," I replied. "Dr. J." said, "There was an eight-footer standing on the logging road about seventy-five feet away. He saw me looking at him and ran up the hill!" I instantly knew that was the footfall that I had just heard! Wow! "Dr. J." just had another full body sighting. How cool! There was no going back to sleep after that event. It was about 5:30 am and I just had to wait till everyone else woke up so I could tell them what had just happened.

Later that morning, "Dr. J." and I shared with the rest of the group what we had experienced. They all thought it was amazing. We then had a light breakfast and then gave a video testimonial for the Doc's YouTube channel. We all wished that we could've stayed another night but it was time to go back home. Little did I know but the day for Nancy and myself was far from over.

Joel Kaminskas

We arrived home about 8:30 pm in Rainier, Washington. It was starting to get dark. We unpacked the truck and thanked "Dr. J." for taking us to SOIA. He said, "Don't be surprised if you have some interaction at home." Well I thought that would be cool. However, what could possibly compare to what we just experienced for three nights out in the middle of nowhere?

Nevertheless, after putting everything away, Nancy and I decided to sit out in our backyard that night. It was about 9:30 pm when we started. It was fully dark as Nancy and I sat out on a bench in our backyard. We started talking to the Xanue. Nancy began to invite them to every Christmas party, birthday party, and holiday that we had on our social calendar. We could hear, in the dead yellow grass around our night sit area, several sets of bipedal footsteps that were approaching us from a few different directions. It sounded like four or five individuals but we were not certain because we didn't see anybody. Nancy asked, "Is that you guys?" Immediately, after Nancy asked her question, we heard a rhythmic pounding on our woodshed which was about seventy-five feet from where we were sitting. It almost had a drum beat to it. It was loud and intentional.

We looked at each other while we were both experiencing complete cognitive dissonance. I thought to myself, "This is what happens to someone else." I felt like I was watching TV and someone was relating their story to me of how a Bigfoot was pounding on their woodshed. The only difference was that it was actually happening to Nancy and me. Being complete novices and not knowing what to do, we sheepishly walked back into our house which was only one-hundred-feet away. We were kind of laughing nervously and apologizing to them while we were doing it. After all, we had just spent three nights at SOIA, located about eight miles up a logging road, a mile up in elevation, and in the middle of nowhere. Now, we were freaking out in our own backyard? You couldn't make this up!

Right there and then, we decided to call "Dr. J." to ask him what we should do because we had no idea. Fortunately, he had just arrived home and answered the phone. Frantically, I told him, "They were pounding on our woodshed!" He responded quite calmly, "Oh, they were just letting you know they are there. If they wanted you dead, you'd be dead. If you went into your house and they wanted you dead, you'd still be dead. So go back outside and apologize to them. Then spend a half-hour with them." I understood the point that he was making. So Nancy and I reluctantly went back outside. We turned out a few lights and profusely apologized for twenty minutes or so. It must've been quite comical for them to watch. Since that time, we have had fairly regular activity on our property with lots of vocalizations and shimmering images. We regularly enjoy hanging out with our locals!

Many thanks to Dr. Matthew A. Johnson and his wife, Cynthia. We have become very good friends with them over the last few years. We have enjoyed many special times together and many amazing experiences with the Xanue. In a nutshell, these experiences have changed my life all for the better.

Kevin Kehne

(Apache Junction, Arizona)

My story is just a little different from everyone else's here in that I've never personally met Dr. Matthew A. Johnson ("Dr. J.") nor have I ever been to any of his locations. What I have to say hopefully will reflect directly to his point.

I have been an avid outdoorsman my entire life. I spent most of my teenage years backpacking the wilderness of Arizona. I joined the U.S. Army in 1987 and I served in Operation Desert Storm. The injuries I received led to me being medically discharged in 1992. I have been married for thirty years this July and I've raised four children. I am now medically retired. I have a lot of time on my hands, which leads me here.

While out on a family camping trip in June 2017, we had found large footprints. We then heard wood knocks and whistles (please understand I'm giving the condensed version at this point). After the trip, I made a report with the BFRO. I met the investigator on site three weeks later. I was chomping at the bit to show him the tracks and where everything else had happened. However, he just wanted to sit and talk.

He explained to me all the different "THEORETICAL CAMPS" in the "BIGFOOT WORLD." I had always believed they were flesh and blood but not an ape. When he told me about the "Supernatural or Woo," I laughed. I responded, "What a bunch of crack pot's!" He responded to me by saying, "If you are going to get into Bigfooting, the best advice is keep an open mind!" My new friend was on the fence about the "Woo." By the end of this trip, he was starting to lean closer to the "Woo" as was I. After driving two hours back home in complete awe, I had to go back.

THE XANUE

One week later, I found myself back up on site all by myself. My new friend would be joining me a couple of days later. I followed his direction of attempting to habituate with the Bigfoot. I later found out that this method came from "Dr. J." No lights, no fire, park my truck in the same spot, set up my tent in the same spot, and place my chair in the same spot, etc.

I had gone for a walk in what I now call "Squatch Valley" looking for signs of them. This is an area of old growth and very little human activity, if any at all. I found a structure. Next to the structure, I found the largest pile of Human Poop I had ever seen. I was excited. I started to spiral out to look for tracks and I found one rather quickly. I followed the direction of that track and came across a large Rattle Snake. My normal behavior is to kill the snake and eat it. However, I had some very strange thoughts enter my head (out of my line of thinking).

I had taken out my phone and started to video record the snake while I was having this conversation in my head, "I'm going to kill and eat you." Then an opposing thought came to me, "Why? This is his home. Look how beautiful he is. He belongs here. Look how old he is. You don't have the right to do this!" I decided to let this one live.

As soon as I stopped the video recording, I had my world shook with the loudest, most powerful voice coming from about thirty-yards away: "WHAAAAA UU WAAAAAA!" It shook me to the core. It sounded like, "What You Want?" I said, "Well, hello my brother." Then he immediately responded with, "WHAAAAAA." I said, "Okay, I'll go back to camp." As I was walking back to camp, I was being paralleled. I started talking to him, "I have a mate and offspring. Do you have a mate and offspring?" This is how I continued all the way back.

That night, I had a "dream" where he came up to me and introduced himself as "Eaden-Gon." He was trying to introduce me to his mate, "Eaden-Gen." However, she was very reluctant to come out from behind a large tree. He kept telling her it was okay and safe. She finally stepped out and was holding what looked like a two or three-year-old. I woke up right after that and sat in my tent until the sun came up trying to grasp what had just happened. I knew it wasn't just a dream. There's so much more that had happened on this trip but I need to move on.

After returning home, I dove into the internet and Facebook to look for answers. I came across a YouTube page and had made a comment about what I was experiencing. I was contacted by someone who is now a good friend and we talked for a while. She directed me to Dr. J's Team Squatchin USA YouTube page. I started watching his video's and thought this guy's nuts. I went about my research and I chose to blow him off.

After spending thirty-two days up at what I now call "Squatch Camp," that year with interactions constantly leaving me beside myself, I decided to revisit the whole "Dr. J." thing again. I watched his four-part video series, "The Great Reveal." I realized that EVERYTHING he was saying was true. I was experiencing everything that he had experienced except the "portal." The big part of it was the mind speak and me being taken by "Indy" (That's what I call "Eaden-gen" because it's easier to pronounce and he doesn't mind me calling him, "Indy") to a Council of Six meeting in my sleep where I was asked, "What do you want from us?" I responded, "I want to learn more!"

In 2018, I spent ninety-five days out at Squatch Camp with increasing interactions, including at home. One such incident occurred in March. I had been out at the Renaissance Festival here in Arizona. I was in a lot of pain and my PTSD was raging at full force due to the crowds. I told my wife, "I'm done." I went home. I had gone to bed early that night. I had just finished my prayers when I felt a light touch on my head and back. I was expecting to see my wife there comforting me. Instead, I was shocked to see a shimmering image standing next to me. I asked, "Is that you Indy?" Immediately, I received a mind speak, "Yes. You need to go to sleep!" That's the last thing I remember. I woke up ten hours later. I felt like a million bucks. Say what you will, IT HAPPENED!!! Indy took away my knee and back pain and calmed my PTSD.

On another trip in 2018, there were four of us at Squatch Camp. I had been walking around and I miss stepped on a flat piece of sandstone. The stone flipped up and whacked the inside of my left ankle on a steel plate. I have two plates and nine pins and screws holding my ankle together. It hurt like hell. It continued to hurt throughout the day. While doing our night sit, Indy and others were around us. I asked them to please take away the pain. About twenty minutes later, I felt a light touch and buzz on my left leg. The pain immediately left.

On another trip to Squatch Camp, I really shouldn't have gone because my back was in really bad shape. However, I knew that I'd be okay after I got up there. It took me all day just to set up my camp. It was all I could do just to walk so I just sat there most of the time. I spent the first night in the tent on the air mattress. I woke up in a lot of pain but I just kept on keeping on. The Xanue were ever present. During the second night, I slept on my cot outside of the tent and the activity was intense. I woke up in a tremendous amount of back pain and went inside the tent to sleep on the air mattress. I asked them if they could please help my back? Otherwise, I'd have to leave and go home the following morning. I wanted to stay there with them in the wild! I woke up in the morning one-hundred percent pain free and full of energy. All that I could do was thank them and I got mind speak, "ZORTH IS HAPPY!" I drove the five miles to where I had service and sent Dr. J a message that "ZORTH IS HAPPY!" I had no idea why or what it had meant. I found it amazing that Indy had mentioned Zorth and this just solidified to me what Dr. J was saying.

Now, I will talk about the Xanue and the different forms of them that I've witnessed, recorded, and have in pictures. Going back to the beginning, I kept seeing these little flashes of light, kind of like how a firefly looks but different. It is bright white twinkles of light here and there. I call them twinkle lights. They always appear where I get the clicks and snaps from as well as bipedal steps. I see them every time I'm out at Squatch Camp and I have seen them at home as well. At first, I thought I was seeing things until my buddy said he was seeing them too. Subsequently, everyone that has been out with me has seen them too.

I've seen the big red Orbs floating around the inside of the branches of the trees. This will blow the mind of anyone who sees it. I've had three daytime sightings of the Xanue in the flesh. I've also had seven-nighttime sightings. I've had at least seven times where I could only see a shimmering image. A couple of them were within ten feet or less of me. The first time I saw the shimmering image, I was all alone. It was my third night out during a bad back trip. I had taken a two-hour nap and had just had a half of a five-hour energy shot. I wanted to stay up late. I was having typical activity, including green eye glow, twinkle lights, knocks, clacks and clicks, along with footsteps.

When I was woken up to one of the strongest zaps I've ever experienced, I thought I'd nodded out for a couple of minutes. However, according to my audio recorder, I was out for forty-five minutes. Anyway, when I was woken up, I could see something about thirty-five feet in front of me. It was the shape of a person but there wasn't anyone there. It looked almost like the Predator movie but different. I kept looking away and then back and there he was. What was really cool was when I could see his eyes start to glow green. Another time, I was sitting and had three of them about thirty yards away. One was positioned to my left, one to my right, and one straight in front of me.

At that moment, I was getting zapped. Then I had the distinct feeling that someone was behind me too. I said, "I know you're behind me. I'm going to stand up." I waited a minute or so and stood up. I said, "I'm going to turn around." Once again, I waited a minute or so then I turned and was immediately frozen where I stood. I couldn't move my arms or legs. Indy was standing about eight feet away and he was massive. What I saw was the shimmering image of a BIG PERSON. He was standing there, looking at me, with those big green glowing eyes. I said, "Okay. Thank you. I'll sit down now." Immediately, I could move again so I sat back down.

It's hard to get the full details of how this all happens with anything shy of my own book, which will one day come. What I will say for certainty is that the Xanue are very real. They exist in different shapes, forms of energy, and have the ability to heal. They are full of love and trust is extremely important to them. The Xanue are far beyond us in their understanding of Love. That kind of Love can only come from

GOD! To try and understand, you have to look into the Quantum World – both spiritual or supernatural.

In closing, I'm grateful that I've been chosen by my local Xanue Council of Six, to have been given a watcher, Indy, and to learn and spread the Love in order to try and help to get US back on track. I can say for certain that Dr. Matthew A. Johnson is who he says he is. The Xanue have chosen him above all. They have also chosen others, like myself, in local areas too. It's an honor words alone could never express.

Alex Kerson

(Bremerton, Washington)

November of 2016, I was Elk hunting with two of my friends. We were in a very secluded area. During the first two days, we saw nothing but beautiful country. As we explored, we found an area that was conducive to our needs. We split up and went our different ways to comeback with the same decision that this will be the area to hunt the next day. At 0400 hours, we were out on the same trail and then we split up and went to our locations. I took the right fork in the road. Rick went left and Marc went straight up the middle.

I started walking the trail. About two minutes later, I had two unknown hunters following me. They kept a respectful distance from me and took the next left fork which left me alone. I kept walking when nature calls. Of course, I respond immediately. After all of this, I walked across to a hillside and sat on a stump. The weather was spectacular and mysterious at the same time.

Around 0530 hours, the sun was peeking through the rolling fog and mist. It was awesome! Instead of walking to the top of the hill like I was supposed to, I elected to go part way. I was comfortable enjoying the sights and weather. When all of a sudden, in my left ear, I hear my name being whispered three times! I checked my phone and it was off due to no signal. I pulled out my Garmin to check to see if my friends were just messing with me. Of course, the radio was totally shutdown to conserve battery power. A trick I learned in the Marine Corps.

I smiled and instinctively looked up to the top of the hill which was wooded. There he was, standing at the top of the hill. He was in his cloaked body with a twenty-foot-tall portal opening right next to him! I was amazed at what I was witnessing! He looked just like the hunter in the predator movie! All shiny and bright, with a pure white eye shine looking straight at me! The reason I could see him was that the portal was so bright it was reflecting off his cloaked body. I was astounded and not the least bit frightened.

I came to the realization that I have just been pushed down the rabbit hole without Alice. I knew that the being in front of me wished me no harm. How do I know this? Because you wouldn't be reading this. He wanted me to see him as he entered the portal. The portal started to collapse and dissipate into a starry mist which shrunk down to about ten feet in height and floated at will down the hill. It reopened at fifty-feet to the right of me to about eight-feet in height. I could see right through it! Nothing went in nor came out. It simply opened and closed. Once again, it turned into a starry mist. However, this time, it totally disappeared and floated away with the breeze. I was pumped. If that portal had been any closer to me, you probably wouldn't be reading this testimonial! I was dazed and enlightened at the same time! I now had personal proof that the Great Creator - God is real! I personally have always believed now I have personal proof! The rest of the hunt was uneventful.

I never heard of Dr. Matthew A. Johnson (Dr. J.). When I returned home, I was looking for information on portals. I found nothing. Library and on the net nothing. Then one day, I was walking around town and came across a metaphysical shop which had all kinds of fascinating trinkets, stones, and books galore! I picked a book and opened up towards the middle and there it was - an article on portals and how the Druids used them. I bought the book and it too changed my life. I needed to know more.

That night I was listening to talk radio and a commercial came on advertising a Bigfoot/UFO conference at the casino in Ocean Shores, Washington. I bought a set of tickets for the weekend and took my best friend with me. Here, were all the Bigfoot hunters with their scary stories and vocalizations, which are cool by the way. Yet none of them could claim the true existence of Bigfoot. Most of them claimed how dangerous they are and warned us to be careful when we are in the woods. I am thinking, "How could they know this? None of them have ever seen one, much less ever interacted with them!"

Then Dr. J. stood up on stage and told his story. As soon as he was telling of his experiences, I knew right then and there that he was telling the truth. His experiences were pretty much like mine. He is the real deal! After he spoke and had his question and answer session, we approached him and asked the big question: "Can we go out with you?" He said no. I don't know you. Fair enough. I understood the gravity of the no. I told him my story. He looked at me and said, "Come to the conference in Bremerton, Washington, and listen to my presentation – The Great Reveal." I was astounded by all these lucky coincidences because I lived in Bremerton!

I went to the conference, bought his book, which in my opinion is the only way to go! It rings with truth! I joined the Team Squatchin USA Facebook Group and I got to participate in a twenty-person study group at his homestead. What an amazing experience! I never saw any orbs. Yet, people were saying they were attached to me. I met the current love of my life, Michelle. We both got to experience the 'big woo'. She had her personal experience with an Orb in her sleeping bag! What a weekend! Finally, I met someone that is as honest as I am!

Since that time, I have received healings as well as witnessing healings! I have never felt threatened at any time. I took a close friend of mine out squatchin. We are like brother's and we have known each other since we were twelve-years-old. He is psychic in his own way. If you lost something, you could call him up and he would tell you where you could find the lost item.

It was around midnight and we are cruising the south end of the Olympic Mountains. I was driving along when I said, "Let's stop here." The stars were bright and clear and it wasn't too chilly. We pulled out chairs and started playing drums. The next thing I knew, Marc stands up, and he is starting to load gear in the car. I'm like, "What's up?" He says, "Can't you hear him? He is telling us to leave and that we are not welcomed and that it is dangerous for you to be here!"

THE XANUE

I was astounded by what Marc had said. I was confused and upset. I started talking to them about how I would not reveal their locations. Also, I was not interested in collecting evidence of any kind. Finally, I shared that I was looking for a personal relationship with them and that we could be trusted. Trust me I was an emotional wreck because I just wanted to meet them. Then there was silence. Then Marc related a message to me. They apologized for upsetting me. Instantly, I totally apologized for my behavior.

Then the questions from one of them and their observations of our past lives were spot on: "Well, we can see from your past that you both were pretty violent." I responded, "No. I've never been violent to anyone. Are you sure?" He responded, "I am sure."

Next thing I knew, Marc stated, "Yes. We were violent when we were young and we have grown out of that stage." I started thinking and they were referring to our childhood past. We were both bullied in school. There comes a time in one's life when you start to turn in kind. I was blown away and I confessed to the cruelty as a youth. After that, we sat and had a very in depth conversation. Personally I could not hear them speak to me. Marc asked them why I couldn't hear them. They said that my brain was muddled from all of the excitement and they couldn't reach me. Of course, that is the story of my life. It was a great conversation. I wanted to know if they are the ones that healed me? Their response was "no." Then they shared that they were everywhere, even downtown. That was where I was living at the time. About three blocks from the center of the town of Bremerton. I was amazed at their response. Just as Dr. J. stated, they are living in the trees!

Marc asked about healings and there was a long pause. They told us to come back in the spring and bring a long table with you. Personally, I was offended by the question. You don't ask a stranger for ten dollars much less start asking favors. We packed up and went home. We never did return in the spring. We waited until late fall to return. When we arrived, we set up cots in the open air on a super moon night at its fullest peak. We had walked a few trails. By the time we got back, we sat around without a fire and just listened.

Alex Kerson

While I was sitting in a camp chair, I could feel this Tarantula creeping up my leg, very slowly. I could feel each leg pressing against my leg. It was twenty-nine-degrees outside. There are no spiders around. I panicked, jumped up, and started slapping the back of my leg! Then I realized that it was a juvenile and I had just blown a great moment to interact. The moment was lost. I looked at Marc and he said, "It's time for bed. It is too cold to sit here." I agreed, took out my portable speaker, and I started to play music. Harp music to be exact.

I put the speaker under my cot so that I wouldn't have to get out of my sleeping bag. I just climbed into my thirty-five below sleeping bag, after I removed my clothes. You get a better response from your bag. It helps to maintain the heat better. Anyway, the moon was out and it was a crystal clear night. The music was playing softly. I laid back and closed my eyes. At that moment, with my eyes still closed, I saw two adults standing on each side of my cot with the juvenile standing at the head of my cot. They were all looking down at me. Instead of panicking, I just opened my eyes. All I could see were stars and trees. I closed my eyes again and they were still standing there. It was awesome!

Then Marc said, "They like your music." I was thinking, "Cool." Then it was lights out. Before that happened, they gave me message to tell Marc in the morning. When the morning rolled around, I saw a spark in Marc's eye that I hadn't seen in a long time. He is the same age as me and has suffered two strokes, two broken legs, and a heart attack. Marc was excited! He said, "Man, you missed it! I tried to wake you up! I saw three of them last night and they told me to leave you alone and that they were here for me. They told me not to discuss with you what we were talking about. I said cool, I was ecstatic for him and his personal experience.

Then I delivered the message I was to relay to him. You would have thought that I gut punched him because his reaction was like – "Wait a minute! That was exactly what we were talking about!" I realized what had happened. They knew him very well. They did not want him to dismiss the experience as a dream. They visit and check on him. His story is truly incredible. I could relate it, yet it is not my story to tell. However, I will tell you this much, you all would like to have his experiences. Bless his heart.

In conclusion, I could go on and on with my experiences with these wonderful people. Just from knowing them, I have met other people who travel the same lines and have never met them much less than interact with them. Yet with the help of these individuals, I have had the esteem privilege to meet Jesus Christ twice! No, I wasn't dying or anything. I was in a meditation circle when he came to me and stated, "Keep doing what you are doing. Your house is ready for you!" I started crying as I am reliving the moment.

I have been bathed in the blue light of their love. I never ask for anything. For me, it is daily contact through mind zapping and personal conversations. I can hear them now and I've been able to for some time. I had to learn how to really listen. Not question what I am hearing. I simply respond to the question. As Dr. J. has said, if you are hearing voices, just ask yourself. If you receive a resounding no, you are in.

I don't call them Bigfoot or Sasquatch. I call them Xanue - The Forest People. I will always have song for them in my heart. They are with me now. What is written is true. Love and light!

Gary Luke

(Atlanta, Georgia)

In February of 2017, I was introduced to Dr. Matthew A. Johnson when I attended the UFO/Paranormal Summit in Ocean Shores, Washington. Matt was one of the speakers. I found him to be an entertaining orator as he shared his experiences with the Bigfoot Forest People. I was intrigued, as at that time, I had no knowledge of Sasquatch. However, I was a believer. There are too many unexplained phenomena in our world so why not a North American Great Ape? In a very short time, I was shown how wrong that hypothesis was because I started having my own experiences.

In April of 2017, my three daughters and I attended Dr. Matthew A. Johnson's Bigfoot University Conference. On Saturday evening, he shared "The Great Reveal" regarding who the Forest People are, where they're from, and why they're here. I must admit, as a novice to the Bigfoot world, I bypassed all the "old school" techniques of research and, apparently, jumped head first on the Woo-Woo train with the head engineer himself - Dr. Woo-Woo!!!

The conference left me with many questions. Therefore, I started my own investigations on habituation and interaction while watching and listening to Matt's YouTube videos and his SoundCloud.com audios. I also listened to and watched many other "researchers", and have read many Bigfoot books. I was approaching this as an investigator to learn the truth, with a very open mind.

Jump ahead to September of 2018. My daughters and I attended Matt and Cynthia's Camp Xanue "Night Sit/Sleep Over" weekend event at their home in Chehalis, Washington. We had a great time! Not only did we meet and become friends with many of the participants, but we now have a bond because of the shared experiences. As hosts, Matt and Cynthia exceed the definition. Throw in the excellent meals provided by our new found friend, Cindy Johnson, and the weekend was complete!

I enjoyed the "get together" in the mornings to record on video what we did or did not experience. It was interesting that thirty plus people in a small area could have so many different interactions! The girls and I heard many vocals, saw the lights, Orbs, had what was explained as an energy scan from head to toe, a physical touch, giggling, an eight-foot plus silhouette from my peripheral of the right side head shoulder arm and leg. Also, there were two footprints 20" x 10" and 40" apart, right in front of the chair I sat in the night before, a small child's footprint and as explained an energy embrace that was filled with an overwhelming feeling of Love. When we finally nodded off, all of us had the most restful sleep. Matt also shared with me, a recording captured one week before we arrived, which was the best audio I have ever heard and it was recorded on his property. It truly was a worthwhile experience. I recommend it to anyone with an interest or curiosity. Go in with a good heart and an open mind.

Since our visit to the State of Washington, we leased some property in Alabama. We have found many signs of the Bigfoot Forest People. I have taken dozens of pictures showing different structures and many faces. However, that subject is a controversial one. I know what I am looking at and what the difference is between real pictures and true pareidolia. No one will ever get a clear picture unless they want you to have one. Quantum Physics baby!!

I have seen the lights and had an energy scan. I heard something dash past me at a high rate of speed that I couldn't explain leaving no foot prints. On a trip in April of 2019, we were staying in a cabin on the Menominee River in the Upper Peninsula of Michigan. The day we arrived, as my wife and I got out of the truck, we were met with a loud "Whoop!!"

Around 9:00 pm every evening, I would go outside, play some music, and enjoy the night. The first two nights were uneventful.

However, I did notice that once I started playing the music, the area got quiet - no night sounds. The third night, as I came outside and stood on the front step, the night erupted! I was surrounded on all four sides with "Whoops" and "Yells" and the 900 lb owls. Also, there was one very odd sounding goose honk. This all lasted for almost a solid five minutes, as I always check such things on my watch. While I was walking away from the cabin to the spot where I set up my speaker to play my tunes, I stood there laughing because it went on for so long. When I said in my normal voice, "Ok", the noise immediately stopped and then became eerily quiet. It was crazy! Not once did I feel uneasy or frightened. I started up the music and played for forty-five minutes. While the music was playing, I had the overwhelming feeling of having an audience. I was not alone. One just knows.

Towards the last fifteen minutes, a very bright softball size brilliant green Orb appeared and lightly hovered and bounced around thirty yards away at the 10 o'clock area on the perimeter. As quickly as it appeared - it disappeared. Then the Orb re-appeared and stayed for several minutes, always slightly swaying. Very cool! The next morning, I walked through the area very thoroughly. I was doing the forensics, as I always do, and not finding any source for the light. I also walked away with the best picture I have ever taken. Without any doubt at all, it's a face – not pareidolia.

I believe in the existence of the Xanue - The Bigfoot Forest People. My journey continues. Thanks Matt and Cynthia. I appreciate you both.

Christine MacDonald
(Nanaimo, British Columbia, Canada)

I have always been interested in the unexplained and unsolved mysteries. I watched many TV shows on these topics. Many years ago, I came across the show, "Finding Bigfoot." I looked forward to what evidence the team would come up with. I watched their techniques and listened to their calls. I was intrigued. I found out that the organization that backed these shows, was having a weekend expedition in the foothills of the Rocky Mountains. I was living in Calgary, Alberta at the time. I signed up, paid my fee, and loaded up the car with hope in my heart that I would have an experience with the Bigfoot.

We had a fun weekend, even with the hail storm that blew over us! I met some great people and will always remember the good times and the stories we shared together. After two cold nights and a couple of callbacks to our whoops and tree knocks, I packed up my car and headed home. I was a little disappointed that we didn't get anything really definitive but I was grateful for the experience.

I continued to watch my shows on the unexplained, unsolved mysteries. All the while, I was thinking to myself, "There has to be more to this Bigfoot thing." I was hooked! I watched the Patterson and Gimlin film over and over again. I went online and watched everything that I could about the Bigfoot Forest People. I was trying to learn more on how to have an encounter of my own. Eventually, I came across a video of a man who had an encounter near the Oregon caves - Dr. Matthew A. Johnson.

I watched his online videos and found him to be very sincere and passionate about what he was experiencing. I believed him. I found out he had a Facebook group - Team Squatchin USA. I joined the group and I followed Matt. When he went out to the Southern Oregon Habituation Area (SOHA), recording with his parabolic microphone dish and put out the gifting bowls, I eagerly awaited the updates. Sometimes I stayed up very late in hopes of a new update. I was not disappointed! He was getting interactions right in his camp! He was recording soft voices and items were being drug through camp. Also, food was being eaten out of the gifting bowls! He was collecting footprints and fingerprints! He was getting results! I followed his page and updates for years. I was hoping that I could attend SOHA one day. Trying to budget a trip from Alberta, Canada to southern Oregon was going to be pricey. Unfortunately, I was never able to attend, as much as I had hoped to.

In June of 2016, my husband and I ended up moving to Vancouver Island, BC. While I was packing and moving, the EXODUS was happening! How thrilled I was to hear about it once my internet was hooked up and I could get caught up! I did a happy dance in my living room! I cried tears of joy! There were 23,542 Xanue people who were brought to the Earth from their dying planet to join the others that were already here. What a glorious day! I thought to myself afterwards, "I wonder what happens now? Will we see more of them? Will we see less of them?"

I continued to follow Matt and his interactions with the Bigfoot Forest People. I was eagerly awaiting updates. One of the videos he recorded, with Cynthia, was announcing that they would be having a gathering in Southern Oregon if one would like to attend. YES PLEASE! So I started my budget and planned on making the trek south to Oregon. I was going! Needless to say, the event was changed. Now, they were going to have it on their property – just outside Chehalis WA. That was a lot closer to me. I signed up for a weekend at Camp Xanue!

Luckily, Matt wrote a book, "Bigfoot: A Fifty-Year Journey Come Full Circle." I figured I had better read up before I attended the Chelalis Interaction Area (CIA). I ordered a copy. When it arrived, I couldn't put it down. It explained a lot. It made sense to me. I was ready for this journey down the rabbit hole, so to speak.

Christine MacDonald

June 2018 at Camp Xanue: I arrived late Friday evening. Matt and Cynthia were kind enough to invite me a day early. I felt very welcomed and we chatted about my journey that had brought me to this point. There were four of us who were allowed to arrive early that night because we lived so far away. We then headed out to do a night sit and sleep out under the stars, near the fire pit. I wasn't really sure what to expect. Yet, in a way, I did know what could happen. I remembered to "be a Navy Seal, strong as steel".

We sat in the darkness, played music off and on, and Matt spoke to them. I heard a distinctive knock and movement by the wood shed. They are here! Matt got up and walked down the path, toward the trailhead (i.e., The 12 o'clock position). Cynthia then got up from her chair and joined him. They nearly disappeared into the darkness. I could still make out where they were standing. That is when I saw what looked like a green mist swirl beside them, to my left. I thought my eyes were playing tricks on me. I began seeing what looked like a faint twinkle of light, here and there, throughout the evening. Close to the ground and then up higher. Not directly in front of me, to the side, in my peripheral.

We eventually retired to our cots for the evening. I was so excited. I wondered if I would ever fall asleep! It was cool that evening. I burrowed deep into my sleeping bag, pulling it up above my head. Nice and cozy, I lay there for a while and began to hear the others, breathing steadily as one does when falling asleep. Shortly after, I heard what sounded to a me like someone heavy was walking beside my cot. I mean real heavy! It was a dull, soft, thud, thud, thud, thud. Am I feeling them walk by? I wondered to myself, "No, it can't be them. Could it?"

I quietly lay there, listening, barely breathing. I'm not sure how much time passed. I began to hear what sounded like a steady whooshing sound. I couldn't make out what it was. It sounded like a high altitude airplane flying above? As I listened, I noticed that the sound didn't change or fade away, like a plane would as it flew by. I continued to listen to this whooshing sound, unsure of what I was hearing. What felt like seconds, I opened my eyes, it was early morning? Did I just pass out? Confused as to how I felt so awake, listening to this sound, then waking up in a blink of an eye and it was morning.

The following day, Saturday, attendees began showing up. We had lunch and chatted and shared stories. It was great to meet everyone. After supper, we had a night sit in two groups. One group was by the fire pit, beside the house. The other group, which I was in, were in the Serenity Meadow. We sang songs, played music, and spoke to the Xanue. I began to notice the soft twinkle-like lights scattered throughout the meadow and in the trees. Other attendees reported seeing them as well. Some were a soft white light, some green, some red.

I then noticed what looked like two faint green eyes at the 3 o'clock position on the trail. The Xanue would have been on the trail on the sloped hill peeking up to the Serenity Meadow. Then I saw a faint red glow coming from the 3 o'clock position, further back in the forest and up higher. It looked, to me, like it was backlit. Kind of like in the movies, when they shoot a night scene in the forest. I also saw a window shaped soft red light, complete with window panes, hovering, further back in the forest, well off the ground.

We eventually retired for the night. My cot was set up in the Serenity Meadow area. I awoke around 4 am. It was just beginning to get light out and I heard two of the biggest freaking owls I've ever heard! Very good impressions. Yet, I knew in my gut it wasn't owls. There was a very deep and bass sounding around the 8 o'clock or 9 o'clock position on the perimeter of the Serenity Meadow. Other attendees later reported hearing them also. About one-half to one-hour later, as it was slowly getting lighter, I heard a bunch of coyotes start yipping and howling. What a way to start the day! We eventually all got up and had breakfast and conversed about our experiences of the night. I really enjoyed myself and planned on attending the following summer.

After attending the June of 2018 Camp Xanue weekend event, I've heard loud bangs on the side of my house; had vivid dreams involving the Xanue which usually involve a meaning or lesson of some sort; have had a tree pop, groan and snap for no apparent reason while in a semi-remote area, with no other people around; had a stick glyph greet me at a campsite; heard weird duck calls late at night; and I found a big footprint by a river during the local salmon run.

August 2019 at Camp Xanue – Friday Night: After the experiences I had the previous year, I was really looking forward to a two night stay at Matt and Cynthia's. I arrived on the Friday evening and decided to set up my cot in the same location as I had been the year before. In the Serenity Meadow, by the trail along the garage, back to the house. I got myself set up then proceeded to the house. I met the small group of people who had arrived earlier. We chatted, exchanged stories, and we got to know each other.

Later in the evening, we did a night sit in the Serenity Meadow. Matt told us that Kontue and Sayreah were with us. One by one, we took turns walking to where they were standing. I did not see them myself. When I went up, I put my hand out and felt a slight warmth and buzzing sensation in my hand and along my forearm. Like an electrical sensation. I thanked them for joining us and expressed how happy I was to be here. I returned to my seat and was told by two of the attendees, Keith and Dawn, that they saw sparkling lights all around my feet as I was standing up in front of Kontue and Sayreah.

A little later in the evening, I was standing up near the driveway into the Serenity Meadow, chatting with an attendee, Andy. We both saw what looked like a faint, dark orange or red brick rectangle shaped light to me. They appeared as eyes to Andy. The brick was about our height, hovering in the darkness. Amazed, we kept asking each other if we were both seeing what the other was seeing. Yes, we were! We thanked them for being there with us.

Eventually, we all crawled into our cots, at various locations throughout the property. I fell asleep quickly. I had a vivid dream of connecting with people and was shown the faces of people. Some, I recognized, others I did not.

Saturday Night: More attendees show up in the morning. There were quite a lot of people compared to the year before. Awesome, I thought. More people are interested in knowing these beautiful beings - the

Xanue. After lunch, we had a meet and greet and introduced ourselves. We discussed the Xanue and Matt went over guidelines and protocols.

About a week before attending, I had a vivid dream. I was with a group of people, I did not recognize anyone, and we were given medallions. The design looked like a First Nations style, yet I could not make out what the design was. It was placed around my neck and, in my dream, I remember looking down at it, on my neck. On the Saturday, during the meet and greet, we were given a necklace from one of the attendees, Steve Bachmann. I recognized this medallion from my dreams! How cool is that?!

That evening, after supper, we were off on our night sits. There were a lot of people in the Serenity Meadow. However, tonight I was off to attend a night sit down the hill near the beaver pond. I joined a small group of attendees: Mike, Andy, Theresa, Debbie, Stuart, and Doug. We got our chairs set up, played music, and spoke to the Xanue. We also danced a bit too. We all heard movement around our sides and behind us. Some reported seeing cloaked figures and movement. I saw some faint twinkling lights to my sides, in my peripheral.

In front of me to the left, by a tree with some grass beside it, I saw what looked like two people hunched down. I could make out the head shape and shoulder shape. This was also seen by others in the group. After some time near the water's edge, I returned up the hill with another attendee, Debbie. We went to the Serenity Meadow where others were going up to greet Kontue and Sayreah. I sat and watched as people taking turns, walking up to them, one by one. I caught movement to the left. It looked to me like a very tall shoulder, head profile, accompanied with movement. We sat up longer, playing music, and Matt spoke to the Xanue. Then we all headed off to our cots for the evening.

Sunday: After breakfast, we gathered in the house and had a conference. People shared their experiences. Matt played some amazing audio recordings. The highlight of the weekend was seeing the healing of an attendee, Ruth Cameron. She had arrived at Camp Xanue with difficulty walking due to numerous strokes. By Sunday, she was laughing, jumping, and running around. Did I just witness a miracle? I think so. I still get teary eyed, remembering her beaming, smiling face, and seeing her run around.

Afterward, I drove down the mountain to get cell reception and make a few phone calls. As I was parked, sitting in the car with the windows up and the air-conditioning on, I distinctly heard two whispering voices behind me. I checked the radio. Nope, it was shut off. I turned around, thinking that maybe someone was walking behind the car, talking to each other, but there was nobody there. I couldn't make out what they were saying. I thought to myself, did the Xanue want to come for a drive with me? Were they watching over me? After making my calls, I drove back to Matt and Cynthia's home with probably the biggest grin on my face! I did not hear anymore chatter from the backseat.

I did some activities in the afternoon and roamed the property chatting with others while we all shared our stories and experiences. That night, during our night sit, we played music and sang some songs. I saw lots of little flashes and twinkles of light. Another attendee who was sitting next to me, Wendy, saw them too. We watched and listened. Eventually, we got up from our chairs and stood facing the 3 o'clock position toward the house. As we were standing there, we distinctly heard movement in front of us. A rustling, like something moving through the grasses. We both heard the sounds and continued to see faint red flashes of light. We crouched down, in a squatting position, asking the Xanue youth to come closer. They did! We heard them directly in front of us! I would estimate that they were one to two feet in front of us! This got me very excited!

As we talked about what we were experiencing, we saw numerous, large flashes of light in the forest to our right, down the trail to the left of the woodpile. At first, I thought it was someone with a flashlight. However, I quickly realized a flashlight does not illuminate a forest like that, nor does a spotlight. It was different. I believe what I was seeing was a portal opening up. Eventually, we called it a night. We helped some attendees with mobility issues get back to the house where they were staying. Another attendee, Debbie, and I, returned to the Serenity Meadow along the trail by the garage.

Upon our arrival back at the Serenity Meadow, we were talking about the night's events and getting ready to retire to our cots. Most other attendees were already in their cots and we could hear them snoring or deep breathing. I then noticed a light in the trees behind the Porta Potties and to the right. I asked my friend, Debbie, if she saw it too. She did. Cool! I asked if she wanted to go check it out, thinking it was possibly the neighbors light, from across the road. She was up for it! As we walked up the driveway from the Serenity Meadow to the Top Lane road, we heard multiple frogs croak in that same section of trees. We did not notice any light to our right, in the forest as we walked toward the road.

Once we did get to the Top Lane road, we saw the neighbor had a light on through a window, the living room perhaps? It was more yellow/amber in color, different than the light we saw in the woods. We heard no one else awake or walking on the gravel pathways or road. We both conversed on this fact for a few minutes as we slowly walked the road to the other driveway toward the house. We then walked back toward the meadow on the trail behind the garage and heard movement in the woods to our right, which startled us. We apologized for being startled and laughed as we made our way back to the Serenity Meadow to go to bed. We did not notice anyone else awake or up walking around.

When we got back to the meadow, the light was there again, in the woods, behind the Porta Potties and to the right. I thought to myself, "Hmmm? Interesting." I did not see any light as we walked the loop around that section of woods. We stood there, looking at this light and noticed it was moving! Very slightly, like it was floating. I asked Debbie if she saw this too. She did! The light slowly floated around, up and down, and then to the left and right, ever so slightly. I heard no noise at all, other than someone snoring off in the meadow. After about a half an hour or longer of watching this ball of light or Orb, my friend, Debbie, went to bed. Although I had lost sense of time during this activity, I had no intention of going to bed anytime soon! I was going to stay up for as long as I could and see what would happen.

I watched as this Orb lightly floated around. I was trying to think of things to discredit what I was seeing. Was it a person? Was it an elaborate light effect? Why didn't I hear anything? There was no humming or electrical sound or crunching on the ground as if one would make walking around. Nothing. I couldn't believe I was the only one seeing this. I heard someone using the Porta Potty and got their attention afterward. I called John to come over and see this. He verified that he saw the light too and thanked me for showing it to him before heading back to his cot. I thought to myself, "How can you go back to bed with an Orb in the forest?" I just assumed that he had seen this before or that he was really tired and just wanted to sleep.

I continued to watch the Orb. It began changing shape. It got bigger and was starting to look like a disco ball. I could see geometric patterns within it - patterns and different colors like a prism. The light was contained; it did not illuminate the forest around it as a lantern might. The color changed to a golden light with reddish edging. It began getting smaller, then became two smaller Orbs! They moved independently then melded back together. It then grew larger and became an inverted triangle. It was glowing in a golden light and becoming larger than the initial Orb. Changing again into two Orbs, they began to get very small and the color changed to a bright red. Now it looked like eyes! The "eyes" moved together, like a person moving around. It appeared to walk and take steps around the area. Yet, it was facing me the whole time.

I thought to myself, "Am I really seeing this? Why don't I hear anything, like crunching, shuffling or twig snapping?" I was in awe. I probably was standing there with my mouth hanging open and eyes bugging out. I was wondering, "What do I do next?" I began remembering things that Matt had told us. They are Beings of Light. They are benevolent. They want us to experience them in their natural form as Beings of Light. I felt no fear at all - just wonder.

The eyes changed back into the original Orb-like shape and golden color. I decided to shuffle quickly to my left and the Orb floated over, appearing to follow me. Then I shuffled back to the right and it followed me again. I thought, "How cool is this?" I am interacting with an Orb! I thanked them for showing themselves to me. I had a bit of a joyful cry. I was grinning, no doubt, from ear to ear. I felt so blessed. I was grateful that I was experiencing this and told them that too. I asked some questions and the Orb responded by floating up and down or by slightly vibrating. It is hard to explain in words. I'm not sure how much time had passed. Maybe an hour or longer. My lower back started to ache. I told them that my back was hurting. I also told them that I wanted to stay up all night with them and that I would as long as I could.

After some time passed, I was having a difficult time standing up. I found myself bent over, resting my hands on my knees, trying to stretch out my back. I took a few steps back, closer to my cot. The Orb changes into the red eyes and the brightness begins to fade. I thanked them for being with me and showing themselves to me and I was a little upset that I was going to go to bed and this night was going to end. Eventually, my back was screaming in pain. I really had to lie down now, even though I did not want to! I backed up to my cot, never taking my eyes off of their eyes. They slowly started fading away to just pinpricks of red light then went dark.

I got myself to my cot and inside my sleeping bag. I was looking upside down to the area where the Orb was, hoping to see any sign of light. I did not. It was all dark and quiet. With the biggest grin on my face, I snuggled in my sleeping bag and fell asleep right away. When I woke up the next morning, I felt great, my back did not hurt. I was telling a couple of the attendees, Debbie and Jill, what had happened to me the night before. I got a bit emotional. I remember telling them that I was not upset or scared. Rather, I was just really overwhelmed and grateful that they interacted with me!

Since returning home to British Columbia, I have had very vivid dreams. Sometimes, the vivid dreams come with messages that I have yet to figure out. I'm sure that I will, in time. I believe they, the Xanue, give you what you are ready for when you are ready for it. I look forward to experiencing more. I trust their judgment.

I truly hope that, for those of you reading this, that one day you will also have experiences with the Xanue. Remember to trust in yourself. Be a kind person, have a good heart, and keep your mind open to the possibilities. You will not be disappointed.

I cannot wait to find out what I will experience on my next visit to Camp Xanue.

Donna Mansfield
(Cottage Grove, Oregon)

I first met Dr. Matthew A. Johnson way back in 2001, shortly after his first encounter with a Bigfoot at the Oregon Caves. My husband and I became members of his organization: The Southern Oregon Bigfoot Society (SOBS). Monthly meetings were provided where like-minded individuals would meet in Grants Pass, Oregon to discuss our favorite topic – Bigfoot.

We were all in the "Old-School" mode of research back then. We would meet up in the forest at a site which was determined to be a hot spot for Bigfoot activity. Then we would try to make contact with them via making sounds, baiting with food, etc. Since we lived near this site, my husband and I would usually be the designated daily food baiters. We would venture out to the site with peanut butter sandwiches, bananas, etc. We placed the items in a bait pile, rang a "dinner bell," and left the area. We would rake the dirt around the bait pile. If a Bigfoot did indeed venture into our bait pile, they would definitely leave footprints. Well, we rarely saw footprints around the bait pile.

We learned later that they were way too intelligent for that. How they got to the food was interesting. They probably would just lay down and stretch their arms far enough to grab things, but we were not sure. The food was usually gone but what or who ate it was questionable. We eventually gave up this quest. I don't know what became of the Southern Oregon Bigfoot Society.

Fast forward several years. I was searching for Dr. Matthew A. Johnson and found a book he had written. I ordered his book – "BIGFOOT: A Fifty-Year Journey Come Full Circle." A few weeks later, Dr.

Johnson showed up on the doorsteps at our home in Cottage Grove, Oregon. My husband, John, answered the door. I was just excited to once again meet up with Dr. Matthew A. Johnson and continue on our quest for knowledge. I read his book and took in every word. Dr. Johnson had come a very long way since our last encounter with him. He certainly did his research and I was so very grateful.

I too wanted to connect with the Xanue. I was a kind person with a good heart and a VERY open mind. I asked them to please connect with me because I sincerely wanted to get to know them. I guess they heard me loud and clear. I believe that they felt that I was one of the humans that they could communicate with. I started having "mind speak" conversations with one Xanue in particular. He told me to call him "Rusty." I began to have vivid dreams of Xanue around my home, inside my home, and communicating with me on a regular basis. On February 6, 2018, I had a mind speak with Rusty who simply told me three words, "Alert, dead tomorrow." While freaking out, I thought someone that I knew would be dead tomorrow. My mother was ninety-three and in memory care. I thought maybe it was her time to go. I accepted the eventual news and went to sleep.

The next day, I discovered my furnace was dead. My gas furnace died. "Alert, dead tomorrow" had happened but not in the way I had expected. Gas is dangerous. I shut it all down and called the repairman. He said we could have blown up! The furnace had a serious problem!

The next night, February 8, 2018, I had the most awesome and mortifying experience of my life. At 12:30 am, I woke up and was contemplating getting out of bed to use the bathroom. I had two cats sleeping around me and a dog about five to six feet away on her bed on the floor. Suddenly I heard a very loud and low guttural growl about a foot away from me. Talk about panic in the middle of the night! After my heart calmed down and was beating normally again, it happened again. However, this time it was right up close to my left ear. Then two more times. It was huge! The lung capacity was tremendous. I was wide awake! The cats shot off the bed so fast.

After the third loud growl, I began to smell a strange odor. The odor was almost putrid but not what I was expecting inside my home from a Bigfoot encounter. The smell was filling the entire room. I was in awe and could not believe what was happening. My husband slept through the entire ordeal with his CPAP machine on. My heart was pounding. It was hot inside the house. My back was hurting, as usual. I had sciatica very badly. Suddenly, I felt something very cold going onto my lower back. I was hot and sweating from fear. Something very cold was being placed on my lower back. I then heard a mind speak, "Lots of nerves, need to reduce inflammation." I heard this loud and clear! WOW! I am a walker and I would always walk in pain. However, the next morning, I walked 3 miles without an ounce of pain!! That was two years ago. To this date, I have not had an ounce of sciatica pain at all! It was awesome to tell myself and to realize that "YES, THIS IS REAL. THEY ARE REAL. THIS REALLY HAPPENED!!!"

Since that initial encounter with the Xanue in my home, we ventured out to Dr. Matthew A. Johnson's and Cynthia's home in Chehalis, WA for a night sit in May of 2018. I am so grateful that Matt and Cynthia have opened up their home to us so we can learn to love and appreciate these wonderful Forest People. We were all welcomed by Matt and Cynthia with open arms and acknowledged. We also attended a night sit and sleep over in August of 2018. Something always happens there. The Xanue want to connect with us.

Between February and May of that year, I had several other encounters within my home. They included loud noises, babies crying, animal sounds, knocking, banging, and little loud "monkey" sounds. One night, our Toyota Camry was moved half way out of the garage, after they managed to open the garage door. My new Toyota Highlander has a lot of high tech gadgets on it that they like to explore. Lights go on and off. Doors click open and lock themselves. Highlander emblem will light up when no one is near it, etc. The juveniles like electronics. At the Chehalis Interaction Area (CIA), early in the morning of the May 2018 night sit and sleep over weekend, I also experienced little "monkey" sounds. The sounds were filling up around my sleeping cot and almost sounded like they were inside my sleeping bag. My guess is that these have been juveniles who liked being around me. I welcomed them and I still do, with open arms. When returning home, I welcomed the same sounds nightly. Also, I always receive a mind speak, "I'm here." I always have visions of them guarding my home.

In June of 2018, I went to have my yearly X-Ray of my kidney stones. I have had both kidneys full of stones. I had yearly checkups, X-Rays, and then I would be given a prescription for oxycodone and was sent on my way for another year. There wasn't anything to be done but give me pain meds in the event the stones traveled. The pain meds would keep me out of the ER until they passed. I had lots of stones removed twice. Also, I have passed many on my own. I knew that time would come again. It's not fun anticipating the most painful experience of your life!

Well, after my X-Ray that day, went to talk to the nurse practitioner, as I usually did. But, this time she said, "They're all gone!" Next, she asked, "So what did you do?" I was in total shock. I was just talking about this with my cousin who had called me a half hour before my appointment. She said that maybe the Xanue got rid of my kidney stones. I thought that would be nice but seriously doubted that would ever happen. Well, that is EXACTLY what happened! I responded, "I have done nothing! I am not a good patient. I don't follow instructions. I don't drink lemon water. I don't watch my diet. I've done nothing."

Next, I told the nurse practitioner that I knew what happened but that she would think I was nuts if I told her. She didn't think I was nuts and wanted to know what I thought happened. So I proceeded to explain my insight into the Xanue. I shared with her what was transpiring in my life since I met these fantastic Forest People. She was so intrigued, that she went to the Team Squatchin USA site and became very interested. I am now kidney stone free! So amazing. Almost 20 years of hell was diminished since the Xanue have come into my life. I am beyond grateful!

I also have had a heart arrhythmia for almost twenty-years. My last checkup revealed that it too was totally gone! I have been taking medication for this for twenty years. What a shocker to know that my heart has been healed too. I ended up giving my doctor a copy of Dr. Johnson's book. She too was in awe of my recovery.

    I am sixty-nine years old. I have absolutely nothing physically wrong with me. Every ache, pain, or medical problem I have ever had, have been dealt with by the Xanue. To this day, they continue to visit me, heal me, help me, and always let me know they are with me. If they use me to teach the other Xanue how to heal humans, then so be it. I was actually told by the Xanue that this is the truth. I love them beyond what words can describe. I thank God for bringing them into my life and for giving me this fantastic gift of knowledge and love. This ride continues for me, and what a ride it is!! There is never a dull moment!

Cheryl Lee McAuley

(Longview, Washington)

Hello. So, you're interested in learning about the Bigfoot Forest People? I will tell you about my adventure, so far, and how it has changed my life. My name is Cheryl Lee McAuley. I have lived in Longview, Washington for almost fourteen-years now. I come from the Midwest where I grew up in the countryside. I was always playing in the woods and fields outside so being outdoorsy, as they say, is natural for me.

Early in 2019, I was looking into the Bigfoot world on YouTube and searching for information. The year prior, I was kayaking on Yale Lake just east of Woodland, Washington and had what I thought may have been an encounter. While kayaking around a peninsula in the lake, I saw an area where the tree leaves and branches dropped over the bank creating a natural tunnel. I headed over to the area in order to kayak through it.

When I was close to the shoreline, I could see the top of a big tree that was in the middle of the peninsula. All of a sudden, the tree started shaking violently and from side to side. This was a fairly thick tree. I could not see farther down to the ground around the tree because the area was too thick with other trees. I stared in wonder as to what could shake a tree that way and why. I was in a remote area and did not see another person on shore. I started to get a bit nervous. I turned the kayak around, knowing that a person could not have the strength to do that. Lying in bed that night, I thought to myself, "What could have been an explanation for that?" Bigfoot did come to mind. However, since I had never had an encounter before, I just decided it must have been something else and I should just forget about it.

Then another unexplainable event happened a few months later. I was walking my black lab, Evie, in the forest east of Castle Rock, Washington. While back into the trail, my dog just started barking at something straight ahead of us. Then she started backing up. I tried to calm her down and keep her still, while I scanned the area for anything she might have seen. I saw nothing. I decided to clear the area, in case it was something like a predator, I did not want to come face to face with. Dogs have a keen sense, better than humans, so I trusted her. We moved on out of there.

After hiking into an older growth forest area, I started sensing something myself. I could not explain it. My dog just had her nose to the ground as I looked straight ahead. All of a sudden, I felt like I was being closely watched. All the hair on my body stood straight up. I looked around in every direction. There was nothing to see but forest but I could still feel something there. Now I started to get the idea of a possible predator in the area. However, my dog did not sense anything at that time. I was getting spooked so I took a hold of her leash and ran out of there. This encounter may not have been Bigfoot related but I don't know. I just know something was there.

Because of these two encounters, I wanted to learn more. My curiosity was getting the better of me. While on YouTube, I stumbled across a gentleman by the name of Dr. Matthew A. Johnson. I listened to his story of how he and his family saw a Bigfoot at the Oregon Caves. I thought to myself, "This has to have some credibility to it as he is a psychologist and had a family with him." I started watching the many videos he has made regarding his encounter and his subsequent research. He was taking people up to his Southern Oregon Interaction Area (SOIA). I thought to myself, "How cool is that to go researching in an area where many people are having experiences."

I thought, "I could not even go to something that far away, but wait!" After watching a few more videos, I found out that he and his fiancé then (now wife), Cynthia, had moved to live just outside of Chehalis, Washington. I also learned that they were hosting weekend events during that summer at their home and property. They call it Camp

Xanue. I was so excited to think that I could maybe find someone who could explain my forest experiences and who saw a Bigfoot himself. I found him on Facebook and contacted him right away. I asked how I could be involved in the camp and night sits in order to experience the Bigfoot Forest People. He told me about his first book and he also explained about the four-part video series: "The Great Reveal." I was excited to find out what this was all about.

After reading Dr. Johnson's first book, "BIGFOOT: A Fifty-Year Journey Come Full Circle," and watching the four-part video series, "The Great Reveal," I became a full believer in what is called the "The Woo." This belief stems from having had several paranormal experiences in my life. To me, these experiences are a normal part of life. However, many people are in disbelief or just plain frightened of the unknown. As a result, these experiences are just left forgotten or denied altogether. Being a believer, and an empath myself, I was ready to go to their property to see for myself. I had prepared my senses to not be frightened or negative about anything. I've learned that love, kindness, open hearts, and open minds are what is needed for these forest people to let themselves be known to you. They do have the ability to read people and to know what kind of person you are and if they want you to know them.

I had also read and heard that the forest people are healers. Having had knee surgery, the year before, I was experiencing pain and limping when walking. Also, I had gained some weight. I was walking as little as possible due to the pain. My situation was taking its time healing. I thought that maybe the Bigfoot Forest People could try something to help me. I was in such pain; I was ready to try anything. I thought that taking pills everyday was not the healthiest thing that I could do. I was only taking them when it was absolutely necessary. I had nothing to lose by asking them for help. I was open minded and read about how they healed Dr. Johnson and saved his life. It was worth a try. I had planned to ask them for help during my first visit to Camp Xanue.

The first visit to Dr. Johnson's home was on the last evening of the weekend they were hosting local folks. I came to help clean up and prepare their property for the up and coming summer camp outs. This was in mid-May of 2019. People brought mowers and weed whackers and just plain elbow grease to help with grounds keeping. When I first arrived, I was greeted by Cynthia. She gave me a big welcoming hug. She showed me around and we chatted. Then she introduced me to Dr. Johnson who was weed whacking. He stopped and walked over and gave me a welcome hug. Upon my arrival, I received hugs from two people whom I had never known before. I could feel that this place was about love and kindness. I felt very comfortable. The area itself had a feeling of positive, loving energy, and the surrounding forest emitted a feeling of welcome. I was excited for the evening to come.

When evening came, I was with the few people left from the weekend. We were sitting, lined up, and facing the path to the woods. It was dark but the moon was out. My eyes adjusted pretty quickly to the darkness. We started to talk and sing. Then Dr. Johnson said we were greeted by Kontue and his two sons, Gouthda and Boetree. They were standing in front of us but in their cloaked form. Many others were in the forest behind them along with their little ones.

This was the very first time I saw eye glow from Gouthda. I actually saw faint red eye glow about eight feet off the ground. I could feel them there but my eyes could not see any shimmering from the cloaked state they were in. Dr. Johnson can see them from all the practice of having spent years in the woods with them during his years of research. I was elated. I started talking with them saying "hello" and that I was "happy to meet you." I asked if they could please help my leg. However, no healing happened that night. Just meeting them was a good thing. I went to bed on my cot. I was smiling knowing that I was in the company of many Bigfoot Forest People. I knew that I was safe. I already loved them and I was ready to go to my next camp out which was to be in June.

Upon arriving at the first summer weekend event at Camp Xanue in early June of 2019, I was greeted by a number of people. They were all very kind and offered their friendship openly. We met and talked about our experiences and what brought us here. Dr. Johnson told us some rules. He explained to us what we should and should not do. He encouraged us to have fun and to not be frightened. We had our run of the property. We could walk down the hill to the wetlands below. We were encouraged to be back on time for dinner. I set up my cot. Then I spoke to the Bigfoot Forest People in my mind. I asked them if they would heal my leg and to help me with my pain. I was waiting anxiously to experience them again.

Night fell and we all met up with Dr. Johnson inside their house. We talked and then we all walked out to the Serenity Meadow. We sat up our chairs and sat to have our evening experience. When we arrived at the Serenity Meadow, many people were already seeing Orbs and young ones in the woods. We gathered around and actually saw the faint Orbs in an area down a path - called the 3 o'clock trail. It was amazing. We would softly talk to them, as you would talk to a young child.

Then, other people were gathering in the front of the Serenity Meadow and facing a woodpile, in the direction of the forest. Matt stated that Kontue was there. He also said that Zorth, the head of the Xanue Council of Twelve, was there too. Zorth was actually there with us. I was one of the people who wanted to go up to the woodpile to say hello. However, with my leg, I was weak and unsure of walking and falling. I had asked another camper, Stuart Barger, to help me walk to the woodpile and go with me. He took my arm and he helped me walk toward where they were. I spoke and told them my name and that I was happy to be there in order to meet them. I told them I was not able to see them cloaked and shimmering. I asked them if they could help me to see them.

At that very moment, a big Orb formed right on the ground in front of us. Stuart and I both saw it. We were amazed. I took a step right in front of the woodpile. I leaned on it and outstretched my hand. I asked if they could please touch my hand. It only took a few seconds and my hand started to tingle and vibrate. It felt like it was very warm. I touched my cheek and could feel the heat. This was very real. This was unbelievable but it was actually happening to me. I was amazed.

THE XANUE

Stuart played a tune that he wrote on his guitar. It was an instrumental written for them. They love music. I felt that the Xanue enjoyed it. I know that we did while standing there in their presence and listening. I told the Xanue that I loved them. I asked them if they would please help to heal my leg and my pain. After we both said "thank you" to them, Stuart helped me back to my chair. I went to bed in my cot that night in awe that I had them touch my hand. I was excited that I had made contact with the Xanue for the very first time.

Upon waking in the morning, I was smiling. I was ready for another fun day at camp. When the June event was over, I drove home excited. I'm still in contact with the friends that I made there. I did not feel any different when I went home. My leg and knee were still in pain and I was limping. However, my excitement and encounter had changed my life. I knew I would be back for the next two campouts during that summer.

When the July campout arrived, I was elated to see some of my friends again that I met earlier in June. Apparently, many people return to Camp Xanue. Dr. Johnson refers to these individuals as 'repeat offenders'. I met a few others that were new. We all talked and mingled and enjoyed our time together. Two particular attendees I noticed were on my mind. After the second night, we all were sitting in the dark and I was praying for a healing for them. I had asked twice before for myself in May and June. Nothing happened. I didn't think about asking again for my own healing. Instead, I found myself praying for the other two individuals.

As one by one people took turns walking to the woodpile to speak with the Xanue, they were starting to disappear. We simply could not see them. Dr. Johnson said that the Xanue were hugging the people and enfolding them with their higher vibrational energy. The upper body parts and entire bodies of these people were disappearing from our sight. Although they were still there, the Xanue's higher vibrating energy was turning the humans invisible. It blew our minds and Dr. Johnson said he had not witnessed that before. This was an amazing experience.

Everyone had their turn and it was getting late. I decided to limp over to my cot with my walking stick and go to bed. As I was laying in my cot, I was under the covers starting to read my book. I don't know why but I thought in my head "If you want me to go to sleep, you will have to knock me out." In about five minutes, I fell asleep on my back. The next thing I remember, I was slowly coming out of sleep and starting to wake up. I was groggy and I heard something rustling around my cot. The next thing that happened was that I heard a deep voice that said in my left ear, "Zorth."

I slowly and barely opened my eyes to see a large, gold ball of energy over my legs. My legs were lifted about a foot up and held there. My entire body was feeling an energy wave going from my feet to my head. I was again knocked out. I woke up the next morning feeling energized like I've not felt in a very long time. I stood up and felt like running. I walked up to the house, in a fast pace, to ask Dr. Johnson if this really happened. I could not believe my leg and knee had no pain. I could walk without limping and I felt great. I was so excited but unsure if I was only dreaming this. All this was new to me and I was a little in shock but very happy.

I was told by everyone in the house who I shared this with that this was real. Dr. Johnson told me that Zorth spoke his name to him also in that same way at SOIA. It happened! I had experienced a healing from the Xanue Forest People and Zorth, himself, was a part of it. I was elated more than words could say. I was so thankful that I drove home after that camp singing all of the way. I felt so much love and happiness. When I was taking my gear into the garage, I walked out to the driveway. Out of the corner of my eye, a beautiful big yellow tiger swallowtail butterfly flew right over my head. Then the butterfly flew off into the forest next to my house. I was stopped in shock as I have collected butterflies all my life and butterflies have such strong meaning to me. This particular butterfly was one of my father's favorite ones. He would always mention this particular butterfly. To have one right there over my head at that time was unbelievable. I have not seen one like that in years. I thought wow, what a beautiful coincidence. Maybe it was not. I thought maybe the Xanue were saying to me, "We are here with you Cheryl." I never forgot that butterfly.

Well, when I was going to the August Camp Xanue, I was being driven by another attendee. There was little space to park because there were about fifty people attending that weekend. When I set my cot up in the little space that I shared with two other attendees, I walked away talking with my bunk mate Regina. Once again, seeing out of the corner of my eye, I turned to look and I saw a big beautiful yellow tiger swallowtail butterfly. It was glittering over our cots. In that very second, I knew it was no coincidence. The Xanue were using that specific butterfly to let me know that they welcomed me back to camp and that they knew I was there.

These experiences have changed my life in a way that has brought me to a place of love, kindness, and giving. I have asked for the Xanue to place it on my heart to help who I can. I have also asked to help get this information out to people and to support Matt and his lovely wife, Cynthia. If you just open your heart and mind and give into the love this world has to offer, you will find the rabbit hole is endless. Knowledge is out there for everyone. Love to you.

Charlene Peters

(Kailua, Hawaii)

I first encountered Dr. Matthew A. Johnson ("Dr. J") a few years ago through a spiritual brother, Robert Quinn. Robert was living in the State of Washington. One day, he called me here in Hawaii and said he had found out about "Dr. J" and his work with The Bigfoot Forrest People and that he was motivated to find out more. Robert was usually led by intuition and certain "knowing" regarding things. He was always ahead of the curve. So when he presented this genre to me, I knew that I should listen to him.

For years, while living in Oregon, I had felt and believed the Bigfoot somehow existed. Not only locally, but around the world too. Bigfoot sightings have been well archived and recorded for eons. Once, I even went into our local forest to try to find them, but to no avail. However, I also knew there were things that were real even if we did not see them. I had great belief in interdimensional worlds and that the veil between our two worlds was thin at the time.

To make a long story short, Robert ended up doing an event with Jodi Wille and me in Los Angeles to help introduce "Dr. J." and the Bigfoot genre. Los Angeles was our stomping ground since the 1960's and it was also a place where everything was possible and could be presented with delight. We did the event. It was a coming out party, of sorts, for "Dr. J" and the Bigfoot Forrest People story in the Los Angeles area. Everyone loved it!

For the next few years, Robert accompanied "Dr. J" to the Southern Oregon Interaction Area (SOIA). He supported "Dr. J" at all of his Bigfoot events in Washington and California. I attended and supported

"Dr. J" when I could. We both believed in "Dr. J" and his story. We started to connect on a frequency with the Bigfoot Forest People.

I live in Hawaii and Robert kept me updated with his experiences that followed with them. He told me about his many healings and encounters. He became totally dedicated to getting to know them. I also ended up connecting with them and had my own encounter with the Xanue when I had to go in for a surgery. Zorth sent them there to be with me. As they say, "What one knows, they all know." There are no limits to where they can travel, be it physically or ethereal.

A few years ago, Robert passed over. I'm sure his story is told with "Dr. J." Robert ended up coming to several of us in dream state and he let us know that he was well. He had decided to work and live among the Xanue tribe as one of them.

Thank you Dr. Matthew A. Johnson for your belief and dedication to this great work. I am blessed to know you and be a small part of that journey and my connection with them. Very Special.

Chris Pettross
(Easley, South Carolina)

It's been a while since my time spent in Southern Oregon and my "Life Changing Experiences" that will forever leave me a committed believer in the existence of the Bigfoot Forest People. Since my trip, there has not been a day that has gone by where that week, those who were present, the subtle little things, the major experiences, and everything else in between, all the way up until this past Fall of 2019 that has not crossed my mind more than a few times each day. The friends, relationships, bonds and also stories I have had the pleasure to experience, share, and have shared with me have been nothing less than a blessing.

Some of the things that I have learned is that "Everything Happens for a Reason". There are no coincidences either. I also learned that the few that I know to have had similar experiences tend to have a lot of the same characteristics or symptoms that normally followed their encounters. What really stood out to me is that I've never shared my incident. Yet, it seems like a carbon copy of details across the country in areas that I have never been to. Also, I spoke to several of these people over the phone and we ended up having more in common in experiences than I had thought.

To start off, I will set the course that always kind of stood out in my mind, prior to my experience, that I chalked up to nothing but I was apparently very wrong. It was the smallest details that seem to have been the bigger key to opening that door.

When we were all on the mountain in Southern Oregon, everyone had decided to head to town for a few hours. I had decided to stay and keep an eye on the camp because of some poachers hunting out of season, that had been driving up and down the mountain that morning. I felt incredibly comfortable being there alone, which is really nothing new to me having grown up camping and so forth in the mountains in Tennessee. That day though, I felt incredibly comfortable. Dr. Matthew A. Johnson ("Dr. J") had offered to leave me "Maggie" for protection. "Maggie" was a .44 Magnum Revolver. I just had absolutely no urge or desire to accept it, despite growing up in a household of firearms. I was just as comfortable with having that firearm with me as I would have been keeping my coat or warm clothes near me to have that time of year, but I didn't desire it.

After everyone left, I built the fire back up in order to warm myself up. I just admired the solitude and beauty of the mountains and the serenity that followed. I then found myself just talking. I felt compelled to just speak whatever was on my mind. I spoke to the forest as if it were a Therapist that had broken down my walls and got to what was really burdening me for many, many years. I had such an emotional dump that I could only release it all through a very long and overdue crying session. I had no idea why I did it? I just knew that afterwards I felt such a relief of burden and weight taken off of my shoulders and an overwhelming acceptance to where I was. I felt like "That Place" was where I belonged.

It didn't matter that I had a family waiting across the Country that I loved more than life itself. I felt as if I could disappear into that forest and not look back without regret or a second consideration to that commitment. I felt a peace inside that I have never known. When everyone came back, I had carried on like nothing had gone on. I didn't tell anyone simply due to the fact that I didn't think it was relative. I got a bunch of burden off of my chest privately and moved on. Well, I was wrong.

That very same night, was the night where I was pulled off of my cot, stood up while still in my sleeping bag, and I felt a very loving urge to go wherever they had in mind to take me. I felt like the Bigfoot Forest People came for me to take me somewhere else for a possible healing or more interaction, but I couldn't get out of my damn sleeping bag to go. When I was falling backwards, I reached out to stop my fall. While doing so, I grabbed onto the forearm of one of them. I was lowered back onto the edge of my cot. I tried to get out and get my boots on, but they were gone. I felt that I missed my opportunity to go further on my interaction because I just couldn't get out of that sleeping bag and get my boots on.

That next day was when one of the members from camp came over to check on me had found my tarp in the woods in one direction, my emergency blanket in another direction, and a small pile of these berries that I had never seen before sitting just a few feet away from my cot. Those berries turned out to be fresh Manzanita berries. However, they apparently were not in season, nor found in that area of the mountain. Also, they're used to treat Kidney Issues. I had gone to southern Oregon with "Dr. J" in hopes of receiving a healing for my Renal Failure due to FSGS.

Later, I spoke to a guy whom we often chat about experiences and theories. He happened to volunteer a similar effect of an overwhelming feeling to have an emotional dump and later that night, he had an almost hypnotic urge to go into the forest with them and not look back. We both concluded that the overwhelming desire to just walk away from everything and everyone could be the reason why possibly we all heard about missing hikers who are never found. It's a theory we pondered on. Did we think this meant we were walking to our deaths? We both agreed "No", but just to possibly "Another Place" if our life here has run its course. I have never felt that feeling since, nor have I had that type of encounter again.

It's kind of odd, and yet interesting, reading about people's experiences in these groups who state that out of nowhere, they had an emotional dump and got rid of all that bad juju. Maybe it's how we are chosen when they come to interact and heal? Maybe it puts us in a very different mindset to accept what they have to offer? After all, we were taught that a positive plus a positive equals a positive. In other words, people are attracted to positive people. Positivity creates more positivity and negativity usually creates more negativity. In short, we need to have the "correct" mindset.

Afterwards, I did find myself seeing, from time to time, an almost "Electric Blue Shimmer" appear in my room. No reason for it. I tried to debunk it or find an answer to explain it, but it got to the point that I just started to accept it.

Over the previous Summer to Fall of 2019, I found myself being almost obsessed with going to the Uwharrie Forest in North Carolina. I felt like I needed to go. I felt compelled as if "I just had to go!" Ironically, this was going on during the week of Friday the 13th and also the Blood Moon that occurred. Just prior to, I was chatting with a small handful of people I kept in contact with and everyone had the same thing to say, "Chris, you were on my mind and felt like I needed to contact you". Even Doc Johnson called me out of nowhere, no reason, but just did. I told him this overwhelming desire and he said "That's the Xanue telling you to go." So I did. At first, I went to a part of Tennessee where I had known of a habitat. I saw Orbs, but that was about it. I felt an urge or inner voice telling me to go to Uwharrie, North Carolina, so I went.

I traveled to a place in North Carolina that I had never been to before. I had plans on my navigation to go to a few spots that a local Bigfoot group had mentioned activity at, but I never found it. Instead, I ended up following my urge and desire going down roads that I had absolutely no idea where they went to, but somehow I knew that's where I was supposed to go. I ended up at a spot that was a hunter's camp. It was isolated and extremely quiet. There weren't even any animals around.

That night, it was incredibly clear. No wind, no rain, no bad weather – just clear skies. I had my cot set up next to my campfire near my vehicle. The trees above were basically my canopy from any type of light weather, if some should roll in. Around 9pm, I heard the sound of wind rolling in over the tree tops. I could see the wind blowing certain trees as it seemed to make its way around the open fielded area. The wind only blew on the tree tops from one direction to the next. It seemed as if the wind was deliberate.

At this point in time, I caught myself fighting to stay awake for some reason. This went on for a while. Around 10:15 pm, I actually got into my SUV due to becoming a bit worried about widow makers possibly being above my cot or the wind blowing a small tree over on me. That was when I looked at the digital clock display and realized it was almost eight hours wrong. I checked my watch that was satellite sync as well as my cellphone. That clock had never been off more than a minute and only an hour for Daylight Savings until I corrected it. It had no reason to have changed or malfunction. It was only wrong that one time and it hasn't happened since.

Here comes the next unexpected twist. I had been speaking to Steve Bachmann, who claims to have the Xanue Orbs living inside him. He called me out of nowhere, completely unexpected, and he said "Go get on the cot. The Xanue know you are there." Now, how in the Hell would Steve know this? Hell, absolutely nobody knew where I was at. Nobody whatsoever. I didn't even know where I was. I didn't know how close I would be to help or anything. I was surprised that I had a cellphone signal.

Well, I stayed in my SUV that night. I woke up because it felt like someone had pushed down on my head and jolted me. It was rather startling to experience that. The next day came and I stayed there and scouted the area a bit more. I was trying to figure out what had been going on? That next night came and it seemed like nothing was happening. I don't remember very much, other than the fire died out pretty quickly. I found myself getting extremely tired and I fell asleep. I woke early that next morning, somewhat on my side, looking up at the sky. I could still see the stars as the sun was about to rise. However, I noticed that there was somewhat of a slanted type honeycomb grid in the sky that was transparent.

I could make out the lines and see it the same way a person can see clear fishing line. I caught myself dozing off again. When I came to again, there was that same grid design in the sky. The only difference was that the sun was coming up, so the sky wasn't as dark, but there it was. I could turn my head a bit thinking, "What if I just have some type of haze in my eyes?" I didn't. I have twenty-twenty vision, so clarity wasn't an issue. Next thing I noticed was that I wanted to get my camera that was in my shirt pocket, but I couldn't move more than just my head a little. I didn't feel paralyzed or numb. I just simply couldn't move. This lasted until that grid disappeared and the sun had risen completely that morning. I know I remember seeing that grid a minimal of three separate times, possibly four times. Beyond that, I do not recall.

The sun had risen and I felt for some reason it was time to change camps. I found one area on navigation that were campgrounds with showers. I knew that I wanted to be close to there. Local groups kept telling me to go towards the lakes, due to recent activity. However, I felt compelled to go to this one area and scout around it. I found a spot across the gravel road. There was some type of work going on where a company had leveled the trees and bulldozed the spot. It was the weekend by then, so nobody was around. Interesting enough though, I had found several tree structures around that immediate area that were not a part of the demo work happening.

That night, I had found cougar tracks and scat. They were fresh enough to be cautious and to keep the fire going. Around 11pm, I noticed a bunch of amber colored Orbs coming through the tree tops and tree line. I thought maybe they were lightning bugs, but they weren't. Then I started to hear a deep and very intimidating growl and grunt just on the outside of camp. The sound was so deep and big in its sound that if it were a cougar, that cat was at least nine-feet tall and over four hundred pounds. This was a totally different type of encounter. No whoops, tree knocks, or anything that were typical of past experiences. No tracks either. Just tree structures as an indication and a compelling feeling to make that specific spot my camp for the next few days.

Well, that growling and grumbling kept on going. I was getting pretty nervous and my anxiety was getting high. I was staring into a dark forest in an area that I had never been to before. Then around 11:20 pm, my heart about came out of my chest when my cellphone rang and it was Steve Bachmann calling me to say, "They are there now. Go to bed on the cot and go to sleep." I'm thinking, "Screw that!' I even put him on speaker as I chatted towards that intimidating growling and grumbling. I was thinking if the Bigfoot hears me and Steve talking, maybe it will go away. He did not sound friendly.

After about twenty minutes or so, it got quiet and everything calmed down. I eventually went to bed. Now, being alone in the forest, and in the pitch black of night on Friday the 13th, during the Full Blood Moon, and knowing Jason wasn't in those woods wearing a Hockey Mask and carrying a machete was somewhat of a relief. However, it didn't stop the anxiety that had been caused. Obviously, I survived to type this information to share in Doc Johnson's book. Therefore, I guess I wasn't in any type of danger other than my own imagination regarding the "what if" factor.

Some of the conversations that I have had with others who have had more experiences than I have, has brought along some very interesting theories for me, at least.

I have come to the conclusion that even the Xanue live by a set of rules. They pick and choose who they help and who they don't help. My assumptions go back to Adam and Eve and the fact that God allowed them to eat whatever they wanted except the apple from the tree. They broke the rules. They sinned. We as a society are made up of sinners. We try to live as if we are not, but we are in some way or another. Even in the Bible, those that were worthy, lived for hundreds of years. We, as sinners, might live to our seventies or eighties. Very, very few people live beyond that. The Xanue are a peaceful and loving species that do not interact with the negativity and sinners that try to hunt them down. Those out to prove something, usually come back with nothing but embellishments and an empty bank account. Those who actively look for them, usually end up being more bitter than accepting of those who have come into contact. Those who came into contact with them and had interactions found a very overwhelming desire to not advertise to the public. They tend not to show off any evidence or trophies or gifts simply because what we were blessed to have experienced was simply meant for our own eyes. It doesn't mean we are not open to sharing information under the correct circumstances, which in my case, to only help educate from my own experiences. There is nothing in this for me to gain. No money, no fame, nada - but just a promise to fulfill that I made to a very dear friend to tell only the truth as I remember it.

I do not have all the answers to what went on? All I know is that I try to debunk, explain, and justify everything that I can before I'm willing to say that it's the Bigfoot Forest People. Granted, there were incidences where I could not think of anything other than the Bigfoot Forest People. Nevertheless, the only way I can remain credible, in my mind, is to try and find a rational explanation. Then I remember that sometimes you have to walk by faith and not by sight.

This is my testimony to what I experienced with the Bigfoot Forest People. It is true, factual, and authentic. I was not under the influence of any substances, alcohol, mood or mind altering drugs. What you are reading is coming from a clear and sound mind.

Thomas Potter
(Carmichael, California)

It all started with a whistle. My wife and I were camped out at 8,300-feet in the Sierra Nevada Mountain Range. It was early November and extremely cold. The campground was officially closed for the season and empty of other campers during that time of year. As we lay in our tent, a nearby distinct whistle could be heard coming from somewhere in the darkness. This subtle event ignited a spark within me to learn more about the Bigfoot enigma.

We traveled to the 2018 International Bigfoot Symposium in Kennewick, Washington. There, I met Bob Gimlin, who along with Roger Patterson in October of 1967, filmed a Bigfoot along the Bluff Creek area in Northern California. It was my first Bigfoot conference. I was impressed by the speakers and their research of this elusive species.

While attending the conference, I met a gentleman named Kevin. He brought up a term that I have never heard before - the "Xanue." He talked of healings, mind speak, portals, and of lights and Orbs associated with these creatures - the supposed paranormal connection of this phenomenon. I was blown away but extremely intrigued. Kevin also brought up the name of Dr. Matthew A. Johnson. This encounter eventually led me to Dr. Johnson's front door in Chehalis, Washington in August of 2019.

Dr. Matthew A. Johnson is a Clinical Psychologist from the Pacific Northwest. Nearly twenty-years ago on July 1, 2000, he and his family had a close encounter with a Bigfoot while hiking on a trail near the Oregon Caves National Monument. He described the creature as being nine to ten feet tall - standing on two legs and estimated its weight at nearly a thousand pounds. He also described it as looking half-human and half-ape. In his book, "Bigfoot: A Fifty-Year Journey Come Full Circle," Dr. Johnson describes his various encounters and research methodology in trying to learn and discover more about these elusive "Forest People."

I read at least a dozen books about Bigfoot before my wife and I headed north to Dr. Johnson's home. I was incredibly impressed by the amount of research and by the number of Bigfoot sightings that have taken place over the years, if not centuries. There are a number of "different camps" and a variety of thoughts and theories about the species as well. I have always been one to have an open mind and not to discount all questionable encounters and experiences at first glance by various eyewitnesses.

We spent three-nights at Dr. Johnson's home in the beautiful forested foothills outside of Chehalis, Washington. I won't go into all the details of what happened there but only what I experienced and saw for myself. We pitched our cots on the forest floor, surrounded by tall trees and a canopy of thick green foliage. The trails on his property are scattered with rocks that glow a brilliant white during the dark hours of night. It has the effect of walking on a blanket of stars and is fascinating to experience for yourself. Because of Dr. Johnson's no-light policy, the glowing rocks will help safely aid you in finding your way around the trails on his property during the darkest hours of night.

Dr. Johnson's property has several giant X's (large crossed branches) - the sign of the "Xanue" (Bigfoot/Sasquatch/Forest People). You will also find small sticks and small branches that are displayed in geometric patterns called "stick glyphs." The stick glyphs are unnatural looking but obviously put together by some higher intelligence.

We slept on cots in the forest, in the open, and under the stars. Around 2:00 am, a pack of wild coyotes sounded off nearby, most likely celebrating a recent kill. All the while, we were just hoping the coyotes would stay away from our cots that we were sleeping on. Mother nature called during the night as well. After doing my business and returning to my cot, I thought I heard a strange "whisper" in my head. It sounded Native American to me. The hairs stood up on the back of my neck and arms. I heard an extremely loud wood-snap somewhere nearby our cots as well. There was no sound of a branch dropping through the trees and hitting the ground though. Then shortly after, five slight tree-knocks were heard. My wife slept through all the strange noises and left me alone to ponder all of this by myself. I basically slept with one eye open the rest of the night and following morning.

The next day we observed a "healing" on the property. After a series of three strokes during the previous year, Ruth, another guest on Dr. Johnson's property, had a noticeable limp and legs braces on. Her husband, David, was often at her side helping her walk and maintain her balance. She had a heck of a time just walking up a flight of stairs. That afternoon, I saw Ruth crying. She was walking! She was running! The leg braces were off! Ruth told me that she had been talking with Cynthia and explaining to her how upset she has been about her health situation. Ruth then felt a weird sensation and vibration in her body.

She told her husband not to help her and began walking normally without a limp. She felt strong and energized. David later told me she walked all the way down the hill trail and back up again. Sometimes running! It was an incredible moment to observe and to witness this amazing healing. Nothing short of miraculous! Things like that apparently happen here on Dr. Johnson's property. It is a special place indeed.

On the third day, I was busy exploring and taking pictures of the large X's and various stick glyphs. My wife had gone down to explore the lower meadow. On the way down to the meadow, she had seen a silver bracelet that had been left on a stump. Thinking someone had lost it, she placed it on a small branch next to the stump, clearly exposing it to the guests who were walking on the trail. She was hoping that the owner of the bracelet would eventually find it.

My wife immediately returned back up the hill trail to find me and take me back down to see the green meadow and forest below. On our way down the trail, she was surprised to find the bracelet now missing and not a person ahead of us. She put her finger on the exact branch indicating where she had hung the bracelet next to the stump just off the trail. We shrugged it off and continued down the trail.

We sat down near the meadow alone for a good twenty-minutes or so. Then we headed back up the trail once again only to find the bracelet back on the branch right next to the stump! Apparently, the Bigfoot can be tricksters at times! I took a few pictures of the small bracelet and left it there on the branch. The bracelet had gone missing again the next day.

We met others at Dr. Johnson's home who were like us. They were wanting to learn more about the Forest People. One very nice Hawaiian couple, who had moved to the Pacific Northwest a number of years ago, told us a story of witnessing lights and Orbs in the woods and forest around their home and property. They discovered large X's and stick glyphs as well. She started gifting food and other items and would receive gifts back such as a pretty leaf, rock, or a stick glyph.

One day the Orbs came into her bedroom where she then recorded them on her cell phone. Her husband also saw the recording. However, by the next morning, the video recording had been mysteriously removed. She also related that she had found small, oily, child-like hand prints on her bathroom mirror. I asked if her children could have possibly put them there. She responded, "We don't have any children!"

I was impressed by the amount of research Dr. Johnson has attained over his twenty-years of dedicated and passionate study of the Bigfoot phenomenon. The number of eyewitnesses to events, encounters, and their personal testimonials are quite intriguing. We saw many unbelievably large footprint-casts and other strange oddities that Dr. Johnson has collected over the years. We listened to sounds that he caught on his parabolic recording devices such as wood nocks, strange howls, and whispers in the night.

I saw a man who willingly opened his home to a bunch of strangers. A man of kindness, humor, and warmth. Also, I saw a man with strong opinions and beliefs in his research and study of the Bigfoot phenomenon. Some guests had disabilities and it was heartwarming to witness Dr. Johnson bend over backwards to help and accommodate them. After having an eye-opening and fascinating time at Dr. Johnsons, we continued on with our foray into the Pacific Northwest.

We actually had two strange events happen to us after we left Dr. Johnson's home. After hiking the beautiful Ape Canyon Trail near Mt. Saint Helen's, we camped deep out on a secluded forestry road south of the shattered volcano. No other people or campers were there at the time and we hit the sack early after a long day of hiking. While my wife was reading a book inside our tent, we both heard a tremendous high pitched scream coming from the forest. I looked over at her and said, "That sounded like a chimpanzee or ape screaming." My wife remarked, "It sounded like a woman screaming or an animal being killed by something." She immediately turned off her reading light and said, "I don't want that thing knowing we're camping here!" I know what a mountain lion and bobcat sound like but it sounded more like an ape scream to me. The next morning, we packed up and headed over to camp near Mt. Adams.

We decided to stay in a campground located on the flanks of Mt. Adams. The forest burned there four years ago. The remains of the burned and blackened trees spread out across the landscape. A creek with clean, cold water from mountain glaciers high above, flowed down from the ancient volcano near our campsite. I set out a gifting bowl in the burned tree line at sunset. I put an apple, a whole bag of peanut brittle, and a peanut butter and jelly sandwich in the gifting bowl. I was hoping that our forest friends would enjoy a nighttime snack.

While setting up our tent, my wife informed me she would like to keep the rainfly off to be able to view the stars and the Milky Way. At 2:00 am, she awoke to tell me that she no longer saw the stars as thunder and lightning flashed in the near distance. We scrambled to put on the rainfly just before the rain started. Shortly after, we could hear twig-snapping and bipedal footfalls around our tent and Jeep. They would walk slowly and then run away. Then they would return again! I would sit up and look out the front of the tent waiting for lightning to light up the area in a brilliant flash but saw nothing! I tried to look out over and over again but I never saw anything.

It was surreal! Then something big and heavy arrived - stomp, stomp, stomp, stomp as it ran past our tent! Well I can assure you that I never went back to sleep again during that long pre-dawn morning! As the sun came up, I went out to check the gifting bowl. The sandwich and peanut brittle were gone but the apple was left. I found a large human-like barefoot footprint and took a few pictures of it as well.

We have continued our research of this phenomenon. In the past two years, we have traveled to many desolate locations around the Pacific Northwest and Sierra Nevada Mountain Range. We have seen strange lights, glyphs, and tree-structures. We have heard whistles, growls, wood-knocks, branch-snapping and screams in the night. The adventure continues.

I am absolutely convinced that something unknown to science lives in the Pacific Northwest and forests across the planet. These beings live on the edge of our perception and there is an intelligence about them. Something more to them and gifted with special abilities that we can only imagine.

Amy Rajek

(Daphne, Alabama)

I was invited to Camp XANUE in June and August of 2019 by Dr. Regina Horne. I have had paranormal experiences with human spirits since I was a child, but had never experienced or considered Bigfoot before this. I was excited to get to meet likeminded people, and to bond over things that most people I had met would never contemplate.

During both visits, I witnessed Orbs and flashes of light in the forest. Upon arriving at Camp XANUE in June, Regina and I set up our overnight sleep area in the meadow facing toward the wood pile. Later after dinner, everyone came out and took turns going down to the woodpile to talk to the Xanue. I went down with Maynard, standing on my right side, and Cindy Johnson sitting in a chair to my left. She and I were holding hands because it was dark. I could not see where to go or stand. I had no idea what to expect or ask of the Xanue since I had never done anything like this before. Before I could figure out what to say, I had mind speak - a male voice and a couple others in the background saying, "You don't have to ask for anything because we already know." I squeezed Cindy's hand very hard because this startled me. She told me to relax.

Afterwards, as I walked back to my chair, I wondered how that even happened. I have never had any mind speak like this before. I witnessed several Orbs, lights and shadow movements during both of my visits. I have some photos with Orbs. Also, Maynard and Regina reviewed a time lapse video from the meadow night sit area and saw a large orange glow come up over the wood pile after everyone had settled down to sleep. This orange glow then divided into five smaller orange areas - two behind Regina's zero gravity chair where she was sleeping, and three behind my chair. They may have been scanning us since we both asked if they could check out our backs for possible healing. I never thought that I would be coming out for any healing, but since we were told that they can do that, it doesn't hurt to ask. I was mainly just there to experience and learn whatever was meant for me.

My most amazing experience happened at the Southern Oregon Interaction Area (SOIA) in August of 2019. After leaving Camp Xanue at Dr. J's home in June of 2019, I had traveled out for this second visit to the State of Washington with a painful fractured ankle. Regina and I were invited to go to SOIA with a small group of people. When we set up camp to prepare for the night sit at SOIA, Dr J (Matt) suggested that, when my turn came to speak to the Xanue at the 12 o'clock position of the base camp perimeter, I should ask them to heal my foot and to mention a few other requests.

Earlier that day, I had found out from my husband's phone call that my grandchildren were moving out of state. I was feeling upset about this when I began sensing a presence near the cars parked at the edge of camp. When I moved over in that direction to check this out, I became involved in a hide-n-seek game with a little cloaked Xanue who eventually went into the bushes beside the cars. I picked a small flower and held it out to him. He reached out and almost took it from me, and he even showed his uncloaked face for a few seconds. I told him that I would go sit down and wait for him to come to me if he wanted. Later on, while we were sitting facing the 12 o'clock position on the perimeter of the base camp area, Matt told us that some small Xanue children had approached us and were standing in front of us.

I began to feel a tingling numbness and shaking on my lap. Matt said that one had climbed into my lap. It made me think of holding my grandchildren and was very comforting. Matt then began to play a song from his recorder ('Celebration' by Kool and the Gang) and the little one jumped down to join some other children who were dancing in front of us. Amanda and I got up to dance with them. They move so fast. They looked like black swirls of energy circling all around us. Matt said that some adult Xanue were also dancing near us.

When my turn came to go in front of Zorth at the 12 o'clock position, I began talking to them all about my foot and soon other topics started coming up. I began to get very emotional and that is when the experience changed into something that I never expected. I began to feel like I was trying to balance on a giant ball. I was pivoting around on top from my waist up. I felt waves of energy hitting me, very strong tingling and vibrations, and then my feet felt lifted off the ground.

Matt said that he could see many Xanue coming to me and wrapping me in their arms. I felt weightlessness, like I was being lifted and swirled around. I felt like I could no longer stand on my own, and I apparently was getting louder and more emotional causing the other campers to worry about me. One camper, Andy, came over to check on me. When he came up and saw that I was shaking, he wrapped his arms around me telling me that I was okay. When he did that, it felt like some sort of energy field around me changed so much that my body merged with his. When we moved apart, it was like trying to pull two strong magnets apart. After that, I felt very weak and I was shaking and sobbing uncontrollably. I felt shaky for the rest of the evening.

I slept very deeply that night since I felt so drained of energy. Regina told me that, from her viewpoint sitting in the chairs facing the 12 o'clock area, she witnessed increasing light flashes and glowing tree trunks with more intense light especially moving up from the 11 o'clock area as I was sounding more and more emotional. She could not hear my words, but could hear my voice getting louder and sounding like I was crying.

For two mornings in a row, I awoke with the shoe strings untied only on the shoe on my fractured foot. I always double knot my shoestrings. By the last day, my foot did not hurt anymore and has not caused me any problems. Ever since I returned home, my pets react to things that I cannot see or hear. I don't know, but maybe the Xanue are around me now. I feel honored to have experienced this, and enjoyed all the good times with great people.

Pamela Roberts-Aue
(Rainier, Washington)

My first actual encounter with a Bigfoot was experienced in a small private forest East of Yelm Washington on July 16, 2013. I had been out walking with my very courageous, loyal, and adventurous Feline, Long Whiskers. I had just completed a small video of Whiskers exploring a large uprooted stump. We were on the way home when suddenly he stopped and starred followed by all his hair raising up on his back. Whiskers began to ever so slowly and cautiously move sideways holding his gaze at a clump of trees and brush. Stunned by this odd behavior, I looked over my left shoulder in his direction of attention and saw nothing. He continued to move towards home in this odd sideways manner with every step being intentionally and cautiously placed. Living in wonder, I looked again and saw nothing, heard nothing and smelled nothing.

Hugely concerned I bent down and gently picked him up and held him snuggly to my chest as he continued to peer over my shoulder with hair still raised. Slowly, we continued to make our way home to our path from forest to yard. Whiskers, very concerned, tried to push away from my arms but I held him firm with soothing assuring words. Moments later, I began to trot home as he never broke his gaze from whatever he was seeing. When I arrived to the clearing of our open yard, I gently set him down. Whiskers turned around facing the trail connection from yard to forest and sat down with a continued stare. Long Whiskers' behavior so spooked me that I scooped him up and put him in our rented twenty-four-foot travel trailer and closed the door. I then collected my other feline and locked all three of us indoors for the rest of the day and night.

THE XANUE

The following morning at 5:15 am will be forever etched in my memory. I was awakened by extremely loud, deep vocals coming from that forest. Startled awake, I lay in the bunk bed with my two cats and listened to this amazing penetrating sound. Moments passed and there was a brief pause in the chatter. Then I could hear a very distant response whose tone was more feminine. Soon all the dogs were awake and barking in nearly a one-hundred-eighty-degree sweep of the neighboring homes. The canine chorus drowned out the intense unique vocal communication to such degree that I could not record what I came to realize were the Bigfoot. The idea of recording the vocals had come from two separate lectures months earlier.

There I sat in an aluminum trailer, locked inside for protection from what? Suddenly, I began to laugh at the very notion of thinking that I would ever be safe from a very large powerful Being whose height would tower over the roof of my sardine can on wheels. The more I viewed the notion of proportions, the more I laughed. Then I stopped and lived in wonder. Wonder what would I do if an ominous intelligent Being would even peer in that top bunk window? Clearly I had no clue.

I followed up on some of the suggested sites offered by the Bigfoot speakers who lectured at the Yelm Library on April 24, 2013 and on June 13, 2013. I found one of the sites and played a few audio files. Suddenly, my cat, Long whiskers, jumped from the top bunk down to the kitchen table. He stood up on his hind legs and listened to the speakers with rapt attention. I told you that he was brave! It was a beautiful July day full of sun. I opened the door and let everyone out to play. I felt very joyful that day from such an extraordinary experience.

Some months later, the same three speakers returned to Yelm to lecture again. This time, many folks had great questions, some of which the researchers weren't so willing to answer. But what to me was funny was that these guys had Bigfoot experiences but could not and did not feel comfortable in admitting that they could not see these Beings. Yet, they could hear them. Also, the Bigfoot even knew the names of the men involved and would telepathically say their names. It was confirmed that my cat did see something. His behavior was like that of a dog, trying to lead its master away from danger.

On September 16, 2016, Dr. Matthew A. Johnson came to give his presentation at The Triad Theatre. I watched Dr. Matt share his story with clarity, emotion and humbleness. Yes, he had his physical evidence, but I was more impressed with his genuine self. His presentation made sense and clarity to my previous experience with Long Whiskers. They can cloak. They move among us invisible to our human eye. I loved that he referred to them as a People. Animal's eyes are structured differently than our own, so they do see things that we cannot see, unless we are trained to do so.

On September 23, 2017, Dr. Matthew A. Johnson gave a continuation of his lecture about two homes up the hill from where I now reside. It was a lovely evening with stories, sharing, food, a fire, and more sharing. At the closure of the evening, Matt delivered messages to some of us from Zorth. When the morning arrived, my body turned to its right side in bed while lightly moaning – I hear the softest feminine voice in English Sweetly ask me, "Are you alright?" I paused for a moment wondering who that was. Merrily, I go about my day because someone in the unseen cared about me and was checking in on me. Dr. Matt returned to my neighbor's house for another informant evening. I told him about the sweet voice and asked him if it was a Xanue. He told me that it was. Visits to my house from my invisible Forest People became more regular and some were even humorous.

During January of 2018, I attended Dr. Matthew Johnson and Cynthia Kreitzeberg's Open House Event. This was my very first night sit and sleep over. This event was so wonderful. First, I met new wonderful people of many backgrounds and I felt like family! Second, because I had my first tagging contact experience. I was sweetly tagged on my back by a juvenile and then a much longer loving contact by an adult.

I additionally attended on May 21, 2018 and on August 19, 2018. Each night sit and sleep over weekend event brought about different experiences for me. The August event for me was much more advancing for me in that I was ready to leave this planet. I actually did not feel I belonged here anymore. I retired to my hammock early in the evening which was away from the group and in the forest. I shared my tears and woes with the woods and God. I lay down. In moments, I heard the vocals of the Xanue- a sort of scream- followed by Coyote howls and I was gone. What occurred was the greatest gift of LOVE I had ever truly received.

I believe that LOVE is a frequency and a state of mind. An individual has to be open to receive it as well as send it. I saw that my hammock was surrounded by female Xanue. They had placed a child beside me, on my left side. What a beautiful child. The child had a beautiful long dark brown coat. I asked if I could touch the child and permission was granted. I was so amazed as to how very, very soft the hair was. I had never been loved by so much feminine energy in all my life! Their love is powerful and truly unconditional.

Since the night sits and sleep overs at Camp Xanue, I have done several sleep outs at my home. I find that the Xanue often arrive between 4 am and 6 am in the morning. I have experienced them entering my home without the use of doors. My cat can see them and she is no longer afraid and neither am I.

Dr. Matthew Johnson and Cynthia Kreitzberg are so generous to open their home and lives to allow for the introduction of humans to Xanue and let the experiences be individually unfolding. Every time I am there, I am at home with my extended family. All the People who attend are amazing, responsible people who all pitch in with chores and clean-up. They maintain respect for each other and the residence. Our time together is priceless! We humans are our own greatest mystery. The Xanue are helping us to remember our latent talents – our connection to nature!

Thank you, Dr. Matthew A. Johnson and Mrs. Cynthia Kreitzberg-Johnson for your unconditional love. Also, for opening your hearts and minds and taking that big leap of courage for the revealing of a great mystery solved. Thank you Zorth and the entire Xanue people for making your connection with the Johnson family to help humanity wake-up, accept love, kindness, and to be open minded. Thank you, each and every one, for the experiences I have had. Let us continue to advance.

Faydra Romero
(Phoenix, Arizona)

I first met Dr. Matthew A. Johnson ("Dr. J.") and Cynthia on December 8, 2017. They invited me to stay at their home which is referred to as the Chehalis Interaction Area (CIA) or Camp Xanue. I won't go into details about the events, since I did a video testimony regarding that evening, and the healing that followed. Please watch it on the Team Squatching USA YouTube channel. The video is titled, "Another credible witness testimonial." Everything in this video is the truth. Sneak peek for those who haven't watched the video yet: The Xanue came to my house and healed me in Phoenix AZ!

Things that make you go hmmmmm: Shortly after my foot healing, my dog Nema wasn't feeling well. She's an older Italian Greyhound rescue. She suffers from the negative effects of not having any fur and soaking in the Arizona sun. I took her to the vet to have multiple growths removed from her body. Her health was declining and she wasn't looking or feeling well. One night while lying in bed, I asked the Xanue if they would help her. I went to bed and never thought much about it again. My hubby was out of town that week. When he got home, he went into the bedroom to see her and yelled at me down the hallway, "What happened to Nema?" Shocked, I ran into the room expecting to see something horrible. Instead, they were playing on the bed. "She looks and acts like a puppy now," he said in amazement. In addition to her new-found energy, within two weeks of having the growths removed, her stitches and scar practically disappeared. I'm not a vet or an expert on how quickly dogs heal. Is it possible the Xanue heard me and helped Nema with her recovery? My opinion is YES. P.S. Nema spelled backwards is Amen. She's our angel from above.

Bumps in the night: I started noticing lots of "new" noises at my house after the Xanues' first visit. What was once a quiet, peaceful home, turned into constant noise throughout the night. One night in particular, my hubby and I were lying in bed. The lights had been out for about ten minutes and there was a loud crash/bang sound. He said to me, "Did you hear that?" I responded, "Yep." "There's lots of noises in our house at night now," he said. I just smiled. P.S. They often come to my place of work and rearrange my desk. They are such pranksters!

A New Creation: This story is harder for me to tell, because it includes parts of my past which I'm not proud of. For my birthday in May of 2018, my grandmother wanted to take me onto the military base so I could pick out a birthday present. She knows how much I love camo! So my hubby, my grandma, and I set out to spend the day shopping at the BX and Commissary.

Upon our arrival, we were directed to the visitor center to get a visitor's pass. This was a new procedure. The base now required running a background check on all visitors. I filled out the visitor request form and handed my ID to the lady behind the desk. Long story short, I was denied access. I left humiliated and angry.

I was angry at God. I'm pretty sure over the next couple days I yelled at Him a lot. I mean, it wasn't fair that my past was still affecting me. After all, doesn't God promise us that we are a new creation in Him? Well that's not how it felt. I said some choice words to Him. After venting and crying for a couple of days, I came to the realization that it's all my fault. We make decisions in our life, and we suffer the consequences, period.

So I thanked God for the life I have now. I decided to take action by submitting a request through the courts for a "Good Clause Exception." This means a judge can remove anything that blocks me from getting a clearance card. So I contacted a lawyer. The first step was for me to submit for a fingerprint clearance card. Then I had to submit the denial letter along with written testimonies from myself and three referrals to the court. Piece of cake. I'm familiar with the process of obtaining the denial letter. I had submitted for clearance cards in the past and received the denial letters. I went to the location to have my fingerprints taken, paid the seventy-five dollars, and anxiously awaited the denial letter to arrive in the mail. Now let me back track for a minute. During my days of feeling self-pity and anger, I pleaded with God to "just make it go away." I also asked the Xanue, if they were allowed to intervene, could they please help me. I was desperate.

About three weeks passed and the denial letter came in the mail. I instantly knew something was different from when I had received them in the past. First, it came quickly. It usually takes about six to eight weeks. Second, it felt thicker, like something other than a letter was enclosed. Upon opening it, I was totally shocked! Although I had applied for the lowest clearance level, I was approved for the highest level clearance. My clearance card was included.

I immediately called my lawyer because I knew I needed the denial letter to apply for the Good Clause exception. Now I didn't know how I was going to get my clearance approved. He laughed at me. Then he said that he's never seen this happen before. He congratulated me and told me to call again if I ever needed assistance with anything else.

Because I knew something very unusual had just happened, I asked the Xanue to please give me a sign if they had intervened on my behalf. They heard me! The next morning, I woke up to a large fingerprint swipe in paint in my hallway. I almost fell over when I saw it. Total shock. I was in the process of picking new paint for our interior and I had samples around the house. The color I had chosen was in my hallway and had been there for over a week. I was waiting on the painters to come the following week. Now, next to the sample on wall, was a new mark that looked like a big finger had been dipped into the paint and swiped a mark down the wall. I took this as one-hundred-percent confirmation.

For the next week, every time I passed it in the hallway, I kissed my fingers and pressed the wall. The amount of love and gratitude I feel is unmeasurable. It's not that I care so much about getting my clearance card, but rather the fact they cared enough about me and my pain to intervene. I don't know how they did it, or how they heard my cries, but they did. This I know for a fact. I also find it cute that my confirmation was a fingerprint. They could have left a feather or rock in my house. However, in this particular case, a fingerprint was a perfect sign. If you are like me and have made mistakes in your past, please know you are forgiven and loved.

CIA September 2018: I made another visit to the Chehalis Interaction Area (CIA) in September of 2018 in order to camp on the property for the weekend. The highlight for me was meeting so many wonderful people from all over the country. It's a blessing to connect with like-minded folks and walk along side of them through this journey. The Xanue want to connect us to each other. This is exactly what's taking place at these night sits held by "Dr. J." at the CIA. Please watch the video on the TS USA YouTube channel. Prior to my visit, I was diagnosed with Nostalgia Paresthetic: A condition that causes pain, itching and skin discoloration to your back. The cause and cure are both unknown. While at the CIA, I asked the Xanue for healing on my back. As of today, March 14, 2019, I still have the condition.

My thoughts on healings: You don't need to visit "Dr. J's" property to get a healing from the Xanue. You don't have to be "worthy" or "special" to receive healings. God loves us all the same and we are ALL worthy. I believe there are trials we go through in life that are part of our life-plan. These trials help us to grow in our faith, to draw closer to God, and to have compassion for others. If you are reading this and you have chronic pain or you have a loved one who is ill, please know that you are loved and not forsaken. Continue to pray to God and also ask the Xanue for healing. If it's within God's will, I believe it can happen for you! I will be praying for you.

Final thoughts: Truth always prevails, and love wins. God bless!

PART 5
A SECOND OPEN LETTER TO MY PROGENY

Dear Biological Descendants

Here I go again. I hope you, my biological descendants, were able to read my first letter to you which is in the back of my first book: "BIGFOOT: A Fifty-Year Journey Come Full Circle." However, if you missed the first book or can't find a copy of it, then most of it is repeated here just to increase the odds that you will have an opportunity to read it.

During this point in time (2020), many people think that your father, grandfather, great-grandfather, so on and so forth, is crazy. They believe that I've lost my marbles. That I'm a few fries short of a McDonald's 'Happy Meal'. My cornbread wasn't cooked right and it is soft in the middle. You get the picture, right? Maybe some of you feel the same way about me too.

I'm sure if some people could get away with it, they would threaten to burn me at the stake if I don't recant. Well, although Galileo understandably recanted to save his own skin, history ultimately vindicated him. He was correct. The sun and planets don't revolve around the Earth. Rather, the Earth and the other planets actually revolve around the sun.

In a similar manner, the TRUTH of the existence of Zorth, the Xanue Council of Twelve, and all of the other Xanue people who live on the Earth does not revolve around the black and white, rigid small box, crystallized opinions, and denial of the naysayers. Instead, their denial revolves around the TRUTH of the existence of the Xanue.

One day, in a similar manner as Galileo, history will vindicate me. Those individuals who are presently in denial of the existence of the Xanue people will ultimately be viewed as the closed minded fools of history. If I can convince you of doing anything, ALWAYS stand up for the TRUTH. Never allow the denial of fools to cause you to compromise your integrity. It is better to be right and to be thought a fool by many than to be loved by many and to actually be a fool (i.e., Never sacrifice TRUTH and INTEGRITY in order to become a card- carrying member of the popular kids club). The TRUTH matters. INTEGRITY matters.

I believe that everyone is a unique creation and that there's no one else on the Earth who is like anyone of us. Yet, my progeny, we share the same DNA and, therefore, we also share many similarities too. When I was a child, I saw some pictures of my grandfather and my father and I couldn't believe how much I looked like the both of them when they were younger. When I look at my sons, Micah and Grady, I can't believe how much they look like me. Although we are very different and unique, we are also similar in many ways. We are merely separated by generations.

With that said, here's what I think you need to know. I truly believe that within our DNA comes the ability to be more sensitive than others might be to the unseen paranormal world. I'm not saying that all of you have been born with this gift, I'm simply suggesting that some of you have possibly been born with this gift.

Why is it important for you to know this? Well, thank you for asking because I'm going to take the liberty to tell you. If you have this gift and you don't know it, then the gift may feel more like a curse. Case in point, in January of 1995, I had a new client come to my office for counseling in Anchorage, Alaska. He desperately wanted me to help him get rid of a curse. I'm always interested when new and unique cases come into my office so I informed him that I was all ears and please tell me what was going on with him.

He said, "Doc, I wasn't able to make it down to my parents' home for Christmas this year in Minnesota. I just couldn't afford the airline ticket. Anyways, I was sitting in my living room and I called them up to wish everyone a Merry Christmas. All my siblings, nieces and nephews, go to my parents' home on Christmas day. All of a sudden,

Doc, I could see all of them. I could see who was sitting where and who was standing where. I could see who was grabbing the next present out from underneath the Christmas tree. I was on the speaker phone and I started telling them everything that I was seeing. They thought I was outside my parents' home, looking through the window, and playing a trick on them. So I told them that I was on my landline telephone at my home in Anchorage, Alaska. I told them that I was going to hang up and to please call me on my landline. Well, Doc, thirty seconds later, my home phone rang and it was my parents. When I answered the phone, everyone started freaking out on me. You've got to help me, Doc. I need to get rid of this curse."

Well, I immediately thought he might be dealing with some kind of psychosis because it sounded pretty darn crazy to me. Then spontaneously, I asked him for his parents' home phone number. I asked, "Your parents are retired right? They should be home right now, right?" He said, "Well, Doc, yes. They are retired. Unless they're out running errands, they should be home."

As I was dialing his parents' home number, I asked, "I have your permission to talk with them, right? They're going to be able to confirm everything you just told me, right?" I was expecting to have him stop me right there and then because I was making a bold move to call him out on his delusional and psychotic thinking. Instead, he said, "Yes, they will confirm everything."

I thought to myself, "Well, calling him out didn't work so now I'll be able to have his parents' input. Perhaps they can help me to gently confront their adult son." When his parents answered the phone, I said, "Hello, my name is Dr. Matthew Johnson and I'm a psychologist in Anchorage, Alaska. Your son is in my office. He told me what happened on Christmas day and he gave me permission to call you and confirm his story."

His parents were on the speaker phone and immediately responded, "Dr. Johnson, you've got to help our son. He was able to see everything that we were doing even though he was at his home in Anchorage, Alaska on Christmas day. We called him back and he was there. He saw who was sitting where and who was standing where. He told us about what was inside the present that one of our granddaughters opened up. Please, you've got to help him."

I thanked his parents for their time and assured them that I would do my best to help their son. After I hung up, my client just sat there with a big 'I told you so' smile on his face. I said to him, I'm sorry but I can't help you get rid of your curse because I don't think it's a curse. I think that you're looking at it all wrong. Instead, I think you have a gift. I am willing to work with you to help you better understand your gift and see how you might be able to use it to help others. If you're willing to proceed down that path, I think I can help you." He agreed to proceed. After a few months, he left my office with a new and positive perspective regarding his gift.

You see, my loveable progeny, I'm sharing with all of you about this curse/gift scenario because my mother, Joann Johnson, struggled with it. She only opened up to me about it. She told me that I was the only one of her four kids who appeared to have it. Although she would secretly expose me to articles and books covering extra-sensory-perception (ESP) and other paranormal phenomena, she dealt with her gift as a curse.

She grew up in a generation where such things were not talked about. Heck, who am I kidding? My generation isn't very keen about discussing such matters either. Nevertheless, although my mother encouraged me to learn more and embrace by gift, she drank alcohol like a fish in order to anesthetize herself and avoid her gift. She couldn't handle it. She turned to alcoholism to cope with something that she could not understand. She wanted me to do better than she did.

During the last few days of her life, my mother lay in a coma in a hospital room. I spent time with her every day reading to her, talking to her, singing to her, brushing her hair, and putting water in her dry mouth. On the day she passed away, she woke up from her coma for a few minutes. Although she wasn't able to talk, she looked at me and mouthed the words, "I love you." She died a few hours later.

We took my father, Art Johnson, home from the hospital and sat down in the living room with him. We were attempting to console his loss of my mother who he had been married to for over fifty years. As I was looking out of the large living room window on to the porch where my mother enjoyed sitting, smoking her cigarettes, and watching the birds on the river, the Christmas lights came on. My mother had Christmas lights hanging all over the porch all year long and never took them down. My dad said to me, "Go outside and turn off those damn Christmas lights."

I walked outside to unplug the Christmas lights from the wall socket, but to my surprise, the Christmas lights were not plugged in. Yet, they were glowing brightly. I immediately sensed my mother's presence near me and I said, "Hi, mom! I love you and miss you already. Thank you for being a great mom to me. I can't wait to see you again in the future. I'll go get dad for you."

I walked back inside the house and into the living room. My father said, "I thought I told you to turn off those damn Christmas lights." I stood there in silence in front of my dad. A few tears were rolling down my cheeks. I responded, "Dad, the Christmas lights aren't plugged in. Mom's outside and she needs to say 'goodbye' to you. I think you need to go outside and talk with her."

My dad just sat there staring at me like I was crazy. He went outside and saw that the lights were not plugged in. He spent about five minutes outside talking to my mom about who knows what. He never told us what he said. When he came back inside the house, the Christmas lights turned off. I don't need any more proof about 'life after death' nor do I need any more proof about the unique gift that some of our biological family members appear to be born with. It's in our DNA.

My youngest son, Grady Johnson, has been involved with my Bigfoot Forest People research since the age of two. At present in January of 2020, he is thirteen-years old. He has seen them. He has talked with them. He can tell when they're around. They have reached out to him on multiple occasions. Ultimately, what he chooses to do with his gift and his relationship with the Bigfoot Forest People is up to him. I have no expectations of him to carry on with my research. His life is his life to live as he wishes. I just hope that no matter what he chooses to do with his life, he will at least consider it a gift and not a curse.

Likewise, Grady's older brother, Micah, also appears to have the gift. Micah was five years old when our family encountered the Bigfoot up on the mountainside above the Oregon Caves National Monument Park on July 1, 2000. His mother strongly discouraged him from being involved in my Bigfoot research.

At the age of twenty-one, Micah decided to join me in the Southern Oregon Interaction Area (SOIA) on two separate excursions during the late summer of 2016. He was motivated to join me after he had his own personal encounter with a cloaking Bigfoot. Both he and his friend saw the Bigfoot while they were sitting in a car, overlooking the city lights of Grants Pass, Oregon.

While in SOIA with me, Micah was able to see and interact with the Bigfoot Forest People. Matter of fact, he was playing his music for them while using my portable Bose speaker. He was dancing up a storm and was surrounded by them. Off in the distance, I saw a Being of Light observing Micah while he was dancing. Eventually, the Being of Light began to mimic Micah.

At the end of our trip, Micah told me that I wasn't crazy after all and that the Bigfoot Forest People are real. Once again, I have no expectations for Micah to carry on with my research either. His life is his life to live. I just want Grady and Micah to be happy and embrace their gifts – not deny their gifts.

With all that said, my dear progeny, I wish the same for all of you. I was only one of four children who inherited the gift from my mother. Micah is one of only three children born with the gift. Finally, Grady was the only child from his mother and he has the gift. If you too are born with the gift, please embrace it. Don't hide from it. Don't deny it. Don't drink or drug it away. You have been gifted by God for a reason and I strongly encourage you to embrace it, explore it, understand it, and use it to help others. In my particular case, the gift was used to help save 23,542 souls (minus the three souls that died within an hour or less of crossing over) during the EXODUS by helping to bring them over to Earth. I know I sound crazy but it's all true.

Last but not least, just as the Bigfoot Forest People are real and live among us, so is God. Zorth openly spoke about the existence of God, Jesus, and our need to be connected to them. He said that we all come from the same God. He said that we all have the same souls but different bodies. Finally, he said that we all return to the same God after we die. Please strive to live in love and to be connected with God, Jesus, and your fellow man. Love, love, love like there's no tomorrow.

Thank you, my progeny, for taking the time to read my book and this crazy impersonal, yet very personal, open letter to all of you. I love all of you. I look forward to meeting you on the other side with God. Until then, cling on to faith, hope, and love. The greatest of these is love.

In the love of Jesus Christ,

Dr. Matthew A. Johnson

(Your father, grandfather, great grandfather, great-great grandfather, etc.)

P.S. To the rest of you who have just read my open letter to my progeny, if you're experiencing something similar, please embrace your gift. Don't deny it or attempt to run away from it. Eventually, you'll have to talk with your progeny about it too. God Bless!

PART 6
HOW TO GET IN TOUCH WITH DR. JOHNSON

Contact Information

Website: www.Xanue.Com
YouTube.Com: Team Squatchin USA
Sound Cloud.Com: Team Squatchin USA
Facebook Group Page: "Team Squatchin USA" and "Planet Xanue"

Twitter: Xanue.Com
Email: BigfootDoctor@Yahoo.Com

www.ingramcontent.com/pod-product-compliance
Lightning Source LLC
Chambersburg PA
CBHW070159240426

43671CB00007B/488